Ernst Wilhelm Nay

John-Paul Stonard
Pamela Kort

ERNST WILHELM
NAY

Ridinghouse

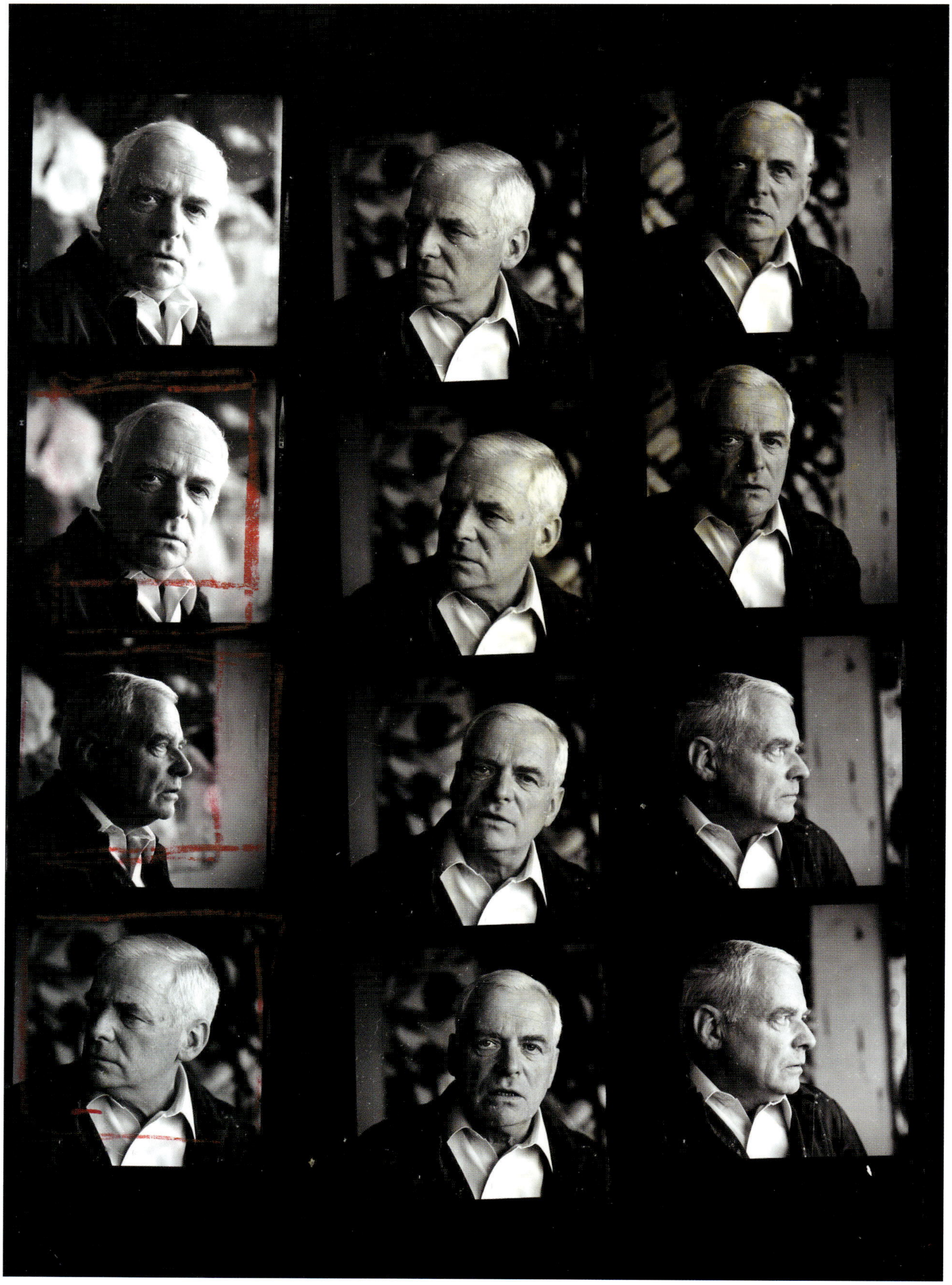

Portraits of E.W. Nay, contact sheet, 1964

Contents

6 Looking Back at Ernst Wilhelm Nay
Norman Rosenthal

13 Ernst Wilhelm Nay
John-Paul Stonard

159 Ernst Wilhelm Nay and the Issue of Content in Abstract Painting
Pamela Kort

186 Index

Norman Rosenthal

Looking Back at Ernst Wilhelm Nay

The name of Ernst Wilhelm Nay (1902–68) does not easily trip off the tongue of English-speaking art lovers, and nor does his work reside in their visual memory. The German art tradition of painting, loosely known as Expressionism, originated at the beginning of the twentieth century with the work of artists such as Ernst Ludwig Kirchner, Erich Heckel or Franz Marc and 'officially' came to an end with the *Entartete Kunst* (Degenerate Art) exhibition in 1937. It only survived in the work of emigrants, and to some extent, so-called inner emigrants. Then, towards the end of the twentieth century, in the eyes of an international public, Expressionism seemed to resurrect itself with artists as world-famous now as Joseph Beuys, Gerhard Richter, Sigmar Polke, Georg Baselitz and Anselm Kiefer, to name but a few. It is precisely in this context of a widely perceived and profound art historical caesura that a re-consideration of the life and work of Nay becomes today an urgent and necessary task. For Nay, it can be demonstrated, is a crucial figure in the history of German painting in the twentieth century who lived through the complex and disturbing vicissitudes of German history. Nay's paintings bridge the two epochs of Expressionism, and ultimately therefore demonstrate the continuity of this most significant of art traditions.

The extent to which political and social events have a direct bearing on art – the zeitgeist, to use that Hegelian term, that now has entered the English language – is a subject that is endlessly debated by philosophers, historians and art commentators.
In regard to the twentieth-century experience in particular, it is a question of intense complexity. In the context of that century, there can be no argument that Nay is a significant cultural and historical figure. Though, in spite of the fact that he understood himself to be a consciously apolitical being, at many moments in his life, both politically and art-politically – as the two separate accounts in this book by John-Paul Stonard and Pamela Kort demonstrate from very different perspectives – Nay was not incapable of adapting himself to circumstances in the interests of his career and the development of his art.

Although Nay died relatively young at the age of 65, he lived through historical phases of immense contrast. A classic and comfortable Wilhelmine childhood was followed by the First World War, the German Revolution, hyper-inflation, the Weimar Republic, the traumatic 12-year period of the Third Reich, Germany's defeat at the hands of the allies and the subsequent occupation, the de-Nazification of Germany, the founding of the Bundesrepublik and finally the Wirtschaftswunder ('Economic Miracle'). That Nay, having arrived at a point where he was unquestionably the most famous artist in Germany, was able to pass back into near-obscurity after his death in 1968 – even within the country itself – is a question that this book carefully considers. Anyone interested in the development of German art in the twentieth century will find it valuable to reflect on the reasons for this. It too is not without its particular ironical twist that the year of his death, 1968, carries itself huge symbolic weight. It was a year in which many of the values that Nay seemed to embody were unceremoniously rejected by the protesting students: A new era was being inaugurated, with its own cultural ground rules and 'sacred cows'. Yet Nay, considered from the perspective of a historical distance of more than half a century, can now be seen as one of the most valuable representatives of the art produced during and after the Second World War. He is an artist who can be looked at again with the utmost seriousness, from an aesthetic as well as a historical perspective.

It was certainly not fortuitous that in 1985, when the Royal Academy of Arts in London staged the grand survey exhibition *German Art of the Twentieth Century: Painting and Sculpture 1900–1985*, a detail of Nay's painting of 1945, *Tochter der Hekate I* (Daughter of Hekate I), was chosen as an emblematic image for both catalogue cover and posters. The image of the painting, the handling of the paint, seemed to sum up all that had gone on before, incorporating as it did in its own idiosyncratic way echoes of the art of Corinth, Kirchner, Kandinsky, Beckmann, Klee and Ernst – just to mention six names that were then, as now, infinitely more famous than that of Nay. However, that ability to summarise an epoch in itself speaks volumes about Nay as an artist, and deserves reflection. And perhaps even more remarkably, within this one image, one can also sense the origins of much art that was yet to come – that were to find expression in the work of such diverse figures as Baselitz, Polke, Kiefer, Richter and many others.

'To write poetry after Auschwitz is barbaric' wrote Nay's exact contemporary Theodor W. Adorno (1903–69), who, as a half-Jewish sociologist, philosopher and musicologist of the famous Frankfurt School, was forced to emigrate from Germany in 1937. He returned to his native land in 1949, at which point he came out with this now oft-quoted but perhaps too simplistic dictum. In spite of his ambition to be a modern artist, Nay's attitude and political stance were the exact opposite of a left-wing Marxist intellectual such as Adorno. By virtue of his family background alone, he more resembled another near contemporary, the somewhat older Ernst Jünger (1895–1998), author of *Storm of Steel* (1920) and *On the Marble Cliffs* (1939), whose novels, essays and diaries extolled in differentiated and cultivated ways the virtues of the German Bureaucratic and Officer Class. The older Jünger achieved fame and prominence in the 1920s. Nay, working as he did, as a young art student in a Berlin bookshop, would surely have known of Jünger well before he met him in France in 1943. Both Nay and Jünger had an ambiguous and analogous relationship with the political morality of the Weimar Republic, and certainly later with that of the Third Reich. Unlike Jünger, Nay was not old enough to have served in the First World War, but he was old enough, aged twelve, to have been affected by his father's death in Belgium in 1914. How this loss disillusioned a young sensitive boy of his class, can only be guessed.

In Berlin, when the war was over, Nay commenced his art studies in the prominent 'Jewish' art school, founded by Albert Reimann. Judging from his contacts and friends, he seemed, perhaps surprisingly for a relatively young man, to lean toward the work of older artists associated with the radical world of the November Group. He would also have known the world of Herwarth Walden's uncompromising avant-garde art gallery, Der Sturm, around the corner from the bookshop where he worked. But he rapidly found himself more in tune with the more French-oriented world of Paul Westheim's art journal *Das Kunstblatt*, which spread popular knowledge in Germany of French artists like Matisse, Picasso, Soutine and later the Douanier Rousseau. By 1933, the year the Nazis came to power, Nay was 31 years old. Through inclusion in exhibitions he had already achieved a certain recognition, and a handful of his works had even found their way into the collection of regional but adventurous museums like Hanover and Lübeck.

The few surviving works of this earlier Weimar period demonstrate successive influences: firstly a kind of German Matisse-ism derived from artists like Hans Purrmann, followed by a French Expressionistic style that recalls the paintings of Chaim Soutine. Having been to Paris in 1928, and perhaps via magazines, he then took cognisance of the newly fashionable Faux-Naifs such as Bombois and Vivin, as well as the Douanier Rousseau, who were being promoted there by the German critic-dealers Wilhelm Uhde and Waldemar George. Later paintings reveal the influence of Max Ernst's Surrealism and a certain affinity with the work of Paul Klee. At this time, for all his critical – but not financial – success, Nay was still finding his way.

It was with two works in the Faux-Naif manner that Nay achieved the great distinction of being the youngest artist to be included in the infamous touring *Entartete Kunst* exhibition that opened in Munich in 1937. Having been cautioned by the authorities in 1933/34, two years later he was officially banned from carrying on as an artist. He began military duties in 1940, serving as a solider in France. In 1935 he had executed a painting entitled *Elchkopf* (Elk Head) (p.33) that would be purchased by the great Expressionist painter of Die Brücke, Karl Schmidt-Rottluff. It was in this painting, and probably in others like it that did not survive the bombing raids of Berlin during the war, that Nay achieved something that became the seed of all his subsequent work. We should be happy that this 'secretly' made work survives. *Elchkopf* demonstrates the influence of Pablo Picasso on Nay. Perhaps its manner is in part derived from the late work – likewise influenced by Picasso – of Ernst Ludwig Kirchner.

In spite of the *Malverbot*, described in this book, Nay found ways to disobey and carry on painting. Whilst in France, he was able to stay for periods in the summer garden house of a French amateur sculptor and paper manufacturer named Pierre Térouanne. Térouanne, who lived in Le Mans, was – through a nephew – connected to the world of Aristide Maillol, the great French sculptor. It was in the garden house of Térouanne that Nay found the space and freedom that led up to the so-called 'Hekate' paintings of 1945–48. Earlier ones, done before and during the war itself (for example *Menschen in den Lofoten* (1938; p.49) or *Komposition mit vier Frauen* (1943; p.63) are exactly the paintings that one can imagine Kirchner might have done had he lived to be a witness to the horrors of the Second World War. We know that in their desperate need for self-protection both Kirchner and Nay would have been happy to have been embraced by the 'New Order', but neither was prepared to compromise their art, so of course, it was not to be. If Nay was at heart deeply apolitical, this did not stop him, in his mature paintings, from making images that are tough, heartbreaking and

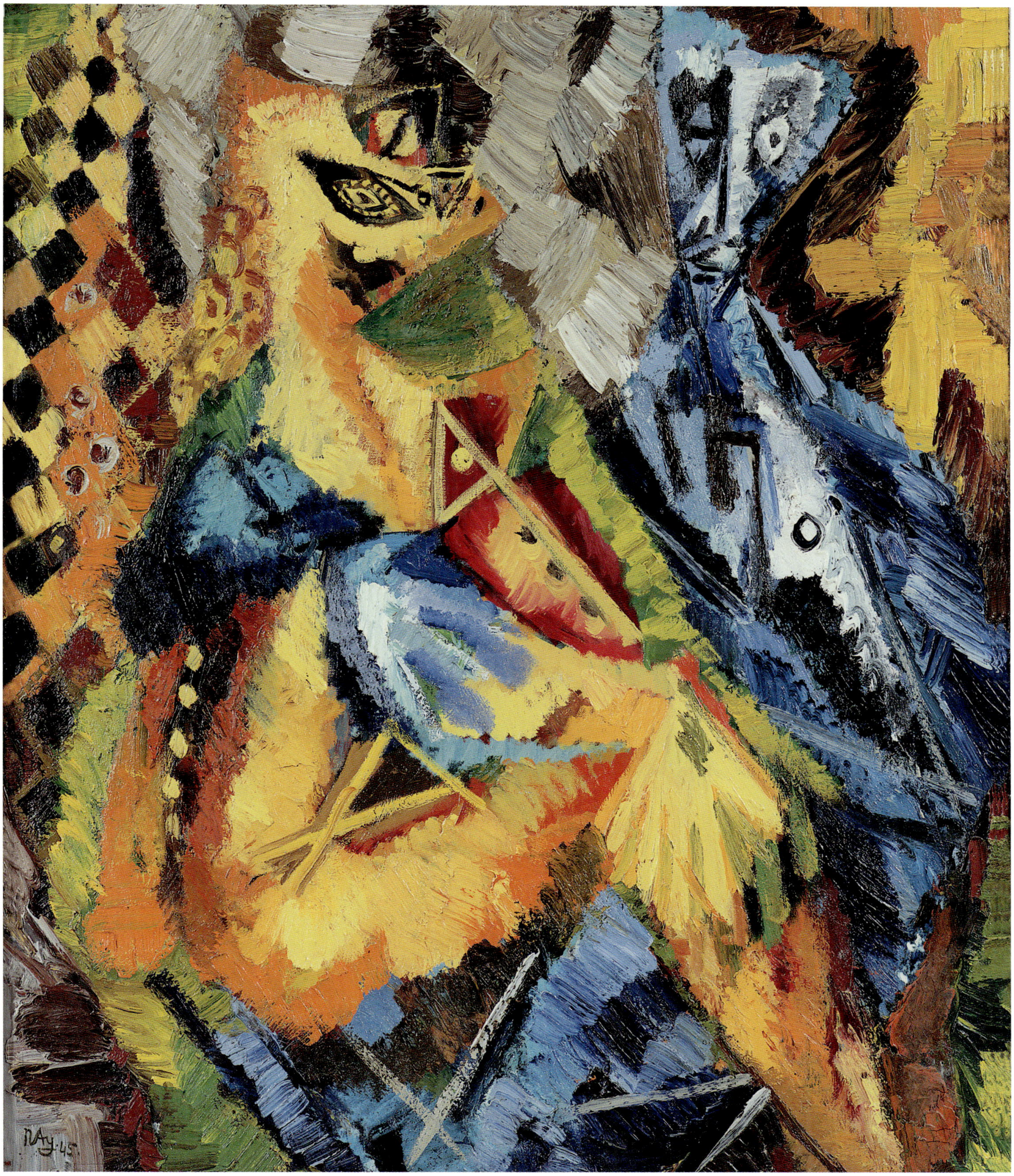

Tochter der Hekate i, 1945
Oil on canvas
98 × 85 cm · 38⅝ × 33½ in

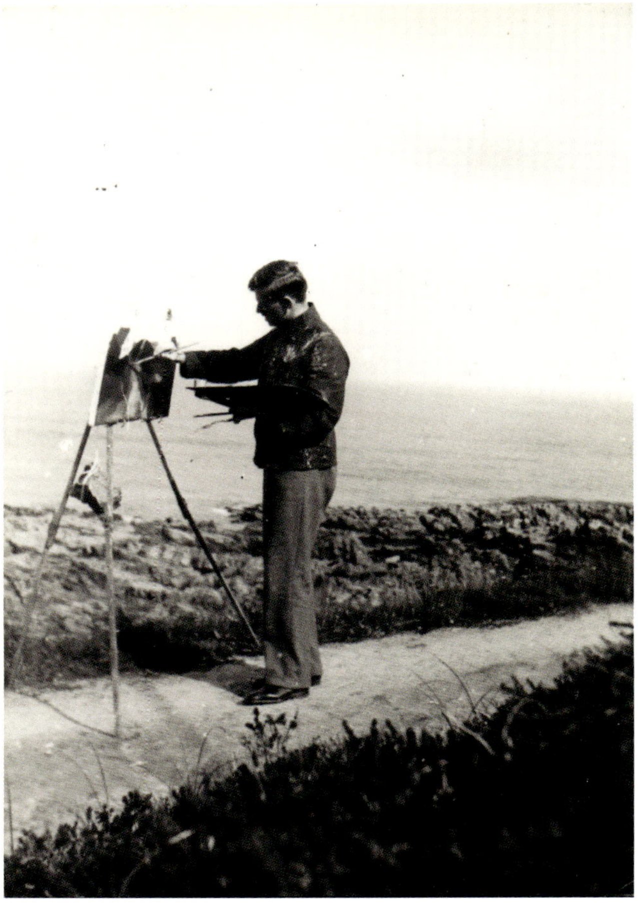

Nay with brush and easel, painting, Bornholm, 1929

desperately sad representations of the human condition of their age – something that even Kirchner himself never achieved in his later work. Perhaps not too much should be read into the titles of these pictures, with their reference to Hekate, the Greek Goddess of Night and Magic. They refer in fact to the daughters of the goddess – something that she, as a virgin, never had. However, Hesiod tells us that, 'when men arm themselves for the battle that destroys men, then the goddess is at hand to give victory and grant glory readily to whom she will'.

Following the war, and after a very short time spent in an American prisoner-of-war camp, Nay returned to Germany – not to one of the flattened cities, but to a quiet village near Frankfurt, untouched by war damage. He was able to quickly establish contacts with museum directors, private collectors, art dealers like Günther Franke in Munich, and most importantly to critics and curators – above all, to the legendary and in his day highly influential Werner Haftmann, who was a leading light of the German postwar art scene and was later to become the director of the Neue Nationalgalerie in (West) Berlin. Nay soon became recognised as the leading painter of Western Germany, adopting, at least on the surface, the now abstract painterly values that almost ubiquitously (with the one notable exception of Werner Heldt's Gris-influenced townscape paintings) defined the Stunde Null (Zero Hour), seemingly the only credible response to the recent terrible past. Nay's career culminated in his very prominent presentations at the first three Kassel Documenta exhibitions in 1955, '59 and '64. On all three occasions did his paintings took pride of place. He was to respond, over a period of two decades, with integrity and increasing painterly confidence, to the international dialogue of Tachist painting that was happening all over Western Europe. Within this, he found his own characteristically lyrical voice, never completely losing a sense of spatial, compositional and coloristic reality and even of figuration. His compositions were hard-edged, reverting often to a softer expressionist touch. However, there is always a calculated mood that emanates from each painting, even when, in the 1960s, he increasingly reacts to the inevitable influence of the New York Abstract Expressionists.

The issue that blighted Nay's reputation in the eyes of a younger generation, however, was his seeming inability, shared with other artists of his generation, to address without ambiguity the disaster that had culminated in 1945 – the defeat, the seeming destruction of all values of civilised German culture that was everywhere evidenced. It seems now clear that the psychological trauma suffered both by the victims and by those directly or indirectly complicit in the ghastly events of the immediate past, was too great for Nay and his contemporaries to fully comprehend and describe. To that extent, Adorno's statement held a great truth in the context of its time. Ultimately, it was to take another generation of artists and creative individuals, who could no longer be accused of wilful blindness towards the past, to begin to work through at least some of the complex questions and provide the answers so urgently required. Such individuals had perhaps been witnesses as children, or even as young soldiers, to the horrors. Those of Nay's generation and even older such as Thomas Mann or Berthold Brecht, who had been 'lucky' enough to emigrate before the war, some of whom would return to West or East Germany after 1945, were amongst the very few who were not directly compromised by the perverted ethics that had made possible and legitimised the criminality of the Nazi regime. The writers of Gruppe 47 (a group of mostly literary West German intellectuals including Günter Grass and Heinrich Böll who were attempting to re-establish the integrity of German literature) were for the most part young enough to be able to avoid accusations of complicity. The same can be said for a younger generation of visual artists, including Joseph Beuys (b.1921), Gerhard Richter (b.1932) and Georg Baselitz (b.1938). Their art could address recent German history much more directly and aggressively, and to a great extent it was this fact that was crucial to their international success.

In his collection of aphorisms, *Minima Moralia*, published in 1951, Adorno attacks the collective cultural amnesia into which he felt that German postwar culture had fallen:

> The thought that after this war life could continue on 'normally,' or indeed that culture could be 'reconstructed' – as if the reconstruction of culture alone were not already the negation of such – is idiotic. Millions of Jews have been murdered, and this is supposed to be only the intermission and not the catastrophe itself. What exactly is this culture waiting for anyway?[1]

He criticises a culture in which:

> Memory is tabooed as incalculable, unreliable, irrational. The intellectual asthma which results from this, which culminates in the breakdown of the historical dimension of consciousness, immediately debases the synthetic apperception which, according to Kant, is not to be separated from the 'reproduction in the imagination', from commemoration.[2]

This could be read as an attack by Adorno, on the meaningless and irrelevance of abstraction, a notion that was shared by many contemporaries. After 1968 it was this perception which was to push Nay, as well as most of his contemporaries in Germany into near obscurity. This was just one symptom of the inter-generational cultural wars that were beginning to rage in the United States and Western Europe in general and – arguably with the greatest consequences – in Germany in particular.

Nearly half a century later, it is perhaps both just and the right time to re-examine the career of Ernst Wilhelm Nay as an exemplary artist of his generation, caught in the crossfire and ever-changing maelstrom of history. Nay was neither a historian, philosopher or a critic, even though he was in touch with many of the leading thinkers of his time, with Martin Heidegger of course – as John-Paul Stonard significantly describes in his contribution to this book – as well as Werner Haftmann, to mention but two. Nay can now be seen to stand for his time and place just as legitimately and authoratively as Adorno. As his very particular career path demonstrates, Ernst Wilhelm Nay was a creator out of expressive necessity – a painter of substance.

London, April 2012

1 *Minima Moralia: Reflections from the damages life*, E.F.N. Jephcott (trans), NLB, London, number 33.
2 *Ibid.*, number 79.

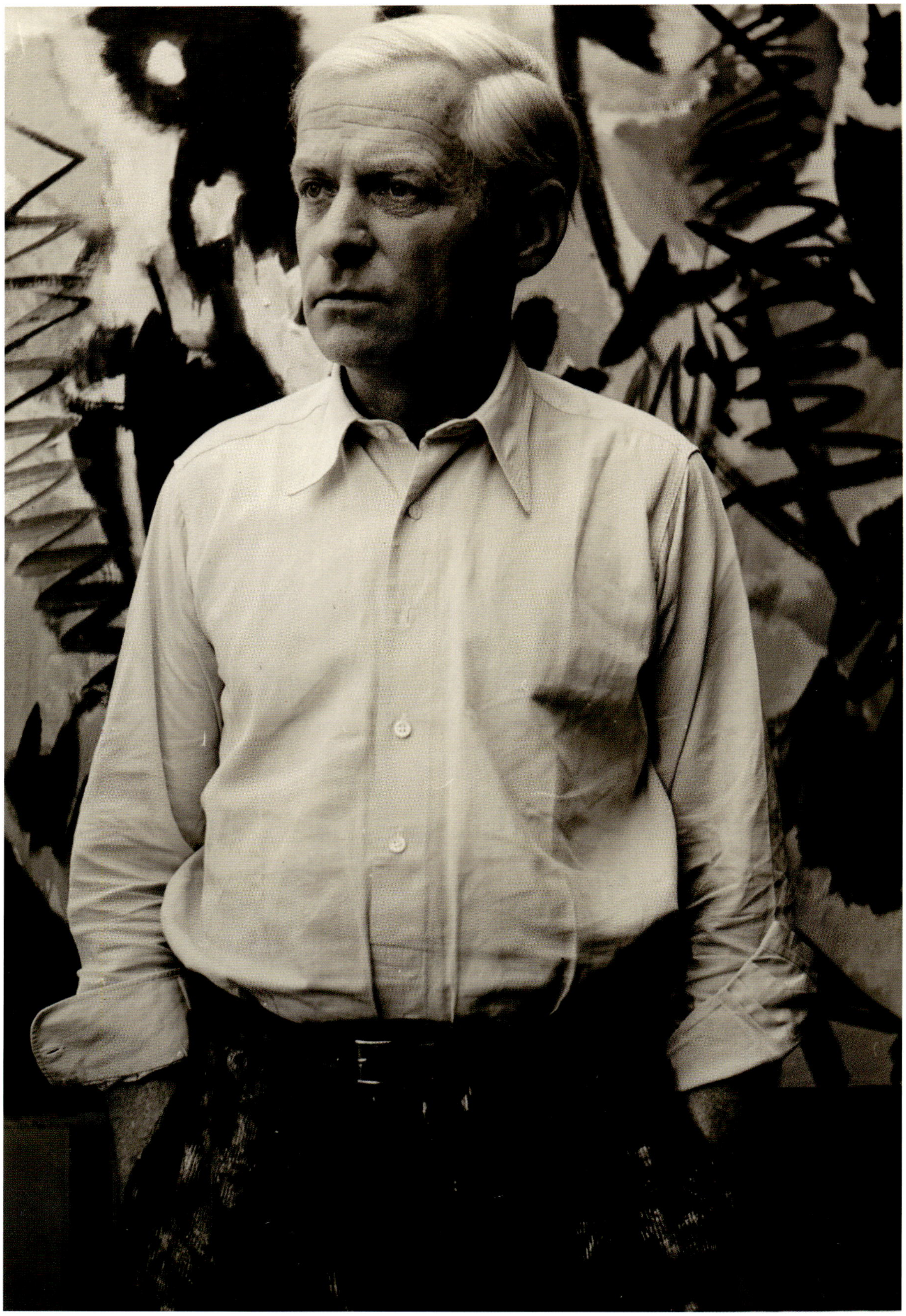

E.W. Nay in front of *Blaue Takte* in his studio, 1952

John-Paul Stonard

Ernst Wilhelm Nay

Introduction

For Ernst Wilhelm Nay, painting was an entrance to a world beyond the visible, a world more real and more vital that lay beneath the surface of appearances. Beginning his career as the chaotic years of the Weimar Republic became the dark years of the Third Reich, it was natural that he should look to art for an alternative reality. Yet his work is neither sentimental nor backward-looking, nor utopian in the sense of providing a vision of the future; rather, it puts forward the imperative that one must always live in the present moment. It is *Jetztzeit* or 'Now-time' painting, to use a word current in intellectual circles during the 1930s.

Nay's *Jetztzeit* was vital to his survival during the early years of his career, and was also the foundation for his later international success. It was the reason why neither 1933 nor 1945 were particular ruptures in the development of his work, and why he was able to produce some of his best works during the war, while stationed as a soldier in Le Mans.[1] It was also the principle that enabled him to continue painting through the destruction and defeat of Germany, amongst the physical and spiritual ruins of his country, at a time when the very possibility of 'German art' was put into question. His paintings, shifting from figurative to abstract forms over the course of his career, are concerned with the sensuous present of the act of painting, with gesture caught in a unique moment of time, recorded in colours, forms and textures.

If it is relatively straightforward to introduce his work, it is harder to convey an image of Nay himself. His painting and writing were to some degree a form of protection from public inquisition. A strong sense of distance pervades his life, not as an aloofness, but as a necessity, a result of having survived the political turmoil of the Republic, the Reich, and the postwar occupation and division of Germany. As Karl Gutbrod wrote, Nay would never use the familiar form of address – *du* – even to close friends: 'he was too afraid of anyone breaking through the protective wall he had created around himself'.[2] The 'sovereignty' that he admired so much in Edvard Munch, after meeting him briefly in Norway, was also a natural part of Nay's character. He was an individualist who defended his work pugnaciously and, although not a solitary character, was never to join an artists' group, such as those mutual-aid organisations that sprang up after 1945. Nay's unsentimental nature went beyond a character trait to become one of the defining features of his art. His second wife Elisabeth Nay-Scheibler has noted his anti-historicist approach to art and life, describing the proximity with which he lived to his own present time, which stretched from his indifference to his own personal history to the highly contemporary choice of architecture and furnishings for the studio dwelling that he had built in Cologne in the 1950s.[3]

Above all, Nay held an unwavering belief in his own painting, its social importance in times of political extremism, and its place

1 Ernst Wilhem Nay, *Lesebuch: Selbstzeugnisse und Schriften 1931–1968*, M. DuMont, Cologne, 2002, p.28.
2 *E.W. Nay, 1902–1968: Bilder und Dokumente*, Archiv für Bildende Kunst am Germanischen Nationalmuseum and Prestel-Verlag, Nuremberg and Munich, 1980, p.171.
3 Elisabeth Nay-Scheibler, 'Without a Filter – Memories of the Final Years', in Ingrid Pfeiffer and Max Hollein (eds), *E.W. Nay: Bilder der 1960er Jahre*, exhibition catalogue, Schirn Kunsthalle, Frankfurt, 2009, p.25.
4 Nay, *op. cit.*, p.310.
5 Werner Haftmann, *E.W. Nay. A Retrospective,* M. DuMont Schauberg, Cologne, 1960, p.161.

alongside the great advances in science and technology of the twentieth century. This self-confidence provided the background for the steady evolution of his work in a series of phases that might be described as 'episodic', given shape by excursions and deviations on various themes that blossom and break new ground for future developments. 'Paintings come from paintings. The work of the painter exists within this continuum', he once wrote.[4] Despite the adverse situation in which this development occurred, from the earliest days of his career in the late 1920s Nay enjoyed the support of many of the most important figures in the art world, who saw in his work an approach to form that could act as a bridge between the difficult world of avant-garde art and a general public. He was often compared to the older artist Ernst Ludwig Kirchner, and indeed may be seen as a bridge between the prewar Expressionist painting of Kirchner, and the resurgence of a type of expressive abstract painting in the postwar era.

Yet Nay's success, despite the extreme circumstances in which his early career developed, and his own strong connections with the institutions of German cultural life, was to be used against him later in his career. He reached the peak of his international success with the installation of three paintings on the ceiling of a gallery at the third Documenta in 1964. By the time of his partial retrospective at the Frankfurter Kunstverein the next year, a public backlash had seriously damaged his reputation. The focus of the attack was not his painting, but rather his role within the official culture of West Germany, as well as the lofty rhetoric that surrounded his abstract forms, a mystical language of transcendence that appeared both exclusive and intellectually questionable.

The stain, which Nay himself had done little to bring upon himself, and which the actual content of his works did not justify, was nevertheless stubborn. Despite having acted more than any other artist as the bridge between 'classic' modernism and postwar formations, and having been central to European abstract painting at a time when American art was dominant, Nay has frequently been omitted from surveys of abstract painting, from Michael Seuphor's pioneering *L'art abstrait, ses origins, ses premières maîtres* of 1950, to the exhibition *The Spiritual in Art: Abstract Painting 1890–1985*, shown at the Los Angeles County Museum of Art in 1986, to John Golding's book *Paths to the Absolute*, published in 2000, to name but a few.

A fresh approach to Nay's painting is now therefore essential. Historical distance, coupled with a range of new archival sources on which to draw, make this possible, and the basis of many claims hitherto made for Nay's work can be set against a more critical standpoint. This book is written from the premise that the 'description of the construction of a painting and its development of colour' does not 'deliver the key to how Nay's paintings are to be read'.[5] It is rather the conflicts from which his paintings arose, and by which they were understood, and their ability to bring forth meaning in a way that neither Nay nor his supporters could fully comprehend, that ensures their continued relevance.

Origins: Berlin

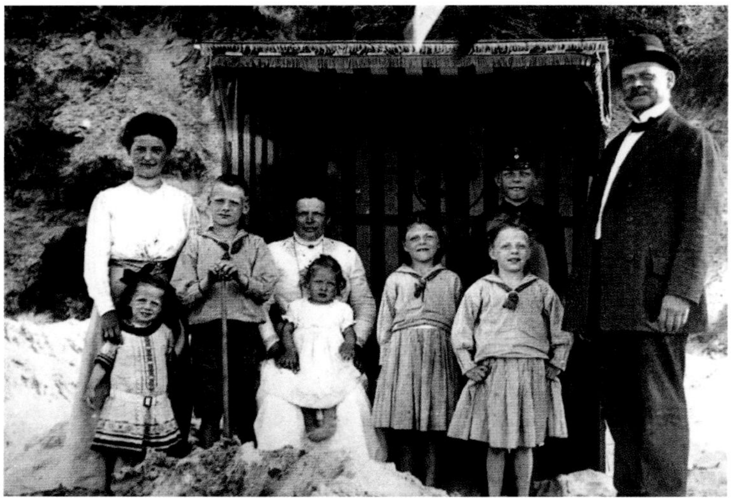

Nay family by the Baltic Sea shortly before the First World War, E.W. Nay third from left

Ernst Wilhelm Nay was born in Berlin in 1902 when the Second German Empire of Wilhelm II was at its glorious height; he spent his childhood witnessing its decline. The Prussian capital was a heady mix of tradition and modernity; of the official culture of the State and the military, and the modern world of advertising and mass culture. Ernst Wilhelm's father, Johannes Nay, was a typical product of the Prussian conservative establishment, a civil servant who had risen to an important post in the Prussian state treasury. His position and income assured a comfortable upper-middle-class childhood for Ernst Wilhelm and his five siblings, including a good education and holidays on the fashionable North Sea coast. In later life, Nay contrasted his father's protestant roots with the more worldly, bourgeois origins of his mother, Elisabeth, née Westphal.

Ernst Wilhelm's Berlin childhood was cut short by the death of his father, killed at the age of 52 fighting for the German army in Belgium in the first months of 1914. His widow was left with six children to raise, and it was a relief when Ernst Wilhelm left the next year for Schulpforta, the 'Fürstenschule', or 'school for princes', a Protestant boarding school near Naumburg (which includes Friedrich Nietzsche amongst its past pupils). Here he received a classical, humanist education. Wandering around the old Cistercian abbey, wrote Elisabeth Nay-Scheibler, Nay must have felt happy to have escaped the war years in Berlin, and the troubled family in Steglitz.[6] Although he appears already to have decided on his vocation as an artist, none of the paintings made by Nay during his schooling has survived.[7] A portrait photograph taken at the time of his leaving examination suggests the confidence and status that his education had provided, a sense of security that was vital for his survival during the 1920s and 1930s, in the face of severe economic hardship and political repression.

On returning to Berlin in 1921, Nay was apprenticed to a bookseller, Gsellius, on Mohrenstraße in the town centre. He derived little enjoyment from this work, and spent most of his free time painting and drawing,[8] attending an evening class at the Reimann-Schule, a private school for fine and applied arts in the Schöneberg district, established by Albert Reimann in 1902.[9] His teachers, including Moritz Melzer, a founder alongside Max Pechstein and others of the Novembergruppe (November Group), were part of the generation that had been involved in the reformist and revolutionary artistic groupings in Germany after 1918.

There are few records of what Nay saw, or what impressed him in these years. He later recollected Herwarth Walden's Der Sturm gallery, located a short walk away from the Gsellius bookshop, at Potsdamer Straße 134a. The gallery was attached to the journal of the same name, run by Walden, the 'prophet and manager of the modern movement' in Germany, and was the centre of avant-garde activity in Berlin.[10] Although no comprehensive list of exhibitions in Walden's gallery exists, it is known that in 1921 they included solo showings of work by Kurt Schwitters and Paul Klee, and from the next year exhibitions of the new Constructivist art from Russia and Eastern Europe, particularly of the Hungarian László Moholy-Nagy. Yet the type of work shown by Walden at Der Sturm was too radical for Nay, who was not naturally drawn to politics as a subject for painting.

Nay left his apprenticeship in 1922 to pursue his career as an artist. Only one work from this early period survives, an introspective self-portrait (Nay destroyed many of his early paintings, throwing them one by one into the canal).[11] The variety of jobs that he took before being forced to return to the book trade fully reflected the new distractions of urban life: working at a department store, the famous Kaufhaus des Westens, and also, with the help of his brother Otto, as a film extra at the UFA studios.[12] Although the Gsellius bookshop offered a sense of continuity with his highly academic, classical education, the temptations of a city whose intense nervous rhythms became a central subject for artists and writers of the time provided a counter-pull. An older generation of Expressionist painters, including Ernst Ludwig Kirchner (1880–1938) and George Grosz (1893–1959), had responded to the boom of the metropolis and the new 'mental life' that it created, 'damned to perpetual becoming' in the words of Karl Scheffler. Grosz's vision of Friedrichstraße, just around the corner from Nay's bookshop,

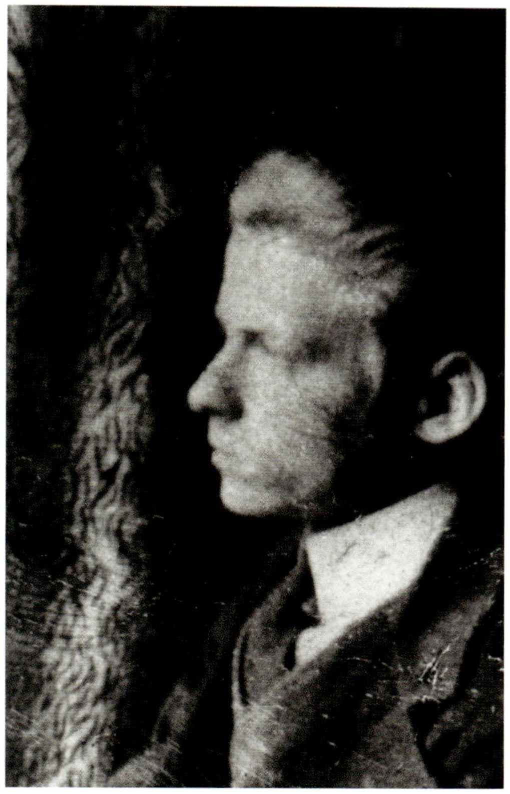

Nay at Schulpforta, 1921

Selbstbildnis, 1922
Oil on wood
40 × 31.5 cm · 15¾ × 12⅜ in

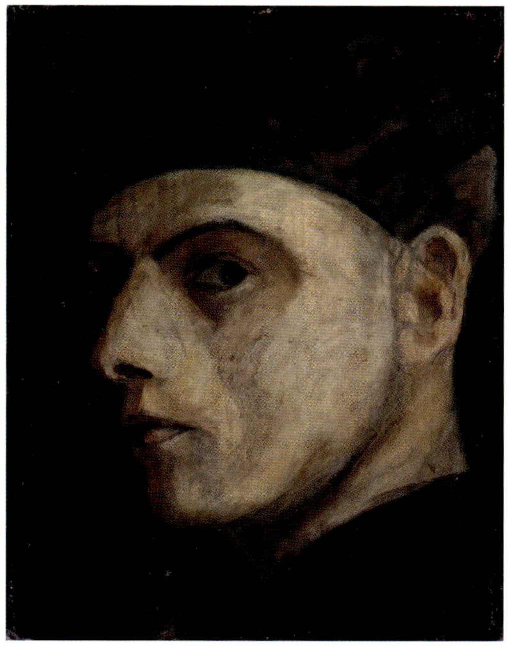

6 Elisabeth Nay-Scheibler, 'E.W. Nay aus der Nähe – ein Lebensbericht', in S. Gohr, J.G. Prinz von Hohenzollern and D. Ronte (eds), *Nay-Variationen. Retrospektive zum 100. Geburtstag*, exhibition catalogue, Kunsthalle der Hypo-Kulturstiftung, Munich, 2002, pp.39–59.
7 *Ibid.*, p.40.
8 Elly (Helene) Nay, *Ein strahlendes Weiß. Meine Zeit mit E.W. Nay*, Hirmer, Berlin and Cologne, 1984, p.11.
9 Swantje Kuhfuss-Wickenheiser, *Die Reimann-Schule in Berlin und London 1902–1943. Ein jüdisches Unternehmen zur Kunst- und Designausbildung internationaler Prägung bis zur Vernichtung durch das Hitlerregime*, Shaker Media, Aachen 2009.
10 Edith Hoffmann, 'Der Sturm. Ein Gedenkbuch an Herwarth Walden und die Kunstler des Sturmkreises (1954)', in *The Burlington Magazine*, no.646, vol.99, January 1957, p.28.
11 Elly (Helene) Nay, *op. cit.*, p.19?.
12 *Ibid.*, p.19.

evokes the frenetic pace of urban life at the centre of the metropolis, 'damned to perpetual becoming' in the words of Karl Scheffler.[13] The city continued its rapid expansion in the early 1920s due to the incorporation of adjoining suburbs, increasing the population to around four million. Yet although Nay was of a generation impressed by the developments of modern life, political and financial precariousness – if not outright collapse – compelled him to appreciate the virtues of stability and order. The value of the Rentenmark on 15 November 1923 was a trillionth of that quoted in 1914. The currency was subsequently stabilised, and the following four years were the 'golden period' of the Weimar Republic, but still significant hardship and poverty were experienced by a large proportion of the population, including a devastated middle class, whose hard-earned savings and war bonds devalued to nothing. It was in this tumultuous context that Nay first gained a foothold in the artistic life of Berlin, and, from around the middle of the decade, enjoyed a number of important official successes.

In 1923 Nay began attending life drawing classes at the Kunstgewerbeschule (School of Arts and Crafts). He is also recorded that year as having enrolled for an evening class in life drawing at the Hochschule für bildende Kunst, which in 1924 merged with the Kunstgewerbeschule to become the Vereinigte Staatsschulen für freie und angewandte Kunst (The Unified State Schools for Free and Applied Art), a reformist institution inspired by the model of the Deutscher Werkbund. Reform was the key to arts education of the period, and to the art world at large – a reform away from the official culture of Wilhelmine Germany, from a hierarchy of the arts and segregation of the fine and decorative arts, which had led to a vast sub-class of unemployed artists. The culture of reform – which found its greatest expression in the Bauhaus of Walter Gropius – was however to have little impact on Nay, who stuck to painting undeterred, despite his lack of success in this early period of going it alone.[14] Economic circumstances meant that by 1924 Nay was compelled to return to full-time work as a bookseller. To continue painting it was vital to secure a place at the Vereinigte Staatsschulen (otherwise known as the 'Academy'), and in October 1924 he wrote in some desperation to the painter Karl Hofer (1878–1955), a professor at the Academy in the western district of Charlottenburg, asking if he could show him some of his work, with the intention of being admitted to his class. Nay later recollected that he took only one painting to Hofer, a portrait of Franz Reuter, completed in 1925,[15] although two other paintings, a portrait of his mother (p.20), and of Ruth Meffert, a friend of Nay's sister, had been completed the previous year.

Nay was registered with Hofer from the summer term of 1925, and from 1928 until the summer term of 1930 was upgraded to Hofer's masterclass.[16] He was marked from the outset as a star student and protégé of the older artist. In 1925 Hofer encouraged Nay to show his *Bildnis Franz Reuter* (Portrait of Franz Reuter, 1925) at the Spring Exhibition of the Prussian Academy of Arts, where Hofer himself had been enrolled as a member two years earlier. This biannual Salon exhibition was one of the principal ways of securing public recognition as a painter, and was an important step for the young artist. Nay's painting was accepted and hung between a portrait by Kirchner and another by Oskar Kokoschka, an unexpected grand statement that confirmed his position as a serious painter. Kirchner was a strong influence on Nay's painting at the time. The painting by Kokoschka, however, might more revealingly have been replaced by a work by the French naive artist Henri Rousseau. During the years 1924 to 1928 (and to a certain extent for the rest of his life), Nay's painting oscillated between two stylistic modes, an Expressionism informed largely by Kirchner, and a primitive, naive figuration that had, less directly, Rousseau as its model. This was by no means unusual: Rousseau's influence on German artists at this moment was considerable. The first monograph on Rousseau, by Wilhelm Uhde, was published in Germany in Düsseldorf, 1914, following the inclusion of his works in the first Blaue Reiter exhibition in Munich, and also with his own room at the Erster Deutscher Herbstsalon in Berlin, 1913, both highly significant exhibitions.[17] Rousseau was considered an emblem of an authentic art, uncorrupted by modern urban life, and well-suited to a conservative, anti-modernist spirit. Furthermore, the French painter offered a model that was not only anti-academic, but also contrary to Expressionism (and remote too from Impressionism).[18] The 'Rousseau School', a term coined by the critic Franz Roh, arose in German art after 1914.[19] Alongside artists such as August Wilhelm Dressler, Ernst Fritsch and Bernhard Klein, Max Beckmann was the most prominent painter to take Rousseau's work as a model for imbuing landscapes and quotidian scenes with a feeling of intimacy and humanity. For Beckmann, Rousseau was 'Homer in the porter's lodge whose prehistoric dreams have sometimes brought me near the Gods'.[20]

It was in this context that Nay's earliest group of paintings developed. Three works, all included in an exhibition at the Lehrter Bahnhof, Berlin, in 1925, and all now lost, show the motif most common to the Rousseau School, a suburban scene with a road winding into the mid-distance.[21] *Landschaft mit Telegrafenmasten*

13 Karl Scheffler, *Berlin: Ein Stadtschicksal*, Reiss, Berlin, 1920, p.267.

14 The reform movement was described by Nikolaus Pevsner as one of the 'most important experiments in art education so far ventured in our century'. Nikolaus Pevsner, *Academies of Art Past and Present*, Cambridge University Press, Cambridge, 1940, p.276.

15 Elisabeth Nay-Scheibler in conversation with the author.

16 These dates contradict the usual chronology of Nay's studies, which claims that he was registered as a master student of Karl Hofer from 1924 to 1928, at which point he left the Vereinigte Staatschulen. Information from Antje Kalcher, Akademie der Künste Berlin, Universitätsarchiv. Bestand 7 (summer term 1923) and Bestand 8 (studies 1925–30).

17 Wilhelm Uhde, *Henri Rousseau*, Ohle, Düsseldorf, 1914. Uhde opened his monograph on Rousseau with a graveside oration glowing with respect. Much of this enthusiasm appears due to Kandinsky's prophetic praise of Rousseau in 1912 as the 'father of the great realism'.

18 By 1920 Hans Siemsen could write in the *Frankfurter Zeitung* that Rousseau was well-known in Germany, and that he was considered a *heilige* (saint), like Dostoevsky. Hans Siemsen, *Frankfurter Zeitung*, 30 March 1920, pp.1–2.

19 Franz Roh, *Nach-Expressionismus. Probleme der neuesten europäischen Malerei*, Klinkhardt & Biermann, Leipzig, 1925. A number of publications appeared in the early 1920s that consolidated Rousseau's prewar reputation in Germany, for example Wilhelm Uhde, 'Henri Rousseau', in *Deutsche Kunst und Dekoration*, vol.47, 1920, pp.17–25; Helmut Kolle, *Henri Rousseau*, Klinkhardt & Biermann, Leipzig, 1922.

20 Max Beckmann, 'On my painting', New York, 1941, lecture given in July 1938 on the opening of the *Exhibition of Twentieth Century German Art* at the New Burlington Galleries in London. Reprinted in *Max Beckmann, Self-Portrait in Words. Collected Writings and Statements, 1903–1950*, University of Chicago Press, Chicago and London, 1997, pp.302–07.

21 *Dorfweg* (1924–25); *Landschaft mit Telegrafenmasten* (1924–25); *Landschaft* (1924–25).

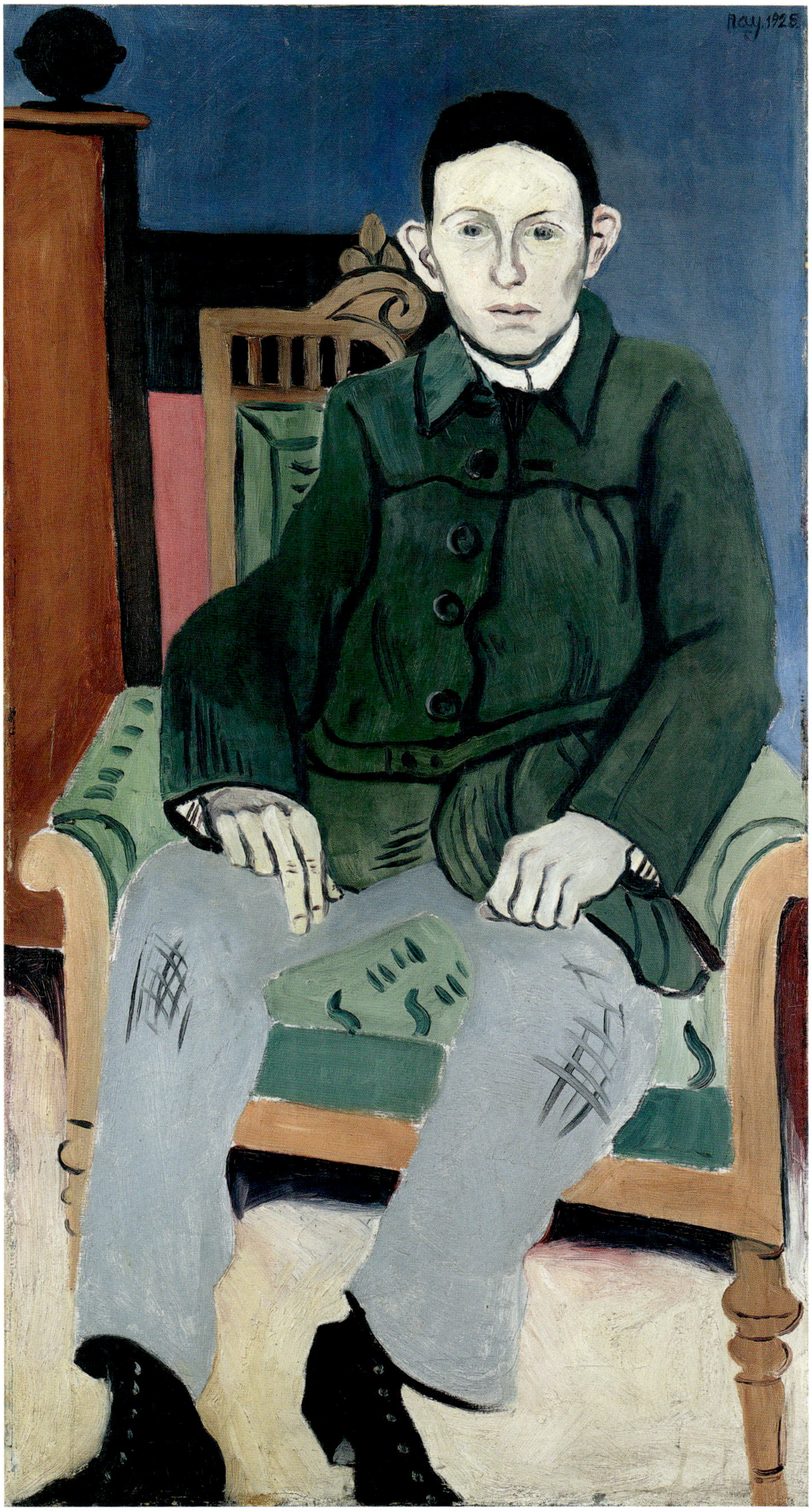

Bildnis Franz Reuter, 1925
Oil on canvas
130 × 70 cm · 51⅛ × 27½ in

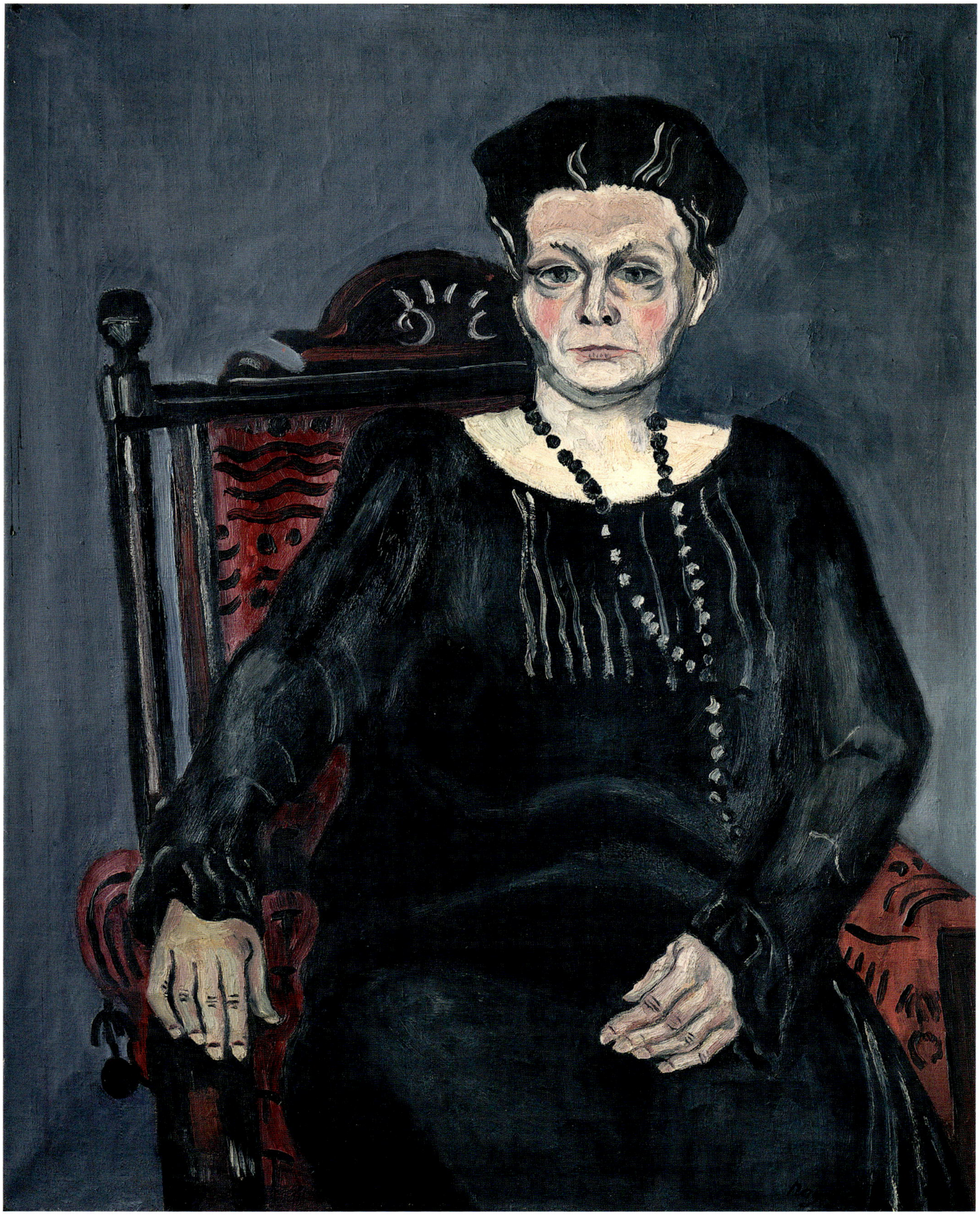

Bildnis meiner Mutter, 1924
Oil on canvas
110 × 90 cm · 43¼ × 35⅝ in

(Landscape with Telegraph Poles, 1924–25) shows a suburban setting, the encroachment of industry and technology on the countryside, with a simplistic style and the pervading sense of anonymity and disquiet. The newly expanding suburbs, with their strange melancholy, quickly evolved into a staple subject for conservative painters, for whom they offered a subject both romantic and quotidian. Of those paintings by Nay from this period that survive, the best-known, *Sandweg* (Pathway, 1926; p.23, top), shows figures in a melancholy setting that might be compared with Georg Simmel's description of the 'stranger', the quintessential inhabitant of the modern town or city.[22] It was a new psychological type, a closed, fearful persona concerned above all with survival. A painting from the next year, *Begräbnis* (Burial, 1927; p.25) shows a crowd of mourners at a suburban funeral. Such depictions of ordinary Berlin life were common amongst painters of the Berlin Secession such as Hans Baluschek, but in Nay's case without the naturalism or sense of high-art 'finish' of what has been termed 'German Impressionism'.

Other paintings show a contrary impulse, deriving from Expressionism, and in particular from the painting of Kirchner. The 1927 *Damenbildnis* (Portrait of a Woman; p.22, top), included in the Spring Exhibition at the Prussian Academy of Arts the next year, appears as a direct homage to the older artist, by that time living in exile in the Swiss mountains. The schematic slit eyes and horizontally striped dress of Nay's portrait refer directly to paintings by Kirchner, although the lack of any colour photograph of this work, now untraceable, makes it difficult to assess how far Nay was experimenting with an expressionistic palette. Nay often compared his comfortable middle-class upbringing to that of Kirchner, who had been born in 1880 to a wealthy bourgeois family. But their fates were only loosely linked through the interest of certain collectors in the 1930s, particularly of Carl Hagemann and then, one year before Kirchner's suicide in Switzerland, the juxtaposition of their works in the 1937 *Entartete Kunst* (Degenerate Art) exhibition. Kirchner's *Winterliche Mondlandschaft* (Winter Moon Landscape) from 1919, taken from the Kaiser Friedrich Museum, Magdeburg, was hung above Nay's *Fischerboote an der Hafenmole* (Fishing Boats at the Harbour, 1930), taken from the Nationalgalerie in Berlin. Another of Nay's paintings to fall victim to Nazi censorship was *Kartenspieler* (Card Players, 1927–28; p.22, bottom), seized from the collection of the Städtische Kunstsammlungen, Kassel, during one of the *Entartete Kunst* confiscation campaigns, and subsequently either destroyed or lost.[23] Showing a group of figures playing cards around a table, this painting reveals a more academic mode present in Nay's work at this time: that of the 'classic modern', which in the case of *Kartenspieler* shows the influence of Hofer's allegorical mode, formally oriented to French modern painting, Paul Cézanne in particular.

Although Nay was reluctant to admit Hofer's influence in later life, and was aware of the limitations of his master's work, it was nevertheless due to the older artist's support that he enjoyed his first successes during 1926 and 1927 in Berlin, Hanover and Munich. Two further encounters took place in his latter years as a student, both decisive for his future. Paul Westheim (1886–1963) was an art critic and editor known principally for the journal he founded and edited between 1917 and 1933, *Das Kunstblatt*. In the 1920s Westheim was an important counterbalance to the overwhelming influence of Walden's *Der Sturm*, and frequently incurred Walden's editorial wrath as a rival promoter of modern German and French art. Like Walden, Westheim was a publicist and entrepreneur who devoted himself to searching out and promoting younger artists working in a modern style. Although Westheim is likely to have seen works by Nay in the exhibitions at the Prussian Academy, it was not until he asked the artist to sit on the jury of a competitive exhibition for young painters, *Junge Maler*, that the two had any contact. A call for entries went out in the January issue of *Das Kunstblatt*, announcing that the magazine was sponsoring an exhibition offering younger artists the chance of a first step into the public sphere. At the end of January, a jury consisting of Nay and two other painters, Heinrich Schwarz and Gustav Wunderwald, selected 100 paintings, which were then displayed in the gallery of the Deutsche Kunstgemeinschaft, in the Berliner Schloss, from mid-February to mid-March.[24] It is clear that Nay as a young, struggling painter was exactly the type of artist whom Westheim was eager to support. In his lengthy review of the exhibition in *Das Kunstblatt*, he highlighted the two works submitted by Nay, a still life, which he compares to the style of Georges Braque, and the landscape painting *Sandweg*. Westheim associates Nay with the German *Eigenbrödler*, or 'eccentrics', 'who develop their own form of expression'.[25] The description is important. At a moment when the first wave of avantgardism, Expressionism, appeared to have exhausted itself, young painters felt a weight of responsibility in deciding which subjects to choose and how to render them. The *Eigenbrödler* style was also identified as *Laienkunst*, 'lay' or 'amateur' painting, a deliberately untutored style focusing attention on the subject matter that was being promoted in the pages of *Das Kunstblatt*.[26]

Nay's *Eigenbrödler* style was comparable with other artists in the *Junge Maler* exhibition such as Karl Döbel, Karl von Appen, and in particular Wunderwald, all of whom had been discovered by Westheim and publicised in *Das Kunstblatt* earlier in 1927.[27] Westheim's reputation in the 1920s was as a promoter of modestly conservative modernist painting, largely influenced by developments in France. He was often criticised in the pages of *Der Sturm* as too reactionary, although Walden's frequent attacks on him were also motivated

22 Georg Simmel, 'The Stranger', in Kurt H. Wolff (ed), *The Sociology of Georg Simmel*, Free Press, New York, 1950, pp.402–08.
23 See Franz Roh, *'Entartete' Kunst. Kunstbarbarei im Dritten Reich*, Fackelträger-Verlag, Hanover, 1962, p.205.
24 See Lutz Windhöfel, *Paul Westheim und Das Kunstblatt. Eine Zeitschrift und ihr Herausgeber in der Weimarer Republik*, Böhlau, Cologne, Weimar and Vienna, 1995, pp.300–01.
25 Paul Westheim, 'Die Ausstellung der jungen Maler in der Deutschen Kunstgemeinschaft, Berlin', *Das Kunstblatt*, 1927, pp.128–44.
26 Franz Roh, 'Malereien von Ringelnatz. Neuer Beitrag zur Laienkunst', in *Das Kunstblatt*, 1927, pp.63–66. See also Nikola Michailow, 'Zur Begriffsbestimmung der Laienmalerei', in *Zeitschrift für Kunstgeschichte*, no.5/6, 1935, pp.283–300.
27 Paul Westheim, 'Gustav Wunderwald', in *Das Kunstblatt*, 1927, pp.2–5. Westheim describes the importance of the model of Utrillo for Wunderwald's depictions of the Berlin in which he lived: 'die Welt der Mietskasernenstraßen und Fabrikanlagen des neuen Berlin', p.2. Wunderwald was born in Cologne in 1882 and was trained as a house painter and decorator, and then as a scene painter. The authenticity of his style was connected with this lack of training and the way in which he captured the 'melancholy' of the city's suburbs, amongst factories and workers' tenement buildings, in Spandau or Moabit.

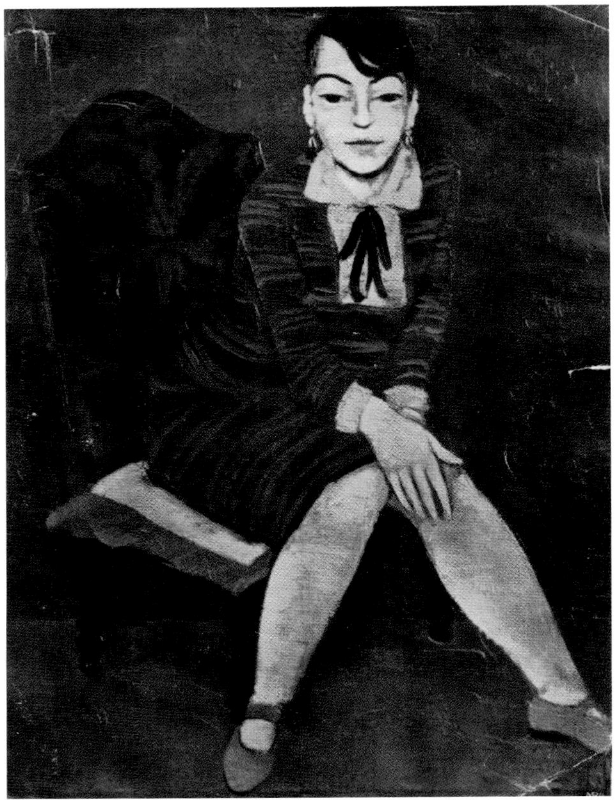

Damenbildnis, 1927
Oil on canvas
117 × 90 cm · 46 × 35⅝ in (approx)
Location unknown

Kartenspieler, 1927–28
Oil on canvas
106 × 135 cm · 41¾ × 53⅛ in (approx)
Location unknown

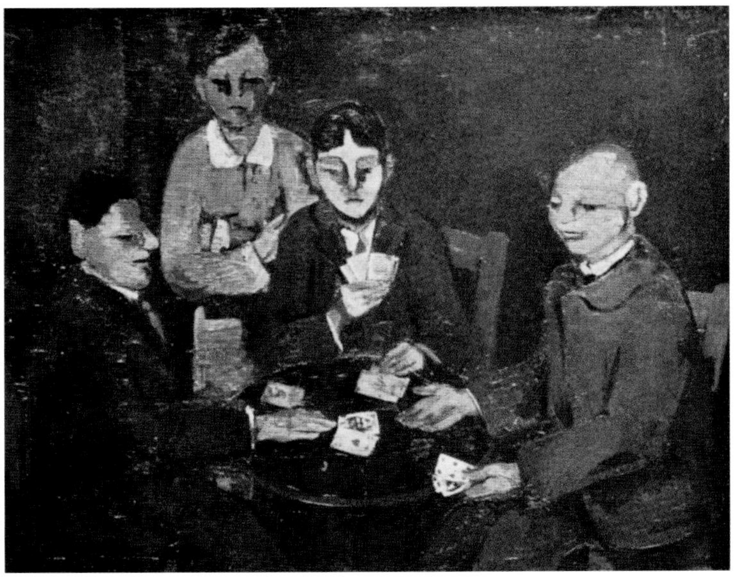

by jealous rivalry.[28] Support of French artists also formed one of the points of the polemic between Walden and Westheim. Walden wanted to retain his privileged position as the source of information on French art in Germany, while Westheim, who made his first voyage to France in 1921, attempted to establish his own credentials as a go-between.

That Nay chose to follow the path of Western influence associated with Westheim, rather than the international trends dominated at this moment by Russian art and the presence in Berlin of Walden, set a pattern that continued throughout his life and work. So too did the successes that he began to enjoy at this moment. By 1927 Nay was known in museum and collector circles as one of Hofer's most gifted pupils, thanks in particular to his yearly contributions to the exhibitions of the Berlin Secession and of the Prussian Academy.[29] In 1927 the Provinzial-Museum in Hanover bought *Landschaft Promenade* (Landscape Promenade), the first of Nay's works to enter a museum. It was also in early 1927 that Nay met his future wife, Elly. His first sight of her, as Elly recounts in her memoirs of her life with Nay, was naked modelling for students at the Academy.[30]

Nay painted what may be seen as his first important work the next year, 1928, an apparently modest still life showing a cauliflower and other vegetables, *Blumenkohlstilleben (Gemüsestilleben)* (Still Life with Cauliflower, 1928; p.26). It was illustrated in an article by Westheim in *Das Kunstblatt* in 1928, alongside another *Eigenbrödler* work by Nay, *Vorstadtstrasse. Blumenkohlstilleben* was the occasion of Nay's first public success when it was exhibited in the Prussian Academy Spring Exhibition of 1928, and received a prize of 1,000 RM. Such a sum would have made a significant difference: in a letter to the councillor Carl Duisberg, thanking him for the prize, Nay emphasised the importance of the money to him at that moment.[31] As a result of the publicity surrounding the prize, the work was acquired by Carl Georg Heise (1890–1979) for the Museum Behnhaus in Lübeck.[32] In his recollections of Nay, Heise recounts admiring the painting *Bildnis Franz Reuter* in the exhibition of the Neue Münchener Sezession in 1928, and seeking out a meeting with Nay in Berlin.[33] He describes the strong impression made on him by *Blumenkohlstilleben*, which he saw during this first meeting with Nay, and which he considered as done in a style typical of the Hofer School.

Nay's friendship with Heise led to a number of further introductions, including Erich Meyer (1897–1967), a medievalist and curator

28 See for example Kurt Schwitters, 'Noch einmal die Gefahr Westheim', in *Der Sturm*, September 1924, p.234.
29 Alfred Hentzen, 'Erinnerung an Ernst Wilhelm Nay', in *E.W. Nay, 1902–1968: Bilder und Dokumente*, *op. cit.*, pp.18–20.
30 Elly (Helene) Nay, *op. cit.*, p.7.
31 It is in this letter to Duisberg that Nay, when explaining his success, despite being only 25 years old, refers to his participation in an exhibition at the Carnegie Institute in Pittsburgh. In fact, no work by Nay was shown at the 27th International Exhibition at the Carnegie Institute, and it seems likely that either Karl Hofer, who had exhibited five works there in 1927 (alongside Pechstein, Heckel and Dix, the latter with his portrait of Hugo Erfurth), or Emil Orlik, a professor at the Akademie der Künste, who showed five paintings in the 1928 exhibition (which ran from 18 October to 9 December), had excited Nay by suggesting the possibility. It may also have been possible that Max Liebermann, who had informed Nay of his prize from Duisberg, had mentioned the possibility, since he was also to show in the 1928 Pittsburgh exhibition, including his portrait of President Hindenburg. E.W. Nay to Carl Duisberg, 4 June 1918, Deutsches Kunstarchiv, Nuremberg (cited hereafter as DKA).

at the Berlin Kunstgewerbemuseum, and Ernst Gosebruch (1872–1953), at that time director of the Folkwang Museum, Essen, and who became a regular visitor at Nay's studio.[34] The network that he began consolidating in the late 1920s, comprising some of the leading figures in the German arts establishment, proved essential for Nay's survival during the 1930s.

Nay was to look back and describe the period between his initial successes in selling works to museums, and his departure for Rome as the result of a residency award in 1931, as the 'quiet years'. In her memoirs Elly Nay writes that he left the Academy in 1928, and continued working in the studio of the painter Hermann Teuber, on Pariser Straße. It may have been restlessness and a feeling of frustration with the Academy, and the influence of Hofer, that precipitated his first visit to Paris in December of that year. Nay wrote that he was particularly inspired by Poussin's 'Four Seasons' cycle in the Louvre, although it is clearly impossible to detect a direct influence on his work. It appears more significant that Nay encountered Surrealist painting here for the first time; this was to have a decisive impact on his work when he returned, and to give a new direction both to his style and choice of subject matter.

1929 appears nevertheless to have been a 'quiet year'. Little is known of Nay's activities and only two paintings survive. It may have been that he was questioning the possibility of continuing to work in Berlin, particularly considering the growing right-wing antipathy to all modern forms, especially those that betrayed a 'foreign' influence. It was far easier to make art outside of Germany – and this is what Nay did, travelling to Bornholm, an island belonging to Denmark in the Baltic Sea, on a painting trip funded by Heise. Of the paintings that Nay made at this moment, only two survive, *Fischerboote an der Hafenmole*, which was bought in 1931 by the Nationalgalerie, Berlin, and *Fischerdorf Teju auf Bornholm* (Fishing Village of Teju on Bornholm Island, 1930; p.27), which was acquired by the Museum Behnhaus in Lübeck. Although the former appears to be a continuation of Nay's earlier *Eigenbrödler* painting, the latter shows a grouping of peculiar, anonymous objects on a beach, including a telegraph pole, an odd ornamental beach hut, and a large object resembling a giant metronome. *Fischerdorf Teju auf Bornholm* shows the first signs of a shift into a Surrealist mode of painting, confirmed by the only other painting completed in 1930 for which an image remains, *Liebespaar* (Lovers, 1930), showing a figure on a bed, entwined with a biomorphic form. The two paintings completed in Bornholm were to appear in the 1937 Nazi propaganda exhibition *Entartete Kunst*. *Liebespaar* was singled out and damned (albeit ambiguously) in the Nazi newspaper *Völkischer Beobachter* in 1933 as a 'masterpiece of vulgarity'.[35]

32 In 1920, at the age of 30, Heise took the directorship of the Museums für Kunst und Kulturgeschichte in Lübeck. He was the youngest museum director in Germany at the time, and was part of a generation, including Hugo Tschudi and Alfred Lichtwark, who had been instrumental in introducing modern art to the general public through museum displays.
33 Carl Georg Heise, 'Begegnungen', in Karlheinz Gabler, *Ernst Wilhelm Nay. Die Druckgraphik 1923–1968*, Belser, Stuttgart, 1975, pp.5–8.
34 Jörg Träger, 'Carl Georg Heise', *Zeitschrift für Kunstgeschichte*, no.43, 1980, pp.113–15.
35 W. Rüdiger, 'Vom deutschen Kunstreich jüdischer Nation', in *Völkischer Beobachter*, 25 February 1933, in Aurel Scheibler, *Ernst Wilhelm Nay: Werkverzeichnis der Ölgemälde*, vol.1, M. DuMont, Cologne, 1990, p.100.

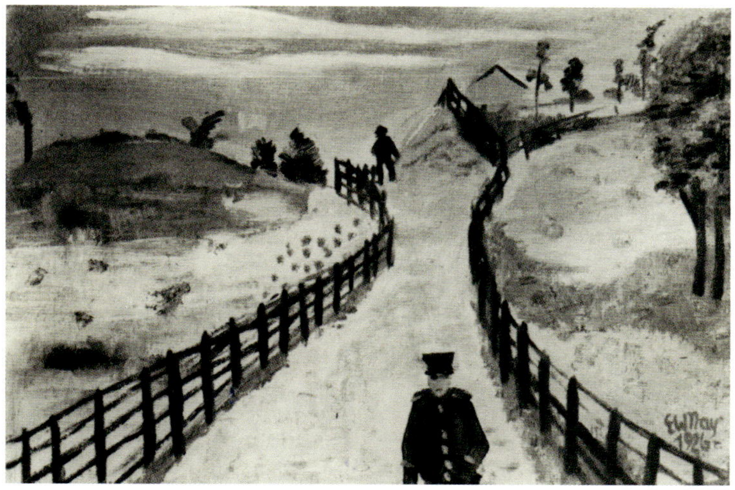

Sandweg, 1926
Oil on canvas
Dimensions and location unknown

E.W. Nay with cat Pieselchen,
Villa Massimo, Rome, 1932

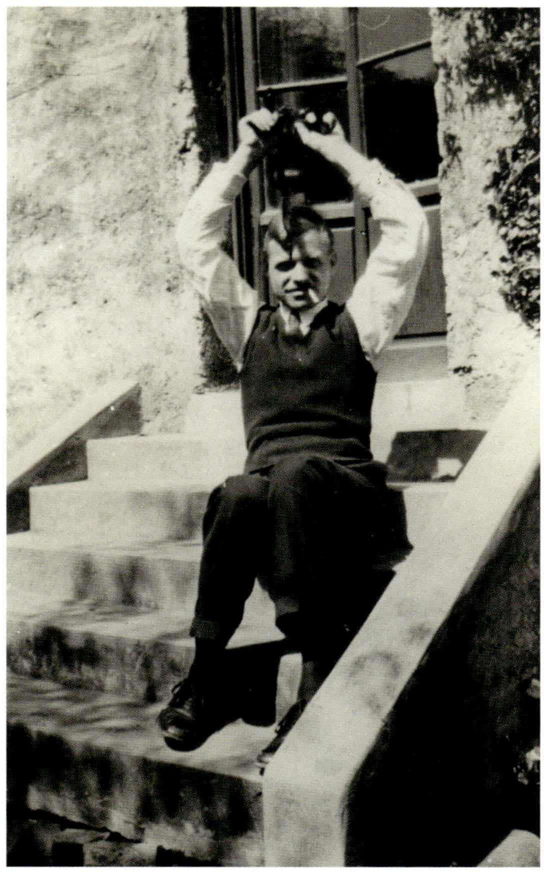

Begräbnis, 1927
Oil on canvas
80 × 130 cm · 31½ × 51⅛ in

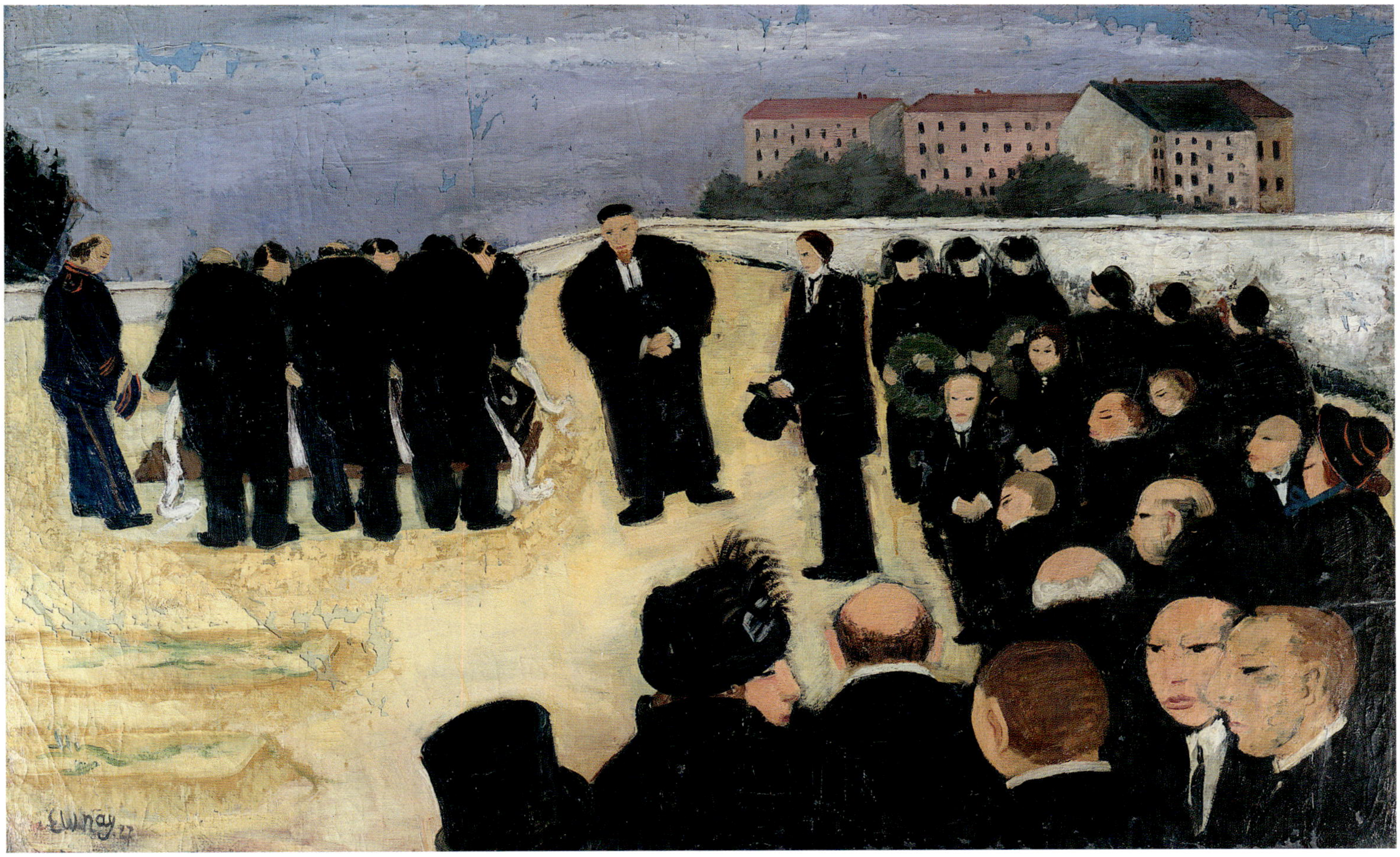

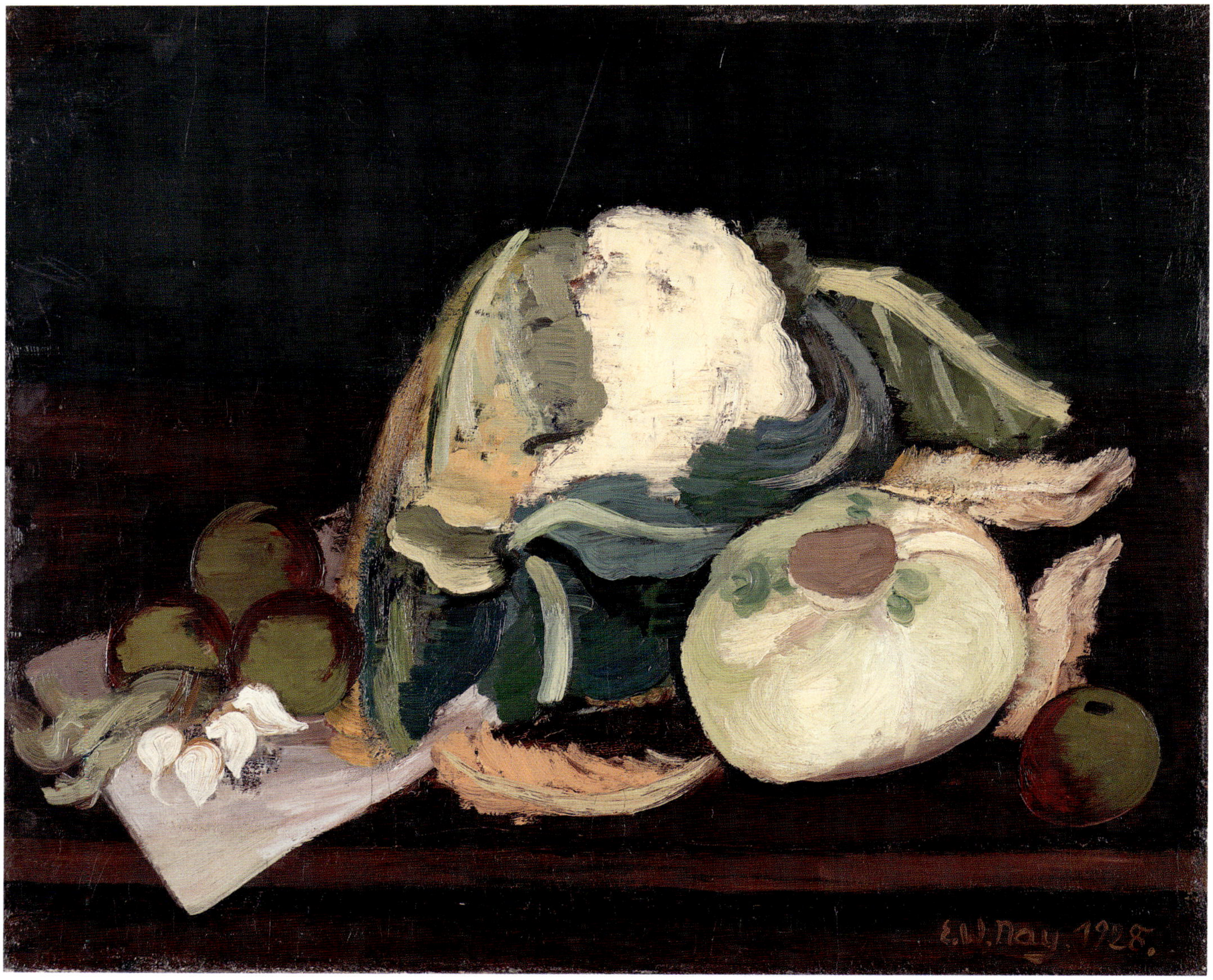

Blumenkohlstilleben (Gemüsestilleben),
1928
Oil on canvas
64.5 × 80.5 cm · 25⅜ × 31¾ in

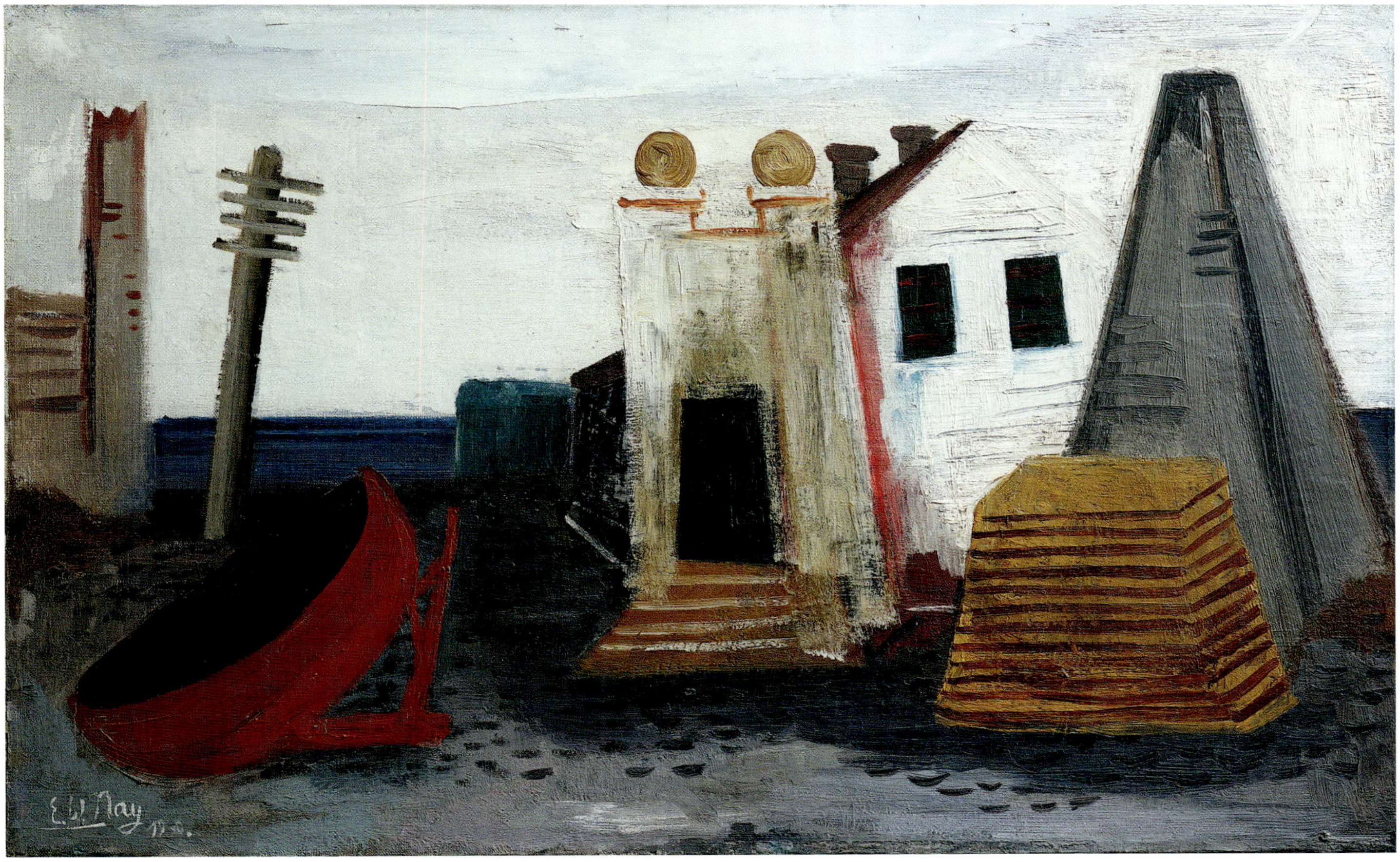

Fischerdorf Teju auf Bornholm, 1930
Oil on canvas
55 × 89 cm · 21⅝ × 35⅛ in

1931–39: Struggle and Survival

Etranger, sur toutes grèves de ce monde,
sans audience ni témoin,
porte à l'oreille du Ponant
une conque sans mémoire

Stranger, on all the shores of the world,
without audience or witness,
lift to the ear of the West
a shell that has no memory

— Saint-John Perse, *Exil*[36]

The autumn of 1931 found Nay painting in a studio of the German Academy at the Villa Massimo on the outskirts of Rome. The Villa had since 1929 (and also once in 1914) been the destination for the recipients of the Rompreis, the equivalent of the famous French Prix de Rome, awarded annually by the Prussian Academy.[37] Nay remained there until summer of the following year. His compatriots studying in Rome at the same time included the artists Hermann Blumenthal, Willi Lammert, Uli Nimptsch, Max Peiffer-Watenphül, Karl Rössing, Josef Scharl and Max Wendl. Karl Schmidt-Rottluff had been a prize-winner two years previously, and the following year, 1933, saw the visits both of Arno Breker, who was to become sculptor for the Third Reich, and the Jewish painter Félix Nussbaum, who was murdered at Auschwitz in 1944.

Nothing hitherto in Nay's work, dominated by the influence of French art thanks to Karl Hofer, and the anti-academic style of *Laienmalerei*, suggested that Rome would be a particularly propitious location for his studies. Indeed, his painting in Rome was influenced more by what he had seen in Paris two years previously than by the antique surroundings of the Villa Massimo. Although few canvases remain from the Rome period – no works from 1931 and only a handful from 1932 are now traceable – the Surrealist influence is clear, harking back to those works made in Bornholm in 1929 presenting the open space of the seashore as a stage on which disparate elements are arranged. *Insel und Mond* (Island and Moon, 1931) features various tentative abstract forms on an island in a night seascape. The style is still that of the *Laienmaler*, giving the work a quiet, mysterious atmosphere.

In a letter to Paul Westheim, published in *Das Kunstblatt* in late 1931, Nay explained that he was moving away from the *realistische Bildformen* (realistic motifs) of his previous work.[38] He was becoming aware of the legacy of Expressionism not in terms of a fragmented pictorial structure with a weight of sentiment, but of a poetic freedom equally found in Surrealism, as he had discovered during his trip to Paris in 1928. Another great revelation had been Ernst Barlach's play *Der blaue Boll* (1926), which Nay saw at the Berliner Staatstheater in December 1930. This, he wrote to Westheim, had revealed a form of mystical expression that he had only otherwise experienced in front of the altarpiece by Hans Memling in the Lübeck Katharinenkirche.[39] Barlach's Expressionist play may appear a strange source of inspiration for Surrealist imagery, but Nay makes clear its affinity with his other sources of inspiration: Picasso, Jean Lurçat, Max Ernst and Paul Klee. His letter is the first statement of a deepening appreciation of the spiritual possibilities of painting, moving away from the everyday materialism of his earlier work.

These first steps into a purely imaginative realm were tentative. The earliest surviving work from the Surrealist period, *Männer und*

36 For this and subsequent references, see: Saint-John Perse, *Exil: poème*, Editions Cahiers du Sud, Marseilles, 1942.
37 See A. Henze (ed), *Deutsche Akademie in Rom, Villa Massimo 1914–1964*, Deutsche Akademie, Rome, 1964.
38 E.W. Nay, letter to Paul Westheim published in *Das Kunstblatt*, no.4, 1931, pp.97–98.
39 The widely acclaimed performance *Der Blaue Boll* at the Berliner Staatstheater on 6 December 1930, directed by Jürgen Fehling, was the first in Berlin, and followed the inaugural performance in Stuttgart in October 1926. The sets were designed by Rochus Gliese.

Rad (Men and Wheel, 1932), shows two figures on what appears to be a beach at night, one of whom runs in fear from a giant wheel, while the other contemplates an aerial geometric form. The small figures strongly recall the paintings of Max Ernst, particularly *Deux enfants sont menacés par un rossignol* (Two Children Frightened by a Nightingale, 1924). Nay's indifference to the Roman *campagna* is reflected in his turn to marine themes in 1932, for example in *Fisch und Muschel* (Fish and Mussel, 1932; p.30).[40] Against a minimal black-and-white background, four elements are suspended, as if collaged, showing natural forms: a fish, a leaf, a shell and a stick. Nay offered an explanation of this work later in life:

> Above the light masculine world, below the dark feminine area ... a fish swims below (penis) without a head! Vertically hangs a brown mussel-form/vagina – above this a diagonal bar – penis – semi-obscured by a helical mussel – vagina, which together provides a definition of the masculine universal world and the possibility (diagonal-spiral) to identify with it.[41]

Despite this tongue-in-cheek Freudian reading, the paintings produced during the short Surrealist period from 1930 to 1933 appear less as psychological evocation than as explorations of the natural world, and stand in contrast with the academic genres and urban imagery that Nay pursued while a student in the 1920s.

The Surrealist period culminates with a sequence of fascinating paintings unique in Nay's oeuvre, evoking a type of expressive Surrealism redolent both of Ernst and Klee and also of Otto Dix. This was however to remain an unexplored avenue. *Rauhreif* (Hoar Frost, 1932; p.31), shows a mollusc-like form on a black ground surrounded by branches and stars, contained in a red frame. A further version of the same subject was lost during the war. Nay's exploration of the natural world outside of the urban academy takes on a cultic, magical appearance, which was to culminate the next year in two works, *Schwarzer Diamant* (Black Diamond, 1933; p.32) and *Elchkopf* (Elk Head, 1933; p.33). *Schwarzer Diamant* places a skull within a symbolic circle, the branches of a tree and corner motifs, all rendered white on black, like a photographic negative or X-ray. It is one of the most striking of Nay's prewar paintings, and shows the last influences of Expressionist culture on his work. (It is also notable as having belonged to the lawyer Carl Schmitt, whose connection to Nay is described in more detail below.) *Elchkopf* is an equally beguiling painting, depicting both the skull and head of an elk, comprised of abstracted motifs and eye forms, motifs that were to persist in Nay's oeuvre.

Nay's period in Italy left little trace on his work, and it seems likely that, as with most young artists, the prospect of a secure income and beautiful surroundings was little incentive to productivity. Certainly, the working holidays that he frequently took

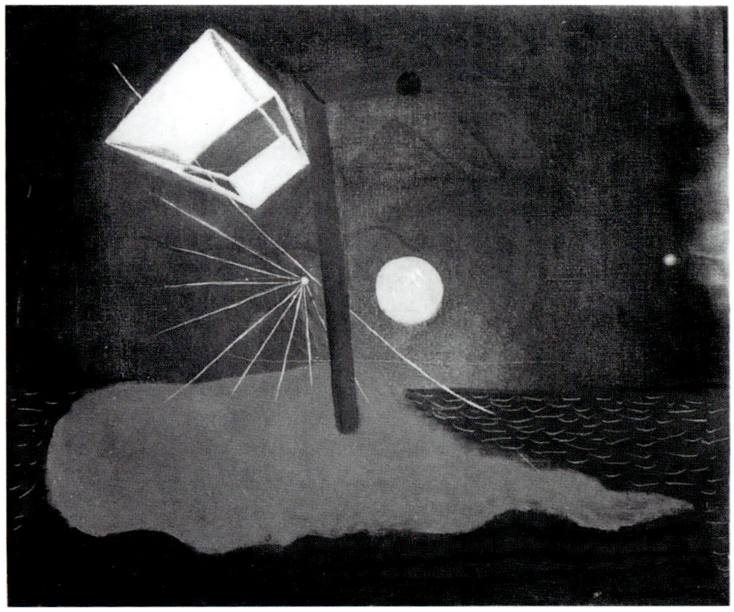

Insel und Mond, 1931
Oil on canvas
Dimensions and location unknown

Männer und Rad, 1932
Oil on canvas
51 × 61 cm · 20 × 24⅛ in

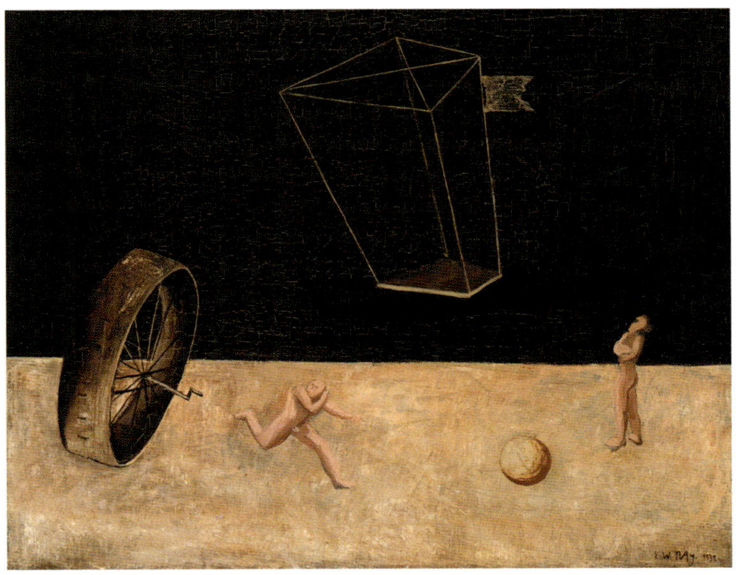

40 *Fisch und Muschel* was acquired by the sculptor Uli Nimptsch, presumably while he was studying with Nay in Rome, and taken to London. Several other works also survived in the Nimptsch collection: *Fledermaus und Leiter* and *Männer und Rad*, both from 1932.

41 E.W. Nay, 'Regesten zu Leben und Werk', 1958, reprinted in *E.W. Nay, 1902–1968: Bilder und Dokumente*, Archiv für Bildende Kunst am Germanischen Nationalmuseum, Nuremberg and Prestel-Verlag, Munich, 1980, p.58.

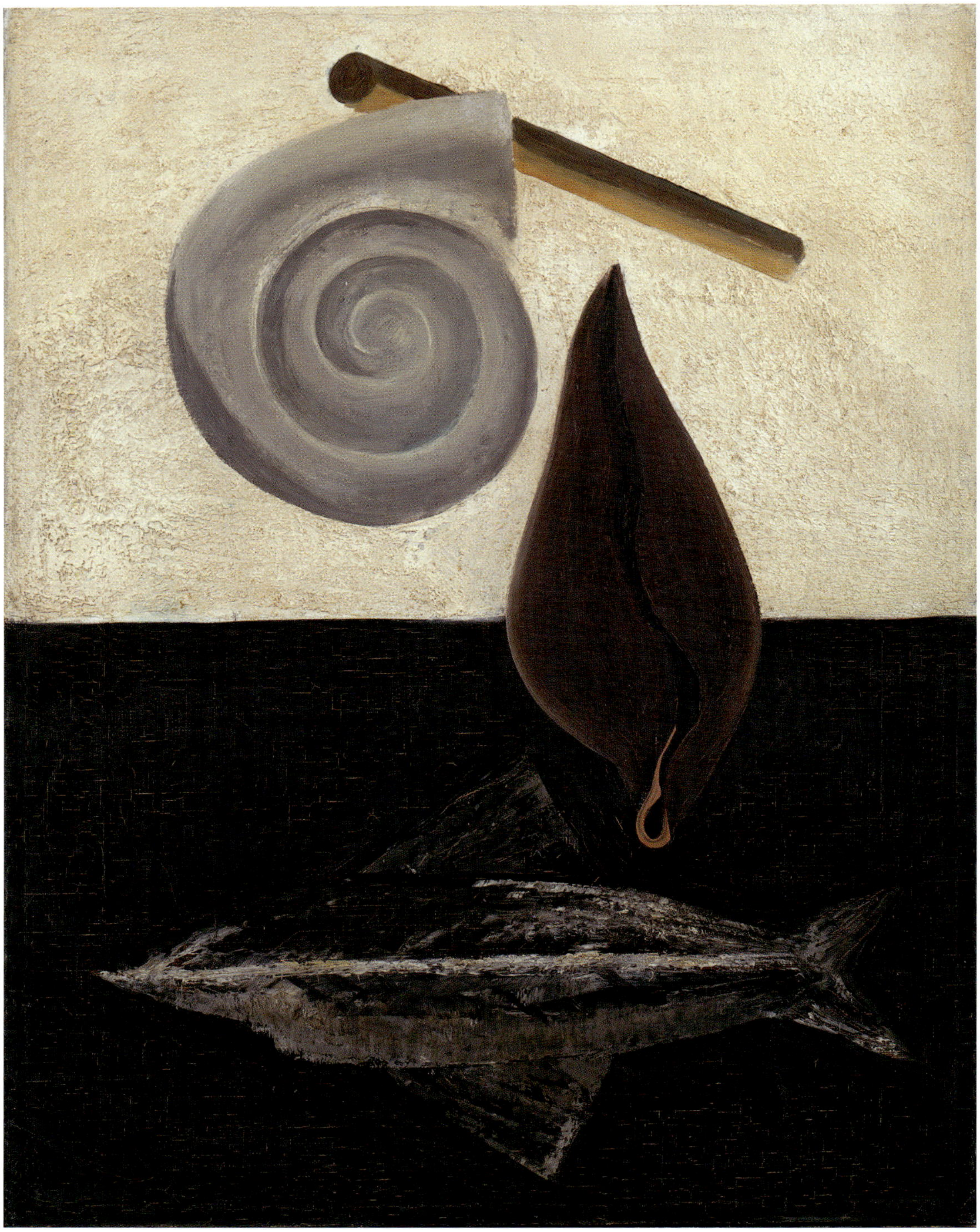

Fisch und Muschel, 1932
Oil on canvas
60 × 48 cm · 23⅝ × 18⅞ in

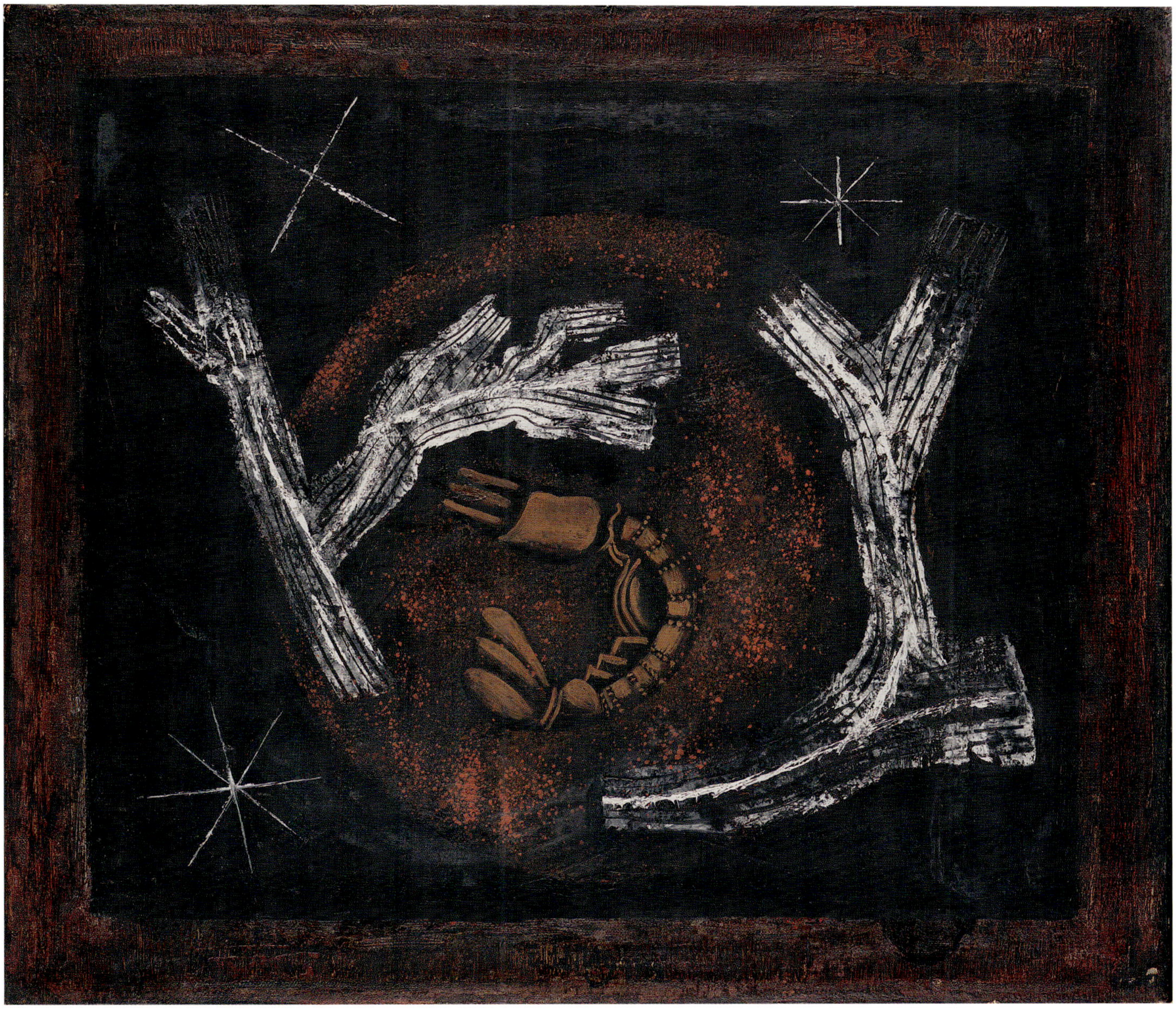

Rauhreif, 1932
Oil on canvas
47 × 55 cm · 18½ × 21⅝ in

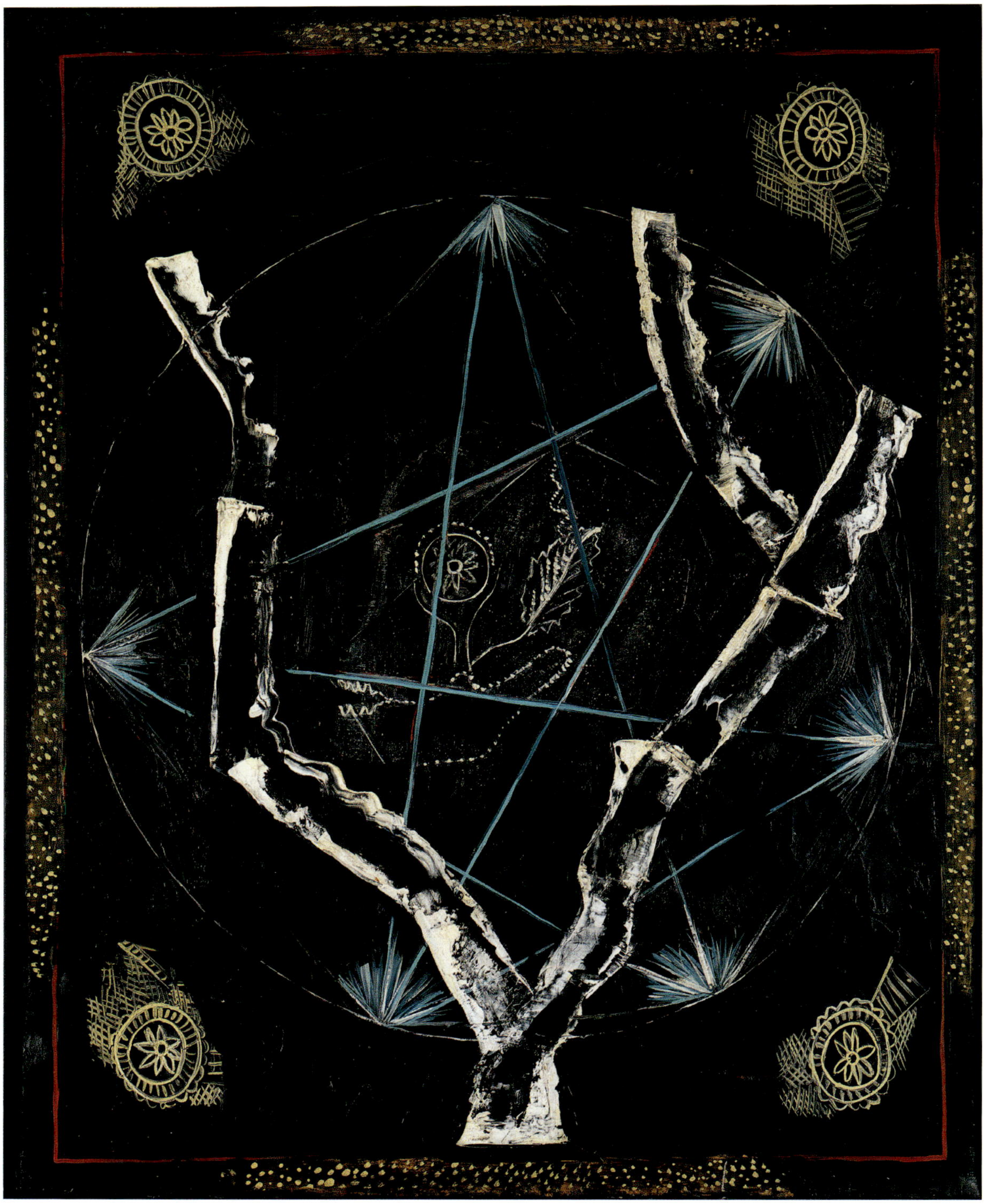

Schwarzer Diamant, 1933
Oil on canvas
70 × 57 cm · 27½ × 22½ in

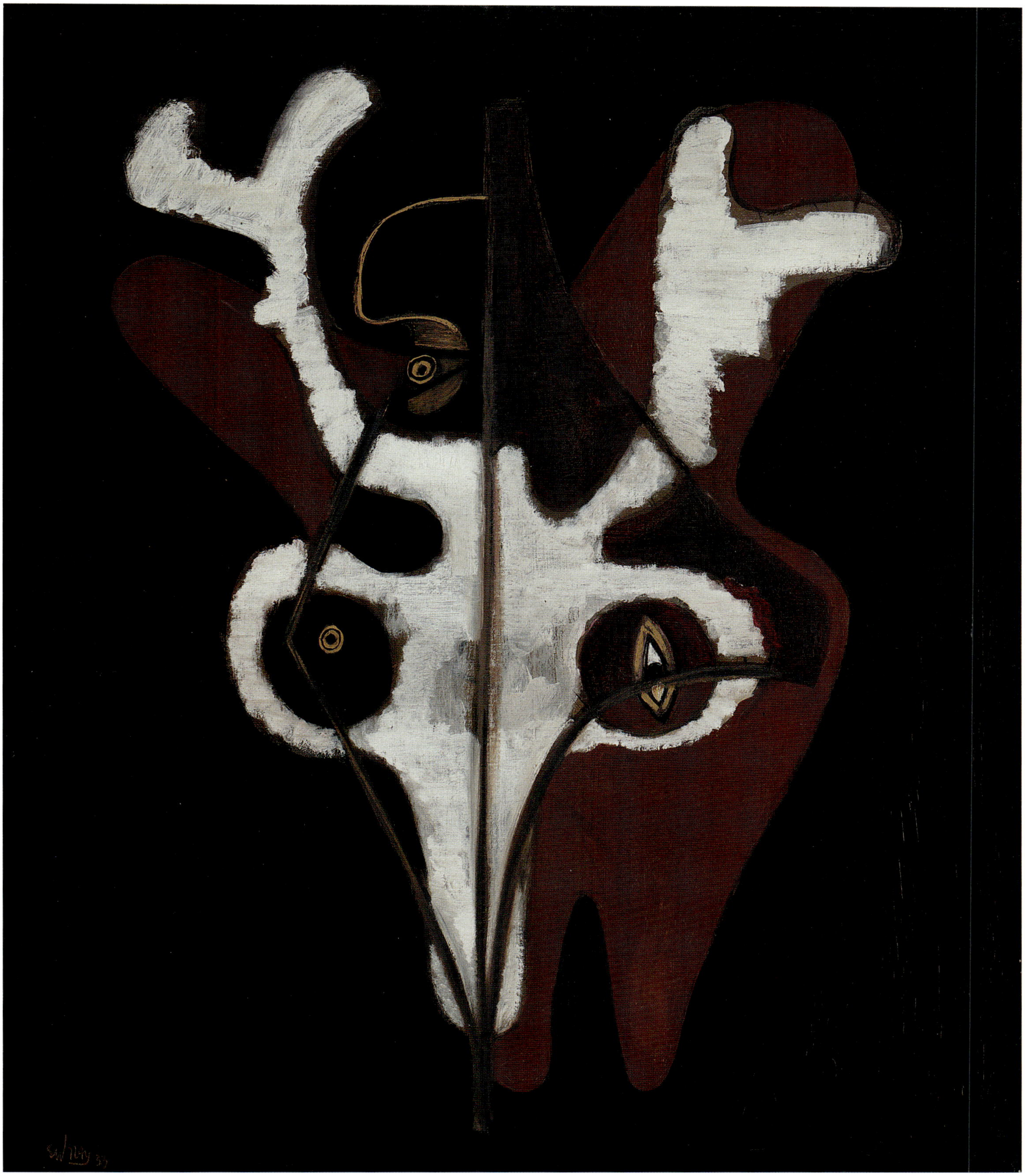

Elchkopf, 1933
Oil on canvas
81 × 70 cm · 31⅞ × 27½ in

in subsequent years were not in the Mediterranean but rather in the harsher climate of the Baltic coast. In addition, the shift in his work in the early 1930s towards natural imagery, at first through the filter of a type of Surrealist nature study, and then in the mid-1930s through an exploration of animal motifs, indicated that the legacy of antiquity and the glories of Rome were of little consequence to him.

Elchkopf thus looks forward to a number of paintings made from 1933 to 1935 depicting animals: *mythische Tierbilder* (mythical animal paintings), as Nay termed them.[42] Of the few canvases that he produced during 1934, the majority show bovine subjects in an abstracted, mythic disguise. *Weiße Kuh* (White Cow, 1934; p.36) is the best known of these.

The escape from urban, academic imagery to the natural world was at least in part a reaction to the mounting discontent in German cities during the early years of the Third Reich, and in particular the growing cultural repression, from which Nay was not exempt. The Germany to which he had returned in the summer of 1932 was experiencing increasing disarray, mass unemployment and financial instability, fuelling Nazi success in the polls. *Der Sturm* ceased publication in that year, when Herwarth Walden fled into exile in the Soviet Union.

Nay had since 1927 exhibited regularly in group shows, principally in Berlin, but also in Hanover, Düsseldorf and Munich; these were generally large events such as those of the Berlin Secession and the Spring Exhibitions at the Prussian Academy. He also showed regularly in group exhibitions at the Kunstverein in Hanover, and at the Glaspalast in Munich, and was included in displays of work by younger artists in commercial galleries in Berlin. From 1931 the dealer Alfred Flechtheim included his works in collective shows, and it was in March 1933 that Nay's name first appeared in the title of an exhibition, *Theo Champion, Werner Gilles, E.W. Nay and Lilly Steiner*, held at Flechtheim's Berlin gallery during March and April – the last exhibition before the gallery was forced to close.[43] This early success came, however, at the least propitious moment to be exhibiting 'modern' paintings. Following Hitler's appointment as chancellor of Germany at the end of January that year, the cultural world entered into a period of unparalleled suffering. The Bauhaus was forced to close in January 1933. Exhibitions of modern art were closed and artists denigrated in the press. The first public signal that Nay's work was also subject to Nazi censorship was an article that appeared in the Nazi newspaper *Völkischer Beobachter* on 25 February 1933.[44] On 13 March 1933 Joseph Goebbels, the minister of propaganda and public enlightenment, formed a new organisation, the Reichskulturkammer, designed to regulate all professional artists. Those who did not belong were forbidden to work, perform or exhibit. On 22 April Nay wrote a long letter to the Minister für Wissenschaft, Kultur und Volksbildung explaining that on neither his father's nor his mother's side was there any Jewish blood, and added a long explanation of his approach to painting anchored firmly in a numinous northern mythology.[45]

No works by Nay were exhibited during 1934 and 1935. Although he had no teaching post to lose, and was not subject to the same degree of vituperation as older artists with more public prominence in the early 1930s, it was only due to a few important contacts amongst dealers and museum workers that he was able to survive for the remainder of the decade. Creating networks of support was a skill that he cultivated out of necessity in these dark years. On his return from Rome in 1932, he had stopped in Munich and met the dealer Günther Franke (1900–76), who was to become one of his principal supporters, particularly during the war.[46] In 1934, Nay was introduced by Carl Georg Heise to the art historian Erich Meyer (1897–1967), later the director of the Museum für Kunst und Gewerbe, Hamburg, who was from the first meeting a passionate collector of Nay's work. He also met a young curator at the Berlin Nationalgalerie in the Kronprinzenpalais, Alfred Hentzen (1903–85), who after 1945 established the Kestnergesellschaft in Hanover, a centre for modern art. From 1955 Hentzen was the director of the Hamburger Kunsthalle. The young art historian Werner Haftmann (1912–99), whom Nay also encountered for the first time in 1934, was to prove decisive for the reception and interpretation of his work after the war, but it was perhaps the meeting with Ernst Gosebruch (1872–1953), the former director of the Folkwang Museum, who moved to Berlin in 1933 after being dismissed from his post by the Nazis, that was to prove the most important for Nay in the period before 1939. That he established contact with such supporters of modern art in so short a space of time was not simply luck: in the face of Nazi cultural policy, supporters of the modern were closing ranks and preparing networks of support and defence.

Some indication of the material plight that Nay was experiencing by 1935 can be gathered from a letter from Gosebruch to the Frankfurt-based collector Carl Hagemann, interceding on the part of Nay for a charitable purchase. Hagemann (1867–1940) was an industrialist, who had since 1925 been a director at IG Farben, but had retired in 1932. Earlier, he had been one of the most important collectors and supporters of modern art in Germany, in particular of Kirchner, with whom he remained in close contact until the artist's death in 1938. Gosebruch played an important role in advising him on purchases, and introducing him to young, relatively unknown artists. His promotion of Nay in this way was in retrospect essential for the artist's survival during the difficult years of the 1930s, most of which he spent living in poverty. Nay, Gosebruch wrote, was not unknown, and had been exhibiting at the Kronprinzenpalais for some years, but the two attic rooms at 198 Hohenzollerndamm in west Berlin where he lived and worked (and for which he and Elly

42 Animal consciousness as a subject for art was also a remnant of Expressionist culture, particularly in the work of Franz Marc. Nay was, to a limited degree, the conduit of this tradition, which was then taken up in the postwar period by the sculptor Ewald Mataré, and more famously by his student, Joseph Beuys.

43 Nay was represented by Surrealist-period works including *Schmetterlinge* (1932).

44 Wilhelm Rüdiger, 'Unsere Generalabrechnung wird fortgesetzt: Vom deutschen Kunstreich jüdischer Nation', in *Völkischer Beobachter*, 56, 25 February 1933.

45 E.W. Nay to the Minister für Wissenschaft, Kultur und Volksbildung, 22 April 1933. Bundesarchiv Berlin-Lichterfelde; RKK 2400 Box 0236 File 18; Nay, Ernst Wilhelm [cited hereafter as BA]. In Beate Marks-Hanßen, 'Innere Emigration? "Verfemte" Künstlerinnen und Künstler in der Zeit des Nationalsozialismus', Berlin, dissertation.de, 2006, p.301.

46 It is likely that the meeting was arranged by Nimptsch, who had been with Nay at the Villa Massimo. See Doris Schmidt (ed), *Briefe an Günther Franke. Porträt eines deutschen Kunsthändlers*, M. DuMont Schauberg, Cologne, 1970, p.160.

payed 28 Marks a month) were still 'unthinkably primitive'.[47] Nay's studio was in one room; the other functioned as a kitchen and bedroom. If he could be likened to Kirchner for his abstract-leaning style, Gosebruch wrote, then the level of material comfort enjoyed by the Brücke artists before the First World War was luxurious by comparison. Despite this, Nay and his wife were upbeat, and it was only through Heise that Gosebruch had understood that they were living hand to mouth. Nay's situation was particularly deplorable due to a throat condition, which meant that he had to undergo an operation in the Charité university hospital at the end of June.

Hagemann reacted immediately, purchasing *Weiße Kuh* for 400 Marks. Nay's stylistic affinity with Kirchner, which Hagemann would have seen from photographs sent by Gosebruch, was an important factor.[48] Gosebruch even described Nay as physically like Kirchner 20 years previously, 'slim and boyish, noticeably young-looking. Decidedly blond'. But in comparison with Kirchner's temperamental nature, Nay was calm and courteous.[49] Gosebruch's intercession for Nay at this time was vital; it was also thanks to him that Schmidt-Rottluff purchased *Elchkopf*. Additionally, he had tried to interest the Berlin-based collector Arnold Budczies, another Kirchner enthusiast who was to become an important collector of Nay's works.

These new sources of income enabled Nay to follow the doctor's orders to spend the summer of 1935 on the Baltic coast. In late July he wrote to Gosebruch from Vietzkerstrand describing the wild, empty landscape, and the primitive nature of the Pommeranian fishermen. Here, as in Bornholm in 1929, Nay used the inspiration of the landscape to produce works expressing essential qualities of nature and 'primitive' human existence. The human figure returned as the principle motif, highly schematised, depersonalised into forms that evoke a 'primitive' instinct and consciousness. The strong identification between the human figure and the landscape was consolidated in a series of paintings of sand dunes, where only the suggestion of eyes remain, as with *Dünenlandschaft* (Dunescape, 1935; p.37). 'I have been working for a long time towards the goal of penetrating through the outer shell of existence to the core of things', Nay wrote to Hagemann from the Baltic coast.[50] In paintings such as *Segelboote nachts auf dem Meer* (Sailing Boats at Night on the Sea, 1935; p.41) he creates images that could not be further from the everyday urban imagery of the previous decade. The nocturnal setting and absence of any sign of contemporary human life suggest the beginnings of an 'inner emigration', an escape from politics and the contemporary world, which was to mark all of Nay's subsequent work.

Hagemann also bought two drawings and one watercolour from Nay's summer trip. His support came at a critical moment.[51] By the New Year of 1936, Nay's medical condition had worsened, and he was once again threatened with the prospect of hospitalisation. Gosebruch wrote to Hagemann to apprise him of the situation, noting:

> It is painful to see such a nice young man, from such a good background (his father worked in the ministry and was killed in the war) and education (Schulpforta), that he by no means rejects, and clearly belongs to the best society, even when he is living in poverty in an attic, and who now cannot even afford 100–150 Marks for an operation that would deliver him from considerable pain.[52]

The operation, for which the philanthropic surgeon did not eventually charge, took place in early February and was successful.[53] Gosebruch continued his valuable promotion of Nay's work by writing to Hagemann again in April 1936 to suggest that he should fund another visit to Vietzkerstrand.[54] The management of Nay's affairs by Gosebruch and Heise came to a head during May, when an *Ehekonflikt* (marital conflict), due, in Gosebruch's words, to Elly's lack of 'spiritual maturity' in comparison with her husband, drove Nay to stay with Heise. Gosebruch wrote to Hagemann to request the money for Nay to travel alone to the Pommeranian coast.[55]

Nay remained in Vietzkerstrand until the beginning of September. He continued making paintings of fishermen departing and returning from the catch, developing the simplified, cyclopic figures of the previous year, now using more varied forms and broken brushwork. Paintings such as *Ankunft der Fischer* (Arrival of the Fishermen, 1936; p.43) develop forms evoking the primitive, elemental conditions, but are also composed on the basis of principles of abstract design that move away from the early construction of a more naturalistic space.

Nay would undoubtedly have welcomed the respite of another summer away from Berlin. In early 1936 he had been summoned to the office of the Reichskammer der bildenden Künste, and asked whether he had altered his style of painting.[56] As a result of this interview he was classified a 'degenerate' artist, and was banned from buying materials (a restriction that he was easily able to evade, so he later wrote, by having other people buy them for him). Nazi cultural repression was in fact to ease off in the summer of 1936, thanks to the need to provide a good image of Germany internationally around the time of the Berlin Olympics. Works by Nay were even included in an exhibition mounted at the Kunstverein in Hamburg on the occasion of the Games, *Malerei und Plastik in Deutschland 1936* (Painting and Sculpture in Germany 1936), a display that was nevertheless forcibly closed when the Kunstverein itself was abolished by the Nazis. Late 1936 saw a considerable

47 Ernst Gosebruch to Carl Hagemann, 22 June 1935, in Hans Delfs, Maria-Andreas von Lüttichau and Roland Scotti (eds), *Kirchner, Schmidt-Rottluff, Nolde, Nay… Briefe an den Sammler und Mäzen Carl Hagemann*, Hatje Cantz, Ostfildern-Ruit, 2004, pp.479–80.
48 See *ibid.*, passim.
49 Ernst Gosebruch to Carl Hagemann, 2 July 1935, *ibid.*, pp.482–83.
50 'Ich habe mich ja langsam dazu vorbereitet, den Kern zu finden und die Schale der äußeren Erscheinung zu durchdringen', in *ibid.*, p.488.
51 The drawings were *Fischer mit Segelbooten (Fischer mit Netzen am Boot)*, 1935, Hagemann 1156; and *Fischer und Boot (Fischer und Segelboote am Strand)*, 1935, Hagemann 1168. The watercolour was *Drei Kühe*, 1935, Hagemann 210.
52 Gosebruch to Hagemann, 20 January 1936, in Delfs, 2004, *op. cit.*, p.523.
53 Gosebruch to Hagemann, 11 February 1936, *ibid.*, pp.531–32.
54 Gosebruch to Hagemann, 17 April 1936, *ibid.*, pp.546–48
55 Gosebruch to Hagemann, 20 May 1936, *ibid.*, p.557.
56 Stephanie Barron (ed), *Entartete Kunst. Das Schicksal der Avantgarde im Nazi-Deutschland*, exhibition catalogue, Los Angeles County Museum of Art and Deutsches Historisches Museum, Los Angeles and Berlin, 1991, p.312.

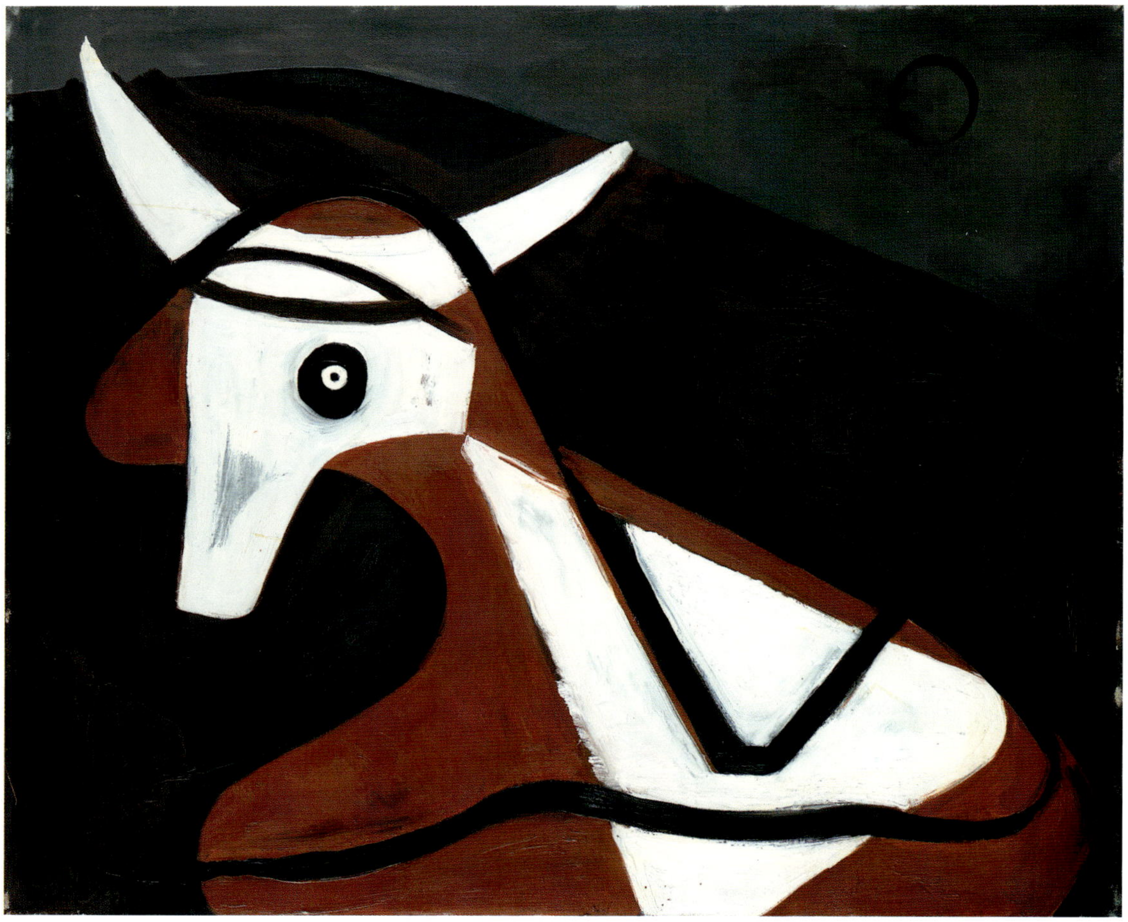

Weiße Kuh, 1933
Oil on canvas
65 × 80 cm · 25⅝ × 31½ in

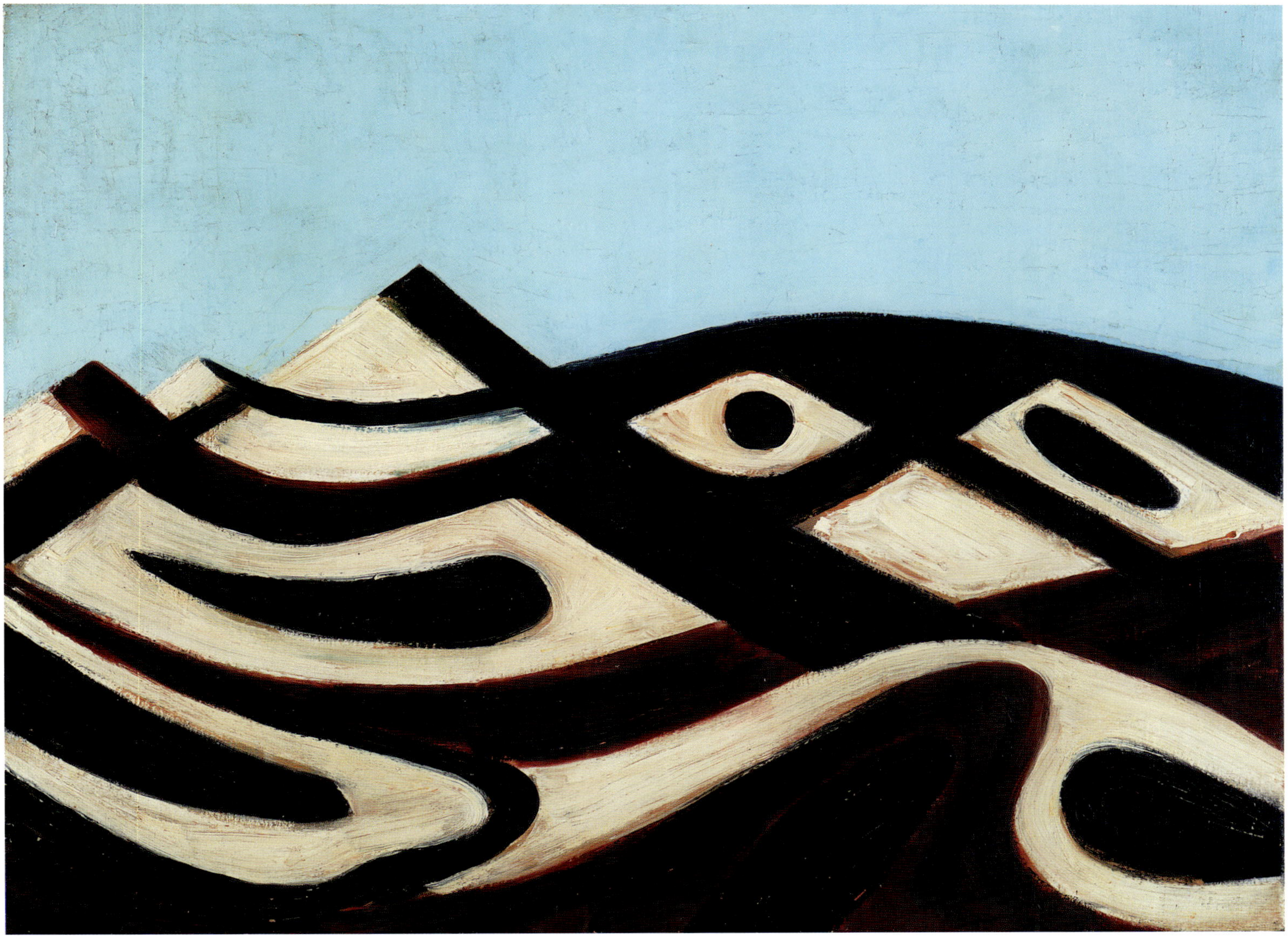

Dünenlandschaft, 1935
Oil on canvas
80 × 110 cm · 31½ × 43¼ in

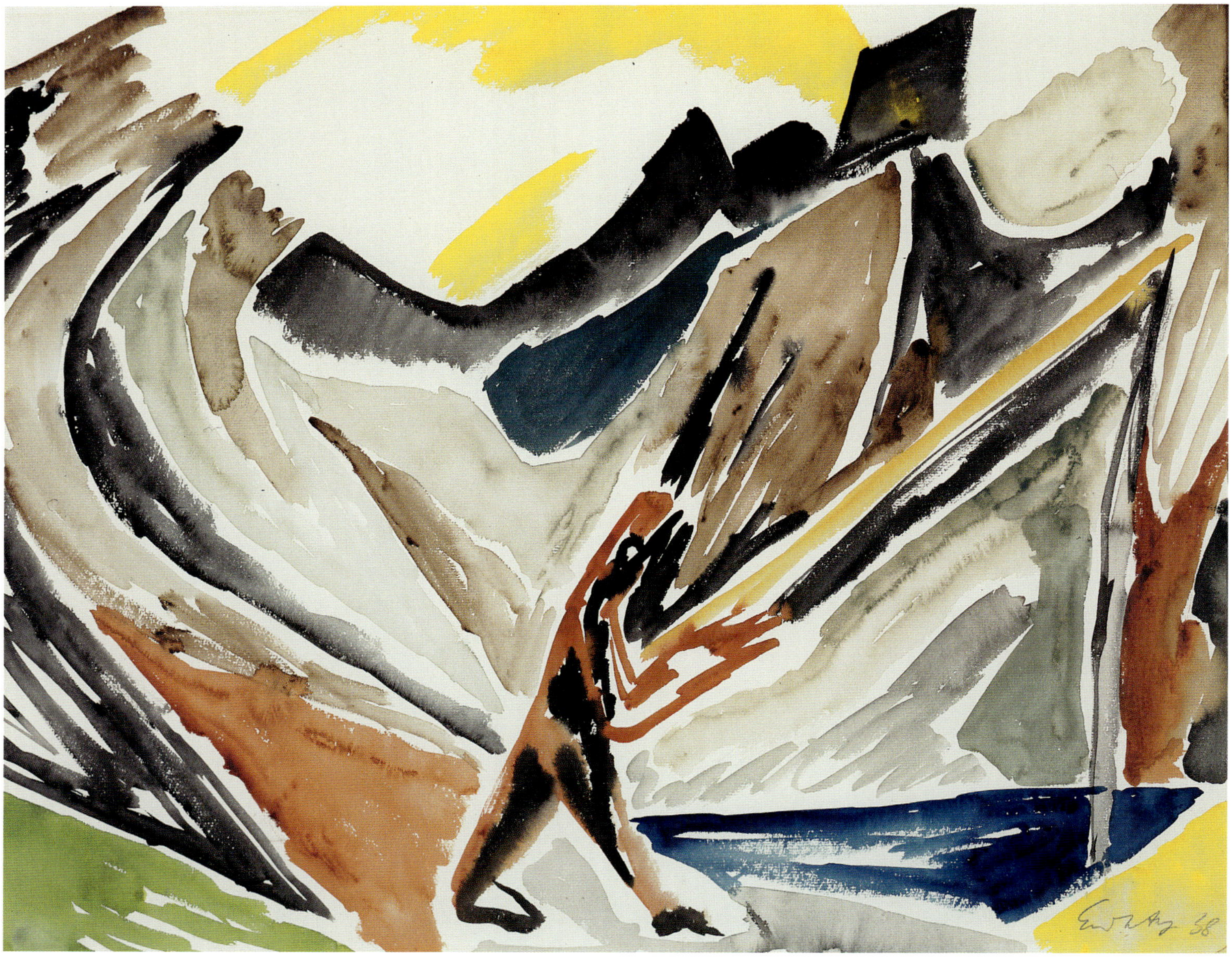

Mann vor Bergsee, 1938
Watercolour
48.5 × 63 cm · 19 × 24¾ in

raising of tension in the measures against modern art. In August, the first modern painting, Kandinsky's *Improvisation* (1912), was removed from a public collection, sold from the Museum Folkwang, Essen, by the director Count Klaus von Baudissin. At the end of October, the modern section of the Berlin Nationalgalerie in the Kronprinzenpalais was closed. During November, Goebbels took the measure of banning art criticism.

Continuing strong support for Nay's painting by a group of influential figures ensured the presence of his works in two exhibitions in early 1937. The first, at the Galerie Buchholz, Berlin, during March and April, was a success, with sales including one watercolour purchased by the Nationalgalerie.[57] An exhibition of Nay's work also took place at the Buchholz Gallery in New York from May to June 1937, thanks to Curt Valentin, who had emigrated that year and opened a gallery in the name of Karl Buchholz.

Nay continued to avoid the worsening political situation in Berlin by travelling during the summer months. At the beginning of 1937, Heise once more intervened as a fundraiser, this time writing to Edvard Munch to ask for money for Nay to make a trip to the Lofoten Archipelago in the county of Nordland, Norway, and within the Arctic Circle. On 6 June Ludwig Justi, the former director of the Berlin Nationalgalerie, who had been dismissed by the Nazis in 1933, wrote to Munch to support Heise's request, noting that the Nationalgalerie had purchased one painting and one drawing by Nay, and that he had developed strongly as an artist since.[58] Justi's letter had the desired effect: on 27 June Nay wrote to Munch to thank him for the offer of 400 Kronen towards his journey. At the beginning of July, Nay travelled to Lofoten, and stayed with the Sverdrøp family. 'The bizarre formation of the mountains and the fjords, the crystal-clear light, the shadowless glowing colours of the extreme north, and the traditional lifestyles of the fishermen and whalers, all had a strong effect on Nay', wrote Elisabeth Nay-Scheibler.[59] The works that he made in Lofoten, including *Fischer in der Brandung* (Fishermen in the Waves, 1937; p.45), were all done in watercolours, and were worked up into oil paintings on his return. In a letter expressing thanks for the financial support, Nay wrote to Munch that the 'tremendous freedom of life is of great importance, and I cannot bear to think about the contrast with my life in Germany'.[60] How much he knew of the rapid decline of cultural freedom in Germany at that moment is not clear. While in Norway, ten of his paintings were confiscated from public collections, and two were exhibited in *Entartete Kunst* (Degenerate Art), the Nazi propaganda exhibition defaming modern art held at the Hofgarten in Munich from 19 July to 30 November. He was the youngest artist to be included.[61]

Nay had written to Munch requesting a visit; Munch's reply, which has not survived, presumably turned down the request on grounds of ill health. When Nay arrived back in Oslo in mid-September, he wrote once again to Munch, thanking him for his letter, describing the 'deep and real sympathy' that he felt for the Norwegian landscape, and expressing regret that he was unable to visit the ailing artist.[62] The visit to Munch later described by Nay must have taken place at this moment, before his return journey to Berlin; or it may even have been the next year, on his second visit to Norway. Nay travelled to see Munch twice at the older painter's house in Skøyen, near Oslo. Although the visit was to become a founding 'myth' within Nay's own biography, his account of it suggests that Munch was, unsurprisingly, not aware of Nay's work, and that Nay found no strong connection with Munch's painting. The lasting impression was rather of Munch's personality, which struck Nay as that of 'the most sovereign individual I have ever met'. The model that Munch provided of obstinate survival, and of dedication to painting as the noblest of callings, was of great importance for Nay.

The watercolours made by Nay in Norway were exhibited at the gallery of Holst Halvorsen in Oslo in late 1937, and their sale helped fund his second visit to Norway the following year. His experiences on the Arctic circle proved to be a turning point for his work, with the emergence of colour as a primary motif, particularly in those watercolours, such as the striking *Mann vor Bergsee* (Man Beside Mountain Lake, 1938), which resulted from the 1938 visit. According to Schmidt-Rottluff, who visited Nay to view the works in his Berlin studio in November, the watercolours had lost none of the 'boldness and explosiveness' (*Kühnheit und Explosivität*) of his previous works.[63] Nay had written to Alfred Hentzen at the beginning of his second stay in Lofoten, describing the extraordinary changing weather conditions, and the intensity with which he was applying himself to work.[64] The experience of being in nature was essential to the development of his work, Nay wrote, describing the affinity he felt with the nineteenth-century German painter Philip Otto Runge. The results can be clearly seen in those paintings he made as a result on his return, such as *Der Angler* (The Fisherman, 1938; p.46), and *Menschen in den Lofoten (Frauen am Meer)* (Figures in Lofoten (Women by the Sea), 1938; p.49).

The influence of Kirchner was redoubled by a visit to see Carl Hagemann's collection at the beginning of 1938, on return from a short return visit to Rome. Nay had expressed particular admiration for Kirchner's painting *Die Sängerin* (The Singers, 1930) to Gosebruch (an enthusiasm that neither the latter nor Franke shared), and would have looked forward to seeing the works of his spiritual master, and also to consolidating his links with Hagemann, who had been vital to his survival during the latter half of the 1930s. Hagemann's collection of paintings by Kirchner had been published in *Museum der Gegenwart* in 1931, and included a range of works from Kirchner's 'late' period in Davos.[65] Later that

57 Gosebruch to Hagemann, 26 March 1937, in Delfs, 2004, *op. cit.*, p.634. Work by Nay was also included in a small group exhibition at the Kunstverein Cologne in April, titled *Zeitgenössische deutsche Künstler (Theunert, Nay, Schröder-Wiborg)*.
58 Ludwig Justi to Edvard Munch, 6 June 1937, Munch Archive, Oslo.
59 A. Scheibler, *op. cit.*, p.154.
60 'Diese herrliche Freiheit und Ungezwungenheit des Lebens bedeuten für mich ausserordentlich viel. Ich darf an den Kontrast zu meinem Leben in Deutschland garnicht denken'. E.W. Nay to Edvard Munch, 11 August 1937, Munch Archive, Oslo.
61 Barron, 1991, *op. cit.*, pp.312–13.
62 Nay to Munch, 16 September 1937, Munch Archive, Oslo. This contradicts the account that Nay later gave of the Norway visit, in which he wrote that he went directly to visit Munch on arriving in Oslo at the beginning of July. E.W. Nay, 'Regesten zu Leben und Werk', 1958, in *E.W. Nay, 1902–1968*, *op. cit.*, pp.65–66.
63 Karl Schmidt-Rottluff to Carl Hagemann, 14 November 1938, in Delfs, 2004, *op. cit.*, p.784. Schmidt-Rottluff visited Nay once again, this time with Hanna Bekker vom Rath, at the end of November.
64 E.W. Nay to Alfred Hentzen, 13 July 1938, in *E.W. Nay, 1902–1968*, *op. cit.*, p.68.

year, Nay reported his shock on hearing of Kirchner's suicide, writing to Hagemann: 'The best spirits are by some inscrutable law also those in the most danger. As you know I had great respect for him, and know that I would have benefited greatly from having had the chance to talk over my ideas with him. Fate has now spoken.'[66]

Despite the worsening political situation, Nay was able in the few years leading up to the outbreak of war to evade Nazi censorship and continue working, a situation due at least in part to his relatively low public profile. In early 1939 he wrote to Hagemann, telling him that he was spending ten hours a day in the studio and feeling at the height of his powers. Hagemann's support, and regular sales of works, had lifted him out of poverty, and made it easier for him to move amongst the 'best society' that Gosebruch had suggested was his natural milieu. Whilst in hospital for a brief period in February 1938, he was visited by the collector Lilly von Schnitzler, the wife of the director of IG Farben, Georg von Schnitzler, who insisted that he take leave from convalescence to show her his studio. Lilly von Schnitzler had first bought works from Nay in late 1937, and appeared keen to increase her collection. It was at her large apartment overlooking the Tiergarten, containing paintings by Picasso, Renoir and Beckmann, that Nay met some of the leading figures in the cultural and political elite of the former Republic; during February 1938 he attended a party where the invitees, according to Gosebruch, included Emil and Ada Nolde, the sculptor Richard Scheibe, the actor Heinrich Georg, 'various nobility', and the lawyer Carl Schmitt.[67] The connection that Nay forged with Schmitt was to prove important in the years to come. The 'many conversations' to which Nay refers in a letter to Schmitt from 1943 probably took place both at Lilly von Schnitzler's salon and at Schmitt's own house in Berlin-Steglitz.[68] These were glittering gatherings of the German political and artistic elite, as well as those from high Catholic spheres, including Werner Sombart, Prince Rohan and Ernst Jünger. Schmitt's affinity with the fine arts, which may be traced back to his early close association with Dada, and Hugo Ball in particular, can be seen in his patronage not only of Nay, but also of Werner Gilles, Emil Nolde and Werner Heldt.[69] His support of Nay was of importance for the artist, both in terms of the social prestige that it brought in the late 1930s, and due to the impact on Nay of Schmitt's remarkably powerful and aesthetically premised political thinking, stimulating an exchange of ideas between the two. Despite Nay's apolitical nature, he may be grouped with Schmitt, and also with the writer Gottfried Benn, as part of a generation who saw the 'National Revolution' as legitimated not by the outward appeal of Nazism, but by the need for an *anthropologische Wende*, an 'anthropological turn', a change in fundamental social attitudes, by which constructive principles of order emerged from the chaos of the Weimar Republic.[70]

Despite these successes, Nay was eager to leave Berlin and spend time away from the politics and the continuing hardships of daily life. Berlin was fraying at the edges, between the horrors of hyperinflation and the growing prospect of war. The writer Friedrich Reck-Malleczewen provided a pungent description of the city, albeit from an aristocratic perspective, in April 1939:

> Berlin smells of war, and strikes me as looking the way a parvenu should: shabby, wan, ridiculous. The menus offer little, the wine is even more questionable than usual, the linen is of doubtful cleanliness. The coffee is miserable, there is no petrol for the taxis, and since repairmen have been drafted for work on fortifications, the hotels are in a sorry state. All kinds of things are now visible under the plushy, stuccoed, bronzed junk which formerly concealed the down-at-heels artifice which is Prussia's natural style.[71]

In March 1939 Nay went to stay with another important figure in the support and promotion of modern art at this time, Hanna Bekker vom Rath, at her house in Hofheim am Taunus, near Frankfurt am Main. Bekker vom Rath held secret shows of 'degenerate' artists at her studio on the Regensburger Straße between 1939 and 1942.[72] This connection was to prove of vital importance for the period after 1945.

Failing to find funds for another summer in Norway, Nay decided at the end of May to take up the offer of a visit to Greece.[73] Through the agency of Carl Schmitt, he had made the acquaintance of two Greek lawyers who had invited him to Crete for the summer.[74] He remembered Munch telling him during his 1937 visit to Lofoten how much the Norwegian island resembled Crete. The voyage never in fact took place, however, and Nay instead departed for the Black Sea coast in Bulgaria on Monday 20 August. Earlier that month the Reichskammer der bildenden Künste had passed a positive judgement on his work, and proposed a monthly stipend for Nay of around 300 Reichsmarks.[75] Germany invaded Poland on 1 September, and, on receiving no response to ultimatums to desist, Britain and France declared war on Germany. On hearing the news, Nay returned immediately to Berlin, arriving on 6 September. It was probably during these last few months of 1939, before embarking on war duties, that he executed a last series of large paintings depicting bathing figures, including *Menschen am Strand* (Figures on a Beach, 1939; p.51), showing a more successful engagement with large multi-figure compositions than those works made on the Baltic coast in the mid-1930s. Here again the influence of Kirchner is clear. They look forward both to the large compositions painted in France during the war, and to the abstract paintings made afterwards.

65 'Die Sammlung Hagemann in Frankfurt am Main', *Museum der Gegenwart*, no.1, 1931, pp.99–111.
66 Nay to Hagemann, 17 July 1938, in Delfs, 2004, *op. cit.*, p.756.
67 Gosebruch to Hagemann, 3 March 1938, in *ibid.*, p.725.
68 At Schillerstraße 2, now Arno-Holz-Straße. See Paul Noack, *Carl Schmitt. Eine Biographie*, Propyläen, Frankfurt am Main, 1993, p.191.
69 *Ibid.*
70 See Dieter Wellershoff, 'Nachwort des Herausgebers', in D. Wellershoff (ed), *Gottfried Benn: Gesammelte Werke in vier Bänden*, vol.1, Limes Verlag, Wiesbaden, 1961, p.643.
71 Friedrich Reck-Malleczewen, *Diary of a Man in Despair*, trans Paul Rubens, Audiogrove Limited, London, 2000, pp.83–84.
72 Marian Stein-Steinfeld, communication with author.
73 Nay to Hagemann, 29 May 1939, in Delfs, 2004, *op. cit.*, pp.818–19.
74 Gosebruch to Hagemann, 2 June 1939, *ibid.*, p.821.
75 Beurteilung der RkdbK, Landesleitung Berlin, 2 August 1939.

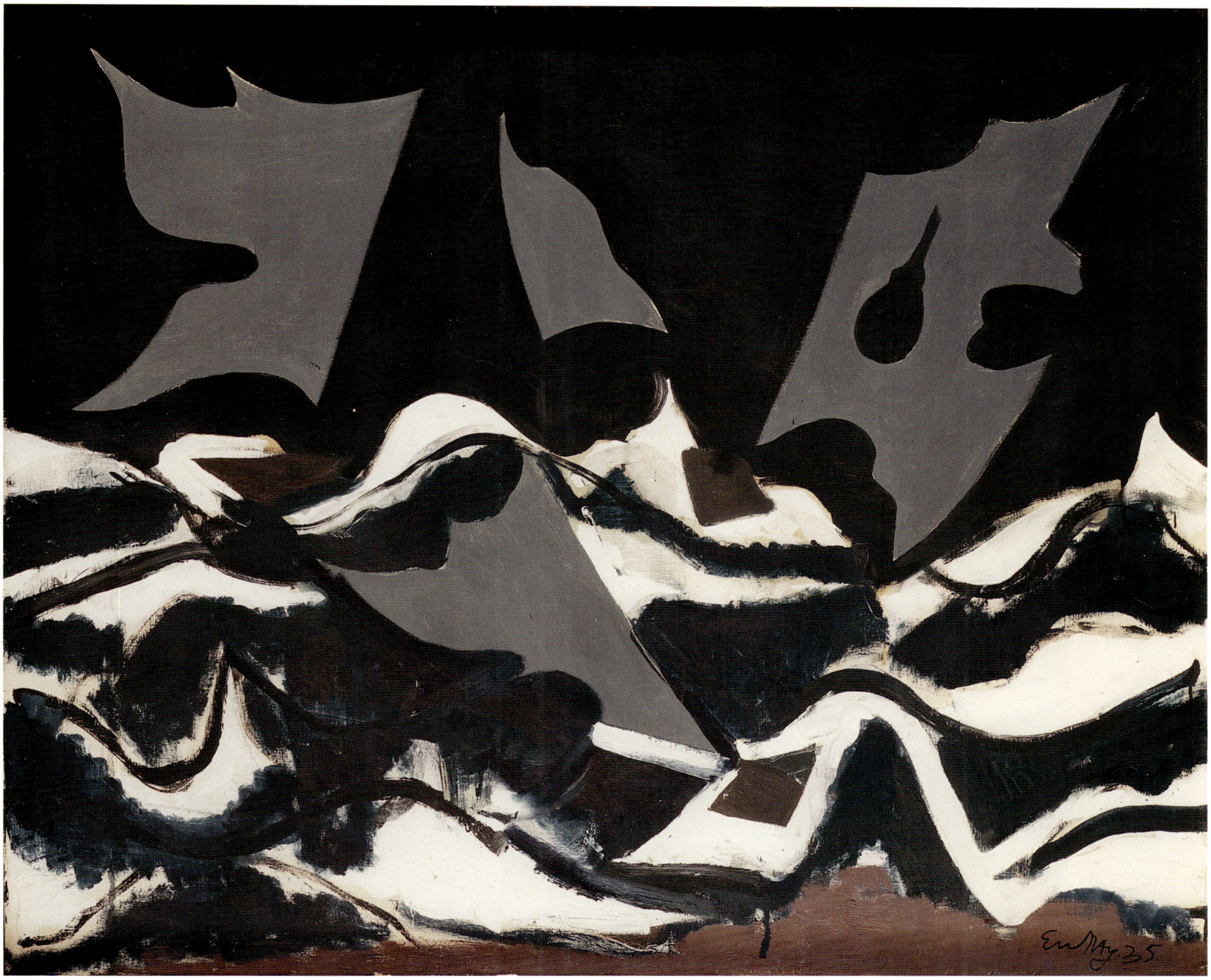

Segelboote nachts auf dem Meer, 1935
Oil on canvas
80 × 100 cm · 31½ × 39⅜ in

Ankunft der Fischer, 1936
Oil on canvas
64.5 × 73.5 cm · 25⅜ × 29 in

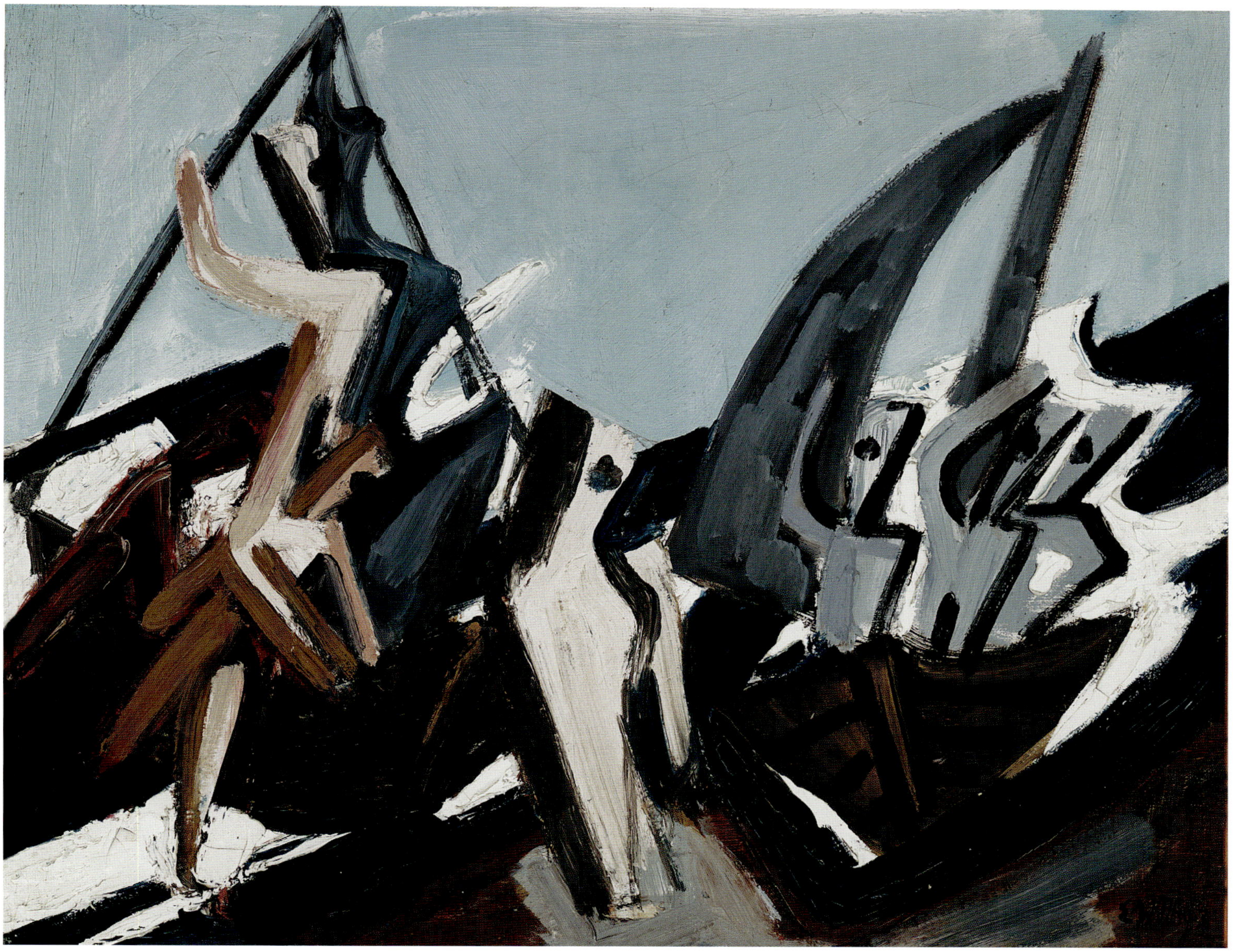

Fischer in der Brandung, 1937
Oil on canvas
100 × 130 cm · 39⅜ × 51⅛ in

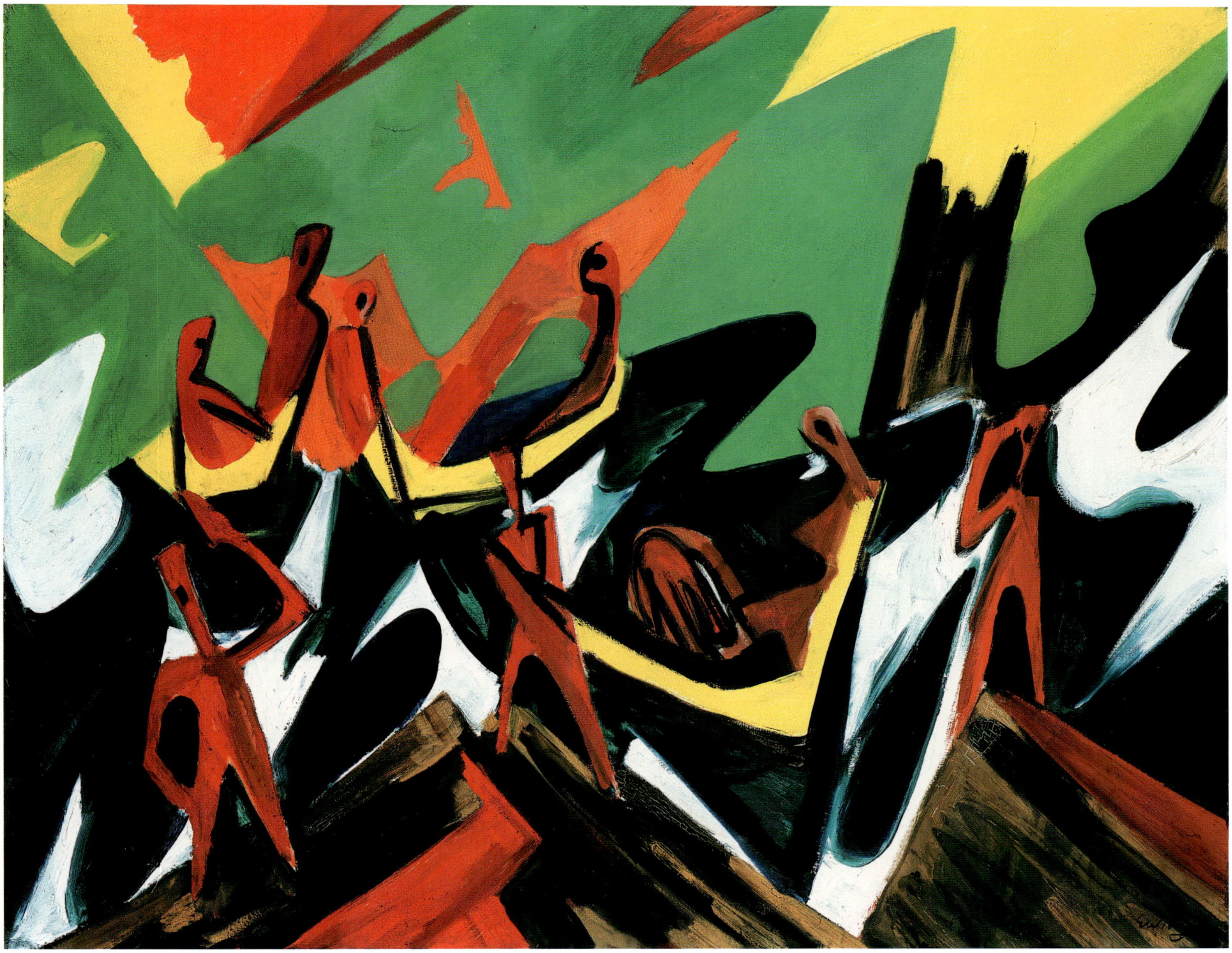

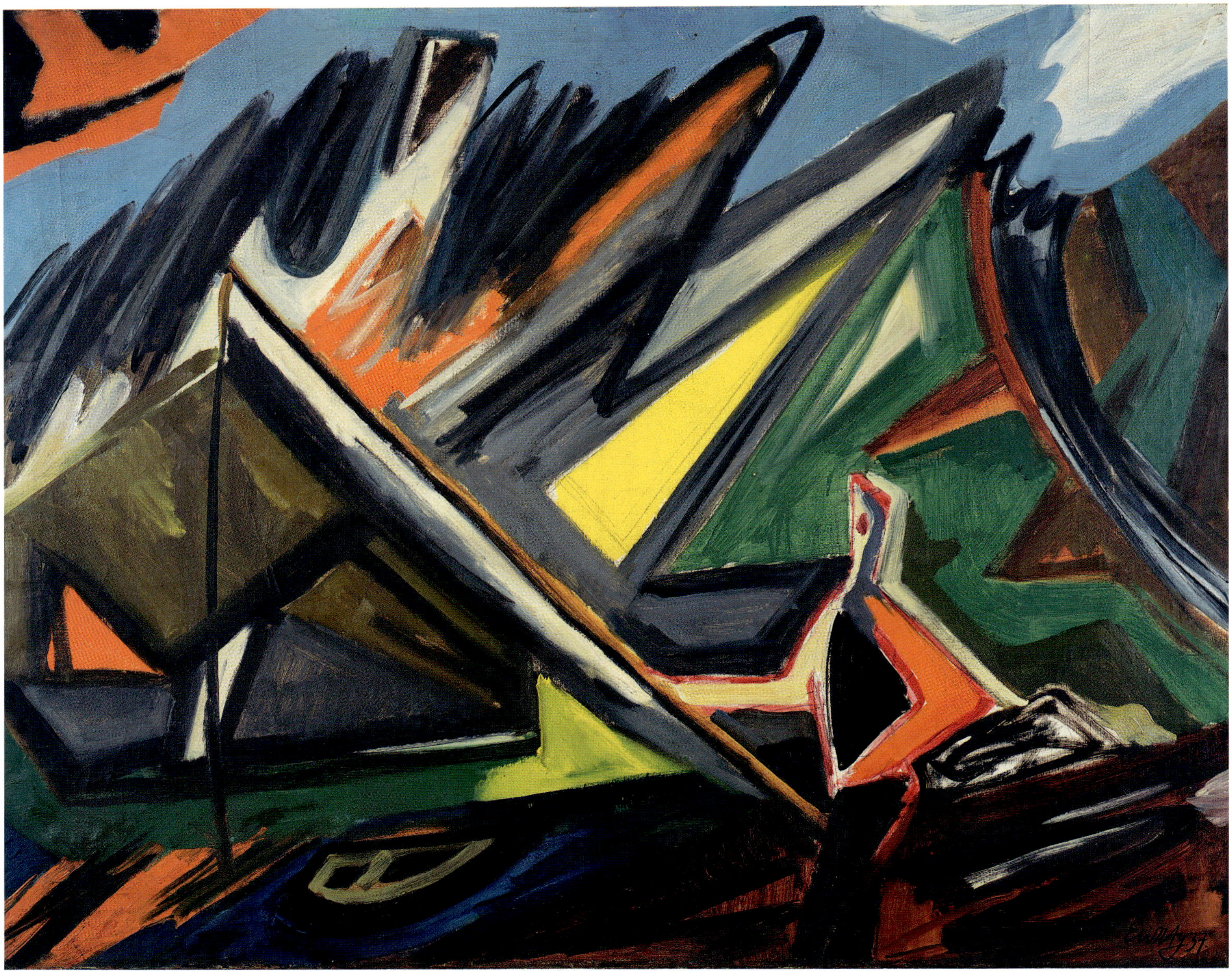

Der Angler, 1937
Oil on canvas
100 × 130 cm · 39⅜ × 51⅛ in

Menschen in den Lofoten
(Frauen am Meer), 1938
Oil on canvas
100 × 130 cm · $39\frac{3}{8} \times 51\frac{1}{8}$ in

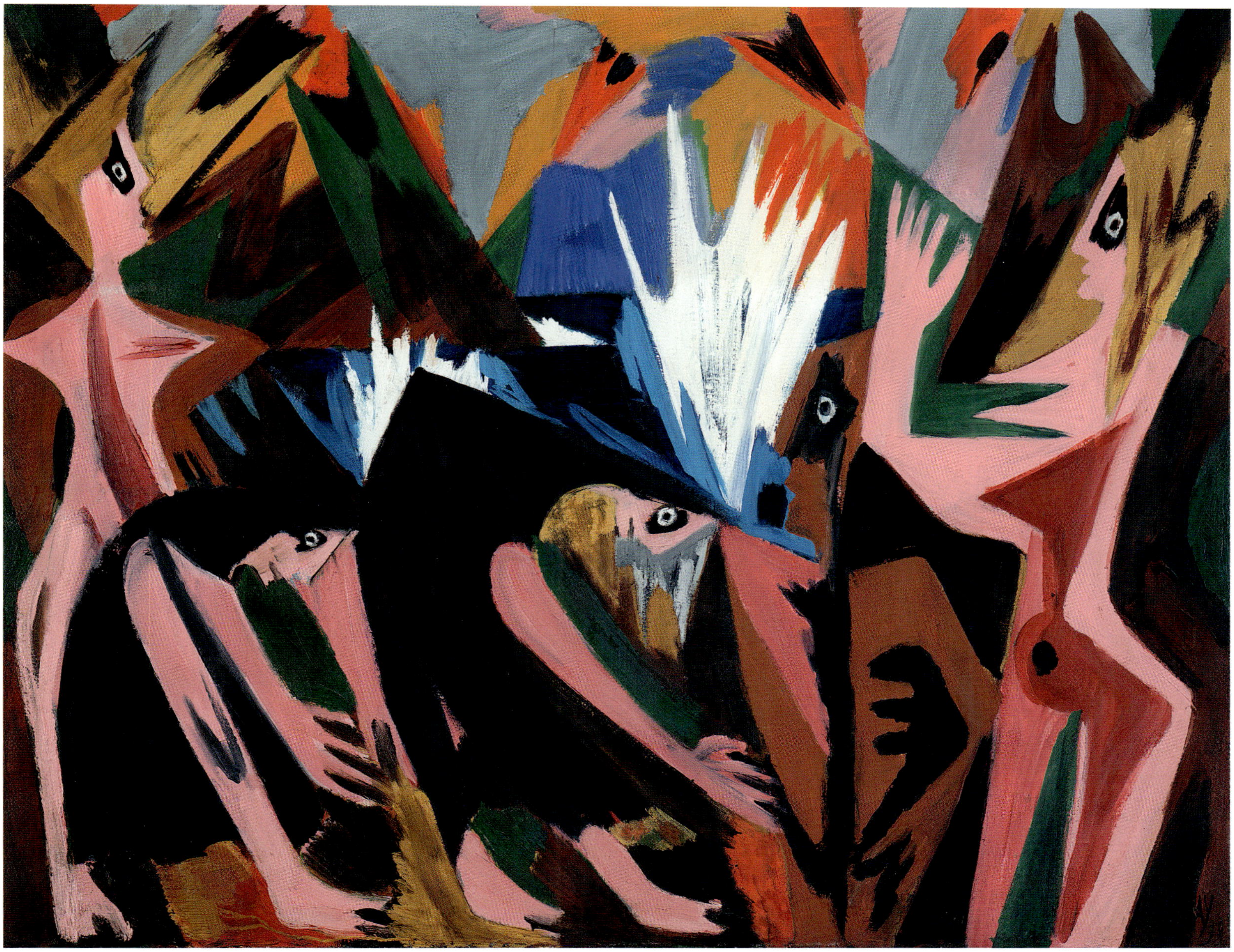

Menschen am Strand, 1939
Oil on canvas
80 × 110 cm · 31½ × 43¼ in

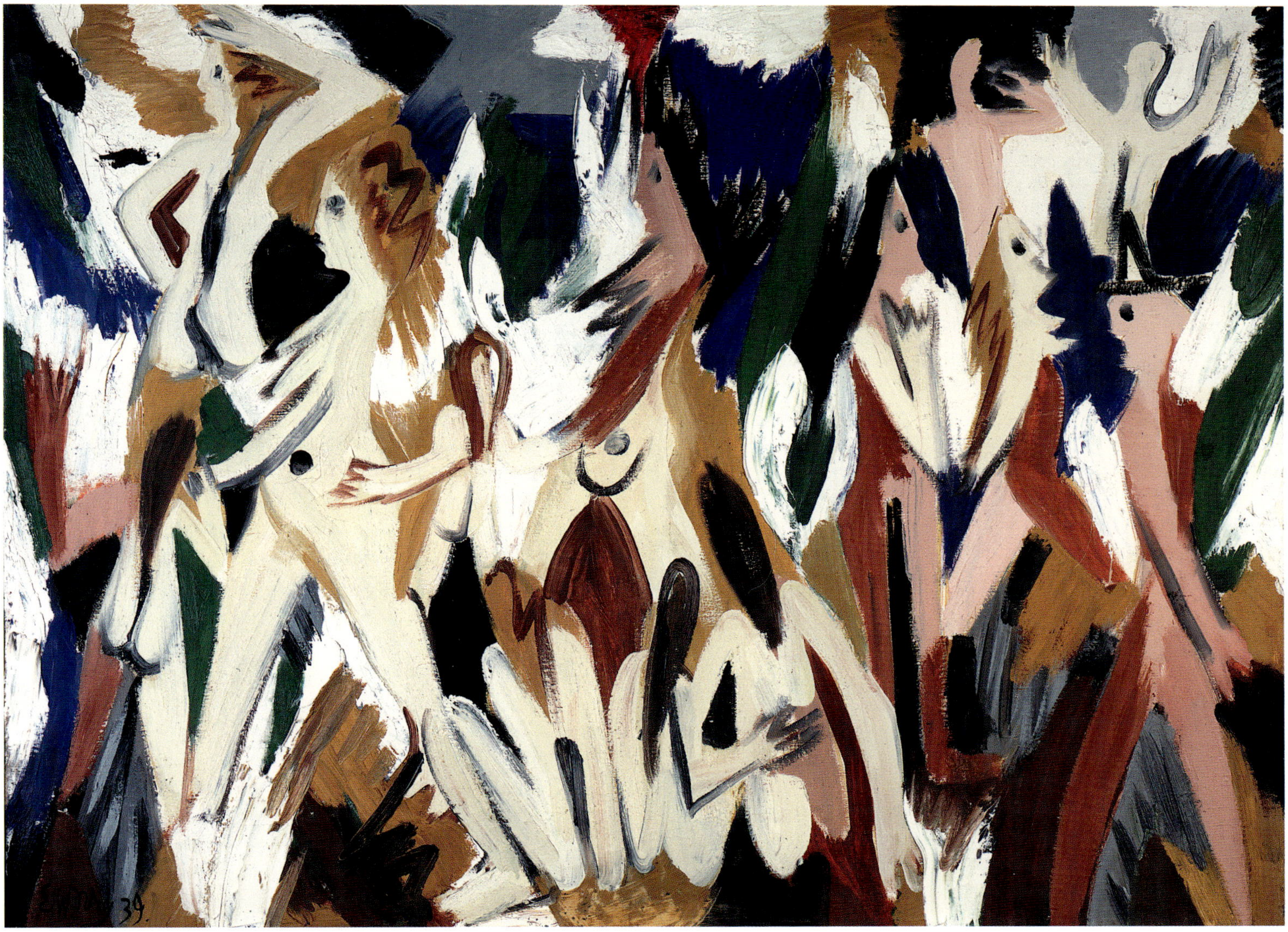

The War and France

Nay is unique among German painters for spending the decisive years of his artistic development serving in the Wehrmacht during the Second World War. He was later to look back and identify the period from 1942 to 1944 as crucial for the evolution of his painting.[76] Although he was not the only artist both to have been represented in *Entartete Kunst* (Degenerate Art) and to have served in the German army, no other artist was able to adapt so readily to the extreme conditions, and to continue the momentum of formal development so successfully.[77]

Despite being one of the best documented periods of his working life, little has been written of his activities during the war. This may seem contrary to his status as a 'degenerate' artist, and demonstrate a degree of alignment with Nazism. It has occasionally been suggested that he made paintings 'in secret' during the war, as if, like Emil Nolde, he was only able to continue his work in a clandestine manner, away from official scrutiny. This is only partly true – he ceased to exhibit his work publicly – but it was largely due to this withdrawal that he was able to continue working in an 'unofficial', semi-abstract modern style. The largest threat to his work was in fact from Allied bombing, which destroyed a number of paintings and personal papers that had remained in Berlin. Indeed, it was precisely because he joined the Wehrmacht, and was stationed in France, that he was able to carry on working, both while on duty and also during periods of leave in Berlin. His status as a soldier protected him from censorship, and as such he joined a long tradition of soldier-painters in German modern art including Franz Marc and Max Beckmann, whose 'degenerate' styles were accepted as a result of having served in the army.

There is little indication that Nay's role in the occupation of France 'tore his heart', as has been suggested.[78] He was utterly indifferent to politics – not due to ignorance but rather to his total allegiance to the sphere of *Kultur* as a higher, essentially religious realm that offered a refuge not only from politics but also from the deadening materialism of modern life. Nay's position may be compared with the 'aristocratic emigration' of other artists from elevated social backgrounds, such as Gottfried Benn. A number of important intellectual connections at this time, particularly with the lawyer Carl Schmitt and the writer Ernst Jünger, helped him develop his ideas, which will be discussed below. As part of a generation that was convinced of some great underlying shift in human life, of which the Third Reich was at first the harbinger but then an increasingly distorted surface expression, Nay was typical of his time. But if it was his belief in the complete distinction between art and politics that enabled him to continue working, the profound experiences of war and the sense of an underlying disturbance in the order of things had a strong impact on his work.

Nay spent the first few months of the war painting in Berlin, and

76 E.W. Nay, *Lesebuch*, *op. cit.*, p.28.

77 Others who were exhibited in *Entartete Kunst* and also fought were Fritz Burger-Mühlfeld, Conrad Felixmüller (who was drafted and taken prisoner of war), as well as Otto Dix and Arnold Topp, both of whom were conscripted to the Volkssturm in 1945. The latter was taken prisoner-of-war by the Russians and never seen again.

78 Fabrice Hergott, 'Malerei wie Poesie konstruieren. Betrachtungen über Nays Verhältnis zu Frankreich', in Elisabeth Nay-Scheibler and Michael Semff (eds), *E.W. Nay. Aquarelle und Goauchen*, exhibition catalogue, Pinakothek der Moderne, Munich, 2004.

was able to keep up sales to collectors such as Arnold Budczies and Hagemann. He began his military service on 1 December 1939, and was posted to a reserve batallion stationed in Schwerin, in northern Germany. In his first letter to Hagemann after his posting, he confessed that barrack life was proving difficult, for the obvious reasons: continuous noise and close-quarters living. He returned for furlough at the end of December.[79] It was at this moment, according to Elly, that she evacuated the paintings remaining in his studio, including many works made in Lofoten, to his uncle living in Bad Muskau on the Polish border in Lusatia.[80] Elly's role in sustaining Nay's market, and managing his stock during his absence was essential, and selflessly conducted. Her memoirs of her life with Nay, in which she describes her experiences of the bombing raids, show the horror of conditions in Berlin at that time.

When his leave was over, Nay was posted briefly to Neuruppin, near Berlin, but then returned to Schwerin at the beginning of February.[81] It was during his next posting, at Meseritz, near the former Polish border, that Nay became active, if unofficially, as a war artist.[82] During March, according to Gosebruch, he was commissioned to paint a *Führerbild*, a portrait of Hitler, on the wall of the cafeteria – which was so appreciated that he was asked to produce another.[83] It can only be imagined in what manner Nay approached this curious commission, possibly abandoning all personal style for a bland naturalism, or adopting a more schematic, expressive style that was not supposed to be considered as 'art'. It is impossible to read anything into this moment other than Nay's complete indifference to politics, and lack of either support or overt antipathy, at this stage, to Hitler. Time and again in his letters home to Elly and others he expressed the wish to be done with the war so that he could return properly to painting.

After a week's leave during Easter,[84] Nay returned to his infantry regiment, and took part in the invasion of France, the Western campaign that had begun on 10 May. He wrote to Hagemann four days before the French capitulation (21 June), from the banks of the Seine, 50 kilometres south of Paris, looking back on his involvement in the lightening invasion of France, and the events that led to the Nazi flag being hoisted on the Eiffel Tower on Saturday 14 June.

> Two heavy days of fighting, which I got through fine. The crossing of the Aisne on 9 June from five in the morning until nine in the evening, and then from 12 to 13 June a night battle in the woods. For both we were in the front line, not more than 40 to 150 metres from the enemy. It was terrible – as were our losses. But those of the French were worse.[85]

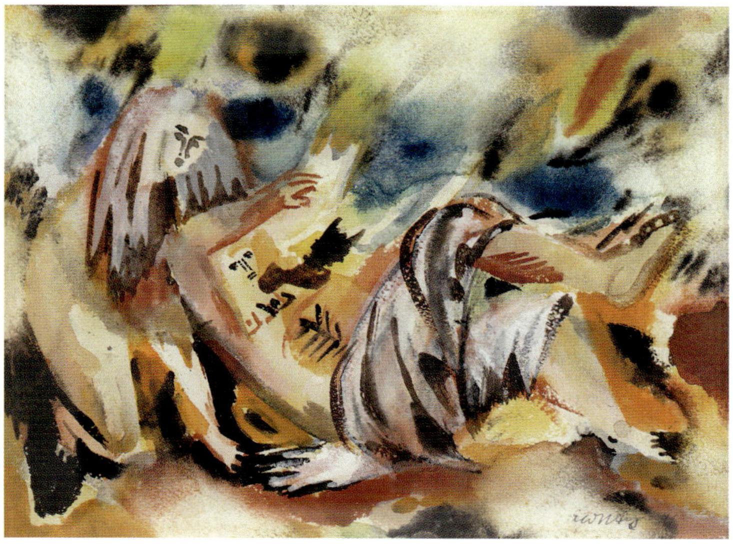

Sommer (zwei Frauen), 1941
Watercolour
23.8 × 32.8 cm · 9⅜ × 12⅞ in

79 E.W. Nay to Carl Hagemann, 14 January 1940, in Delfs, *op. cit.*, p.883.
80 Elly (Helene) Nay, *op. cit.*, pp.115–16. Other works were stored at a villa belonging to Erich Meyer on the outskirts of Berlin, and with Günther Franke at Seeshaupt on the Starnberger See in Bavaria.
81 Nay to Hagemann, 9 February 1940, in Delfs, 2004, *op. cit.*, p.889.
82 Nay to Hagemann, 13 March 1940, *ibid.*, p.895.
83 Ernst Gosebruch to Hagemann, 3 April 1940, *ibid.*, p.897.
84 Nay to Hagemann, 22 March 1940, *ibid.*, p.896.
85 Nay to Hagemann, 17 June 1940, *ibid.*, pp.907–08.

It was at exactly this moment that a 'secret' exhibition of Nay's 'degenerate' work took place in a back room at Günther Franke's gallery in Munich, titled *Von Nolde bis Nay* (From Nolde to Nay). Such exhibitions show on one hand the bravery of certain individuals in the face of Nazi censorship, and on the other the inefficient manner in which this censorship was conducted – as Nay's obvious method of contravening the ban on buying materials suggests, it was not impossible to get around the restrictions. Since Franke himself was also serving in the Wehrmacht at this moment, stationed on the Russian border, the exhibition was organised by Erika Hüetlin, as Nay mentioned in a letter to Franke later that September, in which he also described a letter from an unknown visitor to the exhibition that had reached him at the Front.[86]

By mid-July 1940, Nay was in Brittany, on the coast 'not far from St Malo'.[87] The new collaborationist government of the Vichy Regime had been declared on 10 July, and the northern part of France occupied by the Wehrmacht. By the end of August, on leave in Berlin for three weeks, Nay was predicting a quick end to the war and the occupation of France – with the suggestion that he could perhaps continue his stay there.[88] At this time he was only able to resume his studio work while on leave in Berlin, producing four paintings, at least one of which was a self-portrait, recalling those made by Otto Dix at the beginning of the First World War.[89] Nay's experience of heavy fighting in France had clearly made a strong impact, and he was at pains to instruct Elly on his return that as a topic of conversation it was taboo.[90] One of the two surviving self-portraits of this time, *Selbstbildnis* (Self-Portrait, 1940; p.59) shows some of the dark self-reflection that may have resulted from this traumatic experience. He approached this unusually naturalistic subject awkwardly, with patches of colour approximating a sort of psychic camouflage.

In a letter to Hagemann, written on his return to Brittany in September, Nay describes the important paintings that he had made while in Berlin 'that signal a new direction in my work'.[91] He was referring to the large multi-figure composition *Frauen im Sund* (Women in the Sound, 1940; p.61), and a series of self-portraits, only one of which has survived. However, *Frauen im Sund* continues the series of large bather compositions begun before the war, and suggests that the experiences of being in France had yet to affect his work.

Little is known of Nay's activities during 1941, and few works can be traced. He wrote to Franke in November 1941 saying that he had not been painting recently.[92] Those watercolours that have survived give the sense of time spent moving around the countryside, and an existence not without moments of pleasure, as the pastoral nature of the bathing scenes depicted suggests – see *Sommer (zwei*

Auffindung Moses, 1943
Oil on cardboard
23 × 47.5 cm · 9⅛ × 18¾ in

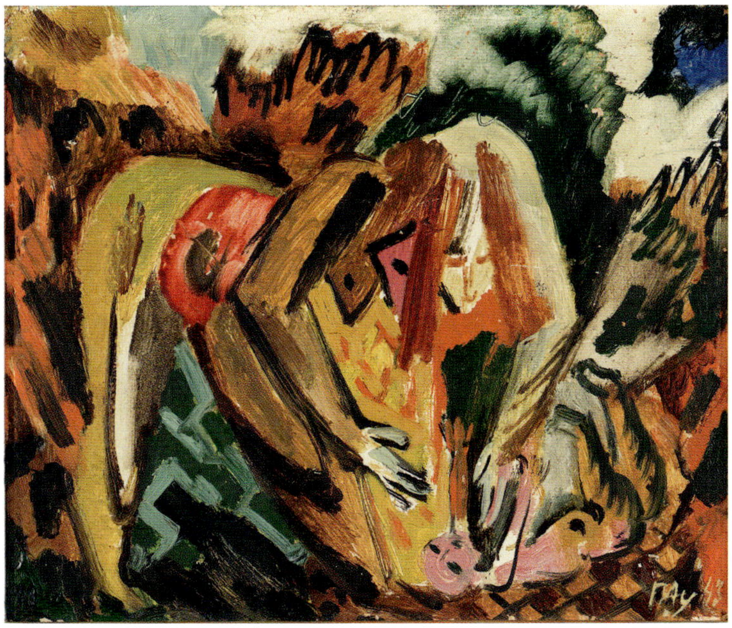

86 Nay to Günther Franke, 15 September 1940, in *E.W. Nay, 1902–1968: Bilder und Dokumente*, *op. cit.*, p.73.
87 Nay to Hagemann, 16 July 1940, in Delfs, 2004, *op. cit.*, p.911.
88 Nay to Hagemann, 20 August 1940, *ibid.*, p.918.
89 Nay to Franke, 15 September 1940, in Schmidt, *op. cit.*, pp.164–65. Scheibler lists only one self-portrait from this moment, and two from December of the following year.
90 Elly (Helene) Nay, 1984, *op. cit.*, p.115.
91 Nay to Hagemann, 22.9.40, in Delfs, 2004, *op. cit.*, pp.922–93.
92 Nay to Franke, 7 November 1941, in

Frauen) (Summer (Two Women), 1941; p.53). During a two-week leave in Berlin in December, Nay painted five more works, including two self-portraits and three landscapes.[93] All except one were later destroyed in bombing raids, the surviving painting being a self-portrait that provides some indication of the appearance of the other missing works in this genre. The style is rudimentary, and the impression given is of Nay reflecting on the hardships of the moment, although it is likely that life in Berlin was more challenging, due to the air war, than his post in the French countryside. Back in Brittany, he wrote in April 1942 to the painter Moering, suggesting that he only occasionally saw his troops, and that otherwise there was 'wonderful summer weather, little sign of the war'. But still there was not much time for painting.

It was around this time, in May 1942, that Nay met Hans Lühdorf, a judge from Düsseldorf serving in the Wehrmacht. Lühdorf had first encountered works by Nay at the home of Carl Hagemann in 1939. He was initially unconvinced, but was more attracted to woodcuts by Nay that he saw in the collection of Alexej von Jawlensky. Lühdorf visited Elly in Berlin during December 1941, and was able to see those works that had not been brought to safety, including early paintings 'in the style of Carl Hofer', and a number of works made on the Baltic coast. All these details were recorded by Lühdorf in a manuscript typed towards the end of 1944, which provides, alongside Nay's letters to Franke, the most detailed record of the artist's experiences in France during the war.[94] The two met for the first time in Auray, where Nay was stationed, before Lühdorf was able to present Nay with the opportunity to be transferred to Le Mans, to work as a cartographer.

Lühdorf was instrumental in helping Nay continue painting in France. In his memoir, he writes that he was able to introduce the artist to the antique dealer Grassin, and to the book dealer Morin, both of whom were interested in Nay's work. It was thanks to Morin that Nay met the amateur sculptor Pierre Térouanne, who in Autumn 1942 was to make his garden studio (the only building that had not otherwise been requisitioned by the Wehrmacht) available to the painter.[95] By September 1942, Nay's war was over. 'As cartographer in an AOK [Armeeoberkommando] one has a very quiet life and lots of free time to paint', he wrote to Franke.[96] A series of larger, more finished gouaches made during 1942 suggest the increased resources available to Nay to paint in Le Mans. Nevertheless he was still able to produce only five paintings on cardboard during the year, most depicting figures in landscapes. The development of a more skilful deployment of monumental figuration is clear from the works made during this year, and sets the stage for the first large paintings on canvas made in France that appeared the next year.

Towards the end of 1942, Nay travelled to Paris, staying with the painter Hans Kuhn. He visited Wassily Kandinsky, who recommended that he contact an art historian, Herbert Herrmann, living in Le Mans.[97] In Paris Nay also became reacquainted with Carl Schmitt and his wife. They discussed Nay's recent work, with the idea that Schmitt could add to his collection, and also talked about Schmitt's most recent book, a short volume *Land und Meer* (Land and Sea), describing the binary opposition between these two elements that has defined human thought and action throughout history.[98] Shortly after their meeting, Schmitt sent Nay a copy of his book. Nay was clearly attracted to the conceptual distinction made by Schmitt, and may have related it to his paintings made in Lofoten and other coastal locations.

In particular, Schmitt's notion of 'space revolution' presented Nay with the possibility of a conceptual link between painting and geopolitics, in turn perhaps sparking the idea that painting could function as part of the war effort. 'Man has a clear awareness of his space', wrote Schmitt, 'which historically is subject to deep-going perturbations ... Each time the forces of history create a new breach, the surge of new energies brings new lands and new seas into the visual field of human awareness, the spaces of historical existence undergo a corresponding change.'[99] This idea of history as a progression of notions of space is carried through to the present day, when, following the conquest of the oceans, the air and the invisible dimension of radio waves, space has become 'the field of man's energy, activity and creativity'.[100]

Nay outlined his response to *Land und Meer* in a letter to the author dated 8 January 1943. 'I am drawing not uninteresting comparisons between your arguments and new problems in space in painting, which I have been working with now for some time', he wrote. His description of these problems, and their solution, is a typical combination of romantic metaphysics and technical terminology through which he created a backdrop for his work. One can extract little that relates to the paintings he was making in Le Mans in 1943, aside from the constant reference to a 'mythical reality', and the need to go beyond illusionism. It is clear that the train of his thoughts was heading towards a spirit of pure abstraction, and it is perhaps surprising that at this moment he did not try to position himself closer to Kandinsky; after meeting the Russian artist in Paris, he may have felt that their works were too close for comfort. Influence is less about likeness than a model against which to react. But the traditionalist element of his attitude, the reason why he could respond so closely to Schmitt's work, kept

Schmidt, 1970, *op. cit.*, p.165.

93 Nay to Franke, 19 December 1941, *ibid.*, p.166.

94 Hans Lühdorf, 'Meine Begegnung mit Ernst Wilhelm Nay', 1944, DKA, IB, 30.

95 Térouanne had, with Harry Graf Kessler and Gaspard Maillol, established Papiers de Montval, a handmade paper fabricant in Le Mans.

96 Nay to Franke, 8 September 1942, in Schmidt, 1970, *op. cit.*, p.166.

97 Herbert Herrmann (1906–66) was closely associated with Willi Baumeister before the war, and in 1940 was appointed to set up a small museum at Kurt Herbert's paint factory in Wuppertal, a refuge for persecuted artists, where Baumeister and Oskar Schlemmer, amongst others, were staying. In May 1941 Herrmann was called up, but during his military service in France gave slide lectures on Baumeister's work. Hermann was not attracted to Nay's work, and it is hardly likely that at this point Nay was interested in that of Baumeister. Marion Ackermann, 'Ereignis/Bild. Einblicke in das Laboratorium der Wuppertaler Arbeitsgemeinschaft', in *Laboratorium Lack. Baumeister, Schlemmer, Krause 1937–1944*, exhibition catalogue, Kunstmuseum Stuttgart, 2007, p.34; Lühdorf, 1994, *op. cit.*, p.12.

98 See Nay to Carl Schmitt, 17 December 1942. Nordrhein-Westfälischen Hauptstaatsarchiv; Nachlass Carl Schmitt, RW 265–10149. Nay refers to works on paper that they had discussed in Paris, and regrets that those preferred by Schmitt and his wife are no longer free. 'But I am working quickly and have already produced 18 more since last Saturday.'

99 Carl Schmitt, *Land und Meer. Eine Weltgeschichtliche Betrachtung*, Philipp Reclam, Leipzig, 1942; *Carl Schmitt, Land and Sea*, trans Simona Draghici, Plutarch Press, Washington, 1977, pp.28, 29.

100 *Ibid.*, p.58.

101 Nay to Franke, 10 February 1943, in Schmidt, 1970, *op. cit.*, p.168.

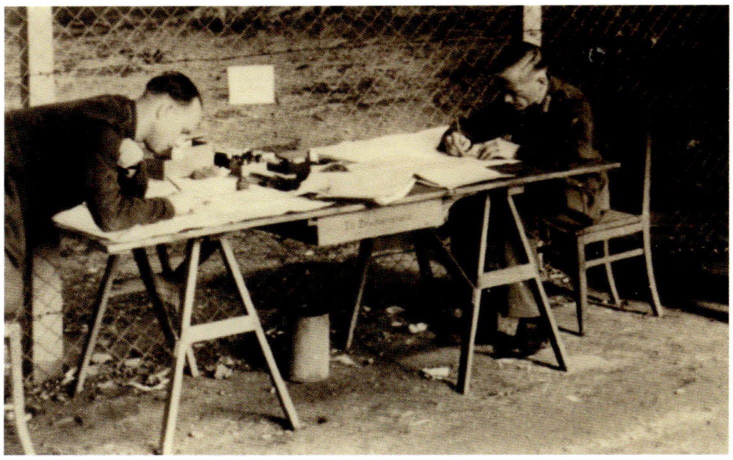

E.W. Nay at work, drawing maps, Le Mans, 1942

E.W. Nay with Hans Lühdorf and Ernst Jünger in the house of M. Térouanne, Le Mans, 1943

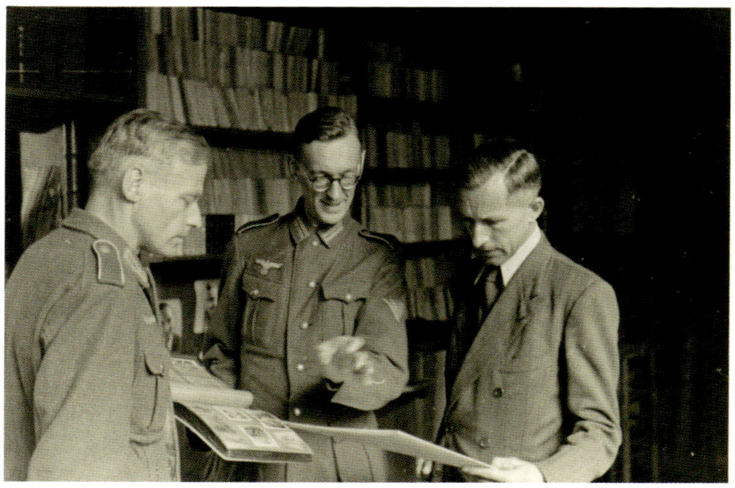

him, at least during the war, within the humanist remit of figurative painting. Despite his indifference to Schmitt's political circumstances, the underlying sense of a spiritual revolution – a combination of romantic nationalism and a rapprochement with the forms of modern life, both in terms of aesthetics and technology – can be read between the lines of his letter to Schmitt.

Nay returned on leave to Berlin in early 1943 (from 18 February to 7 March), bringing nine watercolours, numerous drawings and two paintings. These were amongst the first large paintings made in France and included the important monumental works *Komposition mit vier Frauen* (Composition with Four Women, 1943; p.63) and *Land der fünf Sonnen* (Land of the Five Suns, 1943). On 10 February, he had written to Franke to prepare him for *Komposition mit vier Frauen*, which he considered a major work:

> This painting is a very important station in my artistic development. The rigidity of a large orchestrated composition combines with mellow, soft tones, of a type that can often be found in my early work. The first painting, the *Eichhorn-Bild* (Eichhorn Picture, 1934) that you have, and the paintings from Norway, all the ideas present in these works have now come to fruition. I see in the *Komposition mit vier Frauen* the artistic manifestation of my very being, the first grandiose and comprehensive work.[101]

The next month, back in Le Mans, Nay wrote once again to Franke to alert him to the painting – at that moment stored in Gosebruch's cellar, but due to travel to Franke – as the first fulfilment of *mythischer Wirklichkeit* (mythical reality) in his work.[102] *Komposition mit vier Frauen* does indeed show a new level of synthesis, and also a handling of pictorial space within which figures are dramatically suspended, as if in a shell-burst or in a dream. The closed eyes of the figures only emphasise this impression, and the shield-like depiction of faces and the manner in which the features are drawn recalls those works that Kirchner was making in the 1910s, influenced by Oceanic sculpture. The vigorous, improvised technique of *Auffindung Moses* (The Discovery of Moses, 1943; p.54), one of the first works in the series of paintings made in France, is exchanged for a more highly finished surface that perhaps reflects Nay's more settled situation in his new studio in Le Mans.

The experiences of war were seeping into Nay's work in an oblique, restrained manner – unsurprising for an artist who tended more towards lyrical than expressive abstraction. On 16 March, Schmitt wrote to the writer Ernst Jünger that two weeks previously he had seen Nay's latest work, and found it 'highly instructional'.[103] The fragmentary nature of contemporary painting, Schmitt wrote, was simply a reflection of fragmentary reality. Nay had met Jünger in 1942, and the writer paid him a return visit on 1 May 1943, accompanied by the art historian Fritz Baumgart and a student, 'Fräulein

102 Nay to Franke, 29 March 1943, *ibid.*, p.170.
103 Carl Schmitt to Ernst Jünger, 16 March 1943, in Helmuth Kiesel (ed), *Ernst Jünger, Carl Schmitt. Briefe 1930–1983*, Klett-Cotta, Stuttgart, 1999, p.158.

Lampe'. The visitors were able to see works from the first group of large *Frankreichbilder*, or 'French Paintings'. According to Hans Lühdorf, the visit was not an immediate success, largely due to the unfamiliarity of both Jünger and Baumgart with modern painting. Jünger nevertheless appears to have made stringent efforts to engage with Nay's work, in particular with the symbolic value that Nay ascribed to colour. The writer's rather arbitrary comparison of the motif in the painting *Mit Rotem Arm (Orestie)* (With Red Arm (Orestes), 1943; p.65), with the 'spoke of a flaming wheel', suggests that he was initially at a loss to know how to respond to the paintings. His account of the visit in his diary, however, shows that on reflection his response was positive. The paragraph concerning Nay is worth quoting in full, as one of the most interesting reflections on his work:

> Looking at the paintings I had the impression of the output of a laboratory, of promethean creation, congealing into new form. But I did not reach a judgement, for these are works that one has to consider over time. There was talk about theory, about which Nay, like most good painters, had something to say. Nay is also inspired by Carl Schmitt's *Raumgedanken*. Particularly felicitous was his description of the point in his painting when he had 'achieved tension', as if the painting reached a new state of excellence. This happens also in prose – a phrase, or clause, can achieve special tension, or torsion. This is comparable with the way in which a woman with whom one has been friendly for a long time, suddenly takes on erotic attraction – everything changes.[104]

Before his return to Paris the next day, Jünger once again returned briefly to Nay's studio:

> Finally a second hurried visit to Nay's paintings. They carry the mark both of primitivism and knowledge, and are thus emblematic of our times. Colour is freely used, yet in a manner that brings out their dynamic values. Thus is the arm raised to perform a deed coloured a blood red.[105]

The first half of 1943 was a moment of real achievement for Nay, and his first real floruit. 'I've really progressed', he wrote to Franke in late May.[106] On 14 July he went on extended leave back in Germany, taking 12 paintings with him. He was able to visit a number of collectors, including Hans Dittmayer in Dresden, who purchased *Der Garten des Herrn Térouanne* (Mr Térouanne's Garden, 1943; p.67), an idyllic depiction of the garden in which Nay's studio was located, before travelling to stay with Franke in Munich from 29 July to 1 August.[107] In September, Nay was back in Berlin to deal with the destruction of his studio in a bombing raid – the first heavy raids on Berlin took place at the end of August and the beginning of September 1943 and continued until the end of March the next year. In December, Nay's studio was hit once again, and he returned to assess the damage. He clearly enjoyed his position in the relatively peaceful Le Mans, untouched by aerial bombardment. Jünger wrote to Schmitt in August, mentioning his visit to Nay, whom he describes as 'very happy': 'The State hasn't yet spoilt our artists.'[108] Jünger had paid a second visit to Le Mans, again in the company of Baumgart and Lampe, but since Nay had taken all his paintings back to Berlin, there were only a few works on paper to be seen. Again writing to Franke, Nay describes the generous dinner provided by Morin for the German guests, as well as Térouanne.[109]

The second half of 1943 was equally productive for Nay in Le Mans. On 17 January 1944 he wrote to Franke that he had finished four large paintings, and was working on two more, including *Königin auf Thron* (Enthroned Queen, 1944), which, along with *Aënors Hochzeit* (Aeneas's Wedding, 1944; p.69), represents the culmination of his work in France. Both compositions are dominated by two figures engaged in conversation, in roughly identical poses, but whereas *Königin auf Thron* is rendered with a heavy application of paint, *Aënors Hochzeit* shows a much cleaner, more vivid linear structure. The oscillation of Nay's style between a heavy, quotidian realism and a stylish Expressionism influenced above all by Kirchner, which may be traced back to his first publicly exhibited works of the mid-1920s, continues to inform his painting.

Details of the remainder of Nay's wartime experiences are vague. The Normandy landings on 6 June 1944 signalled the end of the German occupation, although Nay remained in Le Mans for at least another month during the battle of Normandy as Allied troops were establishing a foothold. On the 24 July he wrote to Franke that he no longer had any free time to paint, but was helping Hans Lühdorf complete a memoir of his experiences in France, 'and I'm adding a little of my own spice to it'.[110] No other works are known to have been made after *Aënors Hochzeit*, which according to Lühdorf's memoir was finished in Térouanne's studio at the beginning of August, as the Allied troops were nearing Le Mans. Many German troops were captured in Normandy at this moment. Nay took part in the retreat, narrowly escaping being taken prisoner in Amiens, as he wrote again to Franke on 10 September.[111]

What adventures and hardships took place from this moment until his release from an American internment camp in May the next year can only be guessed. Like millions of others, Nay became one for whom the concept of home was now utterly alien. Simple survival formed the basic premise of life. That instead of returning to Elly in Berlin, he went instead to Hofheim am Taunus near Frank furt to seek out an old friend and supporter, Hanna Bekker vom Rath, suggests that his marriage however had not survived the war.

104 Ernst Jünger, *Über Kunst und Künstler. Aus den Schriften*, Gessler, Friedrichshafen, 1990, p.18; author's translation.
105 *Ibid.*, p.20.
106 Nay to Franke, 28 May 1943, in Schmidt, 1970, *op. cit.*, p.171.
107 Nay reports visits to his studio by Budzcies, Gosebruch, Heckel and Heise to Franke, 23 July 1943, in Schmidt, 1970, *op. cit.*, p.173.
108 Ernst Jünger to Carl Schmitt, 24 August 1943, in Helmuth Kiesel (ed), *Ernst Jünger, Carl Schmitt. Briefe 1930–1983*, Klett-Cotta, Stuttgart, 1999, p.167.
109 Nay to Franke, 17 August 1943, in Schmidt, 1970, *op. cit.*, p.173.
110 Nay to Franke, 24 July 1944, in *E.W. Nay, 1902–1968*, *op. cit.*, p.86.
111 Nay to Franke, 10 September 1944, *ibid.*, p.87.

Selbstbildnis, 1940
Oil on canvas
105 × 80 cm · 41⅜ × 31½ in

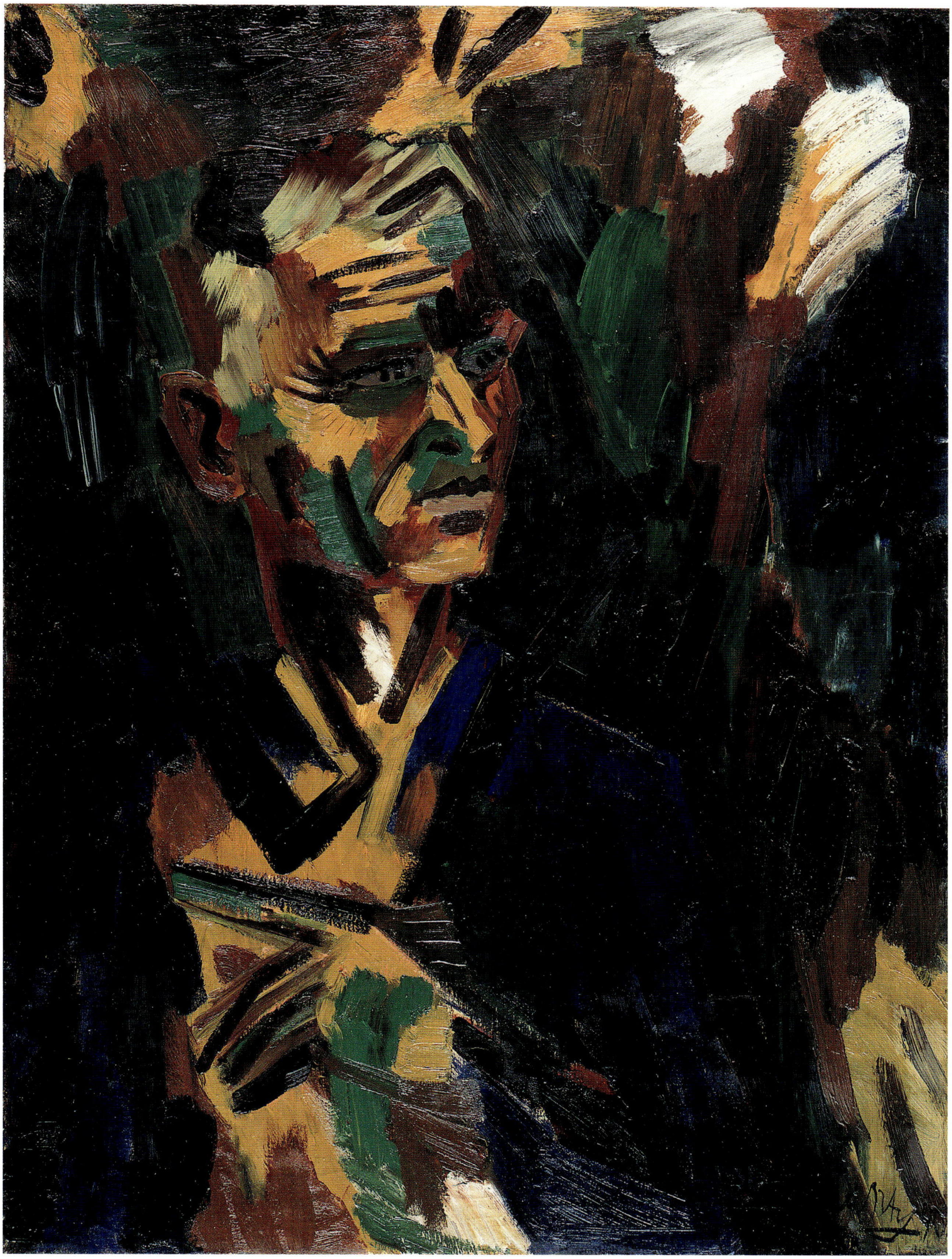

Frauen im Sund, 1940
Oil on canvas
115 × 154 cm · 45¼ × 60⅝ in

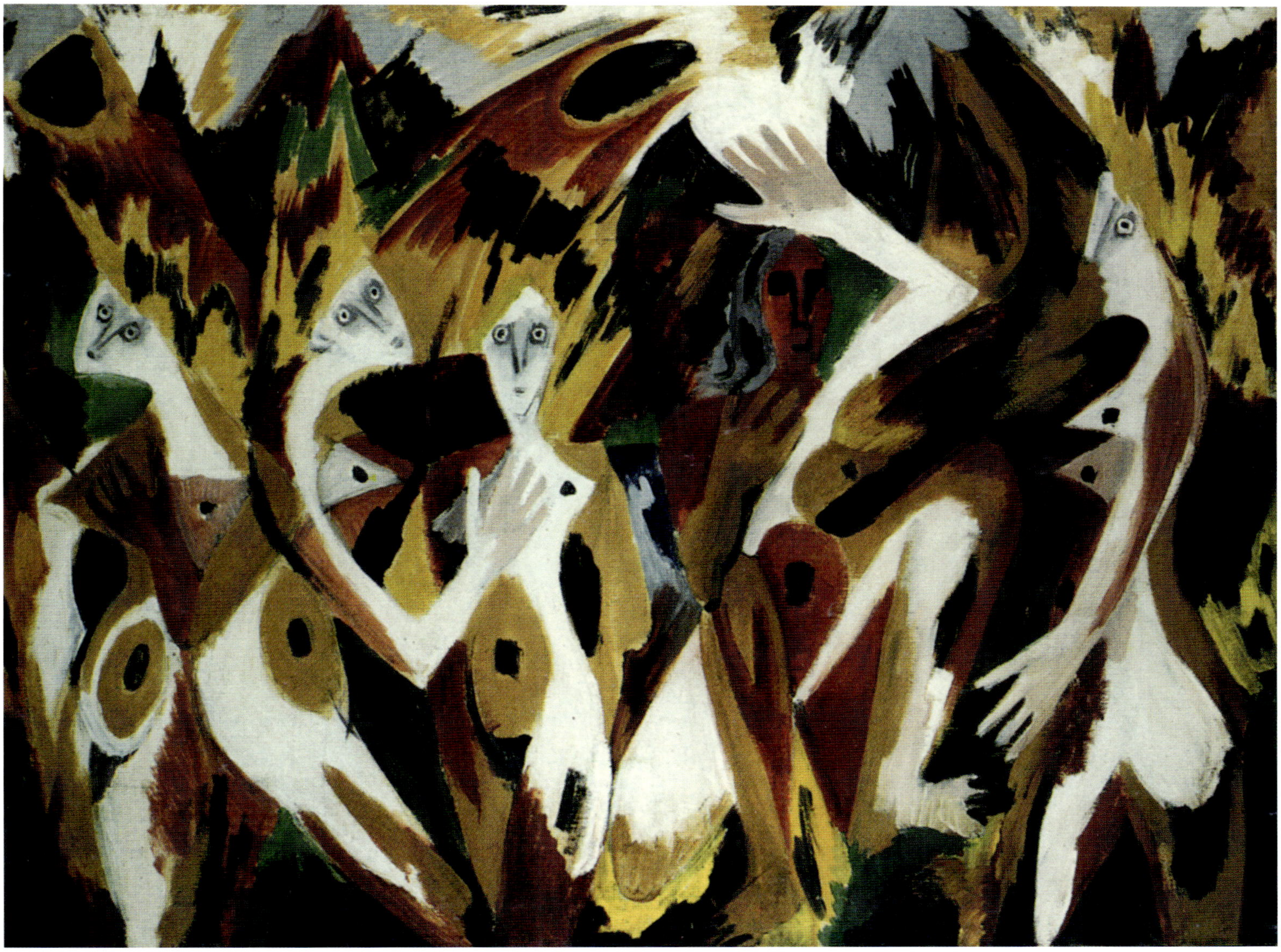

Komposition mit vier Frauen, 1943
Oil on cardboard
79.6 × 103 cm · 31⅜ × 40½ in

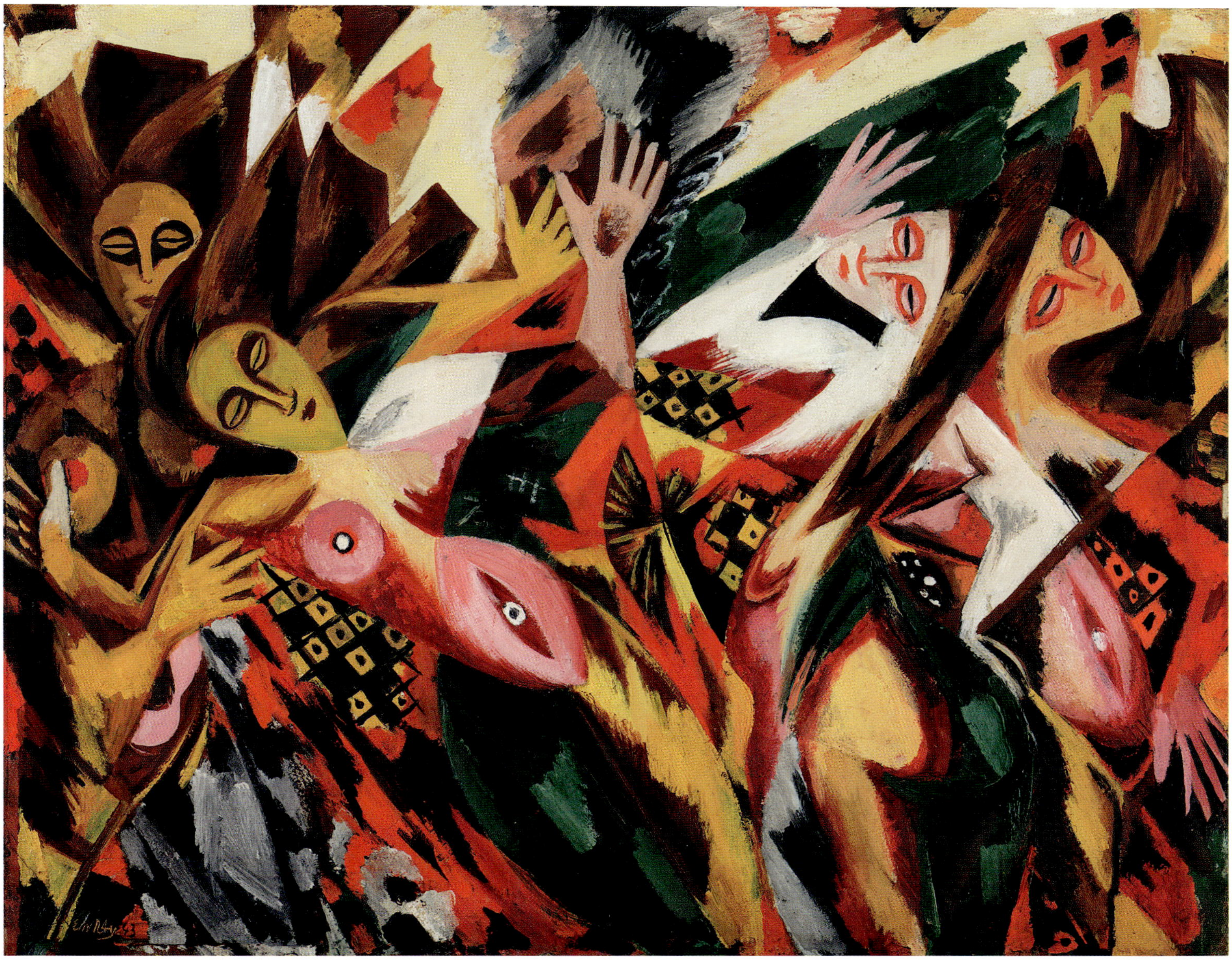

Mit Rotem Arm (Orestie), 1943
Oil on canvas
54 × 72.5 cm · 21¼ × 28½ in

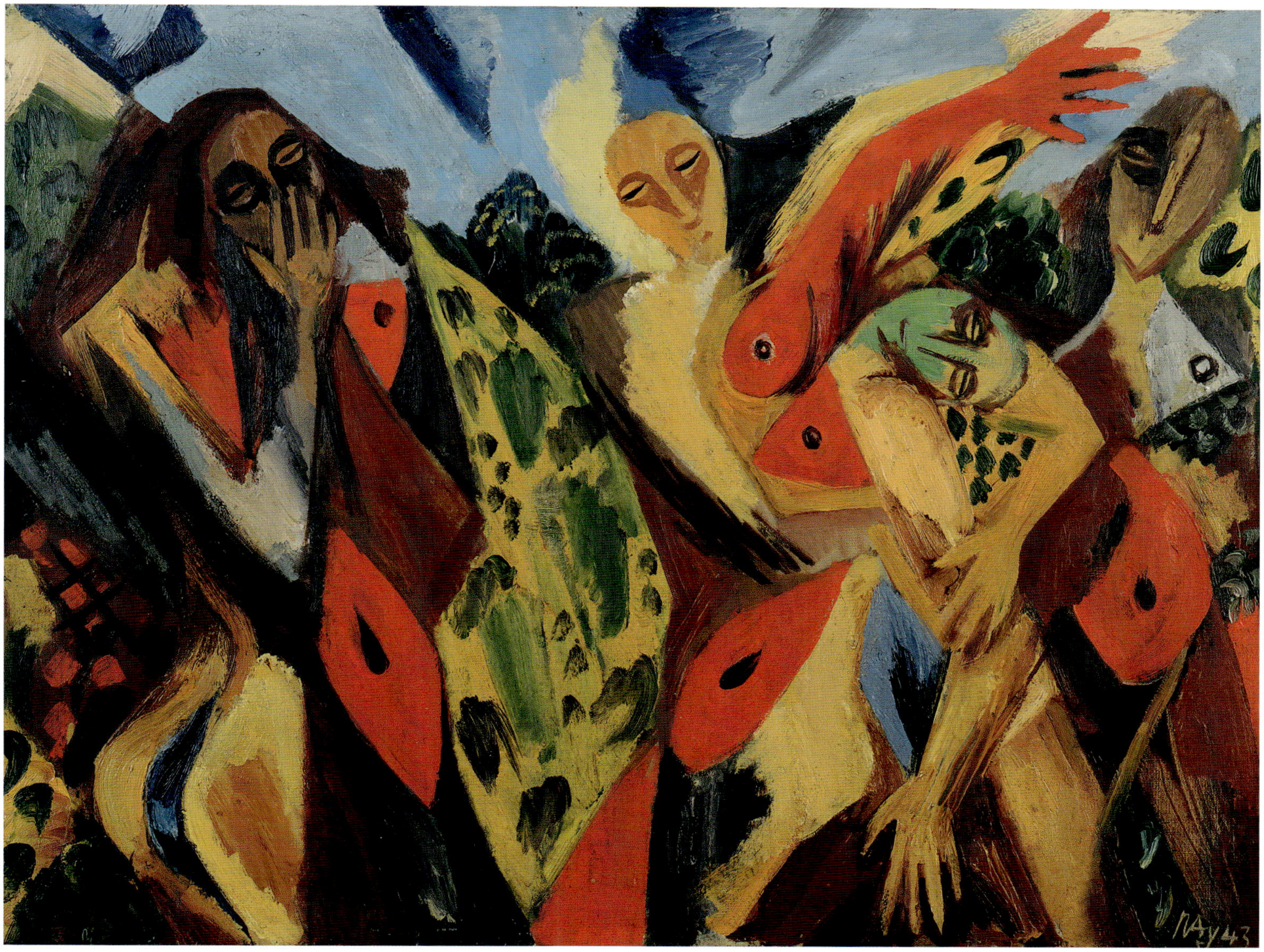

Der Garten des Herrn Térouanne, 1943
Oil on canvas
70 × 91 cm · 27½ × 35⅞ in

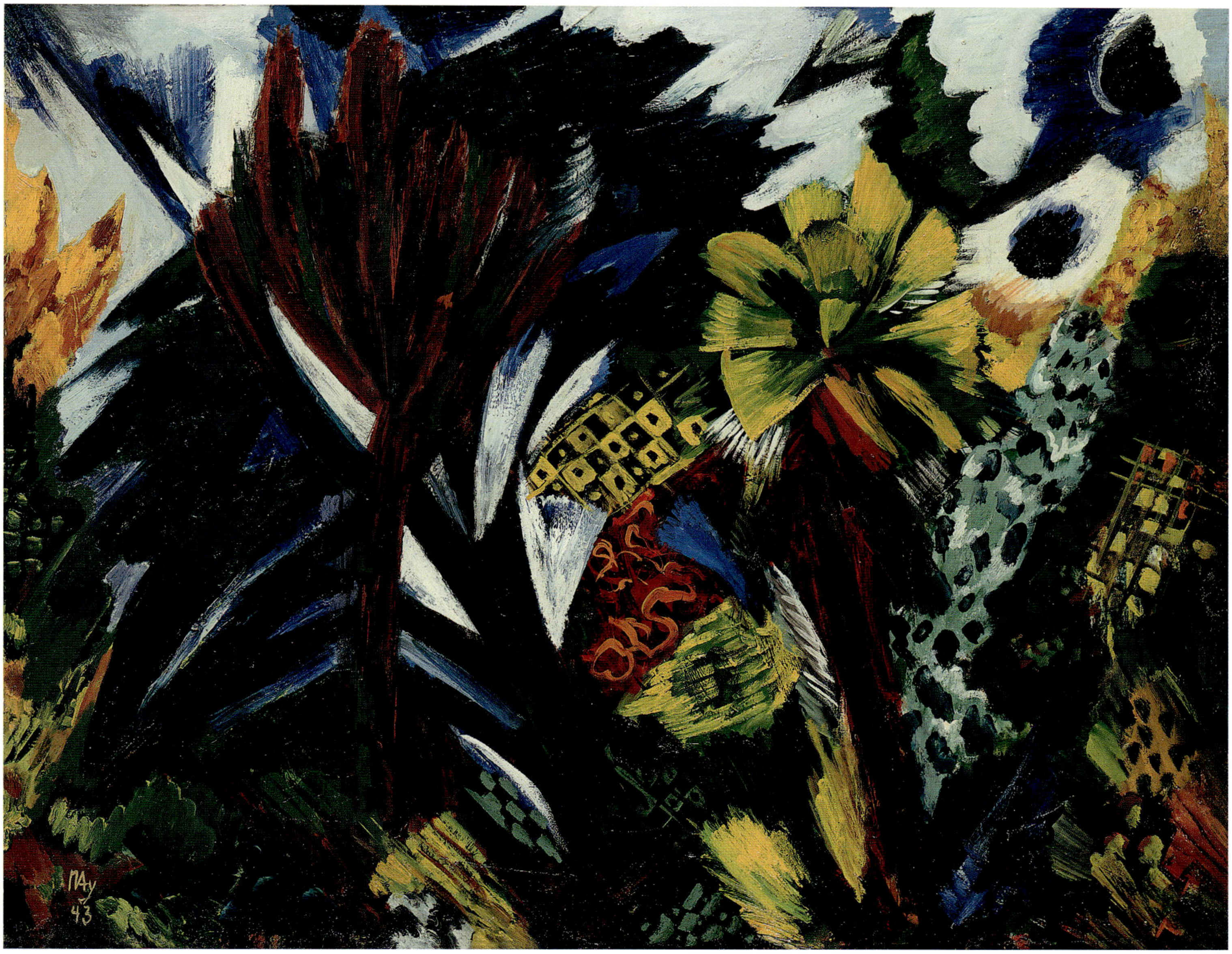

Aënors Hochzeit, 1944
Oil on canvas
73 × 92 cm · 28¾ × 36¼ in

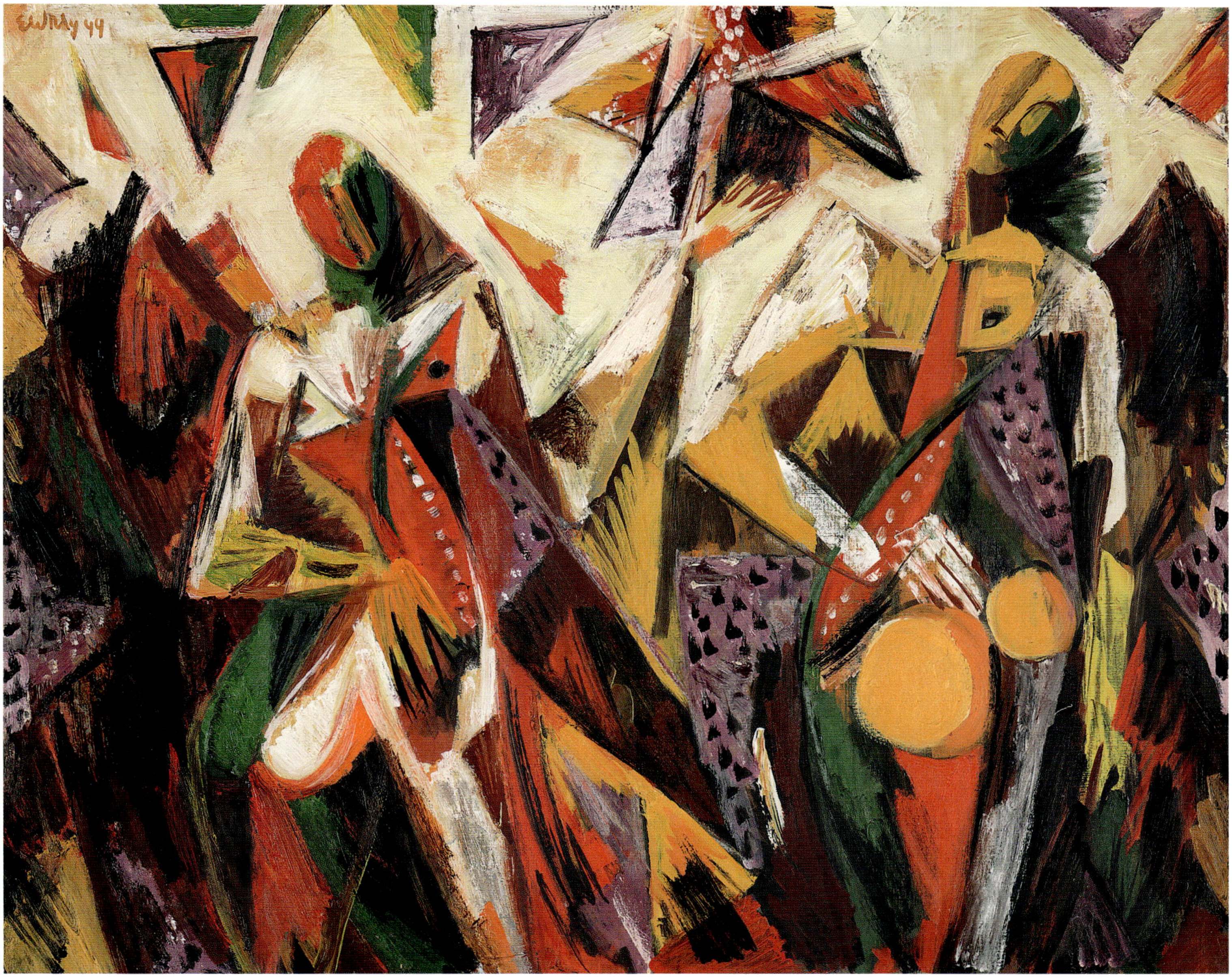

The 1940s: Body and Myth

Et soudain tout m'est force et presence,
où fume encore le theme du néant.

And at once all is power and presence for me,
here where the theme of nothingness rises still in smoke

— Saint-John Perse, *Exil*

As Oskar Maria Graf once wrote, the years after 1945 saw for many Germans the true beginning of exile. There was, it seemed, nothing to return to – towns had been destroyed to the extent that it was no longer apparent where the roads and buildings had been. By some estimates it would take 50 years to rebuild what had been lost. A profound sense of homelessness greeted those returning from exile, or emerging from 'inner emigration'. The DPs, 'Displaced Persons', in their millions in camps or vagrant around Europe, seemed to embody the fate of the continent.

Nay's experiences on his return to Germany in the first months and years of reconstruction unfolded within this context. His painting around 1945 was a direct development of the work that he had made during the war, involving a shift from self-possessed, confident subjects to the pathos of defeat. *Sibylle* (Sibyl, 1945; p.77), shows a single standing figure rendered with impasto swathes of unmixed paint, a heavy and deliberately ugly image recalling works made during the war, such as *Aënors Hochzeit* (Aeneas's Wedding, 1944) (p.69), but as if the human body were now being viewed through a shattered lens. It may seem strange that works made during the war appear more lyrical and fluent, but Nay's ability to remain with the developmental logic of his painting is remarkable, and was to some extent a form of protection from the extreme circumstances of physical existence. He was acutely aware of the difficulties facing German artists at this moment, later describing the period since 1945, particularly in Berlin, as one long *Totensonntag* – a funereal Sunday.[112] Werner Haftmann wrote intriguingly of the 'principle of the desert' that was always at work in Nay's painting, a principle that showed his 'receptivity to existence itself': 'The desert, emptiness as the symbolic form of extension into infinity, into whose breadth man could inscribe the arabesques of his life as a way of confirming reality.'[113] No more fitting description could be offered of Nay's work in the extraordinary situation in Germany after 1945. Allied bombardment had created a desert landscape of destruction that was described by some as a 'moonscape', and interpreted by many postwar artists according to the bizarre disjunctures of Surrealism. Nay's response to this 'ruinscape' was indirect and allegorical.

This was due at least in part to his good fortune in finding a situation in which to continue working, at Hofheim am Taunus, in the purlieus of Frankfurt am Main, within the American zone of occupation. After being released from an American prisoner-of-war camp at the end of May, he made his way straight to Hofheim to stay with Hanna Bekker vom Rath, with whom he spent the summer months. On 15 September Nay moved into a vacant studio that had belonged to the Swiss painter Ottilie Roederstein, who had died in 1937. He described his new situation to the art historian Erich Meyer:

> I have a small, warm room (stove, wood), a large studio that is unheated though comfortable. Two further rooms are uninhabited. I have the little place to myself, it is just outside of the small town with a view over the river Main to the Odenwald.[114]

Klaus Gallwitz has described the idyllic, Arcadian impression of Hofheim, untouched by the Allied bombardment.[115] Accounts of Nay's life at this time are eerily detached from the physical and psychological state of Germany.[116] On the one hand, such disconnection was necessary for creative concentration, but on the other it reveals once again a more fundamental lack of interest in politics and current affairs. 'My world arises and is formed from an all-embracing – if you like – "dream" that is nevertheless the only reality', he wrote to Meyer at the beginning of 1946.[117] Two years later, in a letter of advice to a young painter, Dietrich Voigt, Nay clarified this position:

> Only when you are creating something regardless of your environment can you build something that grows from your inner being. There are too many artists today who only offer impressions from their environment: in a few years they are forgotten. Art is a private activity, and one can only produce works of art when there is no intention to produce something at the behest of those around, be they friends or relatives.[118]

Like most large cities in Germany after 1945, Frankfurt had been largely reduced to rubble by Allied bombardment. The historic Paulskirche had been destroyed, and the Städel Museum had also been severely damaged. The museum was nevertheless an important resource for Nay at this time, who visited Ernst Holzinger (the director of the Städel since 1938) bringing portfolios of watercolours and gouaches made in France during the war, and also more recently in the Hofheim studio, and selling them directly to the Museum. He also met at this time with the painter Louise Rösler, who had studied with Karl Hofer, and the painter Hans Mettel, whom Nay had encountered at the Villa Massimo in Rome during his scholarship year.[119]

Nay's ability to adjust to the postwar situation, quickly re-establishing contacts and a working routine, bears witness to his unsentimental nature, but also to the lack of any prewar reputation with which to contend, unlike Dix and Baumeister,[120] for example. After 1945 the rehabilitation of the reputation of avant-garde artists

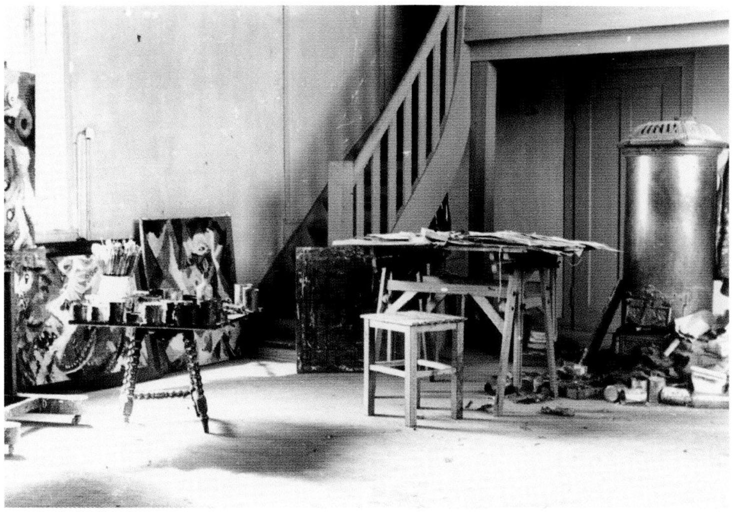

E.W. Nay's studio, Hofheim, 1947

E.W. Nay in front of his drawings in his studio, Hofheim

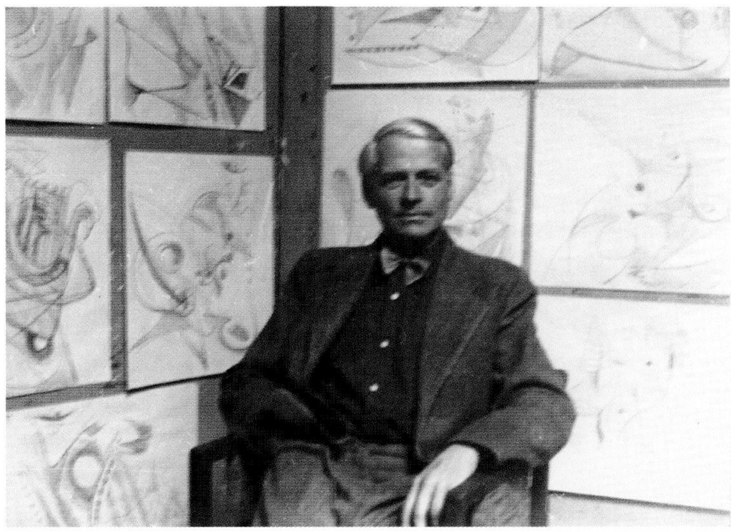

112 *E.W. Nay, 1902–1968: Bilder und Dokumente*, *op. cit.*
113 Werner Haftmann, 'Epilogue', in Haftmann, *op. cit.*, p.23.
114 E.W. Nay to Erich Meyer, 28.12.45, in *E.W. Nay, 1902–1968*, *op. cit.*, p.92. See also the account provided by Hanna Bekker vom Rath, 'Rückblicke auf eine Freundschaft', in *Ernst Wilhelm Nay – Ölbilder, Gouachen*, exhibition catalogue, Kunstkabinett Hanna Bekker vom Rath, Frankfurt, 1970.
115 Klaus Gallwitz, 'Ich stehe auf fließendem Sand', in *Ernst Wilhelm Nay. Die Hofheimer Jahre 1945–1951*, exhibition catalogue, Städtische Galerie im Städel and Museum der bildenden Künste, Frankfurt and Leipzig, 1994.
116 See the account by Doris Schmidt, in *E.W. Nay, 1902–1968*, *op. cit.*, pp.92–97.
117 Nay to Meyer, 25 February 1946, *ibid.*, p.90.
118 The letter begins: 'I'm reassured by the fact that you consider abstract painting too difficult, but I would be even happier to hear that you find painting in a more general sense a very difficult pursuit. The question of whether a painting is abstract or figurative has for me always been inconsequential; I ask rather whether an artist is able to form or not. Here in the West zone everybody is making "abstract" paintings, which results in many stupidities. Every artist needs a guide, particularly when they are young, but I am not sure what model I should recommend for you. As for Baumeister, be careful: he is a famous painter but works in a very simple manner. You may have problems with Klee, unless you approach him solely in terms of style. But whichever you choose, you must be clear that whatever you do you stand for and will defend with your life.' Nay to Dietrich Voigt, June 1948, Deutsches Kunstarchiv, Nuremberg.

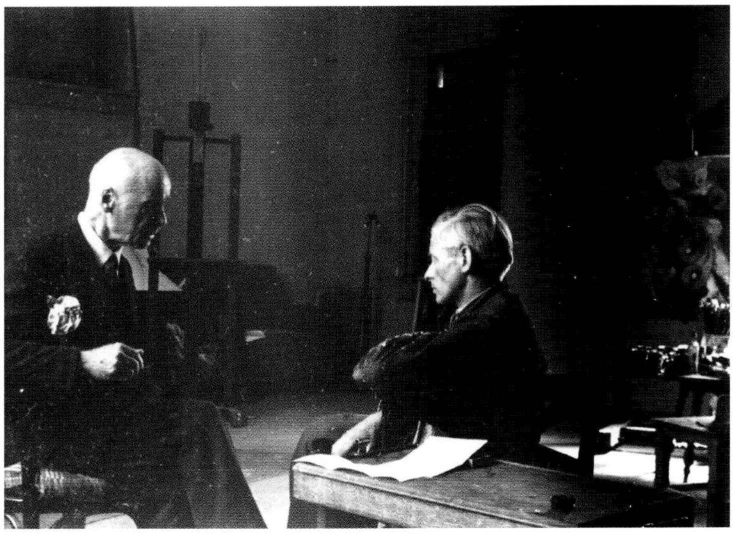

Ernst Gosebruch and E.W. Nay in his studio, Hofheim, 1947

E.W. Nay's studio house, Hofheim, c.1947–48,

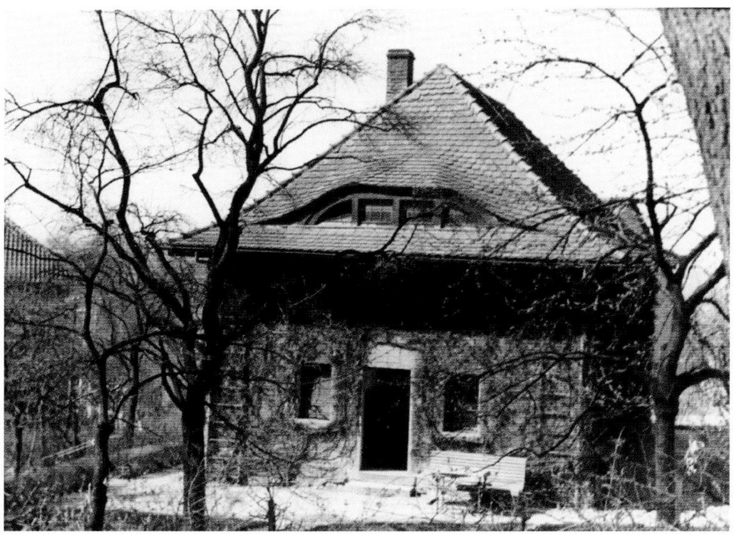

was a key priority, and became part of the 'democratic adjustment' required of Germans in the wake of war. Nay was able to present two important credentials for acceptance as just such an avant-garde artist after 1945: having been represented in *Entartete Kunst* (Degenerate Art), an important sign of martyrdom at the hands of the Nazis, and having served in the Wehrmacht. Themes of tragedy and deliverance underlie the subject matter of Nay's painting throughout the late 1940s. *Tochter der Hekate I* (Daughter of Hecate I, 1945; p.9) is one of a group of works whose titles appeal to the founding myths of European culture, derived from classical antiquity and occidental Christianity, and was taken by Gosebruch to title the works of the period from 1945–48: the *Hekate-Bilder* ('Hekate' paintings). Two monumental figures, differentiated by the colours yellow and blue, dominate the image. The paint is heavy and unmixed, and built up from slab-like marks (which may recall the slow task of reconstructing buildings from the huge mounds of bricks that littered German towns). Many of Nay's works from this period show two figures in conversation, and here the relation seems to be one of consolation. The story, however, is of little consequence. Any relationship to Greek myth is loose: as Friedrich Weltzien has noted, there was no daughter of Hecate in antiquity.[121] Nay's title evokes the various associations of Hecate herself, with crossroads, entrances, doorways and transitions between the worlds of the living and the dead. 'The name *Hekate* stands for [a] descent into a region where the roots of all living things meet and mingle', Siegfried Gohr has pungently observed.[122] As Nay-Scheibler has pointed out, the fact that Nay titled his paintings after completion demonstrates that the titles cannot be considered in any way programmatic.[123] He was rather seeking a general effect in which the pungency and weight of mythology could find expression in a heavy armature of strong colour, and above all, an image of the human body as burdened and riven.

Nay's impressionistic appeal to mythology was part of what made his work 'immanent', as Peter-Klaus Schuster has described it, to the Reconstruction culture (*Wiederaufbaukultur*), for which, as Schuster points out, he was 'in the right place at the right time'.[124] The 'Hekate' paintings must have appeared as a symbol of all that had survived the war.[125] Numerous references to antiq-

119 Doris Schmidt, 'Nay in Hofheim (1945–51)', in *E.W. Nay, 1902–1968, op. cit.*, pp.92–96. Schmidt's assertion that the Städel had retained its political integrity throughout the war has been questioned by recent accounts of Holzinger's activities during this period. He was also a frequent visitor, as Schmidt has recalled (p.96), to the exhibition of paintings from the Berlin Museums, held at that time in the central collecting point in the Wiesbaden Landesmuseum. Four central collection points were established by the American Occupation Forces (the others were at Offenburg, Marburg and Munich) to provide temporary storage for the thousands of Nazi-plundered artworks around Germany and Austria. The Wiesbaden collecting point, which operated until 1951, specialised in German-owned materials from the former Prussian state museums, the Städel Institute and the local museums of Wiesbaden. Work by Nay was included in one of the most important of the exhibitions held at the Munich collection point, *Kunstschaffen in Deutschland* (9–19 July 1949). Organised by the American cultural officer Stefan P. Munsing, the exhibition attempted to provide an overview of German art, with a significant majority of the works being made in 1948. Nay was represented with five watercolours made in Le Mans (individual titles not given in the catalogue), and two oil paintings from 1948: *Apollon* and *Metaphorisches Bild*.

120 Friedrich Weltzien makes this point in *E.W. Nay – Figur und Körperbild. Kunst und Kunsttheorie des vierziger Jahre*, Reimer, Berlin, 2003, p.11.

121 Weltzien, 2003, *op. cit.*, p.215.

122 Gohr, 'Foreword', 1990, *op. cit.*, p.14.

123 E. Nay-Scheibler, 'E.W. Nay aus der Nähe – ein Lebensbericht', in Gohr, *op. cit.*, p.51.

uity and Christian myth in his paintings suggest an unbroken tradition of European humanism. But they also reflect the direct sense of the tragic landscape of Germany, a fact upon which Nay frequently reflected in his letters and diaries of the time.[126] Biblical stories, such as that of Job, were popular themes in contemporary painting, and very literal moral messages and homilies drawn from these sources. Yet whereas Dix used the figure of Job to evoke the theme of undeserved punishment, Nay's references to mythology were never didactic. They were rather part of an appeal to a reconciliatory, universalising rhetoric, an awareness of European culture as a source of reconstruction. Nay spoke often of the European condition, and Werner Haftmann summed up his position:

> Nay knows very well the part played by the primordial, the unconscious, even the barbaric creative forces in man and their liberating function for an understanding of one's own relationship to the surrounding world; but for himself he considers it a binding obligation that the strength of European artist [sic] should be shown in uniting the liberated barbaric forces with the spiritual forces of the conscious mind.[127]

Nay deployed these forces with enthusiasm. There was little let-up in his production, and by mid-December 1945 he wrote to Anne Hentzen that he had completed 16 large paintings, 53 gouaches and numerous drawings, many of which he was able to sell, in particular due to his participation in the exhibition of the Darmstadt Secession.[128] His first solo exhibition after the war was held at the Galerie Gerd Rosen, Berlin, in May 1946. Elly, who had remained in Berlin, was instrumental in organising this show, which Nay was not himself to see.[129] Paintings from Lofoten in 1938 were shown alongside works from the final years of the war, including a gouache study for *Aënors Hochzeit*.[130] The exhibition of his work at the Galerie Günther Franke in Munich five months later included works made since 1943, the earliest being *Legende (Eduards Tod IV)* (Legend (Eduard's Death IV)) made in that year, and was more of a success in providing an overview of the new monumental figurative style that he had been developing. It was undoubtedly one of the most striking showings of any artist in Germany at this moment; few others had been offered the opportunity to develop their work in such extreme circumstances. The exhibition at Franke's was a '*glänzendes Debut*' (glittering debut), as he wrote to Elly that Christmas, and marked the first real public emergence of his work since the war.[131]

The text reprinted in the leaflet accompanying the exhibition was developed from an essay that Nay had written earlier that year, 'Über die Stimulantien und anderes' (On Stimulation and Other Subjects), which summarises both his own approach to painting, and his views on painting in general during this time.[132] He put forward the notion of a expressive, essentially figurative approach, which he set against a type of abstract painting that 'shut out human drama and remained isolated from the world'.[133] The position on abstraction adumbrated here is of particular interest. His distaste at being perceived as an abstract painter can be traced back as far as 1938, when he wrote to Franke:

> I have been thinking about what you said to me, that people regard the new direction in art, which I am part of, as abstraction. But what else would you expect of people who don't have the nerve of a Lofoten fisherman.

Certainly, the works of the 'Hekate' period are more readily comprehensible in terms of a heritage of Expressionism. That Nay is one of the few artists who may be taken as a bridge between the Weimar Republic and the postwar Federal Republic is due largely to the expressive, figurative nature of his work during the 1940s. Expressionism constituted the most vexed focus for the postwar rehabilitation of modernist idioms. Modern German art was synonymous with Expressionism, but it became clear after 1945 that it could not simply be relaunched; not only was there a 'missing generation' of artists, but there were also the problematic overlaps between elements of Expressionist and Nazi rhetoric.

Two of the most substantial accounts of Nay's work to have appeared in recent years take opposing positions on the question of the role of abstraction and Expressionism in his work. The American academic Yule Heibel has provided an account of Nay's unique position as an abstract painter in West Germany who retained an expressive dimension in his work.[134] Heibel contrasts Nay's work with the abstraction being practised by those artists such as Fritz Winter associated with the ZEN 49 group of abstract painters, established in 1949, and the circle of artists around the collector Ottomar Domnick, including Willi Baumeister. She argues that Nay's work 'retains a physical aspect that the metaphysical subjectivism of absolute abstraction discards', and that 'it is vitalism – the expressive, the bodily, somatic, corporeal – that Nay seeks to encounter'.[135] This is certainly unmistakeable in works such as *Sibylle* or *Tochter der Hekate I*, which seem overloaded with bodily vitality, particularly when compared to the floating abstraction of the type produced within the ZEN 49 group, such as the paintings of Fritz Winter. For Heibel, Nay's work holds the key to a critical understanding of subjectivity in the postwar era, avoiding the stasis of abstraction by remaining in a developmental, expressionistic and experimental realm that was linked to historical subjectivity. It is only in comparison with the aloof imagery of the

124 Peter-Klaus Schuster, 'Kunst im Kontext. E.W. Nays ständige Wandlung', in *Bilder und Dokumente*, *op. cit.*, pp.9–10.
125 *Ibid.*, p.9.
126 E.W. Nay describes a 'direct link to the tragedies of antiquity' in a letter to Erich Meyer. Nay to Meyer, 25 February 1946, in E.W. Nay, *Lesebuch*, *op. cit.*, p.29.
127 Werner Haftman, 'Preface. Extracts from an essay on Ernst Wilhelm Nay', in *Nay*, exhibition catalogue, New London Gallery, London, undated (1960), np.
128 Nay to Anne Hentzen, 18 December 1945, in *E.W. Nay, 1902–1968*, *op. cit.*, p.89.
129 Nay to Elly Nay, 12 May 1946, in *ibid.*, p.94.
130 See Markus Krause, *Galerie Gerd Rosen. Die Avantgarde in Berlin 1945–1950*, Ars Nicolai, Berlin, 1995, pp.77–79. Nay wrote later that year to Erich Meyer that the exhibition had not been a success due to the fragmented presentation of his work. Nay to Meyer, 10 June 1946, in *E.W. Nay, 1902–1968*, *op. cit.*, 1980, p.98.
131 Nay to Elly Nay, 17 December 1946, DKA, Nuremberg.
132 The text is dated 5 June 1946 in *E.W. Nay, 1902–1968*, *op. cit.*
133 E.W. Nay, 'Über die Stimulantien und anderes', speech on the opening of an exhibition at the Galerie Günther Franke, Munich, 5 June 1946, *ibid.*, p.98.
134 Yule F. Heibel, *Reconstructing the Subject. Modernist Painting in Western Germany 1945–1950*, Princeton University Press, Princeton, 1995.
135 *Ibid.*, pp.5, 36.

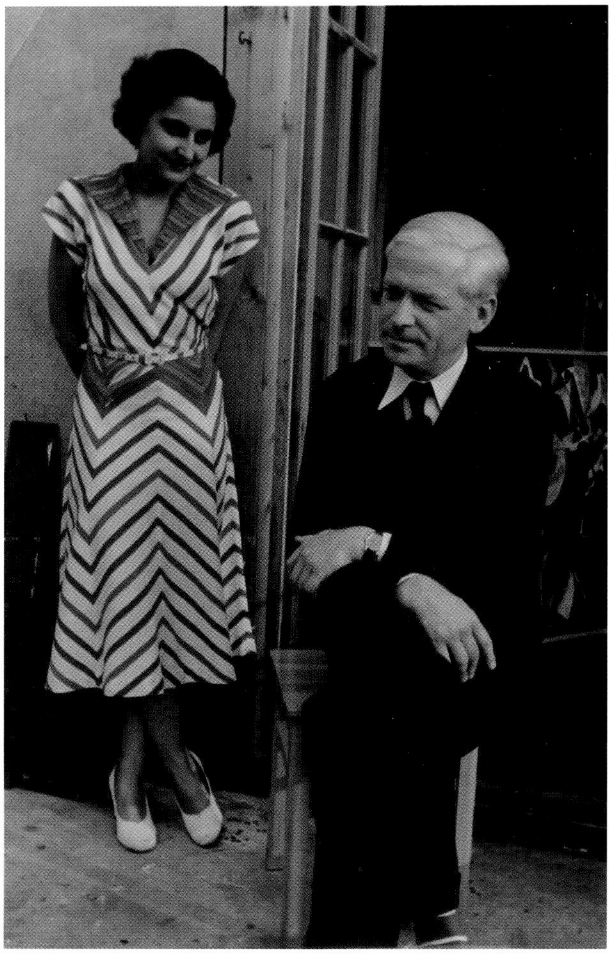

E.W. Nay and his wife, Elisabeth, 1952

ZEN 49 painters that this may become apparent. The crisis of subjectivity that Heibel identifies is essentially one of the validity and value of personal expression in the wake of the war and a crime of genocide that had effectively desecrated the cultural national traditions within which this expression made any sense.[136]

Heibel's arguments concerning Nay's engaged figuration apply only, however, to those works made up to 1949, at which point his imagery began to reflect broader trends of 'absolute' abstraction. Friedrich Weltzien has provided an alternative reading of Nay's work that, while it also focuses on the idea of an embodied abstraction, creates a positive connection with Martin Heidegger, who for Heibel had represented the 'metaphysical approach and ontology' that set the terms for a 'postwar "expressionless" subject'.[137] While Heibel does concede the importance of Heidegger for postwar artists, she prefers to replace the difficult ex-Nazi philosopher with the more intellectually acceptable figure of Theodor Adorno.[138] Weltzien instead situates Nay in a network of *Körperdiskurses*, or discourses surrounding the body, during the 1940s that drew philosophical conclusions from representations of the human form, referring in particular to the writings of Maurice Merleau-Ponty and Heidegger.[139] Weltzien presents this argument as a disinterment of Nay's work of the 1940s from the type of criticism prevalent in the 1950s, referring in particular to the musical, disembodied metaphors used by Haftmann in his monograph on Nay, published in 1960.[140] Haftmann's monograph, Weltzien argues, emphasises the formal, particularly chromatic element of Nay's work and puts forward a teleological, developmental model of his oeuvre, often echoing the artist's own statements about his work, in a way that has shaped views of his art ever since. In addition, Haftmann brings out metaphors that tend to escape direct confrontation with the bodily aspect of the painting, for example the association of Southern with classical serenity and Northern with emotional inwardness, which can be traced back to Heinrich Wölfflin's *Kunstgeschichtliche Grundbegriffe* (Principles of Art History), of 1915.[141]

Interestingly, Weltzien reverses the terms of Heibel's argument, suggesting that the connection between Nay's painting and the discourses surrounding the body in the 1940s, themselves connected with notions of authenticity, humanism, tragedy and so on, was the reason for the strong public reaction against his work in the early 1960s, particularly at Documenta III in 1964, described

136 See, for example, *ibid.*, pp.16–17.
137 *Ibid.*, p.7.
138 *Ibid.*, pp.42–43.
139 Weltzien, 2003, *op. cit.*, for example p.13.
140 *Ibid.*, p.16.
141 *Ibid.*, p.27. Weltzien directs attention to Gert Mattenklott, 'Die Bedeutung der kulturellen Räume und Himmelsrichtungen für die Künste der Zeit nach dem Zweiten Weltkrieg', in Angela Lammert (ed), *Raum und Körper in den Künsten der Nachkriegszeit*, Verlag der Kunst, Amsterdam and Dresden, 1998.
142 Weltzien, *ibid.*, p.17. Weltzien's zeal in rereading Nay's pre-1951 oeuvre in terms of figuration is however over-extended, and depends on a tedious formal description of individual works with no reference to external conditions. The same criticism that Adorno made of Heidegger – that he practised philosophy as if sociology and psychology, 'those two great opponents of the philosophical mind', had never come along (see Rudiger Safranski, *Martin Heidegger: Between good and evil*, trans Ewald Osers, Harvard University Press, Cambridge MA and London, 1998, p.412) – may be transposed onto the type of formal art appreciation that Weltzien is attacking, but which he is ultimately obliged to repeat due to his own lack of reference to the social or psychic conditions of Nay's painting. In the postwar period Marcuse is a key reference for this approach to cultural studies.

below. Where Heibel marshals Adorno to explain the 'rivenness' of Nay's abstraction, Weltzien reminds us that Adorno's *Jargon of Authenticity* was published in 1964, and captured a spirit that summed up a rejection of the Heideggerian rhetoric of anti-rationalism and the body.[142]

The picture that Weltzien provides is more accurate, in particular when it comes to the relative influences of Heidegger and Adorno at this moment. Like many artists, Nay was enthusiastic about Heidegger's writings on art, particularly his essay *Der Ursprung des Kunstwerkes* (The Origin of the Work of Art), published in his first postwar collection, *Holzwege* (Off the Beaten Track), in 1950. Nay recommended it to those who came to speak to him about his painting.[143] Heidegger's description of the artist as the origin of the work of art, and the work of art as the origin of the artist, was taken up by a generation of painters who were faced with the task of recreating not only their own artistic practice, but the very notion of art itself, out of what threatened to be irretrievable ruin. Nay invoked the 'inductive method' to trace the origins of his own painting to a formal, conceptual basis, rather than to a need to represent the visible world (*das Bild als Kunstwerk*).[144] Heidegger's influence throughout the 1940s and 50s was in part due to his continuation of earlier Expressionist aesthetic theories, by which the purpose of art was to render the invisible visible. The appeal of existentialism, and in particular Heidegger's notion of 'homelessness', was strong in the postwar years, for obvious reasons. Heidegger's prewar *Lebensphilosophie*, a life philosophy that fed directly into postwar existentialism and was directed against a soulless materialism, had in the postwar world been transformed into a manifesto for survival.

Nay's professional admiration for the philosopher, by no means unique at this moment, is clear from his letters and diaries. Heidegger's postwar writings, and in particular his *Letter on Humanism* of 1947, often seen as one of his greatest essays, contains a core of ideas that illuminate Nay's painting, and that were directly to inspire him. Nay referred to the essay in a public address that he gave at the opening of an exhibition two years later, in which he alighted on Heidegger's description of the dislocation of European culture at that moment:

> The danger into which Europe as it has hitherto existed is ever more clearly forced consists presumably in the fact above all that its thinking – once its glory – is falling behind in the essential course of a dawning world destiny which nevertheless in the basic traits of its essential provenance remains European by definition.[145]

Both philosopher and painter had roots in an Expressionist milieu from which they had also successfully escaped, by abandoning mysticism for an attempt at systematic expression. Painting as the revelation of a *Kosmisch-Unbewußtes* (cosmic unconscious), as Nay was to describe it, mirrors the Heideggerian definition of art as nature revealing itself: as a way of 'rendering beings manifest'.[146] Heidegger's appeal to language as the 'house of Being', and the importance of thinking as an act that takes place in the midst of being, rather than standing on the outside of it – the sense of remaining in the swim of life – captures the 'immersed' nature of Nay's approach to painting. One may think of Elatic's comment in Plato's *Sophist*, on the matter of 'human art': 'surely we shall allow that as architecture it produces a *real* house, and also as painting, a second house, a sort of waking dream?'[147]

Weltzien's argument for the importance of the body in Nay's work during the 1940s is borne out by critical responses at the time.[148] Will Grohmann's 1948 review of Nay's exhibition at the Galerie Franz, Berlin, is a particularly strong description of a display of works from the 1930s and 1940s that makes no claims for abstraction or, for that matter, for Surrealism.[149] The painting *Gespräch* (Conversation, 1946; p.81), was exhibited at the Galerie Franz, and is typical of works from this moment in showing recognisable figures constructed with largely abstract motifs, in a style that shows the influence of Picasso. Also displayed at this exhibition was *Tochter der Hekate II* (Daughter of Hecate II, 1946; p.79), demonstrating Nay's use of abstract signs to construct human faces and bodies. The influence of Picasso, although diffused through the almost universal reception of his painting as coterminous with modernist figuration, is unmistakable from the early 1940s, and it was only with the move to an exclusively non-figurative idiom at the end of the decade that Nay appears to have overcome the temptations of Picassoism.

A more lyrical feeling enters his painting in 1947. Two works exhibited the next year at the Galerie Dr Werner Rusche in Cologne show Nay's confidence in handling large areas of bright colour. *Kythera* (Kythira, 1947; p.82), recalls the pastoral paintings that Nay made during the war, but the sense here is of a more detailed, close-up view of figures and natural motifs distributed evenly over the canvas. A more generous, complete feeling of form, and a far warmer palette can be seen in *Femme Rose* (Pink Woman, 1947; p.85), a *grand nu* bathed in Mediterranean light. The smoother transitions and harmonious colour of *Femme Rose* look forward to Nay's paintings of the next few years.

This was also the year in which Nay's work began to be shown commercially – he had six solo exhibitions during 1947, in the previous decade he had only six commercial exhibitions in total,

143 For example to Ludwig Baron Döry. See *idem.*, 'Begegnung mit Nay', in Klaus Gallwitz (ed), *Ernst Wilhelm Nay: die Hofheimer Jahre 1945–51*, exhibition catalogue, Städtische Galerie im Städel, Frankfurt am Main and Museum der bildenden Künste, Leipzig, 1994, pp.141–57.
144 E.W. Nay, diary entry, 27 December 1949, in *Lesebuch*, 2002, *op. cit.*, p.52.
145 Martin Heidegger, 'Letter on Humanism', reprinted in D.F. Krell (ed), *Martin Heidegger. Basic Writings*, Routledge, London and New York, 2007, p.244.
146 *Ibid.*
147 R. Klibansky and E. Anscombe (eds), *Plato, The Sophist and The Statesman*, trans A.E. Taylor, Thomas Nelson & Sons, London, 1961, p.182.
148 Weltzien, 2003, *op. cit.*, pp.48–49.
149 This is much more symbolic in its intention – the meaning is more complex than in his earlier works – it is filled with rhythmic, ornamental elements and, albeit to a lesser extent, with echoes of motifs so that it can only marginally be described in terms of abstraction or of Surrealism.
150 The exhibitions were at Galerie Alex Vömel, Düsseldorf (January); Galerie Dr Werner Rusche, Cologne (March); Studio Wuppertal-Elberfeld, Wuppertal (April); Galerie Franz, Berlin (June), and Kunstverein, Hamburg (June), which then travelled to the Overbeck-Gesellschaft, Lübeck (August).

including the covert exhibition at Günther Franke's Hinterzimmer gallery in 1943.[150] A number of important meetings with collectors and supporters took place at this moment. Carola and Günther Peill acquired their first work by Nay, the gouache *Liegende Frau* (Recumbent Woman) in 1947, the year in which it was painted, and first visited Nay in Hofheim two years later. The Peill collection evolved into one of the largest of Nay's paintings, prints, watercolours, gouaches and drawings.[151] It was at this time also that he met the politician and SPD member Adolf Arndt, and his wife Ruth, with whom he kept up a correspondence for the rest of his life.

Although the painting *Der Hirte I* (The Shepherd I, 1948; p.87), has been described by Peter-Klaus Schuster, following Werner Haftmann's description in his 1960 monograph, as a turning point in Nay's postwar work, any of a group of paintings made this year may be taken as a sign of transition to a flatter, less 'somatic' style.[152] *Der Hirte I* shows the development of a clearer set of formal motifs, loosely coalesced into a human shape. Crowds of coloured forms, predominantly the mandorla and an eye-like shape, structure the painting rhythmically, retaining an affinity with the human body through a sense of coherent *gestalt*. The painting can be perceived in one glance as a combination of colour and punctuation, like a living form or functioning machine. The 'crowding' of the canvas is another characteristic of Nay's work of this time, and gives a sense of his intense daily work regime, described in a letter to Erich Meyer written from Hofheim in May 1948:

> I am in the best physical shape, with only nervous stress from time to time, for I am working at the moment in an incredibly disciplined manner. And when it is the case, as recently, of nine paintings in 14 days, then it is a matter of sustaining concentration throughout a ten-hour working day for two weeks without a break, as I paint on Sundays also.[153]

Such intense activity may be a compensation for the relative caesura during the war, and reflects in the densely populated compositions of this time. *Der Hirte I* was included in Nay's exhibition at Günther Franke's gallery in October of that year.

Other works at this time, such as *Zwei Figuren* (Two Figures, 1948; p.89) give a stronger sense of Nay's 'fall' into abstraction around 1949: flat planes, decorative motifs dispersed on the canvas to suggest a field of activity rather than a single unified gestalt. This was also a moment of a significant change in Nay's personal life; during this year, he divorced Elly and married Elisabeth Kerschbaumer, whom he had met as an assistant at Günther Franke's gallery. The sense of a new beginning in Nay's work at this time is unmistakable. Another separation and rebirth took place in 1949: in May of that year, the Federal Republic was founded, and in response the German Democratic Republic was established in October, a *de facto* ending of the Allied occupation and the beginning of the division of the country into East and West.

151 See D. Eimert, et al, *Carola Peill zu Ehren*, exhibition catalogue, Leopold-Hoesch Museum, Düren, 1993.
152 See Haftmann, *op. cit.*
153 Nay to Meyer, 25 May 1948, *ibid.*, p.103.

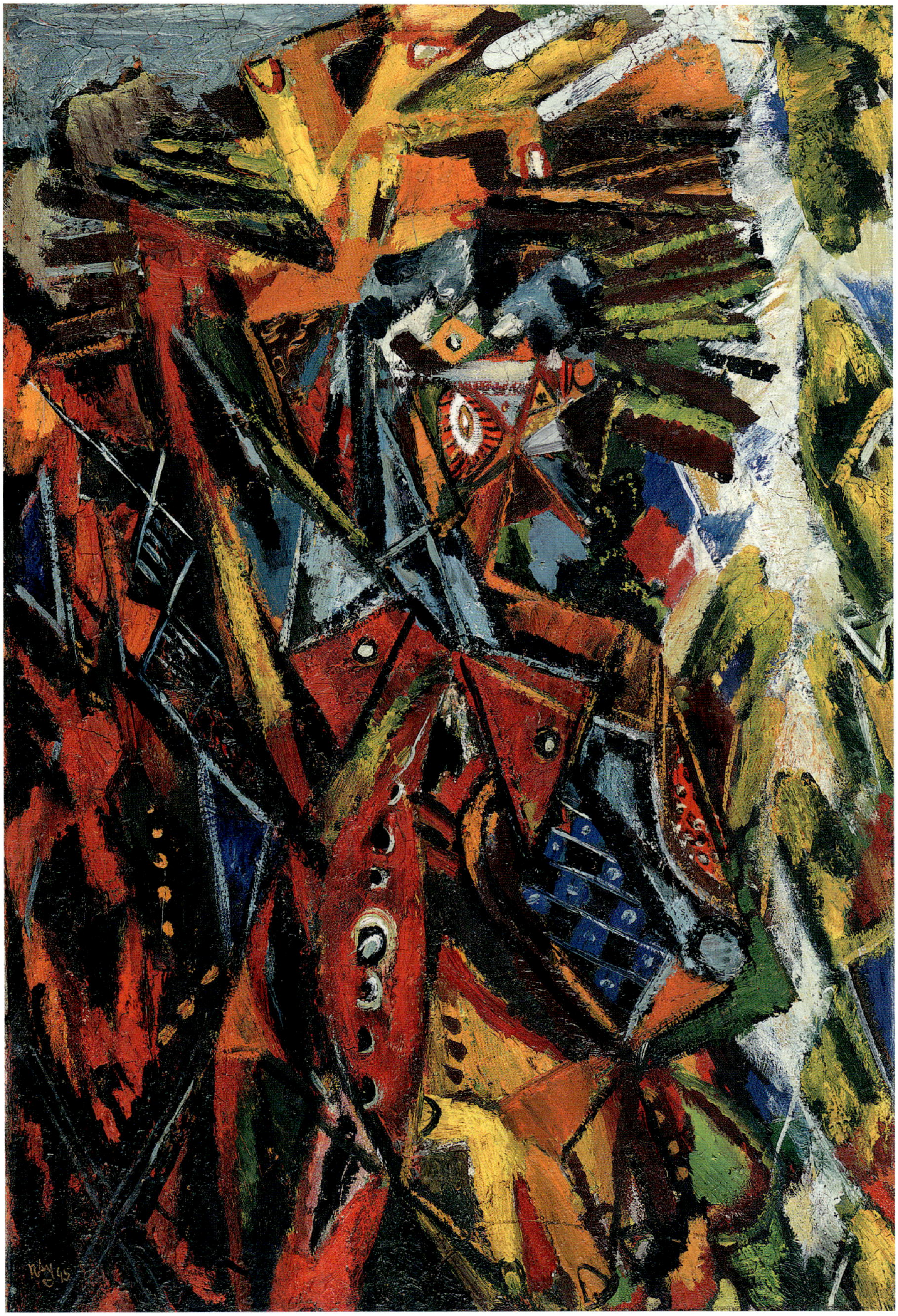

Sibylle, 1945
Oil on canvas
104 × 71 cm · 41 × 28 in

Tochter der Hekate II, 1946
Oil on wood
47 × 38 cm · 18½ × 15 in

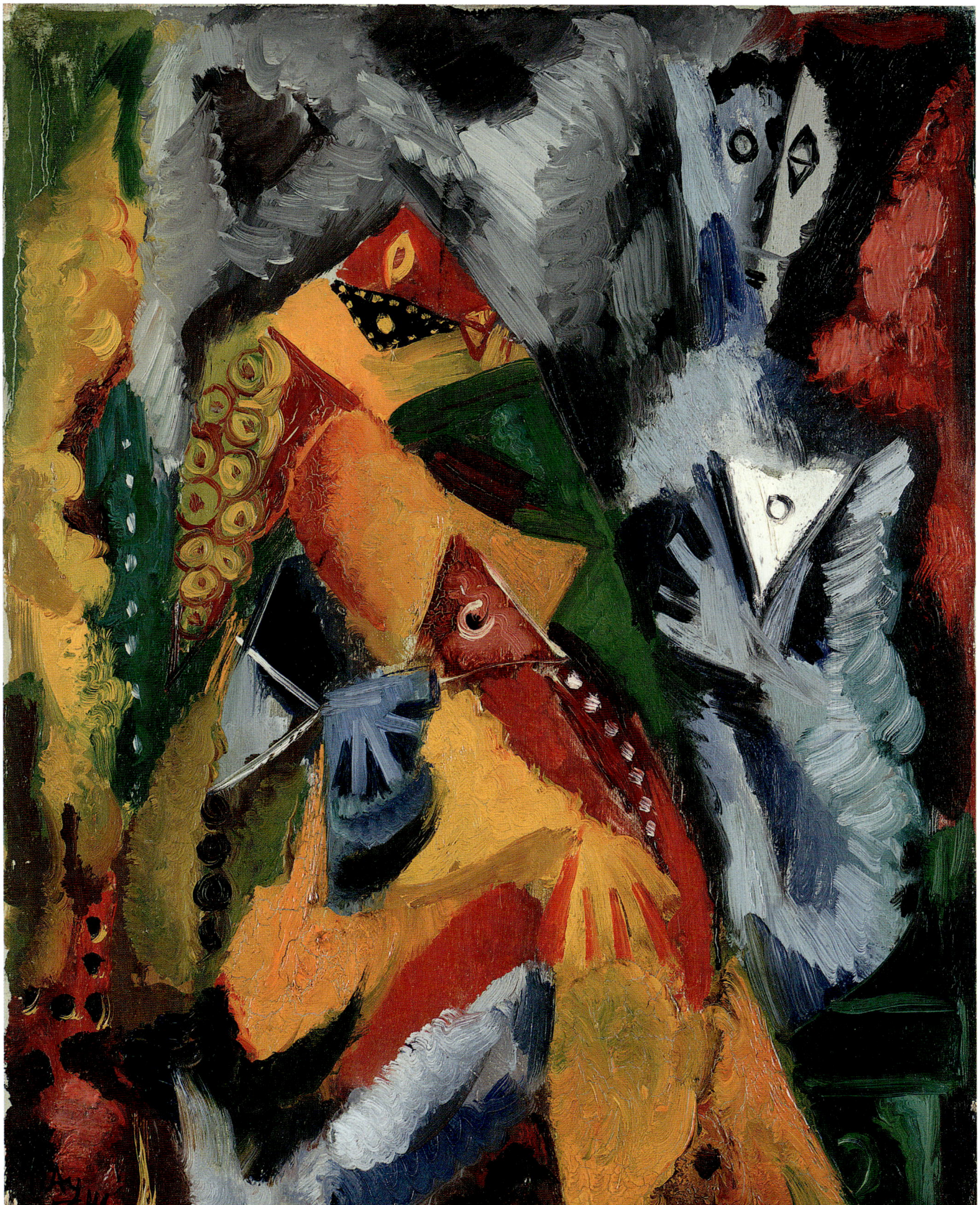

Gespräch, 1946
Oil on canvas
61.5 × 81 cm · 24¼ × 31⅞ in

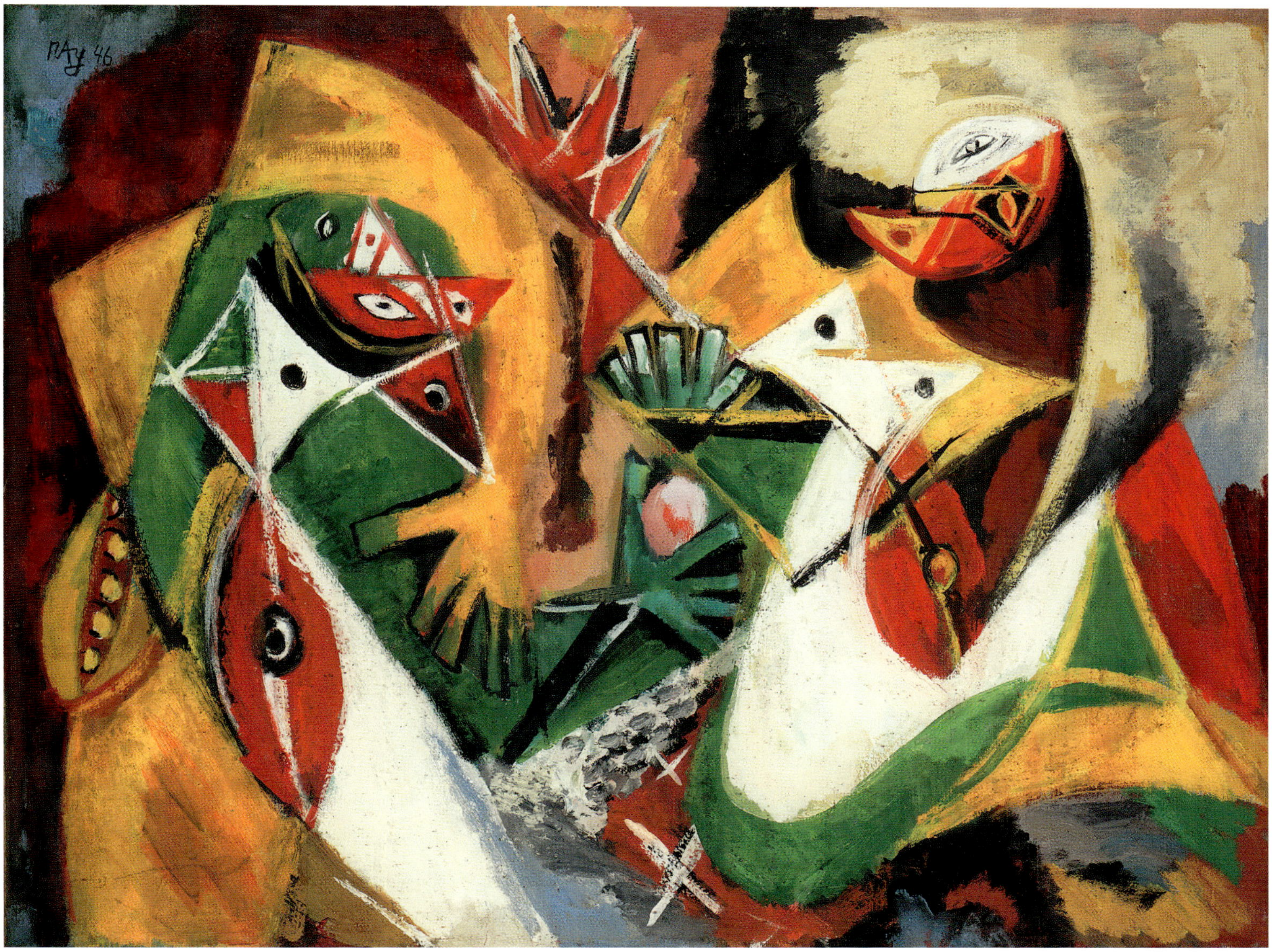
PAY 46

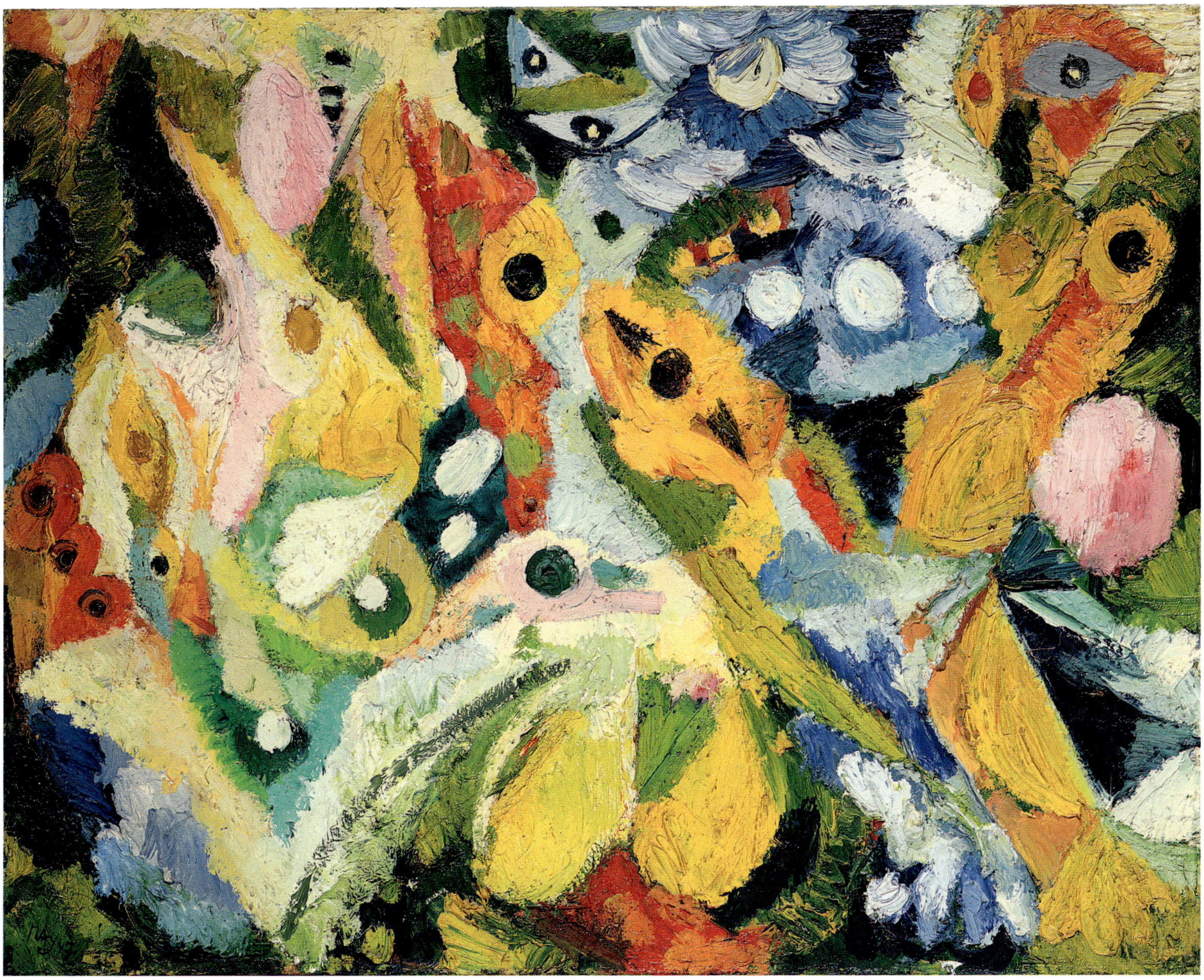

Kythera, 1947
Oil on canvas
80.5 × 100.5 cm · 31¾ × 39⅝ in

Femme Rose, 1947
Oil on canvas
55 × 70.5 cm · 21⅝ × 27¾ in

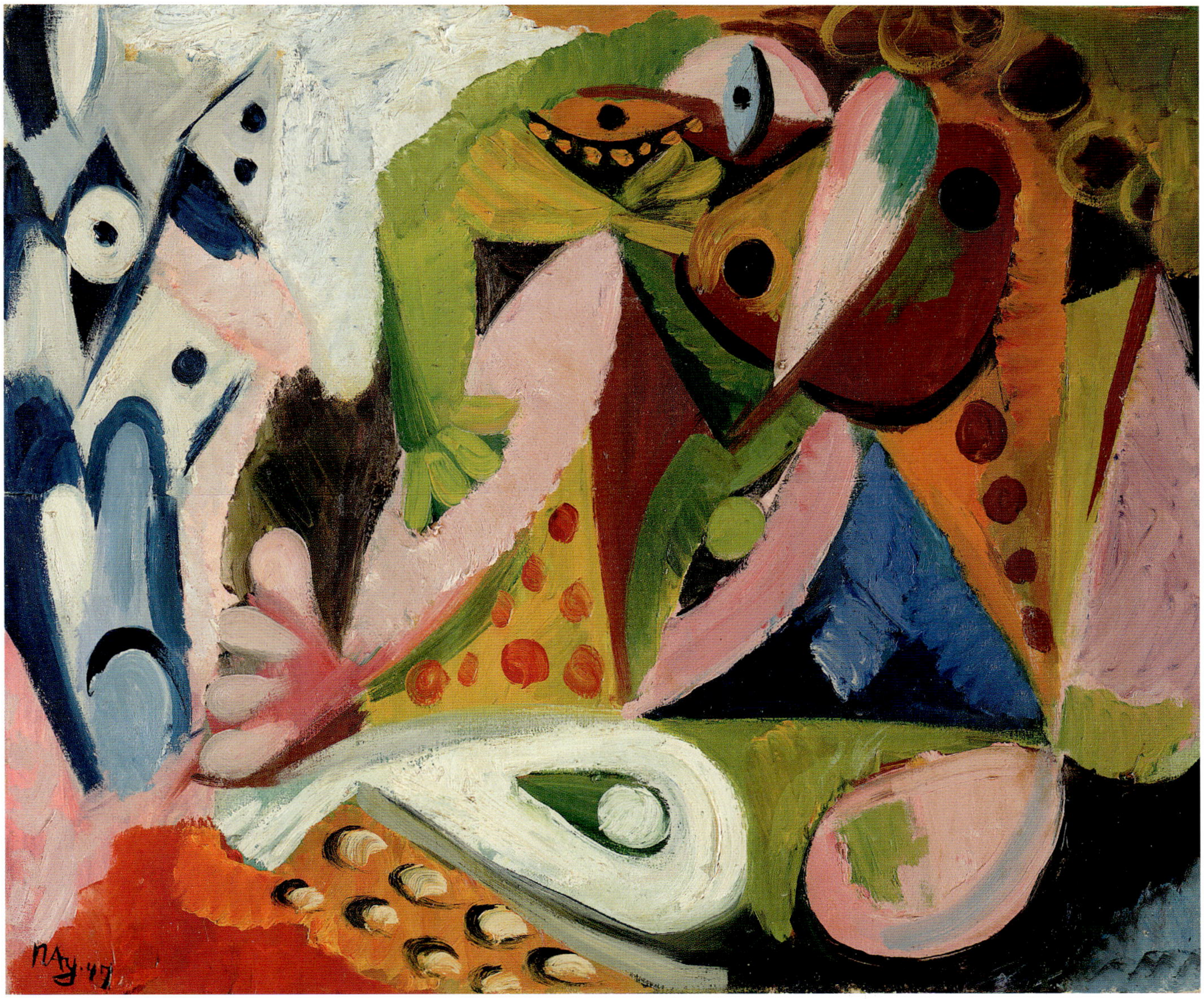

Der Hirte I, 1948
Oil on canvas
116 × 96 cm · 45⅝ × 37¾ in

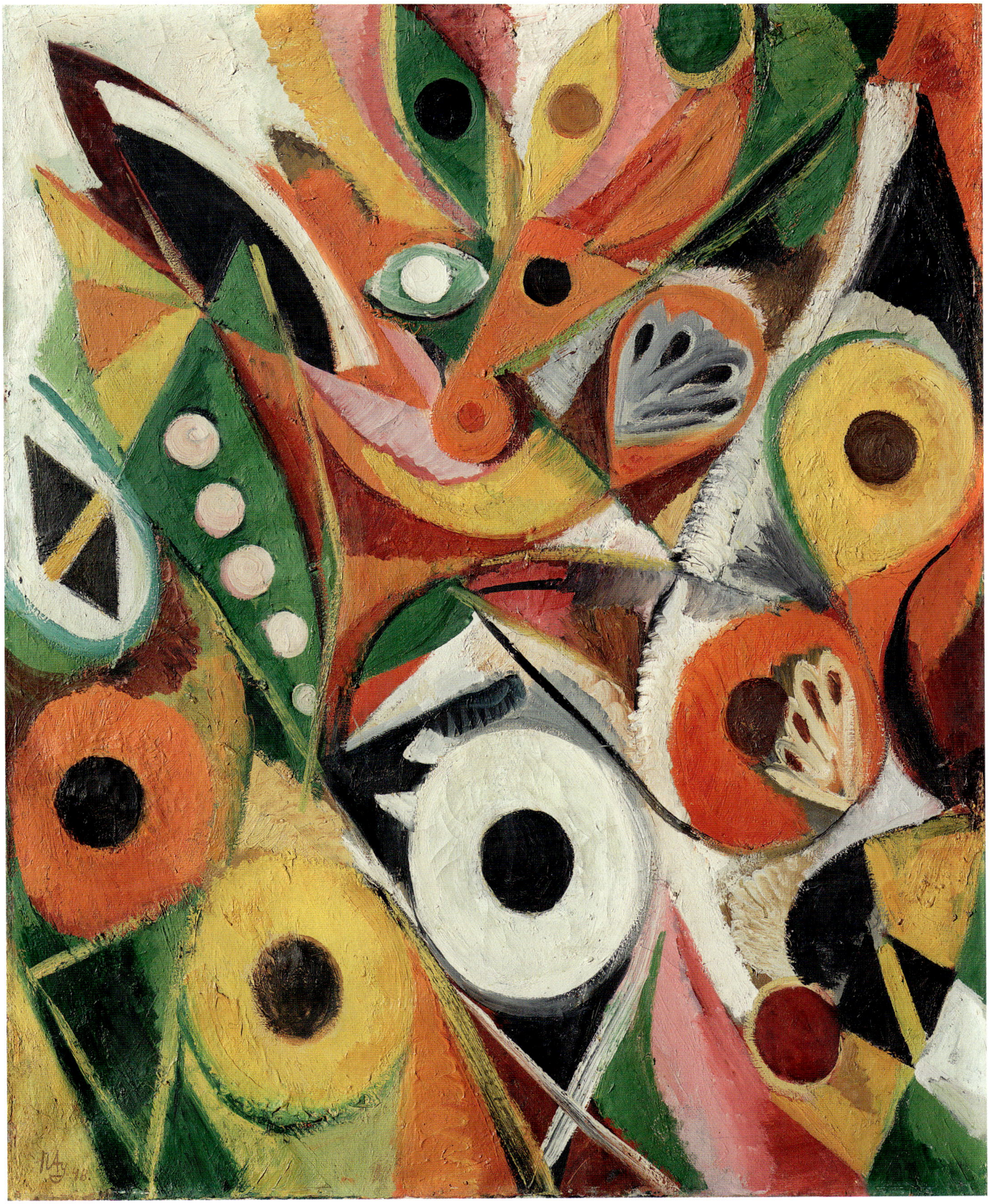

Zwei Figuren, 1948
Oil on canvas
65 × 80 cm · 25⅝ × 31½ in

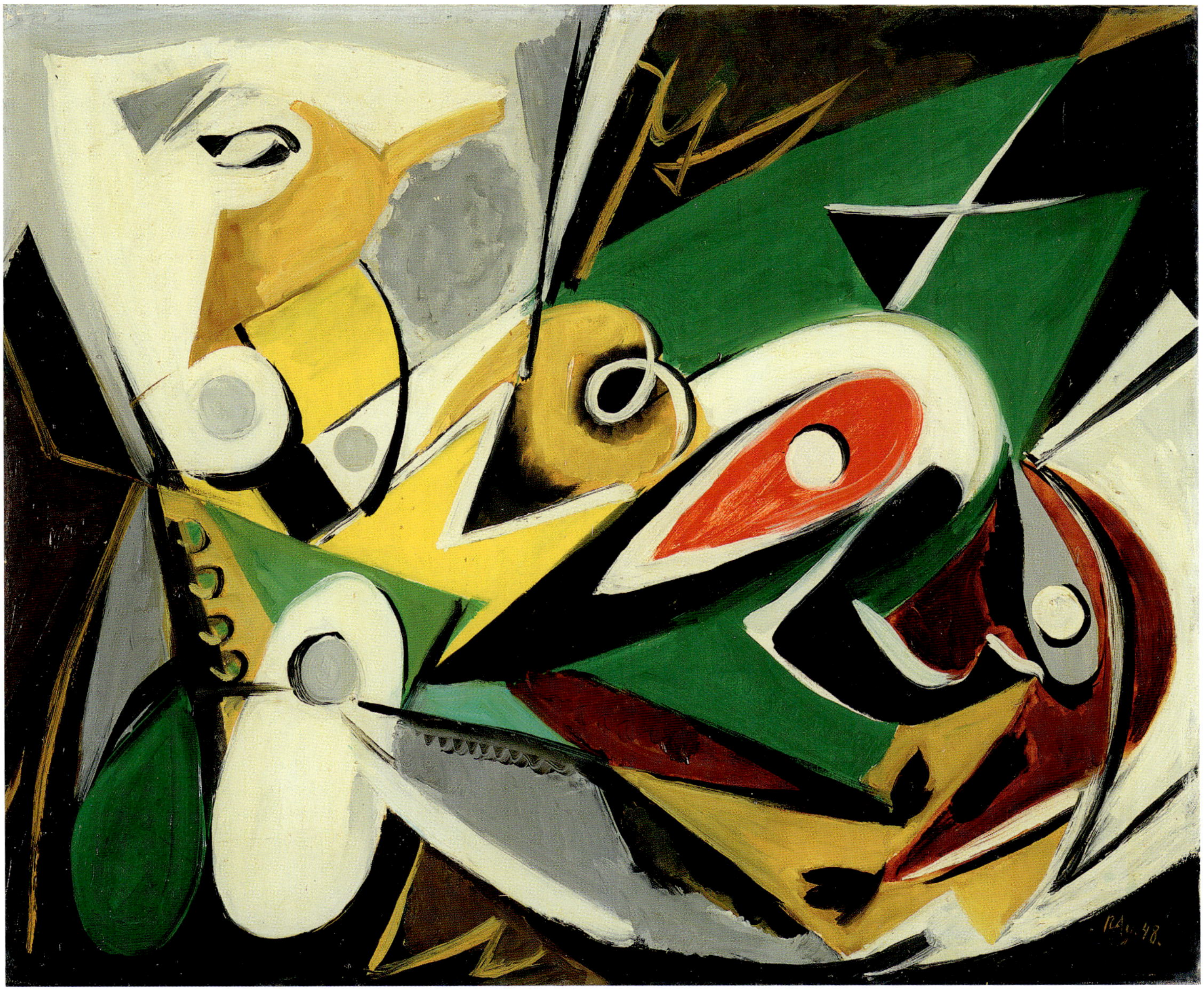

1948–54:

Music, Ornament, Abstraction and the Return of the Body

If the key terms for Nay's work from around 1943 to 1948 were the human body and an 'expressive' figuration, a different set of metaphors were to become important at the end of that decade. Nay's interest in music theory formed the background against which a group of paintings known as the 'Fugal' and 'Rhythmic' paintings were developed from around 1949 to 1954. He was not unusual in this respect; one has only to think back to the close connections between music and art at the Bauhaus, or further back to the musicality of symbolist painting and late nineteenth-century aestheticism. Nay's points of reference were the contemporary post-tonal music of composers such as Pierre Boulez, Luigi Nono (who visited his studio) and Karlheinz Stockhausen. Two books in particular made an impact: Paul Hindemith's *Unterweisung im Tonsatz*, the first two parts of which were published in 1937 and 1939, translated two years later as *The Craft of Musical Composition*, and Igor Stravinsky's *Poetics of Music in the Form of Six Lessons* of 1942, first given as a set of lectures at Harvard during 1939 to 1940, which appeared in German translation as *Musikalische Poetik* in 1949. The music of Stravinsky was of undoubted importance for Nay. Towards the end of his life, he described the experience of *The Firebird* in Berlin, danced by a Russian company, as having a strong influence upon his 'dithyrambic' sense of colour.

In his *Poetics of Music* Stravinsky states the importance of a dogmatic and polemical approach to composition, and stresses that the revolutionary characteristic of his work is not subversive but constructive, guided by the 'stern auspices of order and discipline'.[154] Stravinsky's cultural pessimism, his lament for the modern decline in values, was directed not only towards Soviet music, an example of the 'elementary utilitarianism' that had drawn music away from its foundations, but to 'cosmopolitanism' in general, a 'pathological blemish' detracting from the 'universalism' to which all good art should aspire.[155] His attack on the '*nouveau riche* smugness' of the '*Gesammt Kunstwerk*' [sic] is aimed specifically at Wagner, but also shows what happens when man loses his 'feeling and taste for ontology'.[156] This ontology is best expressed by a description of two types of 'musical experience of time': 'psychological time', which is unstable, allied to emotional impulses or contrasts, and is not self-contained, and 'ontological time', which unfolds according to a principle of similarity and unity. Stravinsky describes the fugal form in similar terms, as a 'pure form in which the music means nothing outside itself'.[157]

It is not difficult to see the inspiration that Nay drew from Stravinsky's account of the conservative basis of experimental, 'difficult' art. The self-contained quality of a fugue, as a pure form of 'ontological time', can be directly compared to the change in Nay's style around 1949, which saw a shift to a more confident, classical deployment of forms and colour. On a more prosaic level, a series of motifs emerged that refer to musical notation and the forms of musical instruments. Crotchets and clef signatures, tuning pegs and the graceful arcs of stringed instruments can be detected in *David und Bathsheba* (David and Bathsheba, 1949; p.92), suggest-

154 Igor Stravinsky, *Poetics of Music in the Form of Six Lessons*, Harvard University Press, Cambridge MA, 1970, p.23.

155 *Ibid.*, p.61.

156 *Ibid.*, p.77

157 *Ibid.*, p.99

ing an operatic meeting of the biblical subject matter and musical metaphor. As with most opera, the actual subject matter is of secondary importance; it would clearly be inappropriate to try and detect any direct reference to the Old Testament book of Samuel. (The story of King David's relationship with Uriah's wife, Bathsheba, was somehow in the air: it was the subject of a Hollywood epic released in 1951.)

A further painting made the same year, *Weiße Sphinx* (White Sphinx, 1949; p.93) recalls the prewar 'Lofoten' landscapes, and even motifs such as the butterfly form in the bottom right, which look back to his Surrealist paintings of the early 1930s; but the division of the canvas surface, and the sense of a complex interlocking structure, show a move to the interior of painting, a more fundamental, 'ontological' approach. The title is taken from the form at the top right resembling the head of a sphinx; Nay was not, however, painting to a subject, but deducing a subject from the painting he had already produced. In a speech given at the opening of his exhibition at the Frankfurt Kunstkabinett of Hanna Bekker vom Rath on 8 June 1949, where *Weiße Sphinx* was shown, Nay described the principles of speculation and 'adventure' determining his approach to painting at that moment.[158] But he also delineates the history of 'autonomous' painting, from Cézanne to Klee, and describes the culmination of this tradition in a new expression and awareness of the 'cosmic-unconsciousness' (*Kosmisch-Unbewußte*) of the contemporary world.[159] This had led, according to Nay, to a type of picture that could be defined threefold, as 'a-perspectival, autonomous, and four-dimensional'. The final characteristic Nay explained by suggesting that the picture was not simply a surface, but a wall within an experiential architectural setting. The 'ontological' form of the fugue described by Stravinsky was read back into painting in a way that answered Heidegger's call for art, as a form of technology, to show the way back to essential being – a point raised by Nay at the beginning of this important speech.

Above all, and more prosaically, music provided a recognisable and accepted language of abstract form with which to describe new styles of painting.[160] The ascendance of abstract painting as a style emblematic of Western freedom and political democracy took place against the background of the division of Germany, and the creation of the Federal Republic of Germany in May 1949; Konrad Adenauer was sworn in as the first federal chancellor in August. Susanne Leeb has concisely described the 'double delimitation' by which abstraction was elevated to a political style after 1945: the need to distinguish the Federal Republic both from the Third Reich and the German Democratic Republic.[161] The possibility of a 'world culture', as Werner Haftmann put it, embodied by abstraction, offered an escape from the trappings of nationalism, and appeared as a continuation of many of the utopian yearnings of early twentieth-century art.

'Perhaps the most astonishing aspect of the postwar artistic situation in Germany', wrote Bernard Myers in the *College Art Journal* in the spring of 1951, 'is its complete lack of direct response to the conditions of the time'.[162] It is nevertheless hardly surprising, he continues, considering the ruined conditions of the country and the fragile nature of the peace, that artists were 'escaping into various types of abstraction or into gentle lyricism'. Amongst a round-up of those artists still working in Germany, Nay is given special mention:

> Ernst Wilhelm Nay (b.1902), who has worked with Hofer and Munch, is one of the best known of the younger Germans and may be classified as an abstract surrealist in the Masson sense. Very strong in emotive quality and unquestionably more than merely competent, Nay gives us the feeling of a certain derivative quality stemming from the other side of the Rhine, as is often indeed the case with the younger German artists.

Myers's description of Nay betrays little knowledge of the figurative painting he made during the war and shortly afterwards, and reduces his work to the influence of contemporary French art. Nevertheless it was through a sort of escapism, or compensation, that abstraction developed both in Nay's work and German art in general during this period.

As we have seen from the accounts provided by Weltzien and Heibel, this disconnection may also be felt in the rhetoric around abstraction. Such language was generally a means of talking indirectly about politics, rather than the making and meaning of the paintings themselves. As Weltzien argued, it is a case of rescuing Nay's paintings from the universalising rhetoric of abstraction, as opposed to restating their allegiance. Apart from political longing, the idiosyncracies of history and the nuances of individual style are more interesting, and conducive to an ongoing history of art. Nay is of particular interest in this respect as an exemplary figure who is also exceptional for his varied response to abstraction as a painterly style, his political disinterestedness, and the continuity of his work throughout the 1940s. The shift in his style at the end of the 1940s appears at least in part motivated by this continuity, with paintings such as *Weiße Sphinx* conveying more optimism, and recalling the experimental work of the 1930s, than the dark, riven nature of his figurative paintings of the mid-1940s.

Nay nevertheless remains an exemplary figure of postwar abstraction. Although the figurative element lingers in his paintings, both in isolated evocations of the human form and in titles that sustain references to heroes of classical mythology (for example *Hero und Leander* of 1949), the gradual disappearance of the human gestalt and the turn to a dispersed, decorative composition, reflects the broader field of painting at this moment, which, at least in an 'official' sense, polarised into figurative and abstract,

158 E.W. Nay, speech at the opening of the exhibition *Nay*, Kunstkabinett von Hanna Bekker vom Rath, Frankfurt, 8 June, in E.W. Nay, *Lesebuch*, *op. cit.*, pp.49–51.
159 *Ibid.*, pp.49–50.
160 This was recognised in particular by the film made in 1953 by Herbert Seggelke, *Eine Melodie vier Maler* (One Melody Four Painters), in which four artists (Jean Cocteau, Hans Erni and Gino Severini were the others), were asked to respond to the Polonaise from Bach's 'French' Suite no.6 in E major, by drawing directly onto film using a felt-tip pen.
161 Susanne Leeb, 'Abstraction as International Language', in S. Barron and S. Eckmann (eds), *Art of Two Germanys Cold War Cultures*, exhibition catalogue, Los Angeles Museum of Art, Los Angeles, 2009, pp.119–33.
162 B. Myers, 'Postwar Art in Germany', in *College Art Journal*, no.3, spring 1951, pp.251–56.

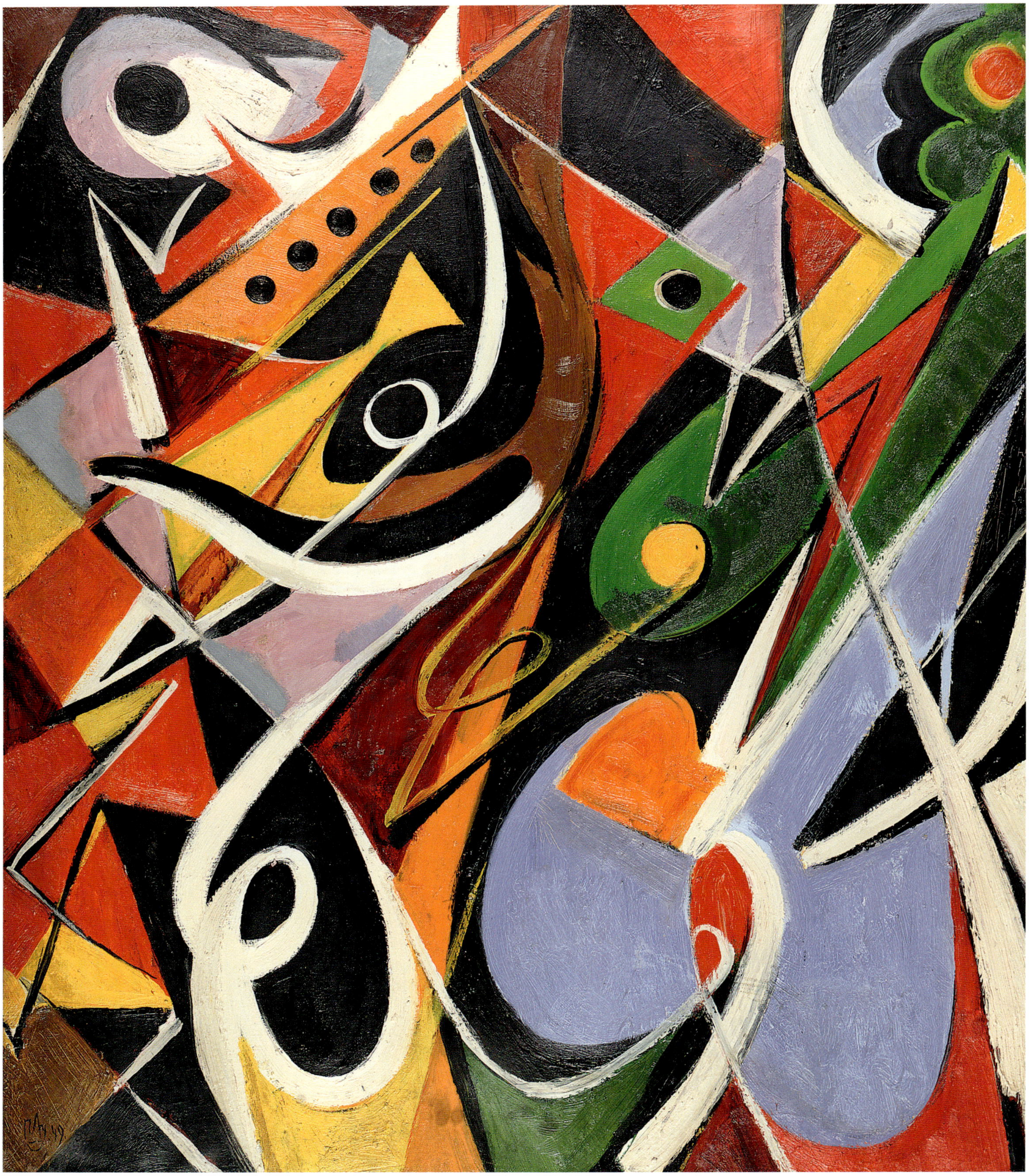

David und Bathsheba, 1949
Oil on canvas
94.5 × 85 cm · 37¼ × 33½ in

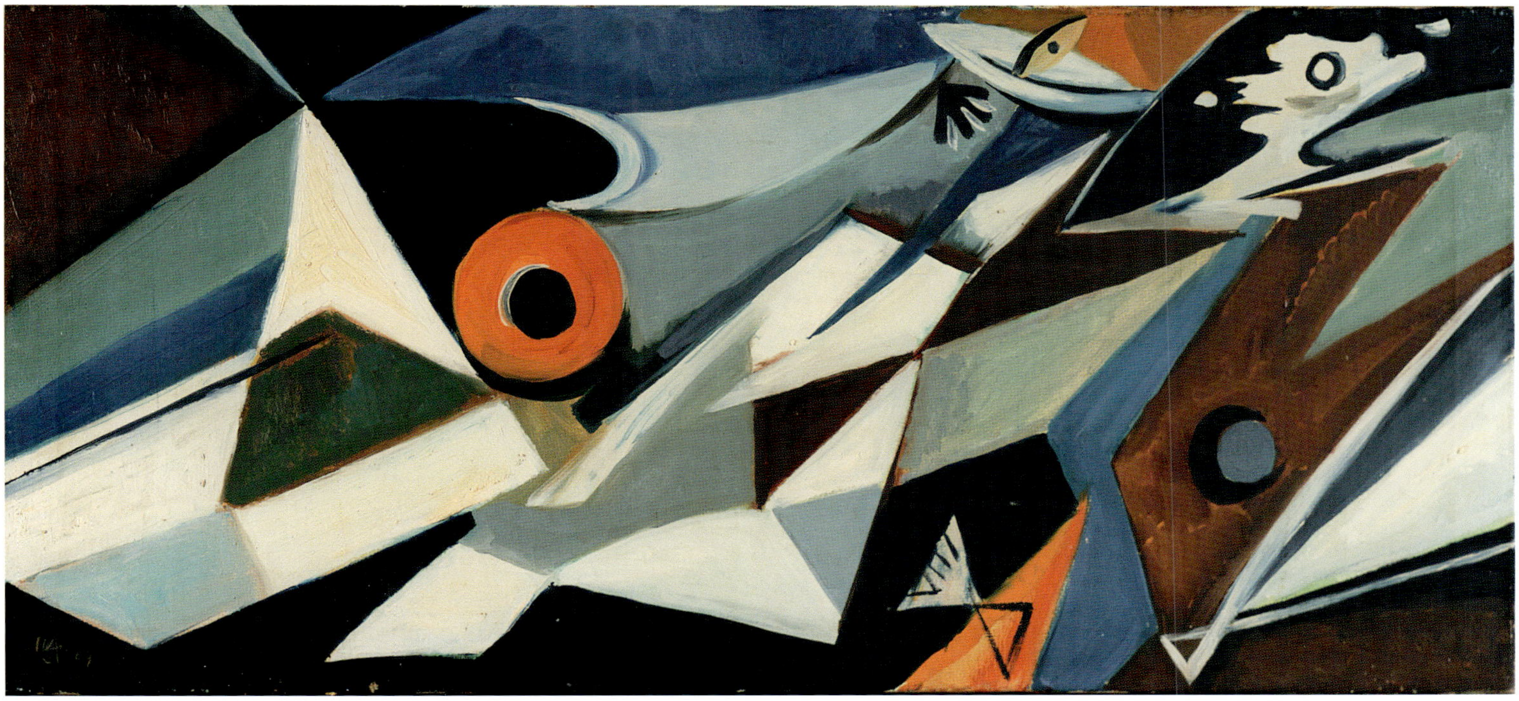

Weiße Sphinx, 1949
Oil on canvas
45 × 100 cm · 17¾ × 39⅜ in

East and West. By 1950 the transposition into an abstract idiom was almost complete. Nausicaa, the temptress of Homer's Odysseus, was the indirect subject of Nay's painting *Figurale – Nausikaa* (Figural – Nausicaa, 1950; p.98), which presents an interlocking surface of flat coloured forms, and the barest indication of a figure rising diagonally from the bottom left. In Greek, Nausicaa's name means 'burner of ships', referring perhaps to the shipwreck that brought Odysseus to the shores of Phaeacia. Such a derivation would clearly have appealed to Nay's unsentimental nature, his aversion to nostalgia or to any return to the past, which was perfectly suited to the climate of reconstruction in the late 1940s and 1950s.

The musical graphemes that dominate Nay's painting around 1950 became increasingly ornamental towards the end of that year and into the next. Black circles and thin lines against bright backgrounds recall the painting of Miró, for example in *Fee* (Fairy, 1951; p.99), a compendium of modern ornamentation. Some hint of the extreme refinement of Nay's later painting can be seen here, particularly in the three dark pod-like forms at the bottom right; but the ornamental feel of this work appears more embedded in the emerging design culture of 1950s West Germany. As such it signals a temporary waning of effect in Nay's work, as if the look of things had seduced him away from his avowal to return painting to questions of being, and ultimately of nature. This, it seems, was simply a result of the overwhelming pressure for all aspects of society to be allied to the task of reconstruction. Paul Betts has described how the 1950s saw the rise of modern design goods as a symbol of renewal and a break from the war economy and imperative of rationing; styled goods became Adenauer's 'insignia of recovery and restored sense of achievement'.[163] *Nierentisch* design culture, so named after the reniform, or kidney-shaped side table by which it was emblematised, was, Betts argues, an appeal to the more painterly side of the Bauhaus heritage, namely the formal language of Klee and Kandinsky, but in a way that could be seen after 1945 in the painting of Willi Baumeister, and also of Nay.[164]

By 1951 it had become clear that it was time to leave Hofheim am Taunus and resettle in a city. Apart from the rudimentary conditions of his unheated studio in Hofheim, he complained in letters to Erich Meyer and to Ruth Arndt of the loneliness of existence in rural retreat. The temptation to move back to Berlin, where he had grown up, was tempered by his nervousness of the embittered cultural politics at the Academy, in particular the stand-off between Karl Hofer and Will Grohmann over the subject of abstract painting. His participation in the 1951 exhibition of the Berlin Künstlerbund, including *Fee*, was the occasion of his first visit to the former capital city since the war. The trip was important for Nay in establishing contacts, notably with Grohmann and the sculptor Hans Uhlmann, with whom he remained in close communication. It was also his first experience of commercial aviation, of Berlin as a theatre of the Cold War, and of the proximity of Russians. 'The journey to Berlin was fascinating', he wrote to Arndt on his return, 'the plane was like a bus journey, 50 passengers, a four-man team with two stewardesses, who served breakfast onboard. 2 thousand metres up – wonderful mountain air'. The return journey was even better:

> It was during the afternoon with clear sunshine and immense cloud-mountains that reached up either side of the plane. Sometimes the plane flew through them, then was revealed wide views of the earth were revealed. Coffee and cakes were served as we flew over Dessau and the Russians.

Nay reported seeing jet fighter planes, and spent the journey with the former Bauhaus painter and weaver Ida Kerkovius. The trip to Berlin must have been a revelation after his wartime experience, and isolation in Hofheim: 'The Berliners very laid-back, the Ku'damm amusing and cosmopolitan as ever, the Gedächtniskirche wonderfully destroyed. The women plainer than in West Germany, but more elegant and cosmopolitan.' He stayed with Elly, and was able to see many of his early paintings once again. 'The highpoint was a studio visit by [the painter] Theodor Werner and the sculptors Hartung and Uhlmann.' He made his peace with Hofer (although this was to be short-lived), and visited Grohmann.

> The opening of the Künstlerbund exhibition was pompous, where I had a certain success, if only notional … The highpoints, according to Grohmann, are Werner, Nay, Winter, Meistermann, Hartung, Uhlmann. At the Hochschule 80 professors, all scheming: provincial art life. They made me just as nervous as the thought of how close the Russians were.'[165]

It was for these reasons that when in October 1951 Nay finally left Hofheim am Taunus, he moved not to Berlin but to Cologne. He had created more than 250 works in Hofheim, and had been able, with the important help of Hanna Bekker vom Rath and Günther Franke, to establish a secure basis for widespread public recognition. Avoiding politics had been essential to his success so far, and Cologne presented the perfect environment in which to expand this public recognition. Cologne was developing into the art centre of the Federal Republic, as Will Grohmann reported in January of the next year: 'Cologne is in luck: after Gerhard Marcks and Ludwig Gies, now Ernst Wilhelm Nay has moved to the old Römerstadt.' Alongside Galerie Der Spiegel, and the important donation by Joseph Haubrich of his collection of modern art to the city, one of the leading figures in the reconstruction of artistic life in postwar Cologne was the dealer Ferdinand Möller. Möller had spent the latter years of the war in the countryside north of Berlin, and, despite calls to return to Berlin after 1945, had chosen Cologne, largely to avoid the difficult political situation in Berlin and the cultural restrictions imposed by the Soviets.[166] His gallery, built in

163 Paul Betts, *The Authority of Everyday Objects. A Cultural History of West German Industrial Design*, University of California Press, Berkeley, Los Angeles and London, 2004, p.4.

164 *Ibid.*, p.13. This type of argument may be traced back to the connection forged by Jost Hermand between abstraction and design in *Kultur im Wiederaufbau. Die Bundesrepublik Deutschland 1945–1965*, Nymphenburger, Munich, 1986, especially p.283. Peter-Klaus Schuster makes this point by comparing paintings by Nay and Baumeister to a furniture advertisement, although it should be pointed out that not only does the advertisement post-date the paintings, but it is also significantly less interesting. See *E.W. Nay, 1902–1968*, *op. cit.*, p.11.

165 E.W. Nay to Ruth Arndt, 28 August 1951, *ibid.*, p.108.

166 See John-Paul Stonard, *Fault Lines*, Ridinghouse, London, 2007, pp.194–95.

the Hahnenstraße by the architect Wilhelm Riphahn, was praised by Grohmann: 'The flat-roofed gallery stands in the city centre, five minutes from the cathedral, and consists of four large gallery spaces with overhead lighting, surrounding a courtyard-garden, providing ample space for exhibitions of painting and sculpture.'[167]

Möller's gallery opened in November 1951 with the exhibition *Die alten Meister der modernen Kunst in Deutschland* (The old masters of modern art in Germany), a striking title that showed how the 'new' art was now part of a tradition, and that its right to existence could no longer be questioned. His exhibition of works by Nay, Georg Meistermann and Uhlmann took place in April and May of the following year. The works by Nay on show were the first of the 'Rhythmic' series that had begun in earnest after his arrival in Cologne at the end of the previous year. Formally, the change in styles is striking: the flat, decorative appearance of the 'Fugal' paintings is exchanged for a more painterly, expressive idiom. *Blüten* (Flora, 1951; p.101), shows a more haptic, nervous paint application, recalling Kirchner's images of Berlin street scenes of around 1913–14, and constitutes a rejection of the flat surfaces and rigid compositions of paintings such as *Fee*. Other works show the earlier 'Fugal' motifs being transformed into something less ornamental, more earthy and 'Rhythmic', as the series title suggests. *Lob des Grau* (In Praise of Grey, 1952; p.103), one of the works included in the exhibition at Galerie Ferdinand Möller, is a combination of modernist ornamentation and expressive vigour, showing the influence of Miró and Kirchner in equal measure. Other paintings demonstrate Nay pushing at the edge of his formal repertoire, as if operating on the boundaries was the only way of sustaining the momentum of his work while expressing himself within the formal language he had developed. *Mit Silberpunkten* (Silver Points, 1952; p.105) is one of his most improvisational and striking paintings. The sense of interlocking surface ornament is entirely abandoned for a free improvisation of form. Nay looked back a few years later and described the change as a 'noticeable loosening of pictorial elements' after a 'period of rigorous constriction'.[168] Although structured composition remained central, rhythm also became important, particularly 'surface rhythm'. Nay conceived of his own development as the development of 'complete clarity of pictorial space', implying a kind of credible, natural picture space constructed with non-representational signs:

> From a 'corrugated' effect to the flat illusionistic space of Realism, to deep pictorial space, finally to corrugated-relief space in the 'Lofoten' paintings ... The 'Hekate' paintings built on this arsenal of forms in a free and poetic and ornamental manner. Then came a more severe, deeper, systematic consideration. The tension, the energy of surface, the colour, from colour to surface, led to an entirely new conception of painting, melodious, dance of surfaces, if you will.[169]

The period from 1949 to 1953, comprising the 'Fugal' and 'Rhythmic' paintings, was in fact the occasion of an ongoing crisis in Nay's work. The development of his painting is less even and assured than before, or in subsequent periods. He appears to be searching for a living motif that would fulfil the somatic, expressive role left vacant by the departure of the human body from his painting, as if after the actors had left the stage the props were somehow being made to come alive.

The call for a new objecthood in painting appears the necessary corollary to the uncompromising move into abstraction of Nay's work in the early 1950s. For Grohmann, reviewing Nay's 1952 retrospective exhibition at the Haus am Waldsee in Berlin on the occasion of the artist's fiftieth birthday, the paintings on display were as distant from the 'so-called abstract painting', as they were from 'so-called Realism'.[170] Nay himself wrote to Grohmann in June 1952 in an attempt to clarify his rapidly evolving 'embodied' abstraction. Is a painting a proposition or a fact? A matter of interpretation or of objecthood? For Nay it was without doubt the latter: an actuality beyond interpretation, a fact that need not be framed merely as a proposition, and therefore with no need for interpretation.[171]

Nay was offered the chance to elaborate this fundamental idea in an unusual context (for him) in 1953, when he accepted a two-month visiting lectureship at the Landeskunstschule in Hamburg, during October and November. He had frequently been called to take up teaching posts in Germany after 1945, all of which were rejected. His acceptance of the Hamburg position was due not only to the short tenure, but also to the fact that it was a post specifically intended for abstract painters – a highly experimental notion at the time (and unthinkable at a later date). The idea came from the director of the Landeskunstschule, Gustav Hassenpflug, who invited leading abstract painters to teach for two months in a painting seminar – Georg Meistermann and Fritz Winter had preceded Nay, and he was followed by Gerhard Fietz, Hans Thiemann and Theodor Werner. Nay's course was devoted to colour, and he wrote to Franke at the beginning of October expressing exasperation at the difficulties of teaching the 'clueless' students.[172] The pedagogic tradition in which he placed himself was unsurprisingly that of the Bauhaus, Klee's *Über die moderne Kunst* (On Modern Art) and Kandinsky's *Über das Geistige in der Kunst* (Concerning the Spiritual in Art) figuring as starting points, in addition, as Werner Haftmann has described, to Mondrian's 'paradigm of the formed surface *gestalteten Fläche*'.[173]

The opening of a Kandinsky exhibition at the Kunsthalle in October (where Nay met Grohmann, as he reported in a letter to Adolf Arndt)[174] appears to have had a strong influence on Nay's work at this moment. He continued to experiment with forms of notation that were on the one hand strongly graphic and on the other suggestive of floating patches of colour, and a more emotive

167 Will Grohmann, 'Das Haus am Hahnentor Deutschlands schönste Kunstgalerie in Köln', in *Neuen Zeitung Berlin*, 18 January 1952.
168 E.W. Nay, 'Regesten zu Leben und Werk', 1958, in *E.W. Nay, 1902–1968*, *op. cit.*, p.111.
169 *Ibid.*
170 Will Grohmann, 'E.W. Nay im Haus am Waldsee', in *Die Neue Zeitung*, Berlin, 20 May 1952, n.p.
171 Nay to Grohmann, 21 June 1952, in *E.W. Nay, 1902–1968*, *op. cit.*, p.112.
172 Nay to Franke, 6 October 1953, *ibid.*, p.117.
173 Haftmann, *op. cit.*, p.160.
174 Nay to Adolf Arndt, 14 October 1953, in *E.W. Nay, 1902–1968*, *op. cit.*, p.117.
175 Friedrich Weltzien, *E.W. Nay – Figur und Körperbild. Kunst und Kunsttheorie des vierziger Jahre*, Reimer, Berlin, 2003, p.279.

aestheticism. *Vom Vulkanischen Grau* (Of Volcanic Grey, 1953; p.107) is one of the most successful and distinctive paintings from this year, and looks forward to the type of work that he would make throughout the rest of the 1950s.

The closing lecture for his Hamburg course, which was reprinted in a later publication on the subject of abstract painters and pedagogy, explored the idea of creating pictorial tension between positive and negative values, where figurative was positive and non-figurative negative. As Weltzien has pointed out, the reference to figurative values was nevertheless deleted when Nay's lecture series was published as *Vom Gestaltwert der Farbe* (On the Design Value of Colour) two years later.[175] Although in the early 1950s Nay had frequently referred to figurative values,[176] and resisted complete partisanship with the followers of abstraction, the statement of his values in his 1955 publication makes clear his full allegiance to abstraction by this time.

Vom Gestaltwert der Farbe was Nay's major publication in the field of art theory, and sheds light on his approach to painting from around 1950 until his death in 1968. Through a description of the formal elements of painting, in particular of colour, Nay demonstrates his growing conviction in the autonomy of painting. *Vom Gestaltwert der Farbe* is also located in a tradition of aesthetic writing that attempts to create a connection between spiritual (*Geistige*) qualities, and the rational, constructive elements of art. Reminiscent of Bauhaus publications both in terms of design and the concise, aphoristic style of writing, it leads through a discussion of the formal elements of painting to a series of simple conclusions: 'Space as pictorial thought is the spiritual projection of the totality of the real.'[177]

The most striking evidence of Nay's new advocacy of abstraction in *Vom Gestaltwert der Farbe* are his descriptions of the 'ahuman' aspect of painting: 'The human is not the concern of the artist. It arises without him, outside of him. Or not. Pictorial form is ahuman.'[178] Before reaching this point the argument explores the basic elements of pictorial form on the assumption that 'pictorial intelligence works differently from ordinary intelligence', and that:

> Artists exist not in the world of the measurable, nor even in the world of sensation, feeling or incantation, but in the world of constructed form ... From the zones of myth one can no longer draw any new secrets; neither can meaning and value be derived from emotion and sensation. The constructed image is the only source of this.[179]

The actual application of these theories is a more oblique undertaking. The tenor of Nay's writing is a combination of Bauhaus certainty and Heideggerian poetry, and as much as it gestures towards his painting, it creates a screen beyond which any further interpretation is unnecessary. In this sense, Nay's writings are highly illuminating in everything that they do not say, and the degree to which they reveal a sort of aristocratic disdain for practical reasoning. *Vom Gestaltwert der Farbe* was as such the basis on which Nay was to resolve many of the problems of abstraction that course through his work during the 1950s, in particular the tension between mystical and rational modes of expression, the notion, perhaps, of painting as a spiritual science. An earlier corporeality was 'dematerialised', in the sense of no longer being subject to the laws of nature – natural colour and light, perspective, gravity and so on.

On the level of technique, the 'dematerialisation' of the human figure was driven to a certain extent by Nay's work in watercolour. Although hardly as prolific in this medium as he was in oil, the simple luminescence of colour enabled by watercolour figured more and more as part of his work in oil from the late 1950s. The importance of watercolour for spontaneously generating motifs can be traced back to the 'Lofoten' period, when Nay produced a number of works in that medium, such as *Mann vor Bergsee* (Man Beside Mountain Lake, 1938), that show an immediacy of execution reflected in the theme of a direct relationship between man and nature. A survey of sorts was provided by the small book published by Piper Verlag in 1956, collecting together 16 of Nay's watercolours, eight made in Le Mans during the war and the remainder in the mid-1950s, as the artist informed Fritz Usinger: 'four were made in Jütland and the rest in Malcesine Hotel Italia room number five, but that is really of no interest'.[180] The Jütland trip was made in the summer of 1954, as Elisabeth Nay-Scheibler has written: 'It rained all week and Nay spent every day painting watercolours in his room, in which for the first time the disk emerged as a central motif.'[181]

The emergence of the *Scheiben*, or disk motif, is one of the most dramatic modulations in Nay's work. In describing the transition, it is difficult to escape musical metaphors: the resolution to a major key, the return of a leitmotif, transfigured by the experience of a journey, perhaps. As always, the transition was slow, like a natural emergence, or the painstaking development of a symphonic idea. Combinations of various idioms during 1954, including *tache*-like marks with linear or chequered forms, led in some cases to paintings that, although successful, did not drive his 'pictorial construction' forward, such as the strange painting *Spuren und Perlen* (Traces and Pearls, 1954; p.109). Other works like *Mit federndem Grün* (With Resilient Green, 1954; p111) show the emergence of the circular motif, in this case defined by outline, or a monochrome painted form with a broken outline, that was to dominate his work for the next decade. *Mit federndem Grün* shows the degree to which the motif enabled Nay to construct a non-naturalistic pictorial space (without perspective construction, depth recession, or implications of gravity), while using naturalistic colour (exploiting the

176 Weltzien points out that as his paintings became more abstract, Nay referred more strongly to figurative elements, citing his contribution to the catalogue of the first exhibition of the Deutschen Künstlerbundes in 1951. Here, Nay explicitly poses an 'embodied' notion of painting (*Körperhaftigkeit des Bildes*), against a psychological interpretation. *Ibid.*, p.280.
177 E.W. Nay, *Vom Gestaltwert der Farbe*, Prestel-Verlag, Munich, 1955, p.26.
178 *Ibid.*, p.25. Nay continues: 'By this is meant that painterly forms establish themselves beyond the realm of human intention: it is irrelevant whether or not an artist chooses in his work to make statements about human intentions that go beyond his artistic or pictorial considerations. This may occur, but is not of relevance for the painting itself. Even when a human concern lies behind the artist's intention, the result first and last establishes itself as a work of art through formal concerns.'
179 *Ibid.*, pp.7–10.
180 *E.W. Nay, 1902–1968, op. cit.*, p.145.
181 *Ibid.*, p.148.

transparency and reflective capacity of the oil medium), and also implying, by way of a minimal morphology, a somatic, or corporeal presence.

Above all, the shift in Nay's painting was one that reflected the great transition in twentieth-century art as a whole – from representing nature in terms of appearance, to depicting instead its mode of operation. The painted image relates to nature not through mimicry (as it had done since antiquity), but by replicating the laws of nature: randomness, complexity, beauty, mystery. As Nay intuited many times in his own writing, the classic prewar model for this approach was Klee – in 1958 Nay averred that Klee's late works, the *Lineamentenbilder* ('Lineament' paintings), constituted the only true pictorial achievement of the previous two decades.[182]

The *Scheibenbilder* ('Disk' paintings) period is generally seen as the 'classic' moment in Nay's paintings, and coincided with his emergence as an artist of national and international repute. In November 1955, he had his first solo exhibition in New York, in the gallery of Henry Kleemann, where he showed ten paintings and 16 watercolours.[183] He had also been awarded the prestigious Lichtwark prize by the city of Hamburg, which occasioned a large retrospective exhibition of his work in the Hamburger Kunstverein. A further survey exhibition took place at the Kestner-Gesellschaft in Hanover. During the same year, Nay was included in the first Documenta exhibition in Kassel. Held in the still semi-ruined Fridericianum, this was the most important exhibition to take place in postwar Germany during the period of reconstruction, and offered a stock-taking of modern art in general, and the German contribution in particular. Nay was represented by three works. *Two Heads* of 1945 was displayed alongside works by Hans Uhlmann, Werner Heldt, Hann Trier, Georg Meistermann and Theodor Werner, providing a context for his work in contemporary German painting and sculpture. In a large central gallery devoted to international (European) abstract painting, his *Gruß an Scharoun* (Greetings to Scharoun, 1955), and *Dunkler Widerhall*, (Dark Echo, 1954) were shown alongside works by Pierre Soulages, Alfred Manessier, Jean Bazaine and Pablo Picasso, as well as Italian artists such as Giuseppe Capogrossi and Giuseppe Santomaso.

At the end of 1955 Nay wrote to Grohmann to describe the 'eventful year' that had passed. He characterised the evolution in his work as a 'softening of my painting style, the resolution of aggression, and [attainment of] the highest level of freedom hitherto'.[184] By the time of works such as *Symphonie in Weiß* (Symphony in White, 1955; p.113), one of the works shown at the Kleemann Galleries at the end of the year (also to be included in the second Documenta exhibition in 1959), the new *Scheibenbild* ('Disk' painting) style was fully established. Rather than using the primed canvas ground as a field on which the painterly event took place, *Symphonie in Weiß* shows a close, jostling mass of forms that suggests interior space, evoking the feeling of flying through cloud formations (an experience on which Nay had commented in his letter to Ruth Arndt, quoted on p.95 above). The 'Disk' paintings are in this sense both intimate and monumental, using a subtle palette of nacreous hues, moving away from tonal contrasts towards chromatic combinations. It was this powerful pictorial model that was to propel Nay's work over the next decade, and also to provide the background to his burgeoning international reputation, but also to the mounting disputes around his status as a leading figure of postwar art.

182 *Ibid.*, p.162.
183 Kleemann had already exhibited work by Fritz Winter and Willi Baumeister.
184 Nay to Grohmann, 1 January 1956, *ibid.*, p.143.

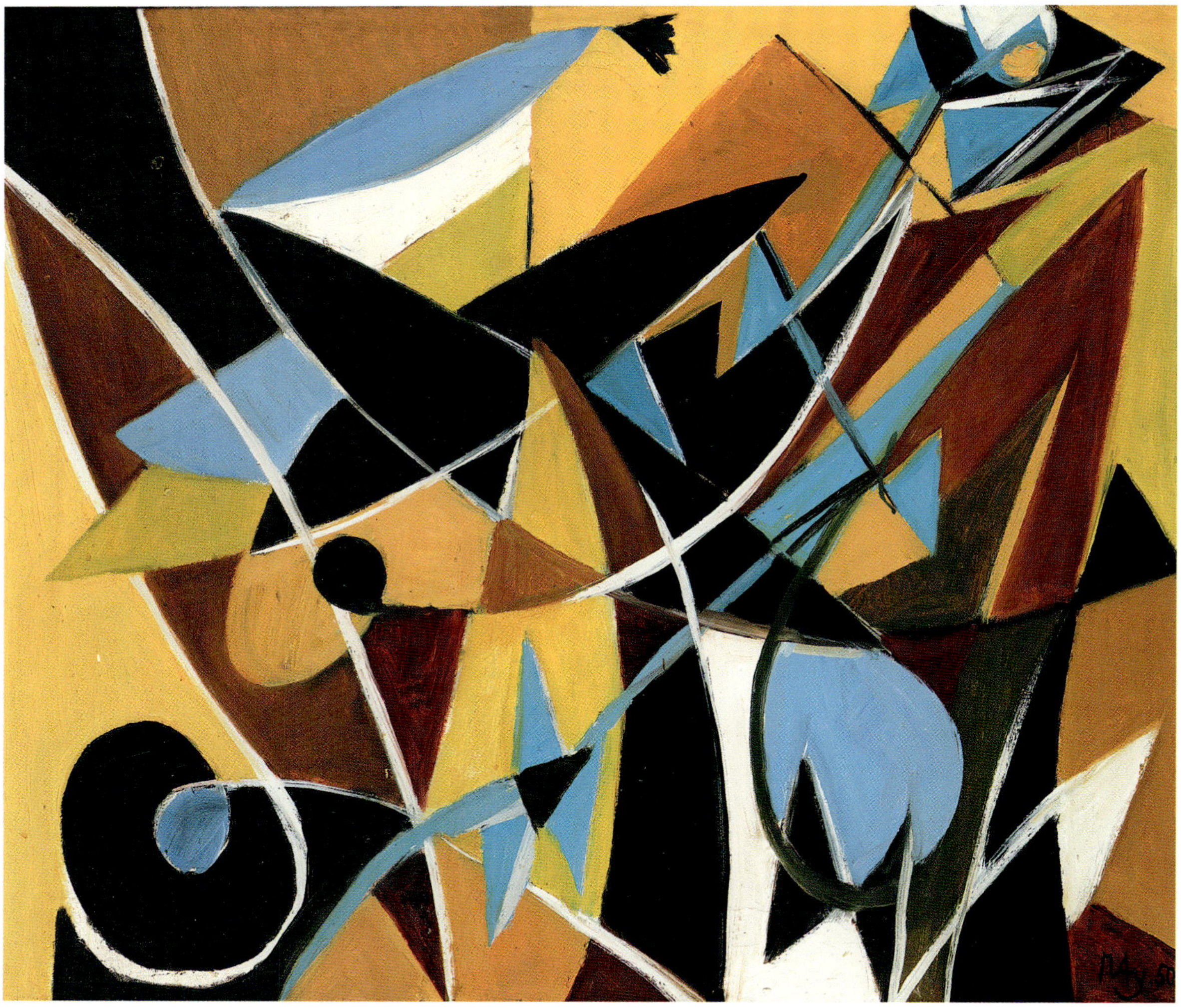

Figurale – Nausikaa, 1950
Oil on canvas
60 × 70 cm · 23⅝ × 27½ in

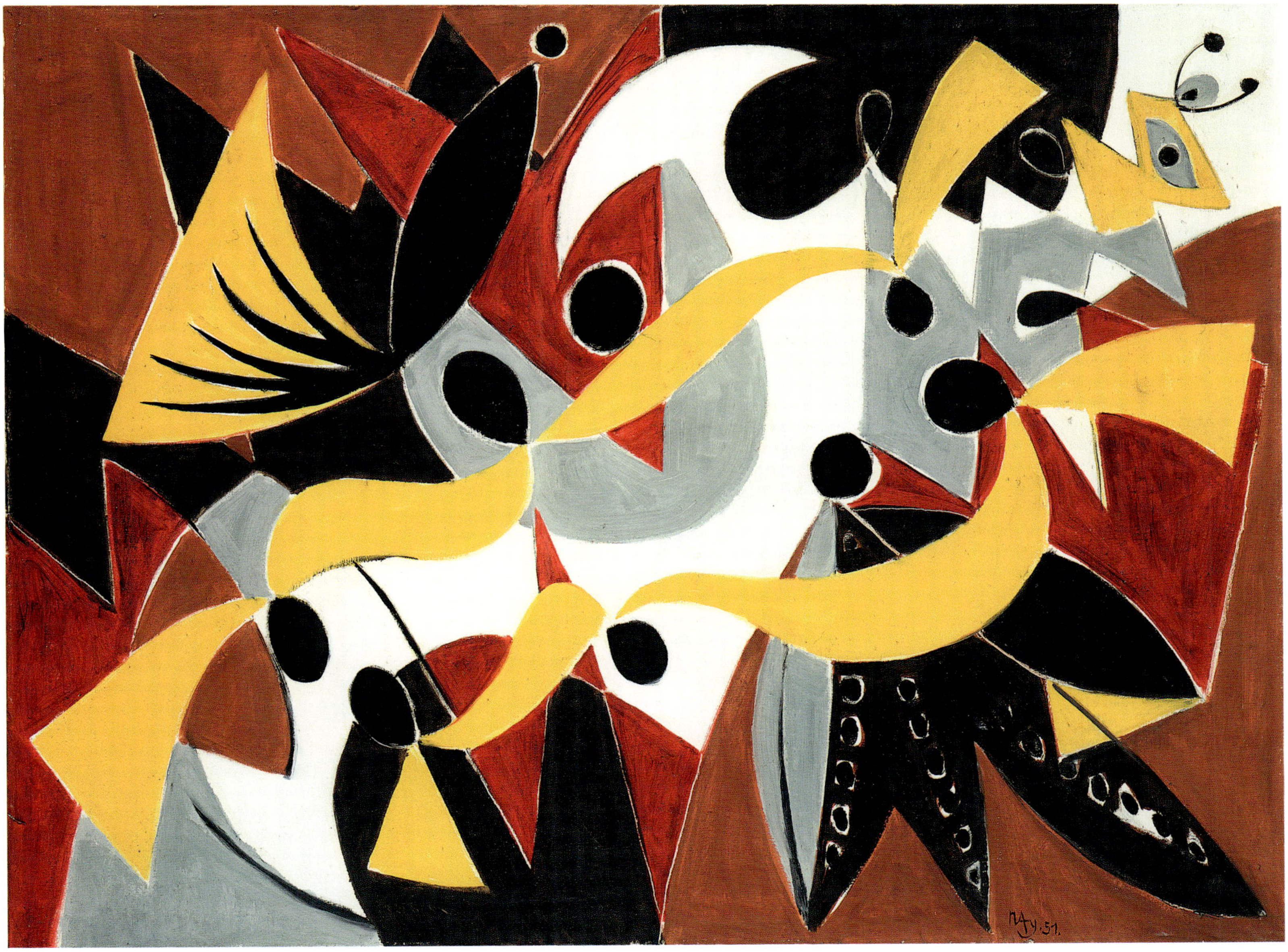

Fee, 1951
Oil on canvas
100 × 135 cm · 39⅜ × 53⅛ in

Blüten, 1951
Oil on canvas
100 × 121 cm · 39⅜ × 47⅝ in

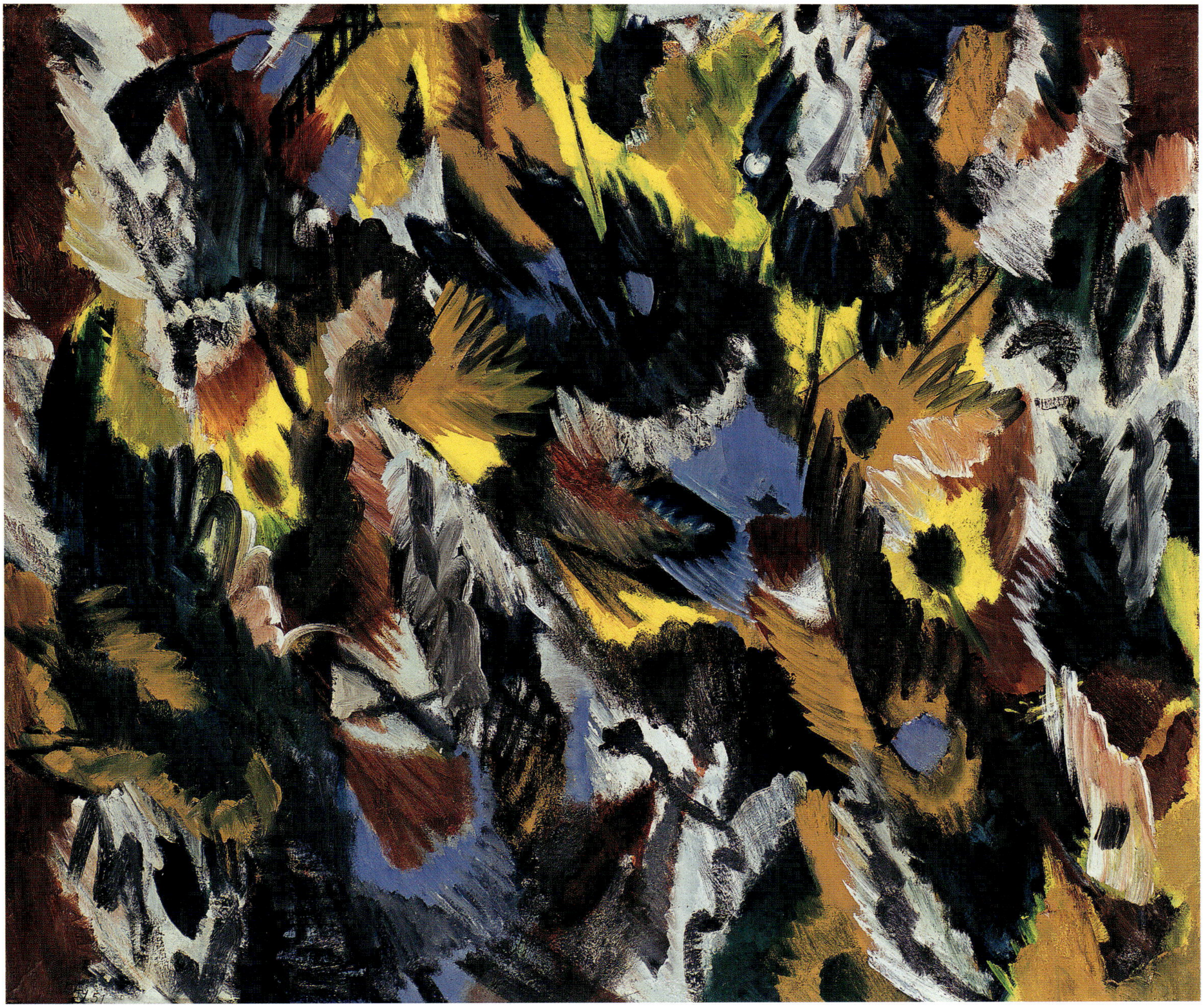

Lob des Grau, 1952
Oil on canvas
100 × 120 cm · 39⅜ × 47¼ in

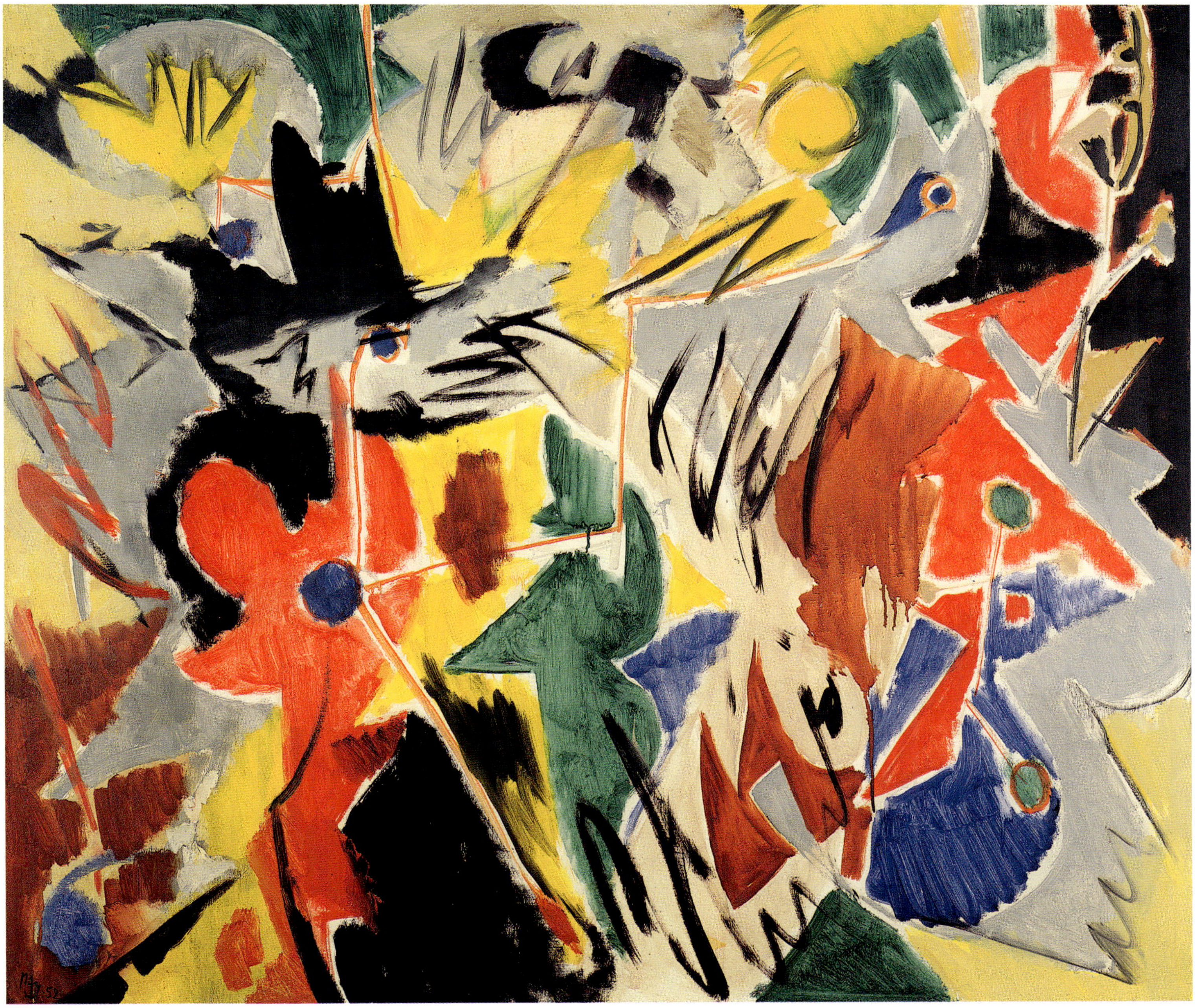

Mit Silberpunkten, 1952
Oil on canvas
100 × 120 cm · 39⅜ × 47¼ in

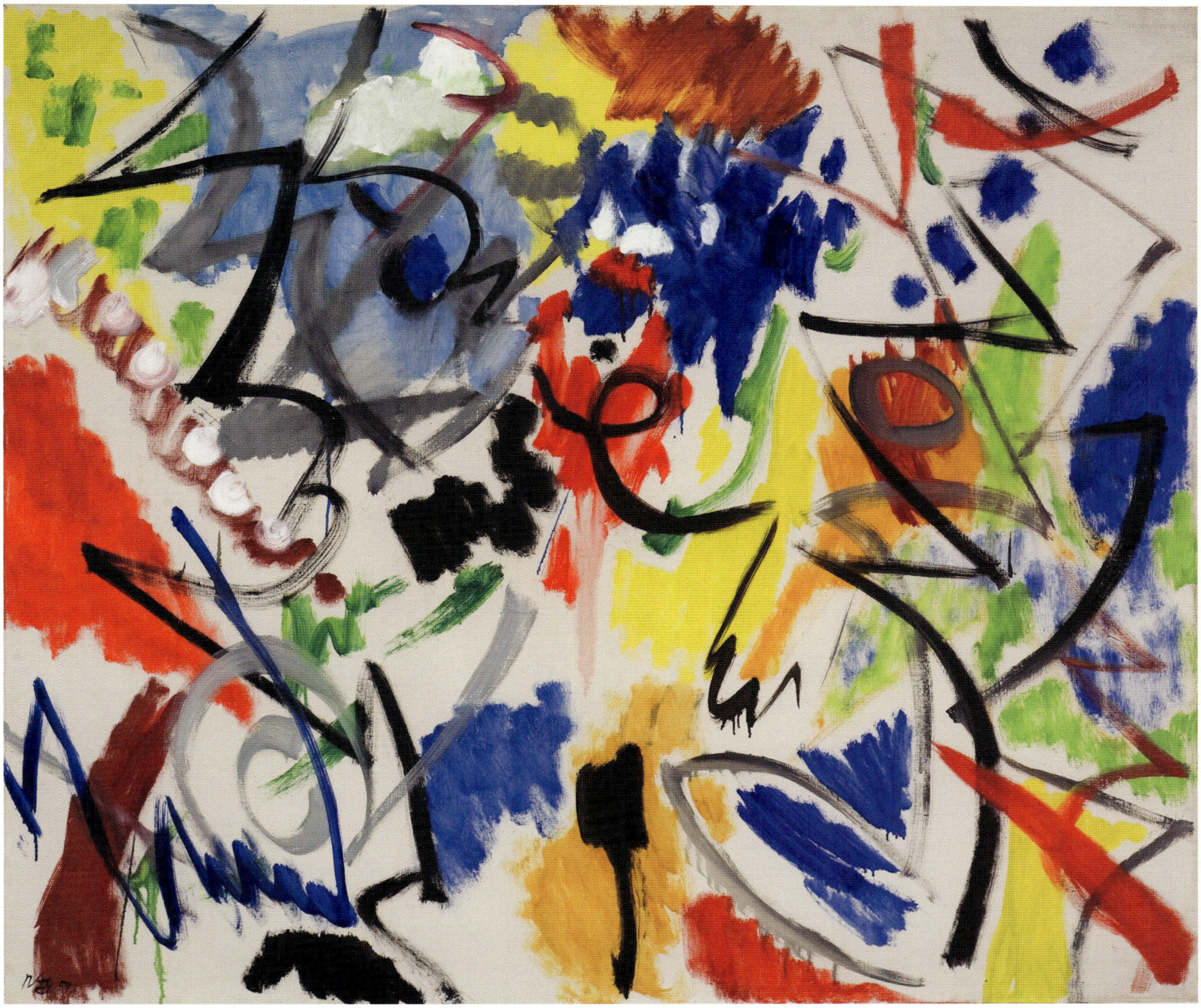

Vom Vulkanischen Grau, 1953
Oil on canvas
101 × 120 cm · 39¾ × 47¼ in

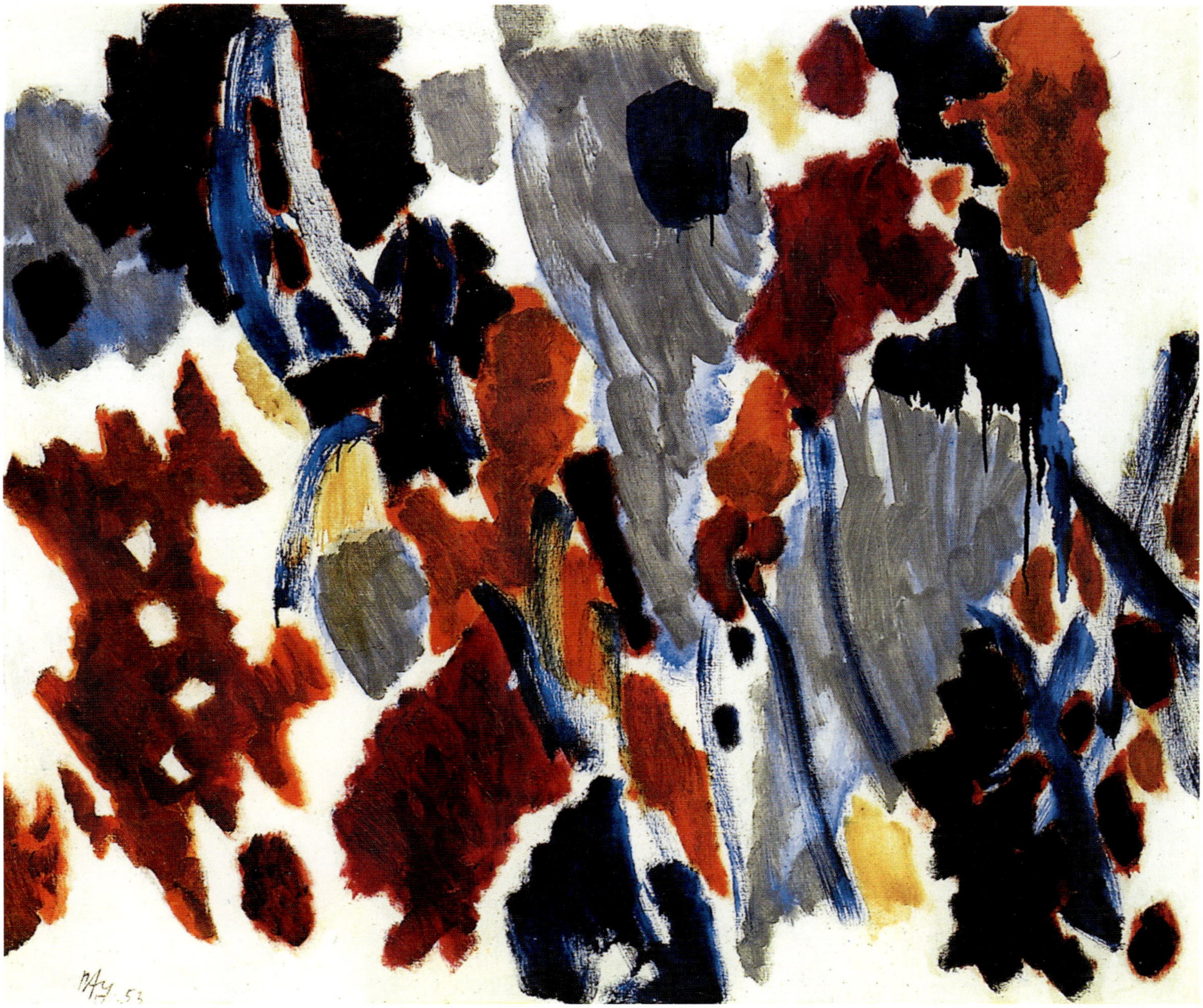

Spuren und Perlen, 1954
Oil on canvas
125 × 200 cm · 49¼ × 78¾ in

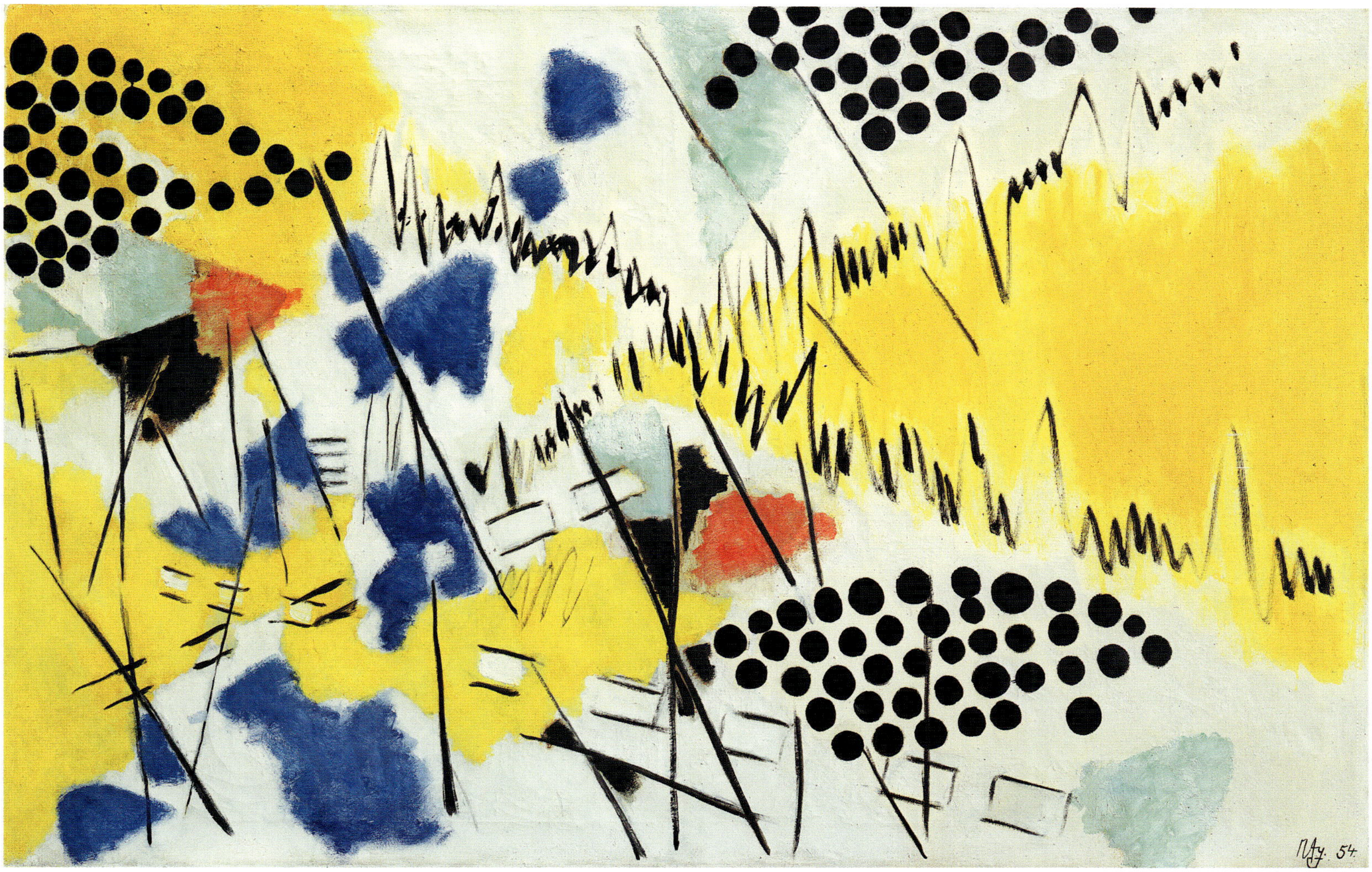

Mit federndem Grün, 1954
Oil on canvas
58 × 70.5 cm · 22⅞ × 27¾ in

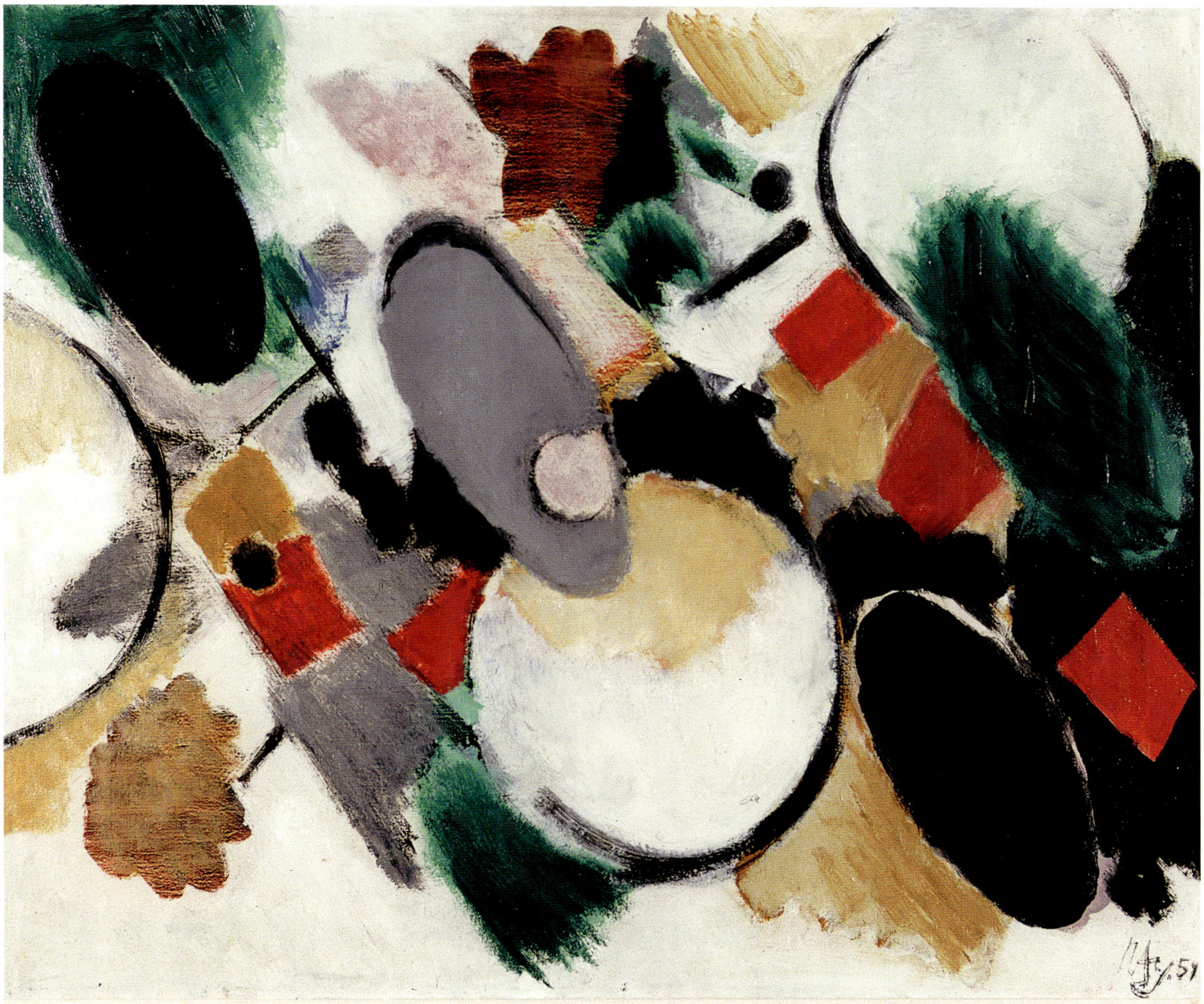

Symphonie in Weiß, 1955
Oil on canvas
124.5 × 201 cm · 49⅛ × 79⅛ in

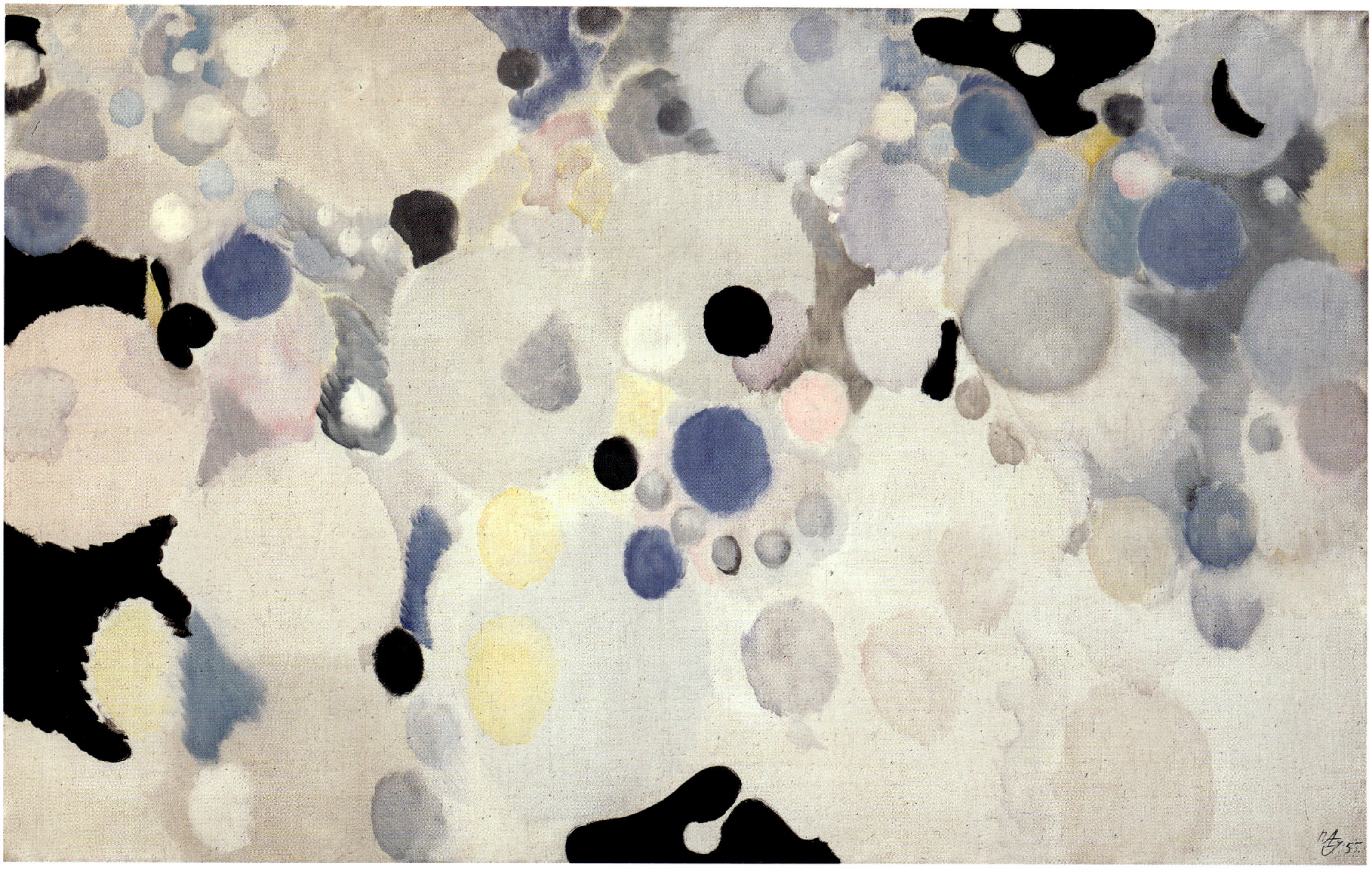

The Freiburger Bild and After

O sables, ô resines!
l'élytre pourpre du destin
dans une grande fixité de l'oeil!

O sands! O rosin!
crimson fate closing its wing case
under a great, staring eye!

— Saint-John Perse, *Exil*

During the summer of 1954, Nay entered a competition to provide murals for Hans Scharoun's designs for a new Staatstheater in Kassel. The monumental, planar qualities of his work meant that it was naturally suited to the requirements of such a public commission, as Werner Haftmann later noted of Nay's paintings of the late 1940s, writing specifically of the 1948 painting *Der Hirte I* (p.87): 'In its flatness and in the broad decorative effect of the colour, it has something of the character of a wall-painting that has been temporarily removed from a ceremonial or sectarian architectural setting.'[185] Although a feature of East German artistic life, which was dominated by collective murals in the Soviet tradition, wall painting was equally present in the West, largely due to the simple need to provide decoration for new buildings. The increasingly large, abstract, 'all-over' nature of painting in the West lent itself easily to such endeavours. In 1960, Arnold Gehlen described the decorative qualities of certain modern paintings, such as those of Jackson Pollock, Jean-Paul Riopelle, Georges Mathieu, Mark Rothko and Nay himself, where the painting is presented as a mural surface.[186]

Scharoun was eventually dismissed as the architect for the Staatstheatre and Nay's commission came to nothing. It was two years later that he was to realise a large-scale, architectural work, possibly one of his best-known, *Das Freiburger Bild* (The Freiburg Painting, 1956; p.121). During the summer of 1956 Nay was asked by the architects Linde and Müller to create a wall painting for the lobby of the new Institute of Chemistry at Freiburg University.[187] The large wall space and lack of any stipulations were extra incentive for Nay to accept the commission. From September to mid-November he worked in situ, but rather than painting directly on the wall, worked on a canvas with the same dimensions. He prepared by making three oil paintings, roughly a third of the size of the final work, as well as a number of watercolours (at least 12). In these works Nay evolved the structure and the composition of the final work, as he described:

> On the one hand it was important to avoid giving the impression of an enlarged sketch, on the other of restricting the proliferation of form. Preparation and improvisation during the process of painting had the following results: the basic structural idea meant that the middle of the painting remained empty, but strong in colour, brick-red. Large areas of colour expand either side of the centre, which relate to each other reciprocally like continents along the Tropics. On the right the darkest disks (Prussian blue) are placed on lighter blues, cobalt, ultramarine, coelin, which are positive values. On the left are grey disks of varying values on Prussian blue. The central red finds itself also in detailed 'potencies' in the top left and right corners. The transition over the red goes from blue to violet accompanied by orange, to cold green in grey (artistic colour changes from bottom right to top left). In the central upper and lower registers, and on the lower left and top right, strong structures of yellow intermingle vertically with orange and red. Brackets, on the left edge in hammer form, on the right edge in the shape of a wedge, aid the integration of surface and rhythm. This is the visual structure of the image.[188]

The preparatory paintings show the development of a dispersed field of coloured disks, which in the final version appear to emerge at either side, creating an empty space in the centre, looking through to a strong red background. The spatial configuration of the painting is 'Neither perspectival, nor flat', as Nay wrote, 'although each colour is presented as a flat plane'. The 'potential volume' of these coloured planes would interest scientists 'who understand nature as a process of transforming material into energy'.[189]

The *Freiburger Bild* was above all Nay's attempt to rival the size and ambition of American painting, and was indeed to hold its own alongside paintings by Pollock when it was displayed at the second Documenta exhibition in Kassel in 1959. It was a major event for the artist himself, who described it in a letter to Haftmann as 'the first picture of our time that shows structure as colour'.[190] As Nay-Scheibler has noted, it was clearly the high-point of the 'Disk' paintings phase, and the best-known work by Nay during the 1950s.[191] The large, panoramic format allows a greater sense of movement across the canvas, and thus heightens the dramatic interaction of colour and depth, and the sense of a complex interior space.

The combination of disk sizes and forms may remind one of the fractal images of nature developed a decade or so later; this sense of a cosmic ordering of the macro- and micro-spheres can be seen in one of the key paintings from 1956, *Sternbalance* (Star Balance; p.123), which was included in the display of Nay's work at the Venice Biennale that year.[192] Haftmann describes the painting as if the

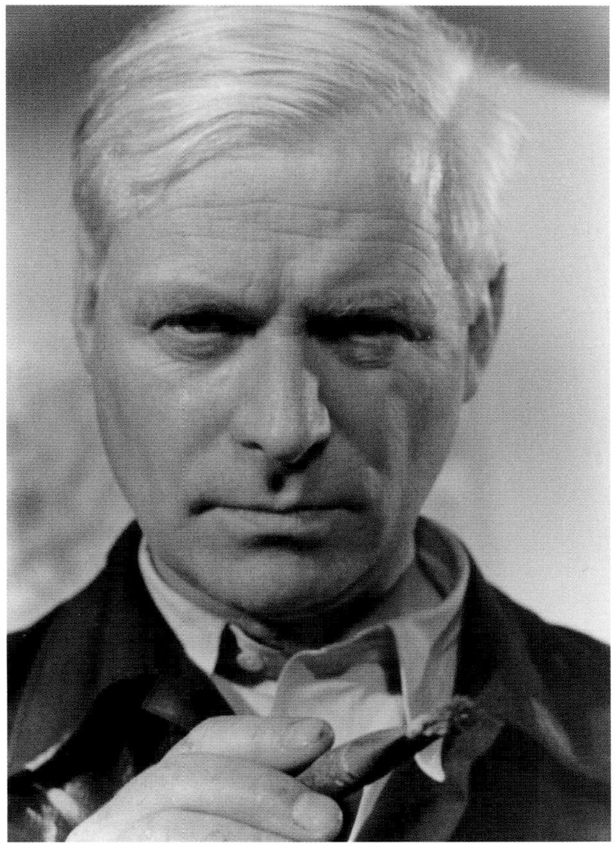

E.W. Nay, 1954

185 Haftmann, *op. cit.*, p.127.
186 A. Gehlen, *Zeit-Bilder. Zur Soziologie und Ästhetik der modernen Malerei*, Athenäum, Frankfurt am Main, 1960, p.98.
187 Haftmann, 1960, *op. cit.*, p.175.
188 'Einmal handelte es sich darum, den Eindruck einer Vergrößerung einer Skizze zu vermeiden, zum andern darum, die Addition, d.h. die Aufzählung von Formabläufen, zu verhindern. Vorarbeiten und Improvisation während des Malens ergaben Folgendes: der tragende Einfall ergab sich dahin, daß die Mitte des Bildes leer gehalten wurde, aber stark in der Farbe, ziegelrot. Zu beiden Seiten der Mitte fügen sich große Farbkomplexe, die sich reziprok in der Art des ›Krebses‹ zueinander verhalten. Rechts die dunkelsten Scheiben (Pariserblau) stehen auf helleren Blaus, die sich (Kobaltblau, Ultramarinblau, Coelinblau) als positive Potenzen verhalten. Links graue Scheiben in verschiedenen Werten auf Pariserblau. Das Rot der Mitte geht zugleich in einzelnen ›Potenzen‹ nach den Ecken links und rechts oben. Die Übergänge über das Rot hinweg weisen von Blau zu Violett mit Orange begleitet zu kaltem Grün ins Grau (artistische Farbverwandlung von rechts unten nach links oben). In der Mitte des Bildes oben und unten und links unten und rechts oben starke von Orange und Rot durchsetzte Gelbkomplexe, die sich vertikal miteinander verbinden. Klammern, von der linken Kante in Hammerform, rechts oben in Keilform, helfen die bewegten Rhythmen als Fläche einzuhalten. Dies die äußerliche Flächenordnung'. E.W. Nay, notes, 17 November 1956, in *Lesebuch*, *op. cit.*, p.161.
189 *E.W. Nay, 1902–1968: Bilder und Dokumente*, *op. cit.*, p.156.
190 E.W. Nay to Haftmann, 13 August 1960, DKA, 1C 97.
191 E. Nay-Scheibler, 'E.W. Nay aus der Nähe – ein Lebensbericht', in Gohr, *op. cit.*
192 A painting by Nay, *Gelbe Sitzende* (1948) had been included in the first postwar Venice Biennale, in 1948, as part of a group exhibition organised in the central exhibition building (which was to become the Italian Pavilion) by Eberhard Hanfstaengl, and a further three paintings were included in the next exhibition in 1950. See Ursula Zeller, *Die deutschen Beiträge zur Biennale Venedig 1895–2007*, M. DuMont, Cologne, 2007, p.364. It was not, however, until 1956 that a more substantial showing of his work took place. Germany was not officially invited to the 1948 Biennale, the German Pavilion having been given over to an exhibition of French Impressionism. Hanfstaengl's small display included work by Otto Dix, Erich Heckel, Karl Hofer and Max Pechstein. See *ibid.*, pp.90–92. Alongside a display of works by Emil Nolde, Hanfstaengl placed displays of works by Fritz Winter and by Nay (12 paintings and six watercolours) to exemplify what he described as 'Northern' and 'Southern' directions in abstract painting in Germany. Eberhard Hanfstaengl, 'Germania', in *XXVIII. Biennale di Venezia*, exhibition catalogue, Venice, 1956, p.387. The display of Nay's work is often described as a solo exhibition, which was not the case. The show also included sculpture by Karl Hartung, Bernhard Heiliger and Toni Stadler.

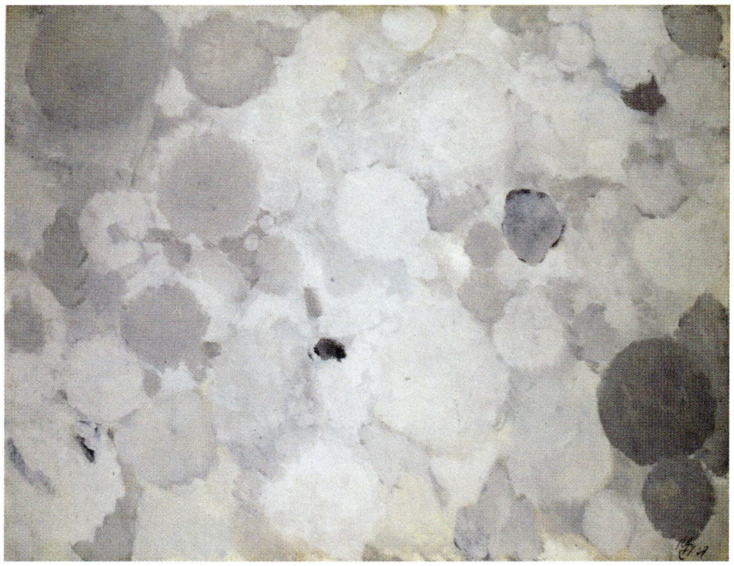

Diamant, 1957
Oil on canvas
89 × 116.5 cm · 35⅛ × 45⅞ in

colours were constructed according to a chemical formula, noting the quadripartite grouping, and also compares it to the earlier *Symphonie in Weiß* (p.113).[193] The scientific context was important for Nay's claim for the immanence of his colour – that it was a direct expression of the contemporary moment – and also for moving away from the dominance of escapist myth during the postwar years. Haftmann wrote a few years later of the important parallel with the spaces and language of modern science for Nay, pointing to his reading of the French physicist Louis de Broglie (probably his *Matter and Light* of 1937) and the German theoretical physicist Pascual Jordan (whose reputation was still highly damaged in 1960 by his former membership of the Nazi party).[194]

Nay was aware of the limits of drawing too close a parallel between the endeavours of art and science. His use of concepts such as potential energy, and the attempt to evolve an objective, critical language for art, was part of a broader shift at a time when science was replacing myth and tradition as the basis for human representation. But if he was constantly searching for scientific exactitude in the language he used to describe colour and space, the terms he deployed would always operate on a poetic, interpretative level. Scientific metaphors nevertheless serve to locate his work in a historical moment where forward-looking technological enterprise, and technocratic notions of social organisation in general, were directing reconstruction.

The search for scientific language, or sets of metaphors, to move painting out of the subjective realm was motivated by the notion that a painting should somehow be socially useful – an idea that had crystallised for Nay around the Freiburg commission. But such usefulness went, needless to say, far beyond technocratic planning. In a diary entry dated December 1956, Nay explains that his systematic, scientific approach to abstract painting was intended to constitute a revelation of man's relationship to nature: 'And thus the relationship of man to himself and to nature is made visible.'[195] This revelation was equivalent not to revealed religion but rather to advances in science and technology. The sense of a shift away from the premises of humanism can frequently be seen in Nay's writing at this time, suggesting that abstraction offered at best only a temporary solution to the problem of change. 'Idealism, Pathos, Heroism, Christendom, Humanism, Law, one must be clear: whether one likes it or not the actual effectiveness of all these ideas has expired', he wrote in 1958.[196]

The degree to which Nazism had been responsible for this change, and the broken society left in the wake of a war in which he had participated, were not questions that Nay avoided. From the moment of the emergence of abstraction in his painting, and certainly during the classical moment of the 'Disk' paintings, disagreeable historical facts are far from the subject matter of his work, but in his private notes he showed himself aware of the

193 Haftmann, 1960, *op. cit.*, p.176.
194 *Ibid.*, p.179.
195 Nay, 29 December 1956, in *Lesebuch*, 2002, *op. cit.*, p.163.
196 'Regesten zu Leben und Werk', 1958, *ibid.*, p.183.
197 *Ibid.*, pp.139–40.
198 *Ibid.*, p.167.
199 *Ibid.*, p.261.
200 *Ibid.*, p.162.
201 *Ibid.*, p.166.
202 Standish D. Lawder, 'Ernst Wilhelm

impossibility of coming to terms with the Nazi past. Shortly before embarking on the *Freiburger Bild* he wrote a short text titled 'On the National Feeling of the Germans in 1956', associating the rejection of national identity amongst Germans not solely with their defeat in 1945, but also with their dependence on a strong economy. Nor does he avoid the question of collective guilt:

> To acknowledge having lived through the Nazi period means for every individual to accept collective responsibility for the period 1933–45. More precisely, this means that every German, Nazi or not, is responsible for what happened, whereas in the preceding years, the time after the Versaille treaty, German affairs were more properly part of a broader Europe. This is the difficult point, and it is because of this that a naturally national sensibility has become distorted.[197]

But if the economy, and also tourism, Nay adds, mask the situation, then it is for intellectuals, specifically artists, to face up to questions of national sensibility – although he adds that there was little evidence of this actually happening, in Germany or elsewhere.

Two years later, Nay reflected once more on the problems facing postwar German society. Again, he commented on the general indifference to the Nazi past, and the widespread sentiment that the Third Reich had constituted some kind of dream, before the current reality of Soviet dominance. Alongside this indifference was a 'vivid interest in all questions relating to technology', which he contrasted with the indolent attitude towards political problems. The increase in specialised labour, necessary within a technologically driven society, led to a decreased realm of influence for the individual, and to political disenfranchisement.[198]

Yet in his descriptions of the Nazi period there is no sustained criticism of the regime, or indications that he thought of emigrating. Haftmann's inclusion of Nay in a list of artists of inner emigration is unrealistic, and, without detracting from the hardships suffered by Nay throughout the 1930s and 1940s, does little to honour those who were forced to emigrate, or, like Oskar Schlemmer, did not survive the Third Reich. For Nay, politics and art were immiscible. Engaged art was for him an *Unding* – an absurdity. 'Art cannot be political, social critical or otherwise', he wrote in 1965, a line he held consistently all his life.[199]

Throughout November and December 1956, Nay developed his notion of the disk as a 'potential energy form'[200] that was organised according to a 'planar choreography' (*Flächenchoreographie*).[201] A long series of paintings that echo the basic structure and strong, saturated colours of the *Freiburger Bild* carried him through to the next year. The scientific metaphors fall away, however, and in paintings such as *Diamant Rot* (Diamond Red, 1957; p.125), it is rather an intense aestheticism that animates the 'planar choreography'. A detailed description of the 'Disk' paintings was offered by the American writer Standish D. Lawdor a couple of years later, in which the theme of 'liberation' was central. 'Nay's circles of color have unrestricted freedom of movement. They quietly float and glide upward and outward, sometimes fusing, sometimes separating. Physical density, architectonics, weight and gravity, are absolutely foreign to Nay's pictorial concept'.[202] For which reason, Lawdor suggested, Nay was 'one of the most atypical German painters'. *Diamant* (Diamond, 1957), shown shortly after completion at an exhibition of Nay's work at Günther Franke's gallery in Munich, is one of the most fugitive images in Nay's oeuvre, and takes the idea first presented in *Symphonie in Weiß* two years earlier to an extreme.

Towards the end of 1957 the disks begin to break up, and the scale of the painting becomes more intimate. Titles continue to suggest a sensuous aesthetic appeal rather than a scientific, materialist spin. Throughout 1958, the late *Scheibenbilder* period, Nay experimented with the scale of the disk motif, and intensified the experience of colour. *Rondo* (Rondo, 1958; p.127) is one of the most striking works of this year, and in particular recalls the influence of Emil Nolde. Although Nay had moved away from the rhetoric of subjectivity underlying Expressionist painting, he had by no means relinquished any of its effect.

The second half of the 1950s saw an opening up of cultural exchange in Western Europe, as well as the arrival of a new cultural dominant – the New York school of painting. The touring exhibition of work by Pollock, and the large abstract paintings on show in *The New American Painting*, which circulated in Europe during 1958–59, confirmed the dominance of art from the New World.[203] In the wake of the first Documenta exhibition, the West German art scene became increasingly international during the late 1950s, with the Rheinland as the new cultural centre. It was Nay's good fortune that he achieved the first peak of his success as a painter at this moment. His work had been included in the 1956 exhibition *A Hundred Years of German Painting 1850–1950* at the Tate Gallery, and the next year at the comparable exhibition *German Art of the Twentieth Century* held at the Museum of Modern Art, New York. The large 'Disk' painting *Parabel* (Parable, 1958; p.129) was one of the works included in Nay's show at the Galerie Les Contemporains, part of *Expo 58 – 50 ans d'art moderne*, the 1958 Brussels World's Fair, where his painting *Alpha* (Alpha), made the previous year, was included in the exhibition display. A room of his paintings was displayed at the 1958 São Paolo Biennale. Also in 1958, Nay travelled to America for the first time, on the occasion of his second exhibition at the Kleemann Galleries.[204]

Despite this rapidly accelerating exposure, and accumulation of important honours, such as nomination (by Hans Scharoun) to the Berlin Akademie der Künste in 1956, and prizes, notably the Guggenheim Prize in 1960, Nay remained essentially a private figure. The gallerist Bernd Klüser has drawn an interesting contrast between Nay and the younger artist Joseph Beuys – both, he argues, made their most interesting work between 1950 and 1968, and both, it may be added, were strongly affected by their experience of fighting during the war. At the end of his life, Nay's thinking

Nay. An Evaluation of his Recent Paintings', in *Art Journal*, vol.21, no.2, winter 1961, p.101.
203 Sigrid Ruby, 'Have we an American art?', in *Präsentation und Rezeption amerikanischer Malerei in Westdeutschland und Westeuropa*, VDG, Weimar, 1999.
204 Nay's first exhibition at the Kleemann Galleries was in 1955. Thereafter exhibitions in 1958 and 1959 consolidated his reputation, and led to a number of museum purchases.

was surprisingly close to that of Beuys, considering the divergence in the type of art they were making. 'The artist today is like the shaman of the Siberian people, who is able to heal himself and treat himself psychoanalytically through pictorial formulations that, detached from his own personality and individuality, may be used therapeutically by others, consciously or unconsciously' Nay wrote in 1967–68, perhaps making conscious reference to Beuys's experiences as a fighter pilot cared for by Tartars after crashing his plane in Siberia.[205] Yet whereas Beuys was an entirely public figure who framed his art as an ongoing public project, Nay did not cultivate a public persona, or change his essentially private approach to making art.[206]

The impact of New York painting on Nay's work in the late 1950s was decisive. At the second Documenta exhibition in 1959, he was able to compare his work to the monumental products of Abstract Expressionism by the likes of Pollock and Mark Tobey. Represented by seven works, including *Symphonie in Weiß* and the *Freiburger Bild*,[207] Nay was given 'top billing', in the words of one American critic, and was able to outdo his American rivals at least in terms of the 'dubious measure of success' suggested by size ration: Nay with 16 square metres against Barnett Newman with 13.1 and Clyfford Still with 11.9.[208]

'Tachism is dead', Nay wrote in a diary entry two days before the opening of the exhibition; Constructivism was also dead, and it was against the new yardstick provided by American art that he was to measure himself: 'The spiritual movement of art has found a new form of expression in the work of Nay'.[209] Such uppercase egoism was justified: his showing was a critical success, and confirmed his international reputation; what Picasso had been for France and Pollock was now for America and Henry Moore for England, Nay was for Germany. The art dealer Harry A. Brooks described how he visited the 1959 Documenta, looking forward to seeing Moore's monumental sculptures in the still semi-ruined Fridericianum, and at the same time discovered the 'astonishingly dynamic' works of Nay in the painting section.[210] Brooks was to be Nay's most important contact in America, organising exhibitions of his work at Knoedler & Company, where he was on the board in 1962 and 1964, from which a number of American museums were to purchase works. A further exhibition of 'last paintings' was held at Knoedler & Company after Nay's death in 1968.

Nay's response to this new international arena of painting, and to New York in particular, emerges in his writings in a series of reflections on a new impersonality and universality in art. One of the most striking formulations appears in the term 'nomadic collectivism' (*nomadischer Kollektivismus*).[211] Nay saw that the striving towards the future of an earlier avant-garde was, by the late 1950s, transformed into a politics of migration and travelling: the attempt to reach distant audiences. To describe the contemporary human condition as nomadic was not only to suggest a post-political definition of humanity, beyond geo-political boundaries, but also to take up the concept of *Unbehaustheit* – homelessness – as it appeared in the writings of Heidegger. Heidegger's explanation of the 'homelessness' of contemporary man remains the most important element of his thinking in relation to the experience of artists at this moment. Within the context of postwar reconstruction, his connection between dwelling and thinking, and by extension, expressing oneself in language, which found its most distilled expression in the 1951 essay 'Bauen Wohnen Denken' (Building Dwelling Thinking), was in effect a poetic meditation on displacement and the severe housing shortage at the time. The terminology that Nay was to develop of a 'nomadic collectivism' in the late 1950s, was inspired at least in part by Heidegger's conceptualisation of this material plight.

After the death of Willi Baumeister in 1955, Nay was the leading painter in Germany, as an exhibition combining the work of the two artists at Kunstmuseum Basel in 1960 showed. According to Arnold Rüdlinger, writing in the exhibition's catalogue, Nay was the legitimate heir to a tradition of Expressionism that he had reinterpreted in abstract forms.[212] For an international public with only a dim awareness of what was occurring in Germany, and still little disposed to treat German art with much sympathy, Nay was one of the few positive points of reference.

1960 also saw the first solo exhibition of works by Nay in London, at the New London Gallery on Old Bond Street during December. The show was well received, if with circumspection. An anonymous reviewer in *The Times* described Nay as 'a typical colourist in the north German Expressionist tradition', who in his work of the 1930s and 1940s revealed himself as a painter of 'marked, almost ruthless energy in imaginative compositions and landscapes'.[213] The reviewer alighted upon the musicality of the 'Disk' paintings, suggesting that 'mood is being orchestrated and picked out in chords almost as though the disks of colour were banks of massed organ stops'. The praise was all the more valuable for a German artist: 'From the early *furor teutonicus* to the present mood of lyrical vitality, the achievement in this exhibition is impressive.'[214] For Edward Lucie-Smith, reviewing the same exhibition, Nay could be a clumsy artist, but was also 'honest'. The effect of recent work 'is to set up a kind of slow rhythm – the eye is drawn from one patch of colour to another, into the canvas and across it'.[215]

Nay's painting during the early 1960s, the end phase of the 'Disk' paintings period, becomes increasingly gestural, and also develops heavier, darker colour scales, such as with *Metagrau* (Meta-Grey, 1961; p.131). The transformation of the disk motif during this period provides the energy for the development of Nay's work into its final phase, alongside a more and more sophisticated use of colour. The disk is increasingly represented by a quick, blocking-out gesture, suggesting a semi-transparent form. *Lob des Grün* (In Praise of

205 Nay, *Lesebuch*, 2002, *op. cit.*, p.314.
206 B. Klüser, 'Ein Brief zu Nay und Beuys', in *E.W. Nay, 1902–1968*, *op. cit.*, p.32.
207 The five other works were: *Stellar Chromatisch* (1955), *Gelb und Purpur*, *Ontario Blau*, *Omega* and *Instrumentation in Gelb* (all 1959). See *II. documenta '59. Kunst nach 1945*, vol.1, *Malerei*, exhibition catalogue, Museum Fridericianum, Kassel, 1959, pp.292–97.
208 Lawder, 1961, *op. cit.*, p.101.
209 E.W. Nay, 'Meine Idee von der D(ocumenta) II', *E.W. Nay, 1902–1968*, *op. cit.*, p.168.
210 Harry A. Brooks, 'Betrachtung eines Amerikaners', *ibid.*, pp.178–81.
211 For example, *Lesebuch*, 2002, *op. cit.*, p.178.
212 A. Rüdlinger, untitled preface, in *Willi Baumeister Ernst Wilhelm Nay*, exhibition catalogue, Kunsthalle Basel, 1960, np, sides 3–4.
213 NN, in *The Times*, London, 2 December 1960, p.20.
214 *Ibid.*, p.20
215 Edward Lucie-Smith, in *Art News and Review*, no.23, 1960.

Green, 1961; p.133), is one of the key paintings of this important period, and indeed one of Nay's greatest works. The disk motifs are used to construct an increasingly dark interior, with the suggestion of an inner light. Although not a major work from the period, the painting *Licht in Dunkel* (Light in Darkness, 1961) provides a clear statement of this pictorial idea. A shimmering tonal drama animates the surface of these canvases, combined with a far more rapid execution giving a heightened urgency and immediacy.

Evolving alongside the disk motif was a renewed concern with biological forms, looking back to Nay's paintings of the 1930s – cyclopic, humanoid shapes, or a welter of disembodied eyes. A number of works from 1962 could demonstrate this change, but one of the dominant paintings of this period, *Rotklang* (Red Sound, 1962; p.135), shows the energy that Nay was applying to the surface, and the close-packed forms, as if signalling the birth pangs of a new period of work. A slow awakening to self-awareness appears to govern the way in which disks become eyes. Nay was aware of the change in his painting as part of a broader, more fundamental shift in the relationship between art and nature. 'An epoch that began with Expressionism and Cubism is fundamentally over', he wrote in March 1962.[216] Myth, magic and religion were no longer the sources of painting. He was becoming increasingly aware of the way in which his painting could provide an equivalent for natural processes, rather than imitating natural appearances. His own notes on this topic during the years 1962 and 1963 constitute some of his clearest and most interesting writings on his own painting, and suggest a resolution, to a certain extent, of his own approach to abstract painting as a utopian, apolitical activity: 'My art makes visible a new stage in the consciousness of mankind, a hitherto unknown accord of man and nature. Man experiences himself and nature as universal – he dispenses with subjectivity in favour of a universal oneness.'[217]

By 1963 the sense of a new period in Nay's work had fully emerged, characterised by rapid execution and a reliance on the unconscious accidents of paint application, and simple, eye-shaped motifs. *Weiße Quelle* (White Source, 1963; p.137), comprises a series of quickly drawn oculiform shapes against a series of rapid gestures done in white, black and lemon yellow. By the next year, the motif had become the dominant sign in Nay's painting, and the *Augenbilder*, or 'Eye' paintings, as they were collectively titled, were fully established. The confidence that Nay had in this new motif is unmistakable. *Rhythmen und Kürzel* (Rhythm and Code, 1964; p.139), comprises a series of variations on the motif, done with a single, unhesitant paint application. Nay's own international reputation was at a peak, and there could be no more clear sign of the power and confidence of his vision of painting than the works that he made during this year.

216 E.W. Nay, draft for a foreword to the catalogue of the exhibition *E.W. Nay – 60 Jahre*, Museum Folkwang Essen, 1962, in *Lesebuch*, *op. cit.*, p.215.

217 'Meine Kunst macht eine neue Bewußtseinsstufe des Menschen sichtbar, in der heutige und kommende Mensch eine bisher unbekannte, neuartige Übereinkunft seiner selbst mit der Natur erlebt. Er erlebt sich und Natur als Universum – er verläßt die Subjektivation zugunsten seiner universalen Einheit'. Nay, 3 March 1963, *ibid.*, p.236.

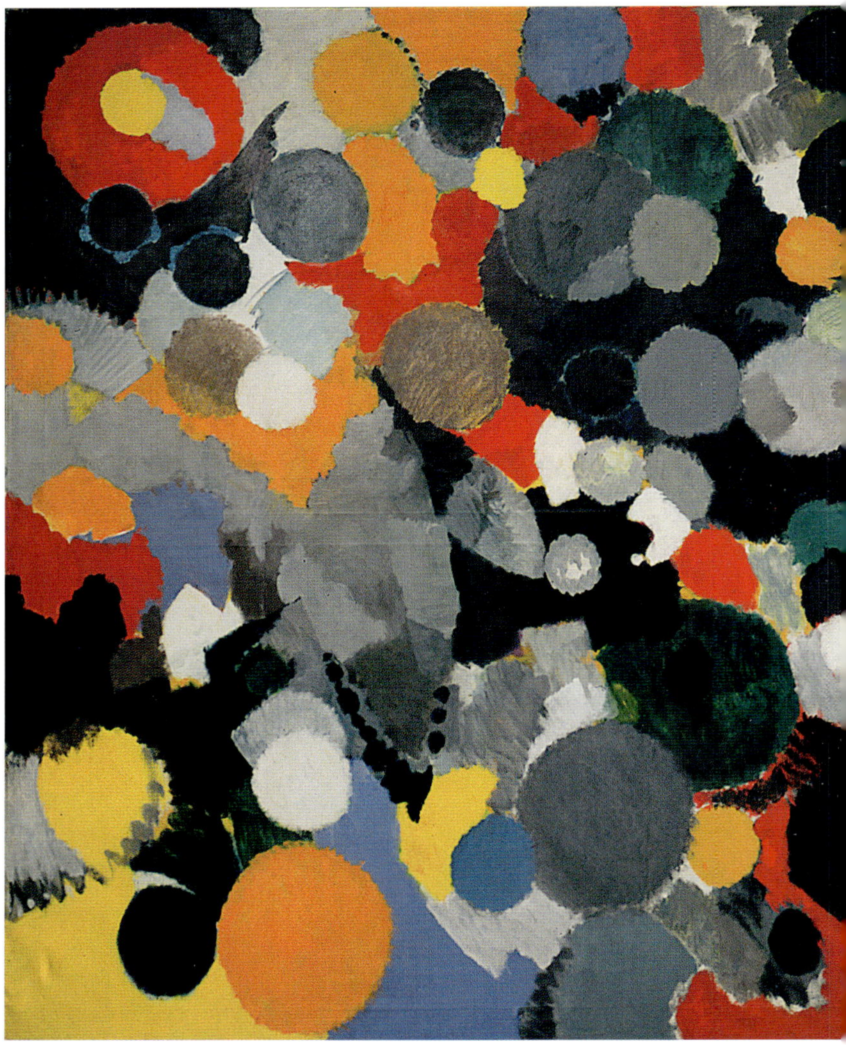

Das Freiburger Bild, 1956
Oil on canvas
255 × 655 cm · 100⅜ × 257⅞ in

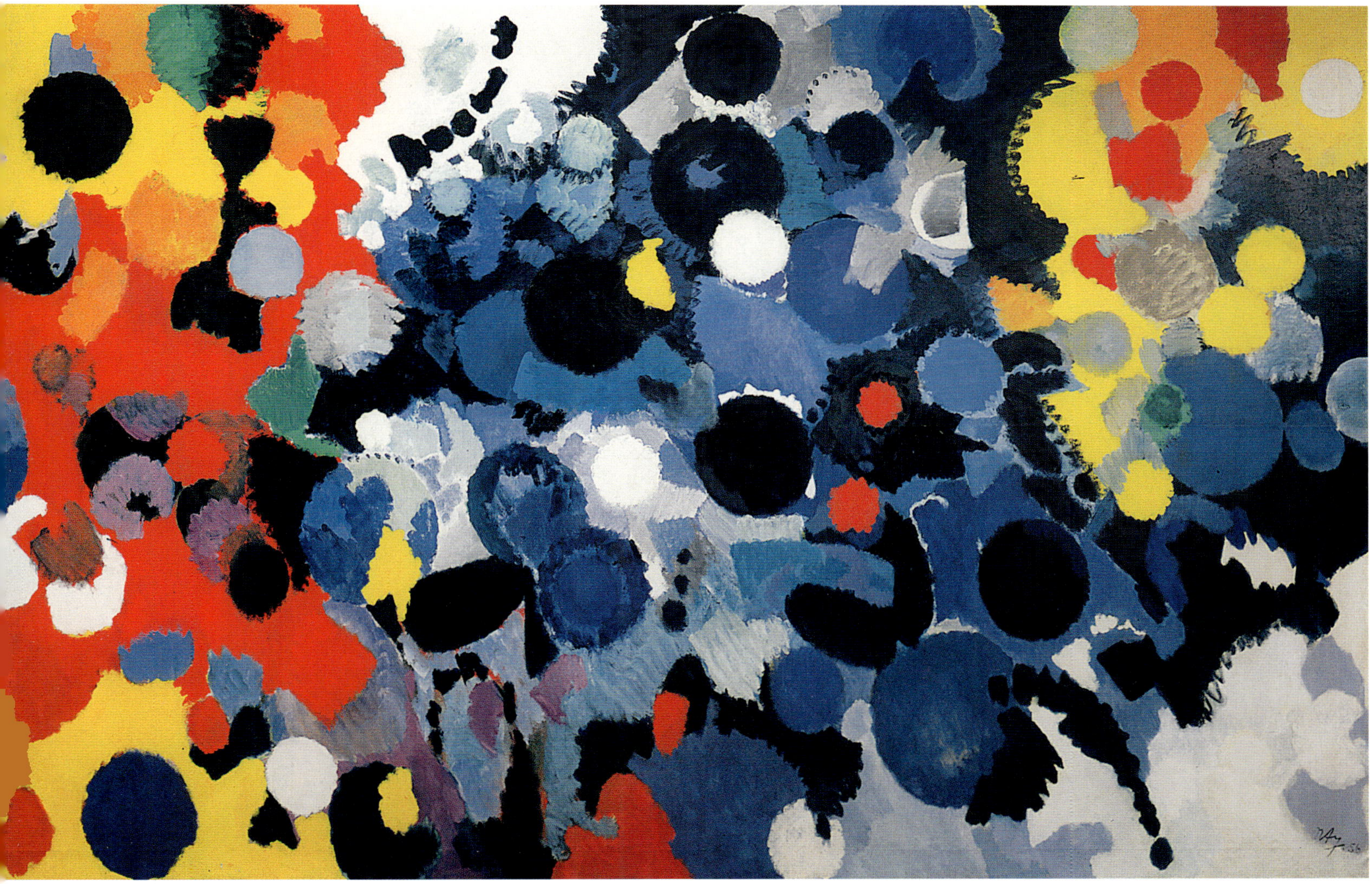

Sternbalance, 1956
Oil on canvas
125 × 200 cm · 49¼ × 78¾ in

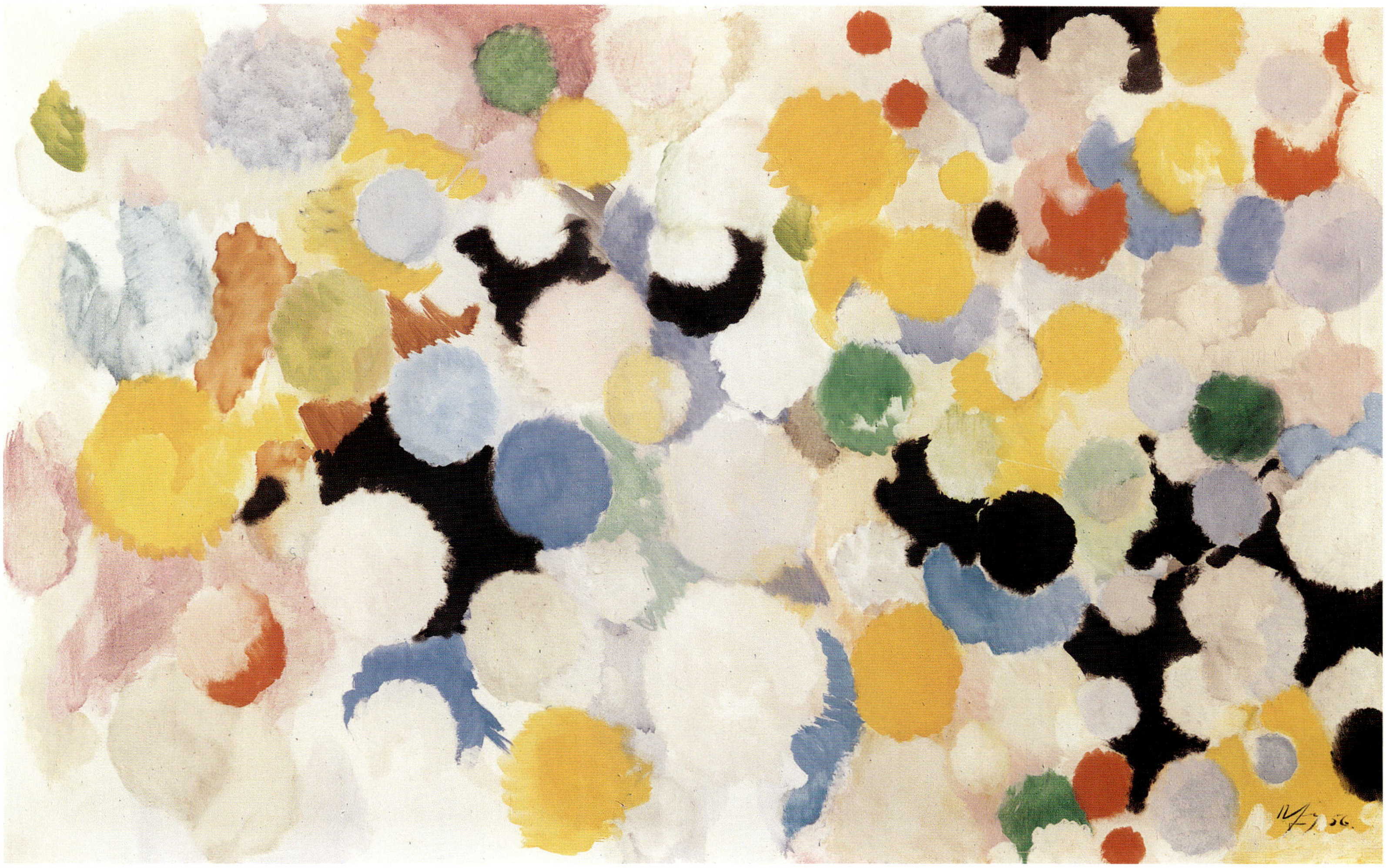

Diamant Rot, 1957
Oil on canvas
116 × 89.5 cm · 45⅝ × 35¼ in

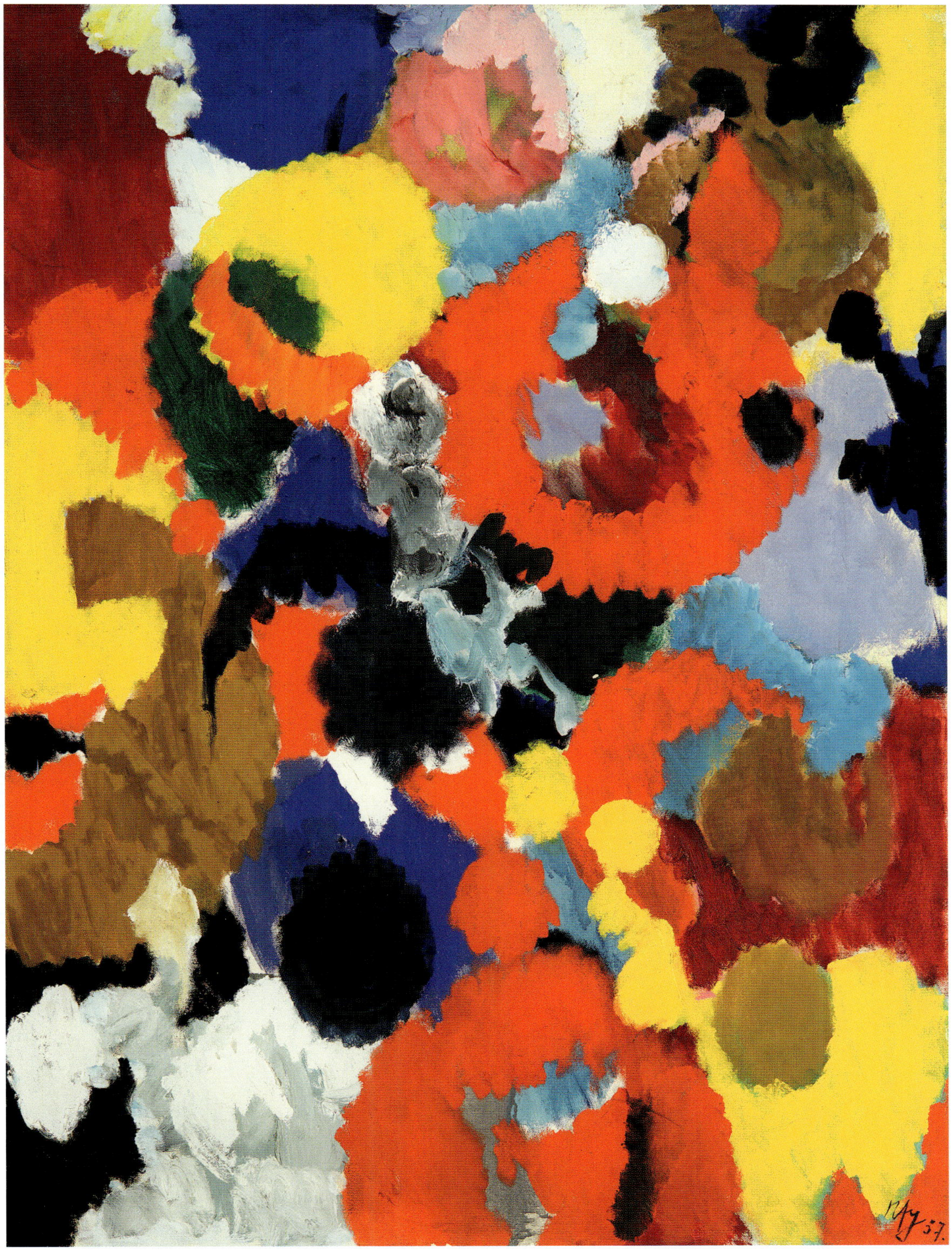

Rondo, 1958
Oil on canvas
89 × 116 cm · 35⅛ × 45⅝ in

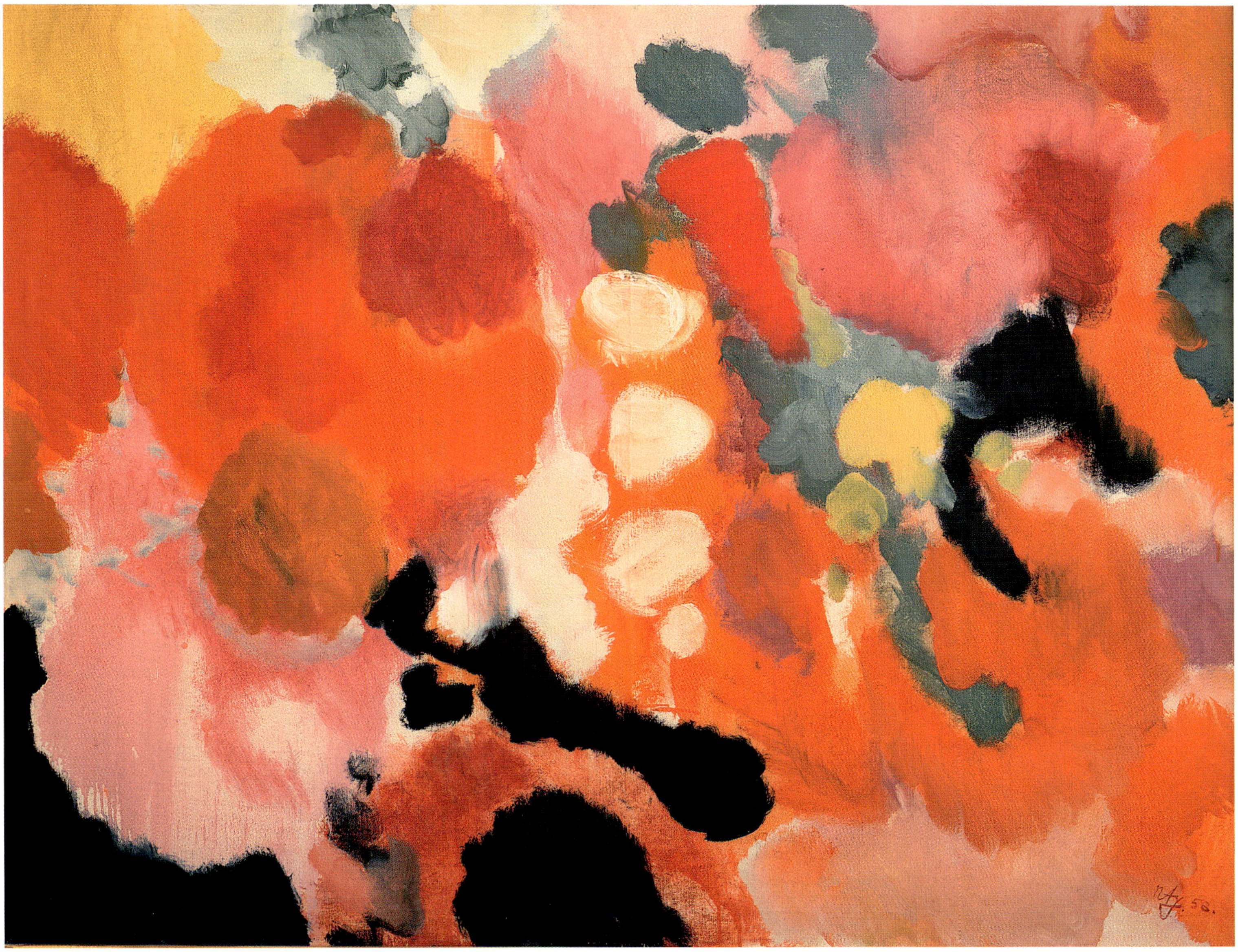

Parabel, 1958
Oil on canvas
117 × 81.5 cm · 46⅛ × 32 in

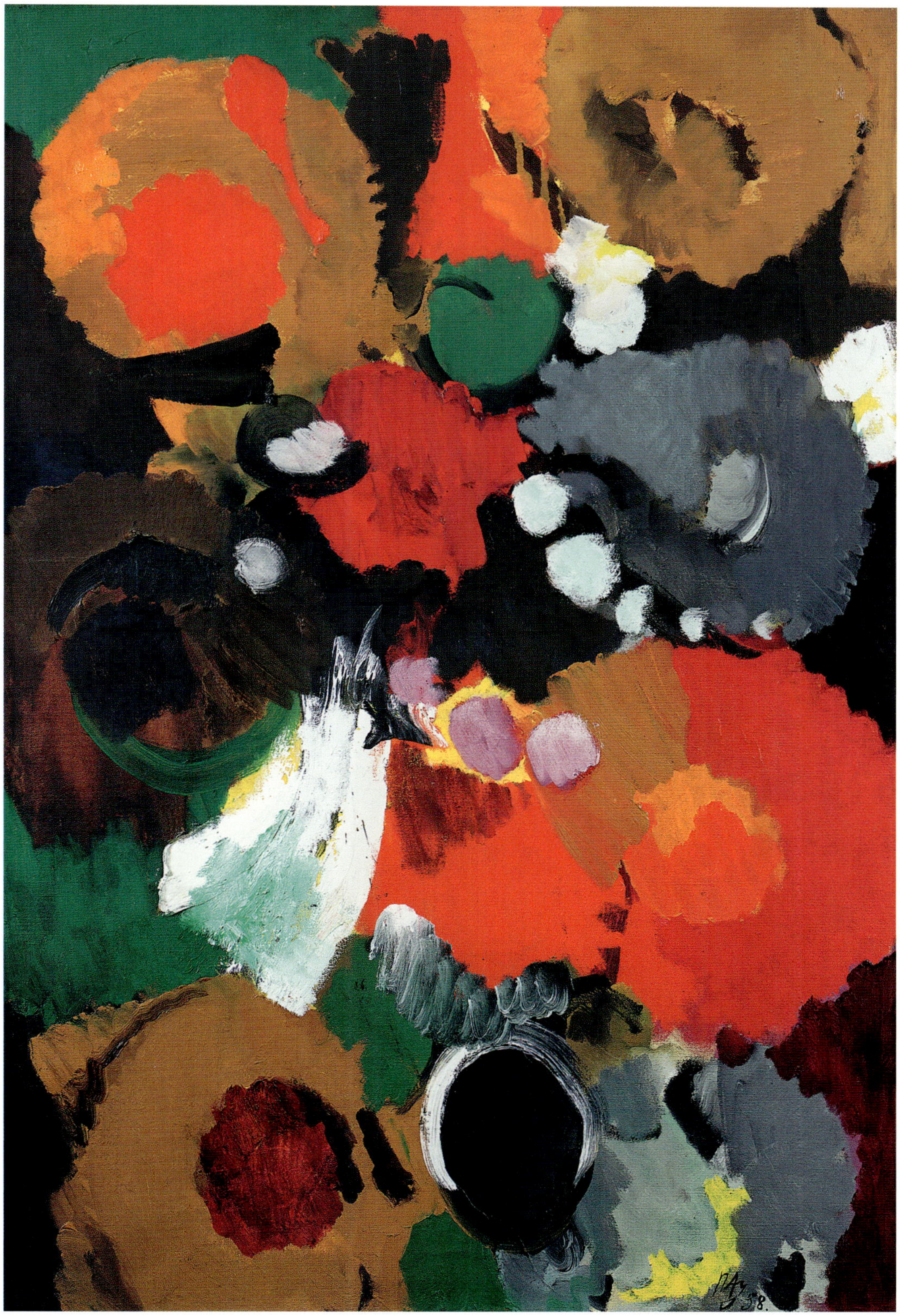

Metagrau, 1960
Oil on canvas
150 × 100 cm · 59⅛ × 39⅜ in

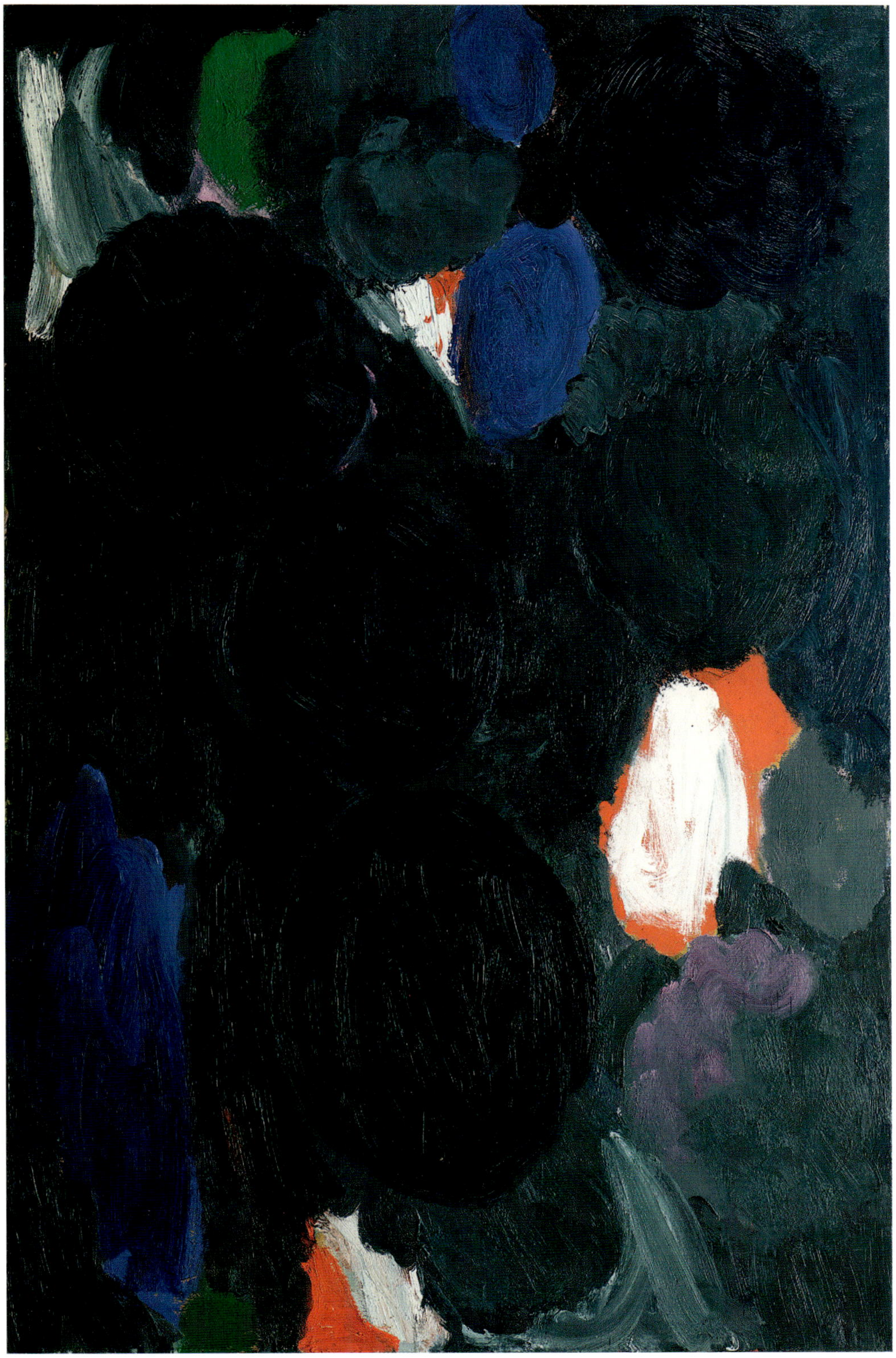

Lob des Grün, 1961
Oil on canvas
240 × 190 cm · 94½ × 74¾ in

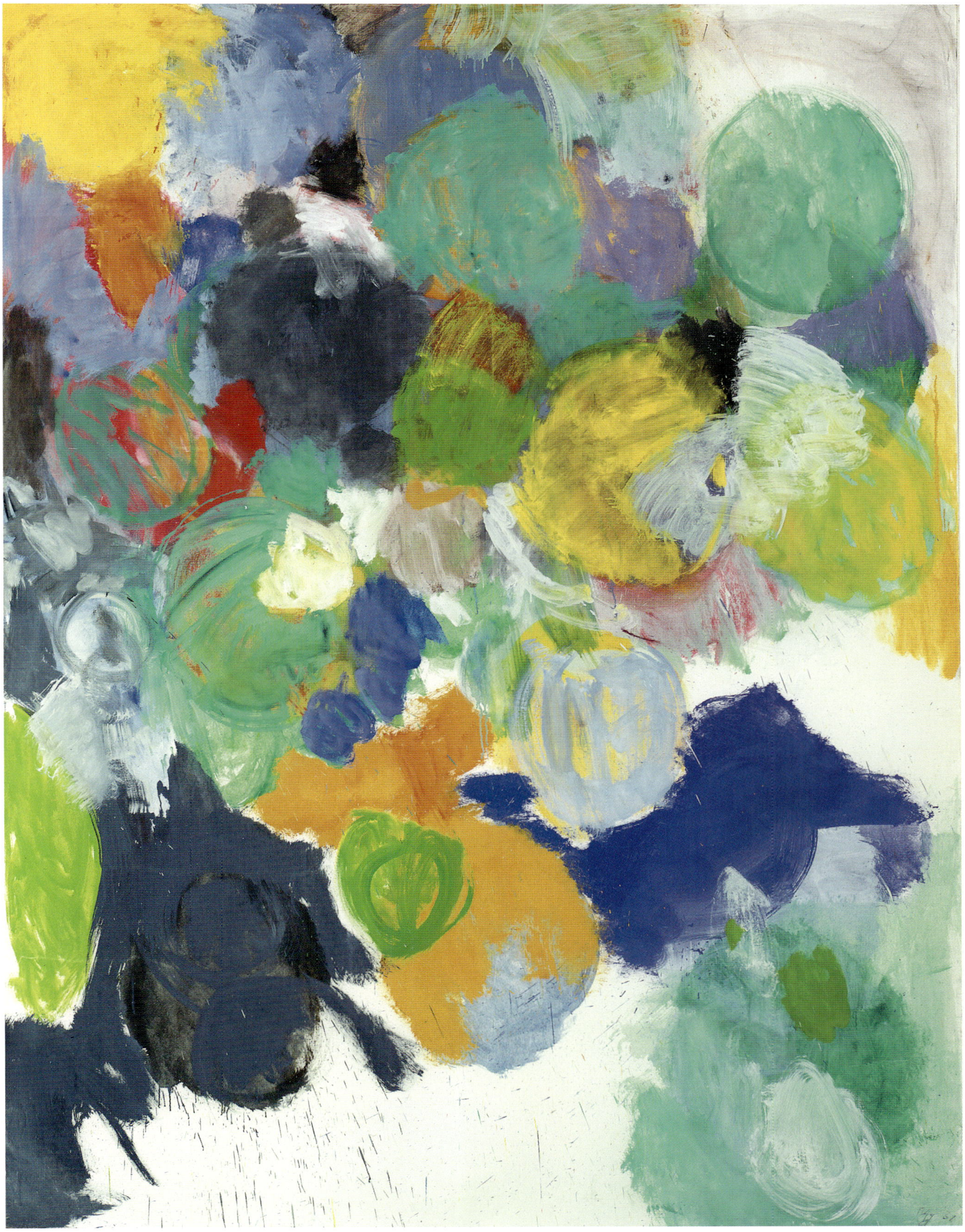

Rotklang, 1962
Oil on canvas
240 × 190 cm · 94½ × 74¾ in

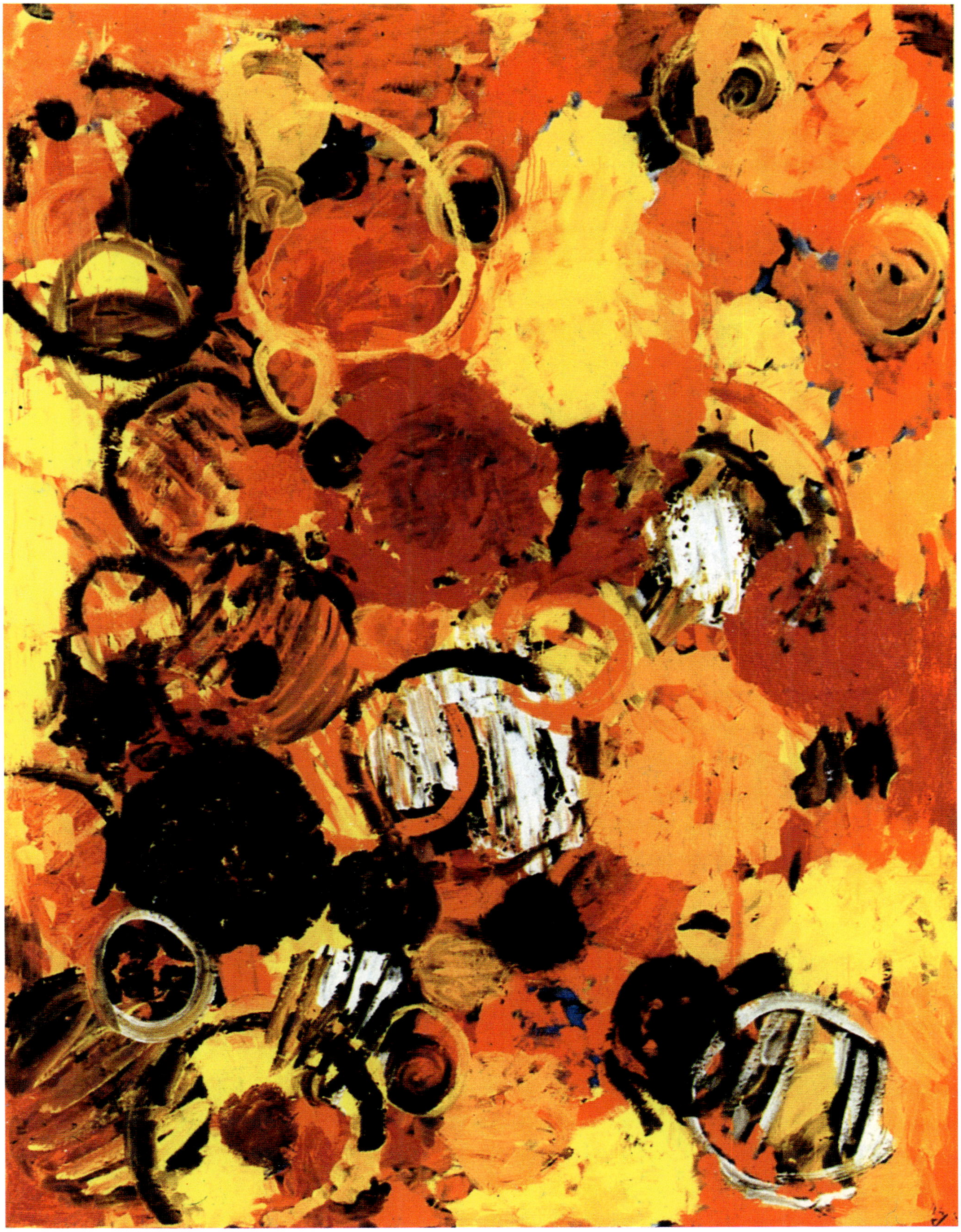

Weiße Quelle, 1963
Oil on canvas
140 × 200 cm · 55⅛ × 78¾ in

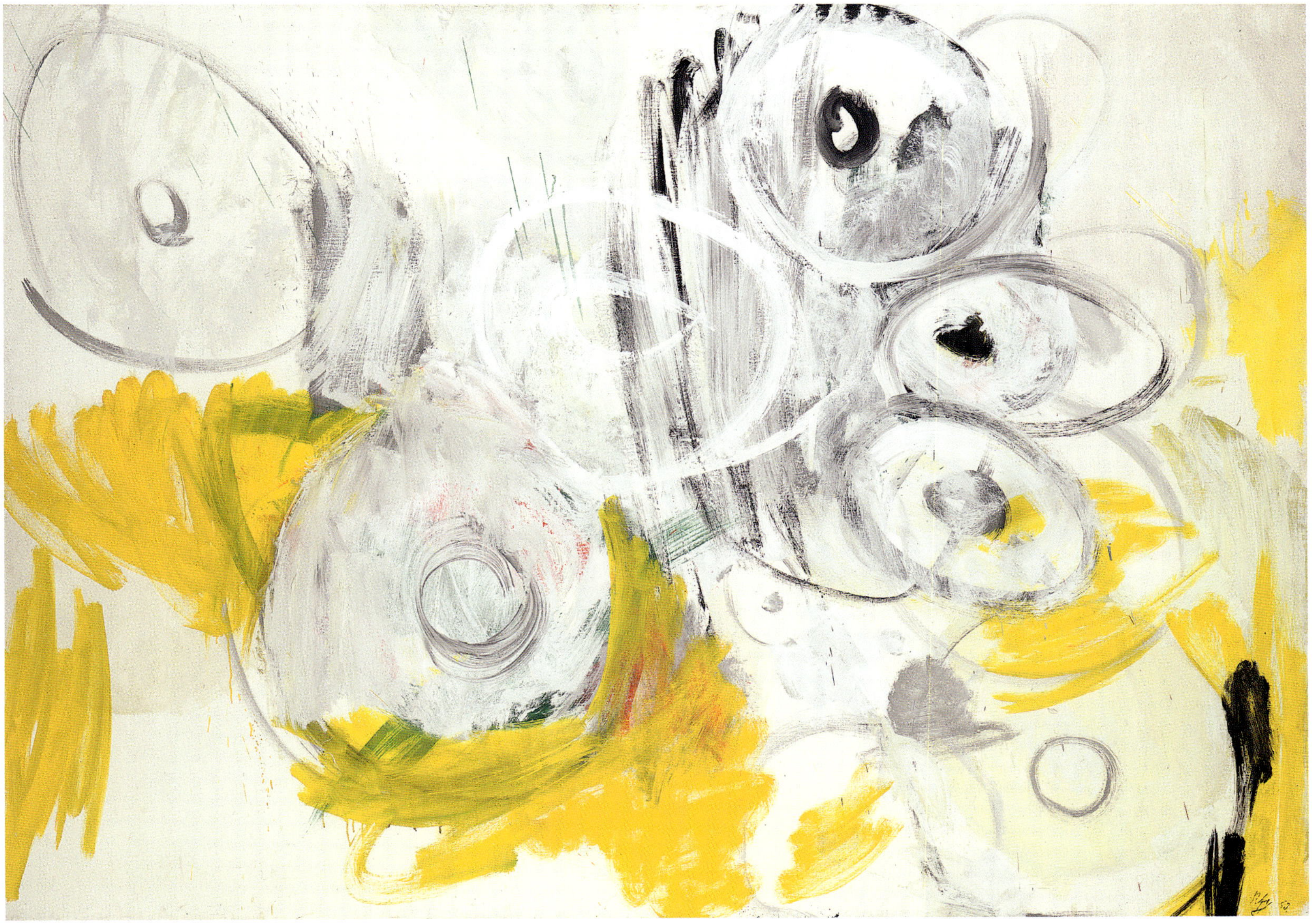

Rhythmen und Kürzel, 1964
Oil on canvas
200 × 160 cm · 78¾ × 63 in

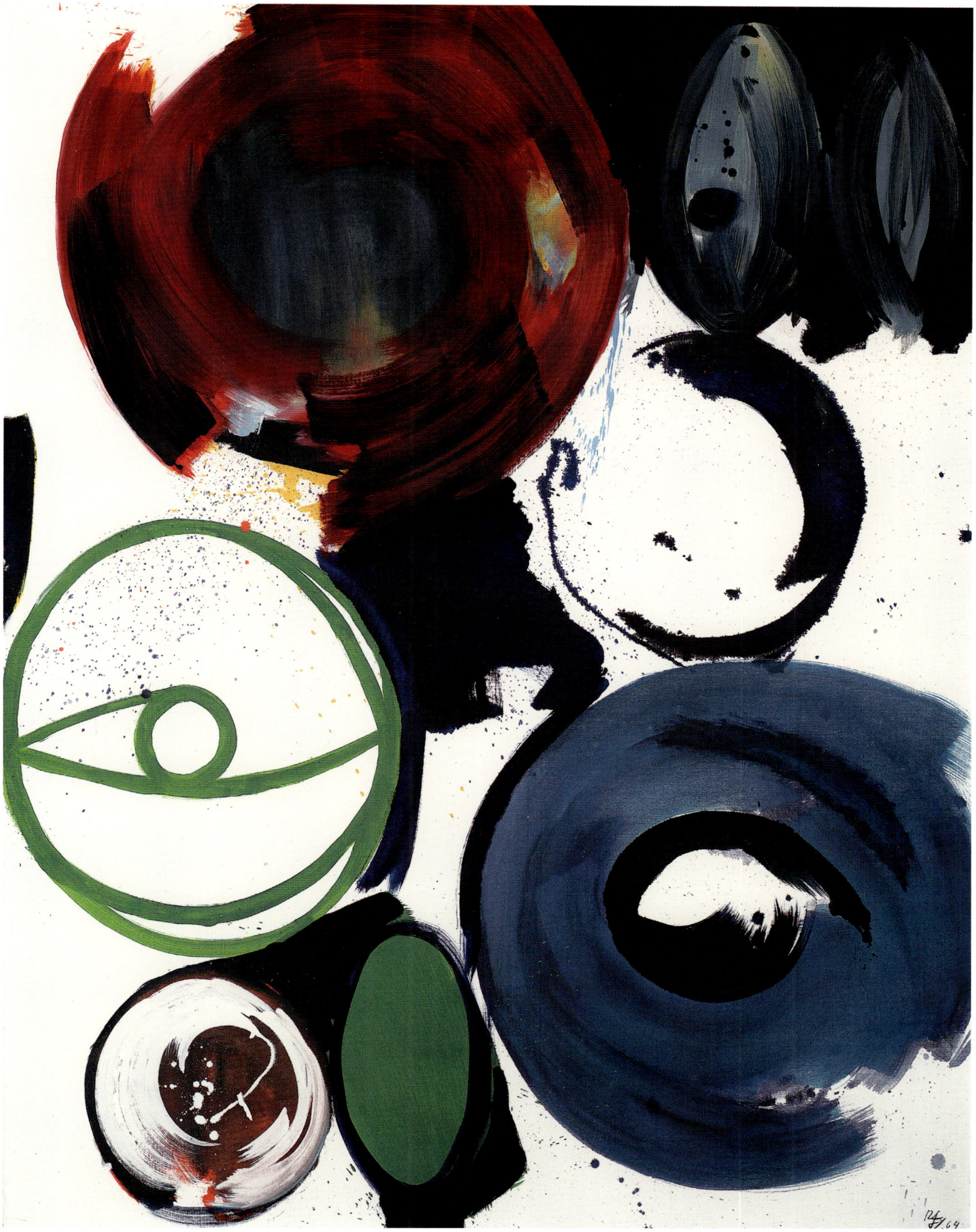

1964 and After

1964 was a crucial year for art in postwar Europe. A new generation of artists was emerging with the intention of turning everything on its head. In Düsseldorf Gerhard Richter was developing a form of painting using printed sources and a 'photographic' technique. In the same city, since the late 1950s the Zero Group had pioneered new forms of sculpture, painting and performance, claiming a new beginning for art – a postwar renaissance. In Berlin, Georg Baselitz was creating his 'Hero' paintings, monumental battle-scarred figures wandering through ruined landscapes. An international group of artists, writers and musicians were coming together under the banner of Fluxus for performances and happenings, such as the Aachen 'Festival of New Art' in the summer of 1964, where Beuys was a prominent participant. Figurative art was back, as well as a realism that looked not to nineteenth-century precedents but to the popular culture of everyday life. These two new movements were given extensive coverage at the important exhibition *Neue Realisten & Pop Art* (New Realism & Pop Art), shown first in The Hague and Vienna, and then at the end of 1964 in Berlin, which documented the shift towards a new, often satirical spirit of popular culture in art.

1964 was also a pivotal year for Nay, witnessing the most important exhibition of his work during his lifetime, the display of three large canvases at Documenta III. They appeared in the section of the exhibition titled *Bild und Skulptur im Raum* (Paintings and Sculptures in Space), and in the catalogue were collectively titled 'Drei Bilder im Raum' (Three Paintings in Space).[218] The daring display of the canvases, hung at angles from the ceiling, to be viewed as a continuous band, was the idea of the exhibition's organiser Arnold Bode. As Dirk Schwarze has pointed out, the radical 'skying' of the paintings was intended to reflect Nay's own stellar reputation.[219] The artist was initially reluctant to respond to Bode's idea, and it was only at the insistence of the latter that he eventually produced the three canvases, measuring four metres square, significantly larger than any work to date. Titled *Documenta Bild A (Rot-Grün)* (Documenta Painting A (Red-Green)), *Documenta Bild B (Blau-Rot-Gelb)* (Documenta Painting B (Blue-Red-Yellow)), and *Documenta Bild C (Weiß-Schwarz-Grau)* (Documenta Painting C (White-Black-Grey); pp.141–43), they constitute the height of Nay's 'Eye' paintings phase, and are characterised by strongly differentiated, striking colour schemes in the first two of the series, and a predominantly black and white, graphic rendering in the final canvas. For the display, they were ordered *A*, *C*, *B*, so that the orange-yellow-green combination of *A* was separated from the blue-yellow-red of *B* by the quieter, more simple *C*.

The dramatic impression of the hanging can today only be surmised. One critic suggested a range of associations, from the eye of God, to the sense of oppressive surveillance famously conveyed in George Orwell's novel *1984*.[220] But one might also think of the

218 *Documenta III. Malerei und Skulptur*, exhibition catalogue, Fridericianum, Kassel, 1964, p.271.

219 D. Schwarze, *Die Kunst der Inszenierung, oder, als Arnold Bode Ernst Wilhelm Nay in den Himmel hob*, B. & S. Siebenhaar Verlag, Berlin, 2009, p.7. This short account of the genesis and reception of Nay's Documenta paintings was published following an exhibition at the Schirn Kunsthalle, Frankfurt, for which Bode's 1964 installation was reconstructed.

220 Wolfgang Rothe, article in *Sonntagsblatt*, 23 August 1964, *ibid.*, p.31.

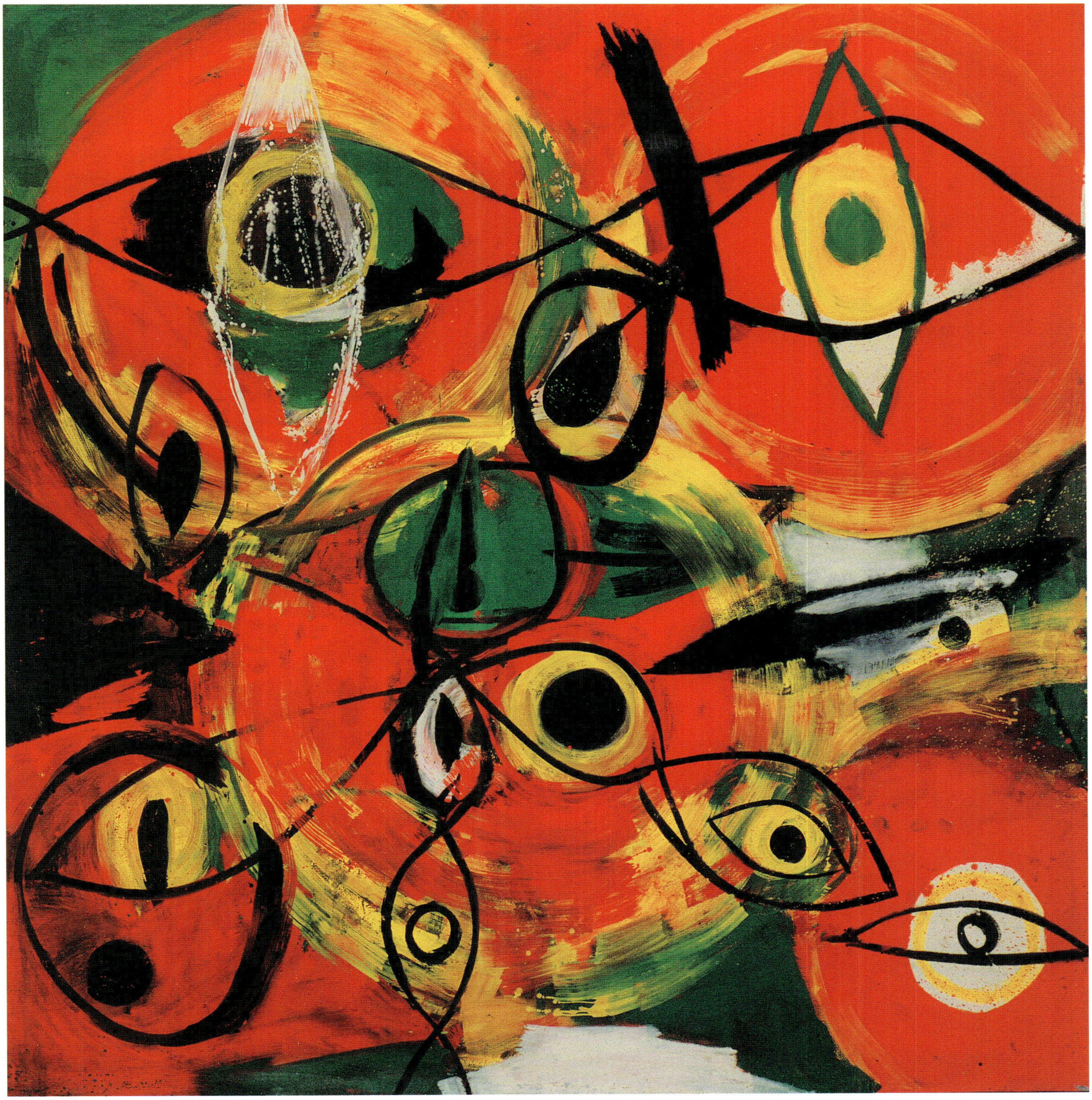

Documenta Bild A (Rot-Grün), 1964
Oil on canvas
396 × 396 cm · 155⅞ × 155⅞ in

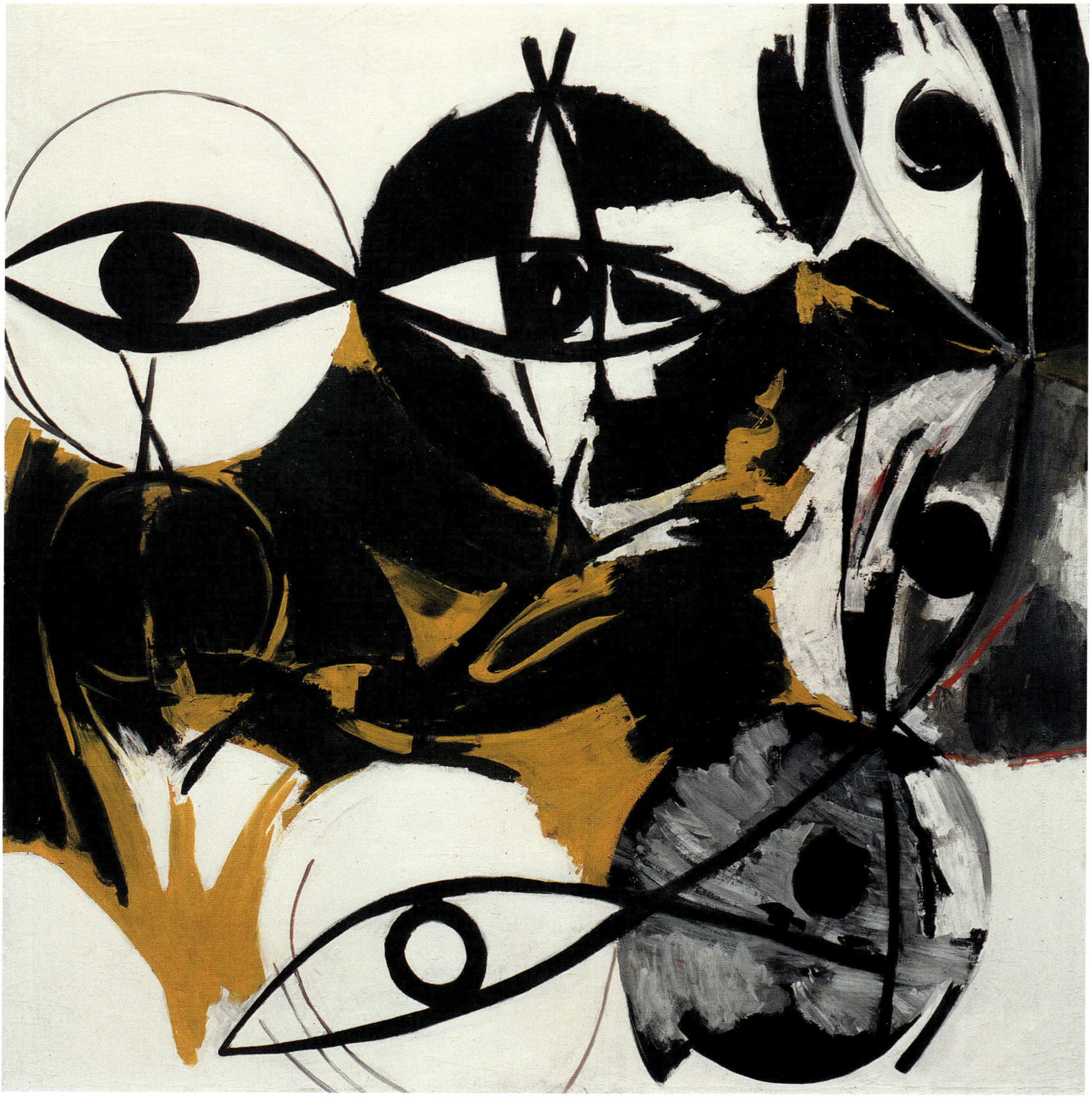

Documenta Bild C (Weiß-Schwarz-Grau),
1964
Oil on canvas
396 × 396 cm · 155⅞ × 155⅞ in

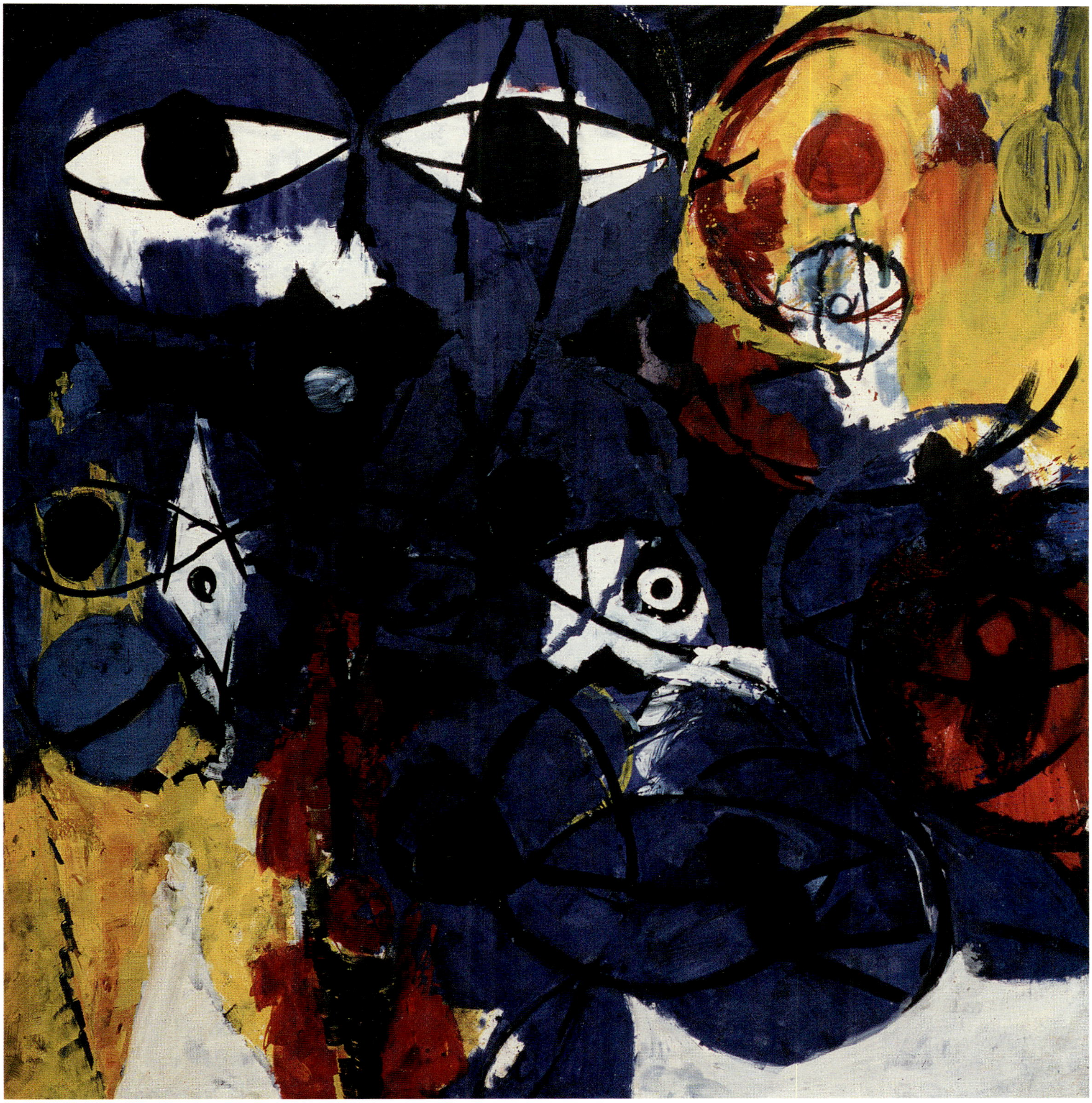

Documenta Bild B (Blau-Rot-Gelb), 1964
Oil on canvas
396 × 396 cm · 155⅞ × 155⅞ in

psychological scars of aerial warfare, and the Allied bombardment of German cities during the war. An ominous stillness is combined with a sense of oppressive threat. Siegfried Gohr has described the transition from the 'Disk' paintings to the 'Eye' paintings in cinematic terms: 'the speed of execution slows to the point that the disks, which had rotated freely and frictionless in the pictorial space, come to a standstill and seem to gaze at the viewer through enigmatic eyes'.[221] Certainly, the effect of this still, penetrating gaze would only have been increased by the unusual display.

Nay was represented in Documenta III by six further paintings from the 'Eye' paintings series: *Die Nacht* (The Night), *Traum* (Dream), *Himmelsrichtung* (Heavenward), from 1963, and *Quell* (Source), *Meteor* (Meteor) and *Das Licht* (The Light), from 1964. Six drawings were also included.[222] Bode's room, however, overshadowed these works, and indeed most other contributions to the exhibition. His intention was not necessarily to provoke public opinion, but rather to elevate German art to an international level, a programme that he had been pursuing since the first Documenta exhibition in 1955, where the main exhibition room was dominated by two paintings on opposing walls: Picasso's *Girl with a Mirror* (1932–33), and Fritz Winter's *Komposition vor Blau und Gelb* (Composition on Blue and Yellow, 1955). A similar tactic was pursued at the second Documenta by comparing Nay's *Freiburger Bild* with American works of a similar scale and abstract nature. When he commissioned the three paintings for the 1964 Documenta, he clearly had in mind as competition the three canvases completed by Sam Francis for the Kunsthalle, Basel, *Drei Wandbilder für das Treppenhaus in der Kunsthalle Basel* (Three Murals for the Stairway of Kunsthalle Basel, 1956–57), which he included in the 1964 exhibition in the Fridericianum, compelling visitors to judge the works alongside each other.

The uncompromising nature with which Bode pursued his programme could not in the end avoid controversy, although it was not from international critics, but from a German audience, that voices of dissent first arose. A critical article titled 'Nay's disks – a closer look at a typical German painter' by Hans Platschek was published in the newspaper *Die Zeit* in September 1964. Two years previously, Platschek had written a short book on contemporary painting, *Neue Figuration*, which promoted artists such as Wols, whose approach to abstraction was informed by Art Informel, rather than pursuing the 'absolute' abstraction of Nay. Platschek's prime target in his article was, however, not Nay's disks, nor his painting at all, but rather his reputation, the rhetoric around his work, and the uncritical response to it by an 'initiated' audience. This reputation was based on an ideology of transcendence, he held, shored up by a vague mystical language that Platschek exemplifies by quoting at length from Haftmann's 1960 monograph. The irrational, expressive dimension of Haftmann's text is scurrilously compared with that of the Nazi architect Paul Schultze-Naumburg, whose writings on racially pure art were an important part of Nazi cultural ideology. It was Nay's indifference to the contemporary state of Germany, and the official protection given to a 'backward-looking utopia' that invoked Platschek's ire (as well, it must be said, as the fact that his own works had not been selected for inclusion in the exhibition).[223]

The public debate triggered by Platschek's article was extensive. The painter and critic Klaus Jürgen-Fischer, who had published a review on Documenta III in *Die Zeit* in July 1964, was invited by the Berlin newspaper *Der Tagesspiegel* to sum up the debate, and produced an even more embittered attack on Nay's painting, in which he criticised in particular the attempt to reconnect with Expressionism.[224] From a later perspective the debate appears as an echo of the discussions around Expressionism in the 1930s, and part of broader disputes about 'transcendent' modes of painting in the postwar period. It brought nothing to an appreciation of any individual work by Nay, and was instead the focus for an attack by a younger generation on the conservative institutions of reconstruction; in this way, it was symptomatic of broader changes occurring in German cultural life. In some respects it was simply a sign of a gathering confidence, and a reaction to a period in which all efforts were directed towards reconstruction and levels of competition amongst artists were low. Platschek's concentration on Haftmann's prose also showed the degree to which Nay had exposed himself to *ad hominem* criticism by the ease with which he negotiated official culture; but such criticism left his work untouched, and may even be said to have acted as a stimulant. The dispute had both positive and negative outcomes: although it placed a strain on the artist, it meant that 'everyone was talking about Nay', and his own public standing increased significantly.[225] It should be stressed that it is impossible to understand the change in his work that took place around 1965, and all subsequent responses to it, without taking these reactions to his paintings of 1964 into account.

The distinction between criticism of the 'official' nature of Nay's art and an appreciation of its actual qualities was nowhere more evident than in the most extraordinary attack on Nay, from the English critic John Anthony Thwaites. In an article published in America in 1965, Thwaites mounted a bitter critique of postwar German art, on the basis of its servility to foreign influences (unwittingly echoing the conservative criticism of those such as Carl Vinnen at the beginning of the century), its repression of personal expression, and its dependence on official promotion of second-rate artists. Nay, Thwaites wrote, is the 'chief of all class B celebrities'.[226] 'He is the darling of the Hollow Men of the museums and the art historians, who play a unique part in the German art world.' Thwaites refers to Nay's retrospective exhibition at the Frankfurter Kunstverein earlier in 1965, noting that it demonstrated his 'popularity in circles of power'. Although his ability to handle 'large

221 S. Gohr, 'Ernst Wilhelm Nay – Ein Essay', in *Ernst Wilhelm Nay*, exhibition catalogue, Stedelijk Museum, Amsterdam, 1998, p.32.
222 *Frau mit Spiegel* (1947), *Handzeichnung* (1964), *Ohne Titel* (1961), *Handzeichnung* (1964), *Paar* (1947) and *Handzeichnung* (1956).
223 See Alfred Hentzen, 'Was heißt "künstlerische Weltgeltung"? Zu Platscheks Kritik an E.W. Nay', in *Die Welt*, 3 October 1964. See *E.W. Nay, 1902–1968: Bilder und Dokumente*, *op. cit.*, 1980, pp.257–59.
224 Klaus Jürgen-Fischer, 'Der Fall des Malers E.W. Nay – Ein heftig geführter Beitrag zu einer heftigen Diskussion', in *Der Tagesspiegel*, Berlin, 5 November 1964, *ibid.*, pp.255–57.
225 Elisabeth Nay-Scheibler, 'Without a Filter – Memories of the Final Years', in Pfeiffer, *op. cit.*, p.28.
226 John Anthony Thwaites, 'Germany: Prophets without honour', in *Art in America*, vol.53, no.6, 1965, pp.110–15.

polychrome areas, keeping the sharpest contrasts well in equilibrium' gives his painting an 'air of authority', and allies him with the 'decorative painters of the past', it is nevertheless based on a 'trick of borrowing'. Thwaites's criticism dissolves when he attempts to describe the paintings aside from the condition of their reception. The 'trick of borrowing' is nothing less than the normal list of influences by which any modern painter (with the exception of Picasso) might be described. 'His sources are as various as Nolde, Beckmann and Kandinsky, and a series of 1964 leans heavily on late Picasso. Yet the assimilation to Nay's manner is impeccable.' For Thwaites, this indicates neglect of 'creative talent', although the point is not developed. In the final count, Thwaites's article, like Platschek's, constituted an attack not on Nay's painting (which both obliquely praise), but on his reputation.

Those artists whom Thwaites saw as a remedy to the 'official culture' of postwar art were necessarily of the younger generation, such as Richter. The shift in climate was certainly evident at the third Documenta exhibition. For the first time, works by a second generation of postwar American artists were on public view, notably Robert Rauschenberg, represented by two paintings, *Axle* (1964) and *Exile* (1962), and Jasper Johns, with three paintings, *Periscope (Hart Crane)* (1963), *Flag in Orange Field* (1957) and *Highway* (1959). The new relation to reality proposed in such works formed an explicit criticism of the expressive abstraction of those, such as Pollock and Nay, whose paintings posited a different kind of reality and a different kind of relation. Yet however one may want to characterise the 'new realists', there was one important characteristic of their work to which Nay was uniquely attuned to respond: the direct, unsentimental nature of their relation to the lived moment. It is on this basis that the transition in Nay's work around 1965 is best explained.

This change was, alongside the shift into 'absolute' abstraction in the late 1940s, the most dramatic that Nay had undergone. The 'Elemental' paintings, as they came to be known, of the three final years of his life, are characterised by large flat areas of even colour, and simple yet highly evocative and unique forms that appear sometimes biological and elsewhere more emblematic. As Ingrid Pfeiffer has pointed out, the 'Elemental' paintings are to an extent a resolution of the demand first raised in *Vom Gestaltwert der Farbe* for colour and form to be indistinguishable[227] – in other words, for a sense and feeling for colour to determine in a profound way the extent and topology of the painting's appearance.

The emergence of these works signals the resolution of many of Nay's concerns, but one in particular – the attempt to create a direct and actual image, rather than one that deferred in any way to illusion, or acted as a symbol of anything apart from itself. Any hint of illusion through the accident of paint application is dispensed with. In an important document written whilst staying on Crete in 1965, Nay described this as a 'non-academic, autodidactic art' that could be characterised as romantic, rather than classical, and could be compared with Natural Science, but also with the self-evident truths of mathematics.[228] Nay termed such a form of painting 'concrete', setting it against the 'realisms' of the day: Surrealism, Pop art and Op art. Only a concrete art that did not attempt to access reality through representation could claim to be relevant to the 'scientific age' that Nay defined as the present.[229] Nevertheless, as we have seen, such distinctions count for little, and it was his ability to respond positively to the shift in climate in 1964, rather than retrench himself further in the gestural abstraction of the 'Disk' paintings, that gives the 'Elemental' paintings their value.

The format and appearance of the 'Elemental' paintings was swiftly developed in variations that appear to present either closed or open forms. *Nachtblau* (Night-Blue, 1965; p.147) features two dark blue oculiform configurations floating on a black ground, and a white organic mass that suggests bioluminescence. Cooler colour combinations and a thin paint application, which in places appears almost like an ink stain, give a brooding quality to such works. Other paintings, by contrast, create a strong sense of openness and luminescence, such as the large work *Der Morgen* (The Morning, 1965; p.148–49), commissioned for the Schulkollegium, Münster. *Der Morgen* is a late manifesto painting, a summary of the pictorial ideas that Nay developed in the final three years of his life. Vertical bands of repeated forms defined by a single, unmixed colour move with a steady rhythm across the canvas, pushing forward into the space of the viewer, rather than suggesting a pictorial space – the painterly space stops at the white surface of the canvas.

The 'Elemental' paintings with the most startlingly reduced format can be seen the next year, with works such as *Gelb mit blauem Band* (Yellow with Blue Band, 1966), contrasting a cool grey band and white motifs on a bright yellow background, and to an even further extreme with *Sinus* (Sinus, 1966; p.151), showing a central very dark brown form abutted by two abbreviated yellow forms, implying circles or loops cut by the canvas edge. Pfeiffer has described the environmental quality of the 'Elemental' paintings, showing how each implies an extension into the surrounding space; it is in this way that the monumentality of Nay's previous work is transformed in images that seem to modify, rather than add to, the space in which they are displayed. Nay himself referred to this dilatory quality as 'open Nomadic', a type of borderless expansion that equated with freedom.[230] He may have been thinking back to the philosophy of borders developed by Carl Schmitt in his *Land und Meer* (Land and Sea), or to his early experiences in Bornholm, or on the Baltic coast; or to any of the freedoms of his early years, free from political or material burdens.

Indeed, although there appears on the surface some congruence between the flat, clearly defined forms of the 'Elemental' paintings and the work of Hard Edge painters such as the German artist Karl Georg Pfahler, or the American Ellsworth Kelly, on close inspection there is little that is 'hard' in Nay's forms. The thin paint application contains many subtleties of gradation, and the edges of his forms are uneven, drawn by hand. The large polychromatic areas to which Thwaites had referred were ultimately defined by an older tradition of oil painting, rather than the pop effect of acrylics. Nay

227 Ingrid Pfeiffer, 'E.W. Nay – Topicality and Timelessness', in Pfeiffer, *op. cit.*, pp.7–17.
228 E.W. Nay, notes made while staying on Crete, June 1965, in *Lesebuch*, *op. cit.*, p.263.
229 *Ibid.*, p.265.
230 *Ibid.*, p.279.

himself gave a trenchant description of the spiritual, decorative quality of these works when in 1965 he remembered a combination of influences that he had felt during his twenties: Henri Matisse and Casper David Friedrich. 'The artist of pure form, and the pure magical artist.'[231] Three other painters whom Nay cites as having influenced his late works were also from an older generation: Robert Delaunay, in his Orphist paintings, dealt with natural appearances and colour values in the same way, whereas František Kupka and Otto Freundlich are also invoked as forerunners of a type of abstract painting that mixed analytical with mystical goals.[232]

Nay's productivity in the last few years of his life was extraordinary. The simplicity of the format of the 'Elemental' paintings allowed for numerous variations, and the sense of a new image-world opening up. The titles become increasingly descriptive of the works, rather than suggesting an interpretation. The pageant-like quality of *Doppelspindel-Blau* (Double-Spindle-Blue, 1967; p.153) is typical of the best works from this period, where colour and form are precisely calibrated to provide the maximum of evocation with the minimum of representation. Nay continued to experiment with different ways of applying the broad flat areas of paint, taking particular care to avoid any rigidly decorative effect, as with *Phiole* (Phial, 1967;). The remarkable innovation of this series continued into the final year, with paintings such as *Polychromatisch II* (Polychromatic II, 1968; p.155), developed from a painting completed the previous year, and evolving an entirely new palette that suggested yet another new departure.

The 'Elemental' paintings constitute a synthesis of Nay's exploration of painting's flatness and decorative qualities, a combination of the intuitive and analytical sides of his personality. Yet they also reveal his sense of something coming to an end. The influx of American art, and the end of a European model were associated with the passing of an older idea of painting. Nay could not accept popular culture as a source for serious art; he saw it as a turn to 'banality', for which both America and England were responsible.[233] Pop art and its cognates were at best symptoms of a shift away from outmoded ideas of pathos, idealism and transcendence, clearing the way for a new type of art. Against this was set a tradition of abstract painting, defined by the therapeutic task of revealing to man his own humanity. Only at the end of his life was Nay able to reduce his thinking about painting to this simple formulation, recalling Heidegger's powerful description of art as a moment of nature becoming aware of itself. 'Humanity steps into the light of day nowhere more clearly than in the liberating discoveries of abstract painting', he wrote.[234]

Nay died on 8 April 1968. At his funeral Haftmann related a comment that the artist had made just a few weeks earlier, when Haftmann had said what a dark day it would be to hear of the death of Picasso. Nay disagreed – 'he said that every true painter dies and is reborn with each painting they make, because each painting should be invested with life and render the death of the individual as a mere biological misfortune'.[235] That for Nay, life and art were inseparable was clear to Haftmann. Indeed, that his final paintings seemed themselves to contain the sense of an ending, had filled Haftmann with anxiety at the end of the previous year, since they appeared to herald Nay's death. Haftmann had last seen Nay in Berlin, when he had shown him his new museum – the Neue Nationalgalerie, designed by Mies van der Rohe. But the last great work heralding a new era of museums, collecting, and display was not to be – for the first time Nay was not there, living in the moment, in the *Jetztzeit*.

231 *Ibid.*, p.265. A large collage by Matisse, *La Perruche et la Sirène*, had been included in Documenta III.
232 *Ibid.*, p.274. Delaunay's influence on German painting in the early years of the century was marked.
233 *Ibid.*, p.315.
234 *Ibid.*, p.316. 'Der Mensch tritt nie deutlicher zutage, als in der freiesten Erfindung der Abstraktion.'
235 Werner Haftmann, 'Totenrede für Nay', Cologne, 10 April 1968. Reprinted in *E.W. Nay, 1902–1968*, *op. cit.*, pp.231–32.

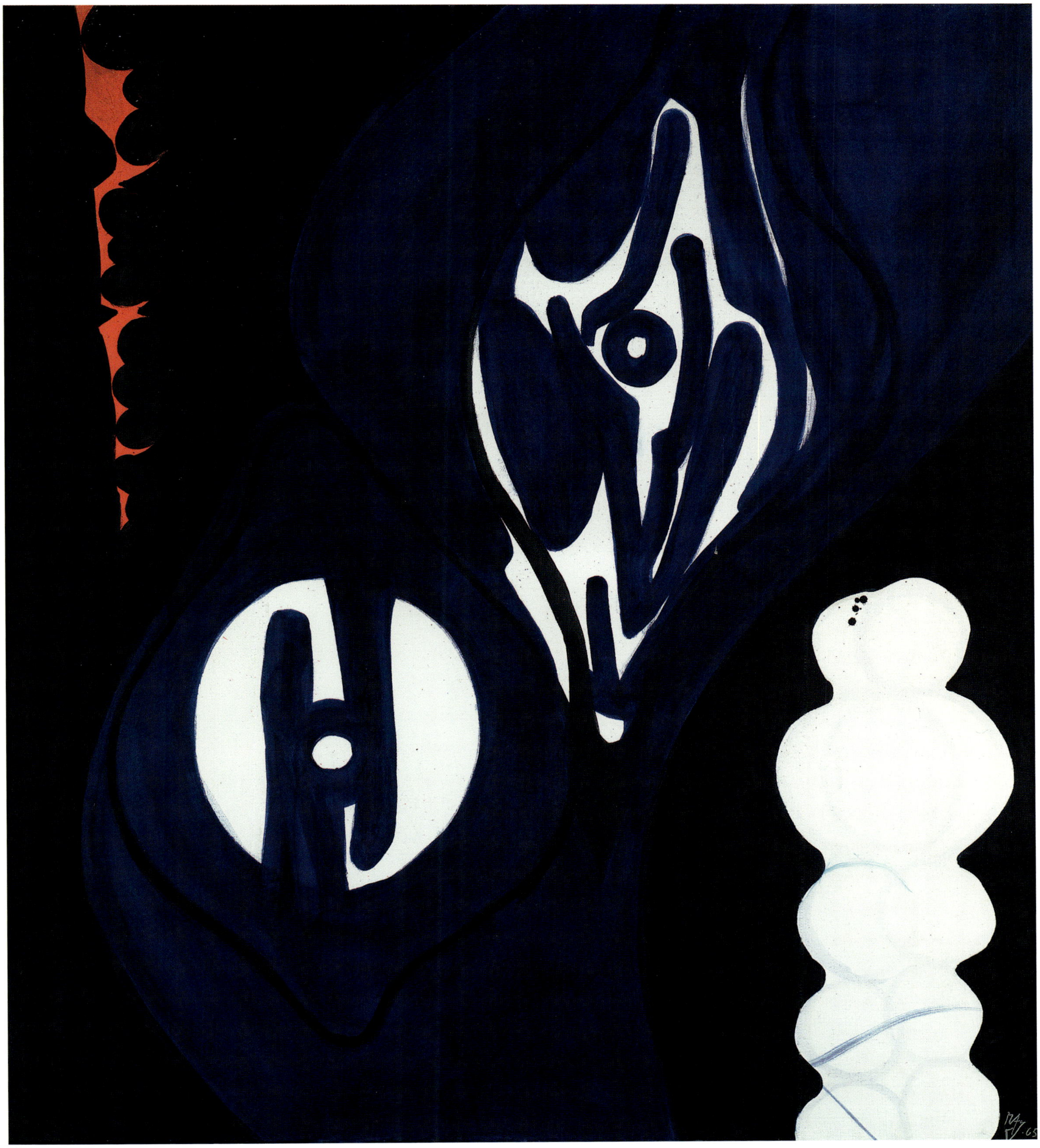

Nachtblau, 1965
Oil on canvas
162 × 150 cm · 63¾ × 59⅛ in

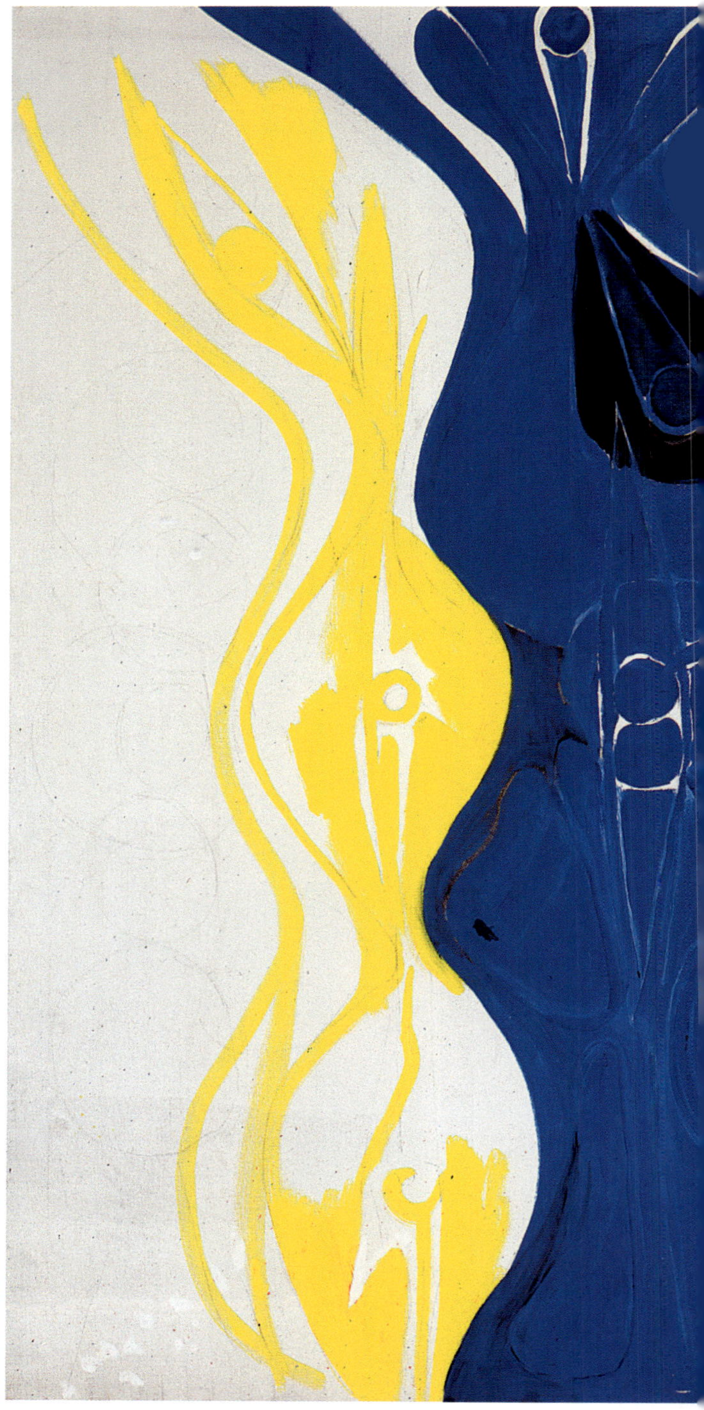

Der Morgen, 1965
Oil on canvas
190 × 340 cm · 74¾ × 133⅞ in

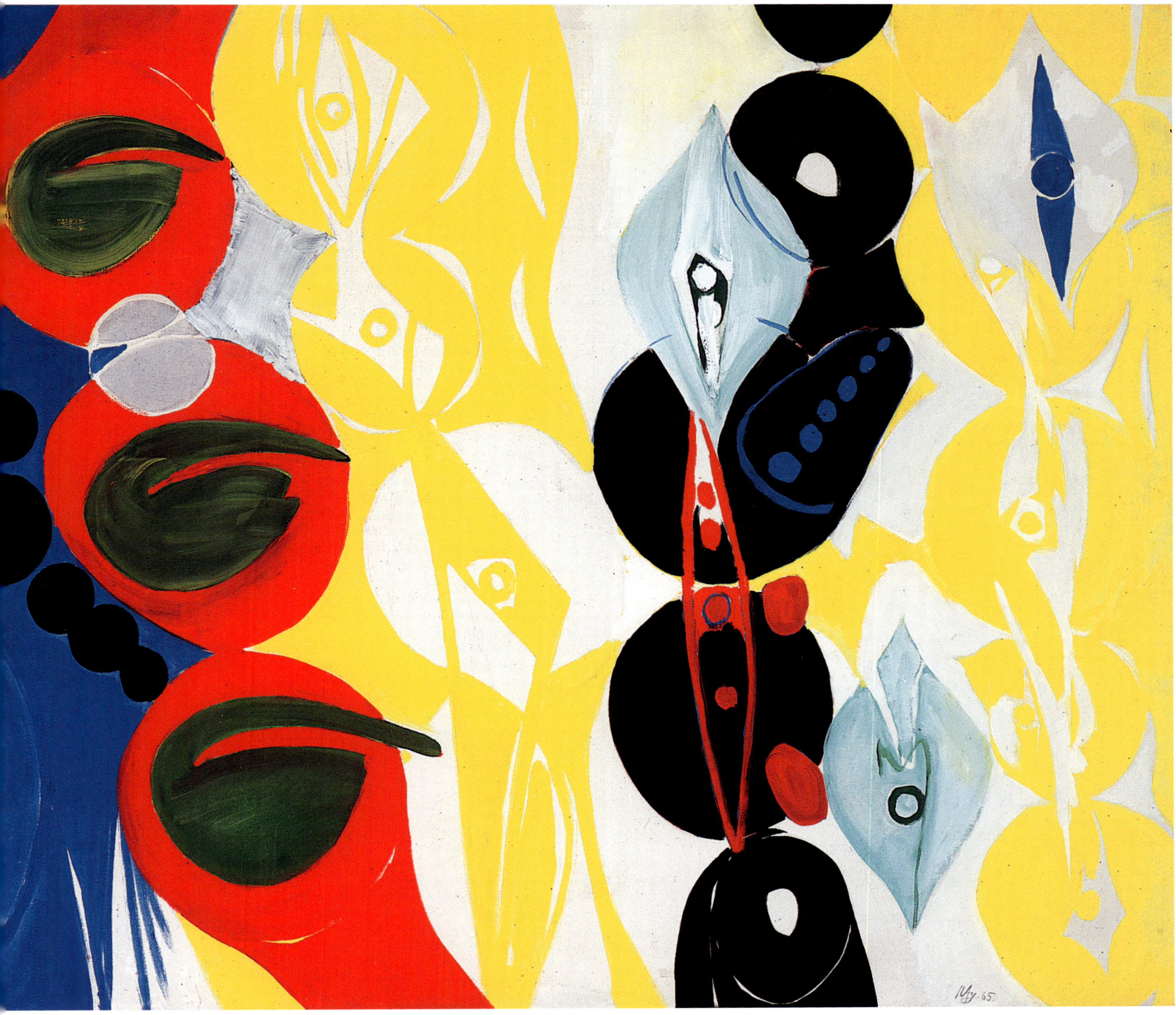

Sinus, 1966
Oil on canvas
162 × 150 cm · 63¾ × 59⅛ in

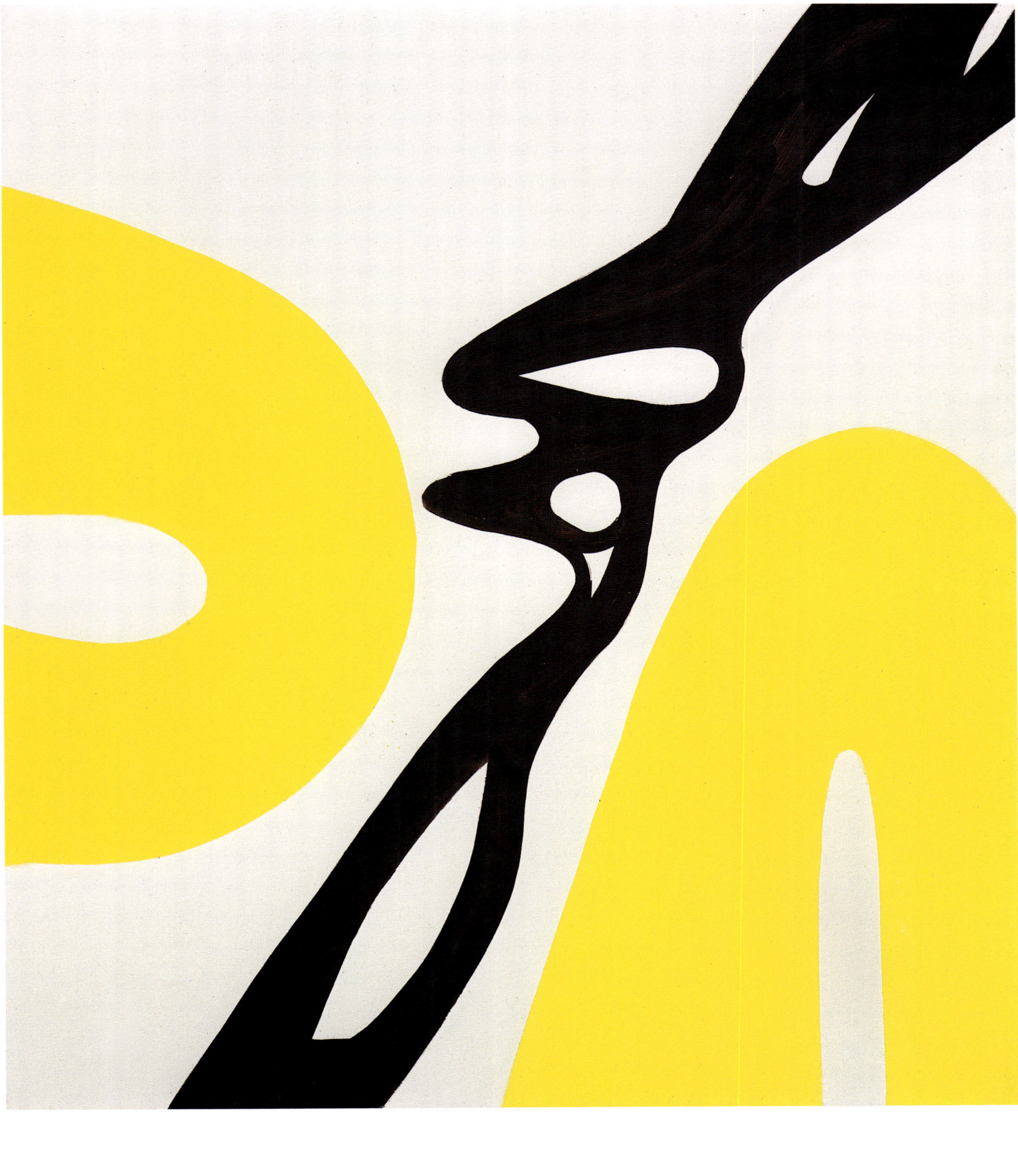

Doppelspindel – Blau, 1967
Oil on canvas
200 × 192 cm · 78¾ × 75⅝ in

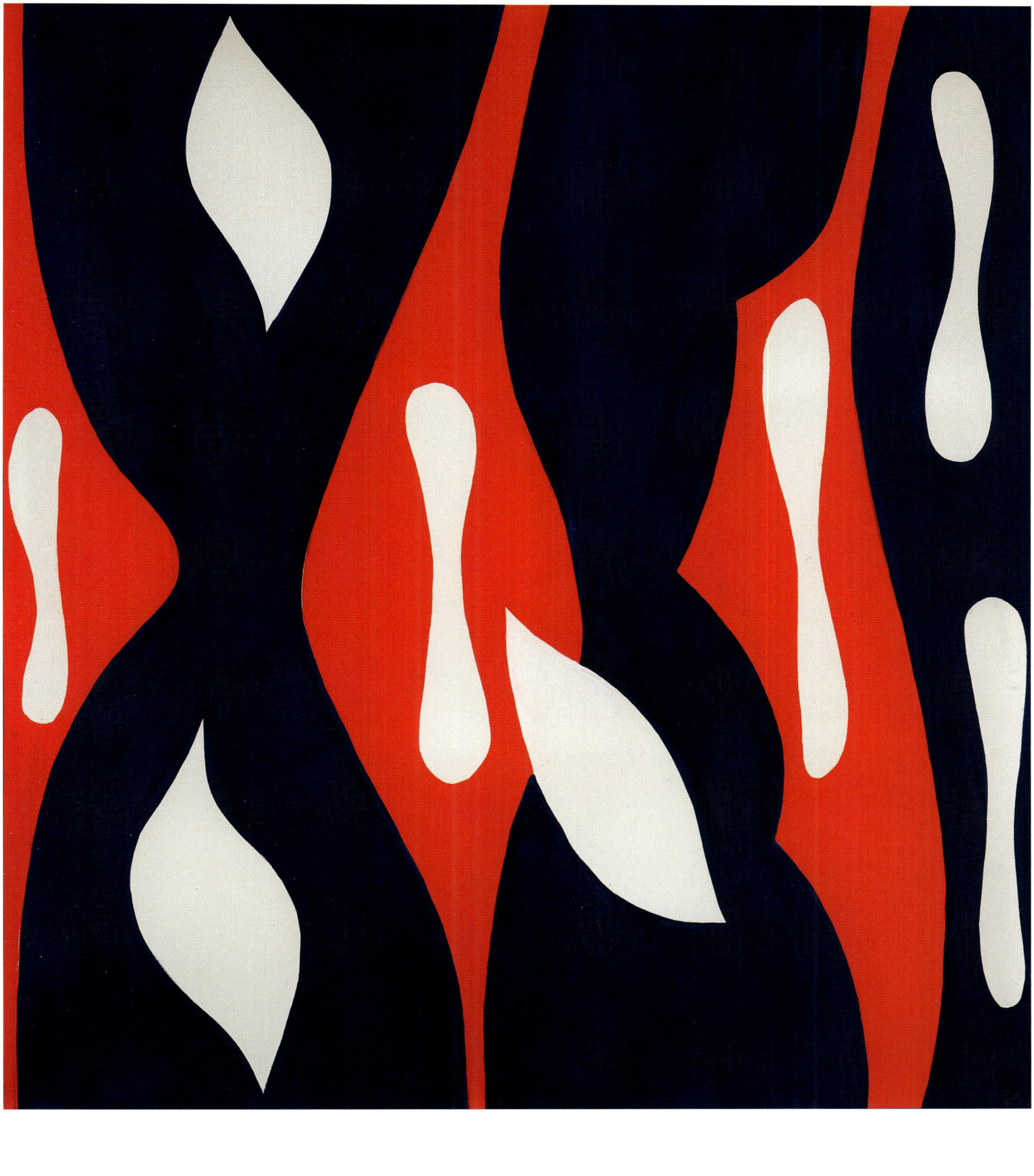

Polychromatisch II, 1968
Oil on canvas
130 × 120 cm · 51¼ × 47¼ in

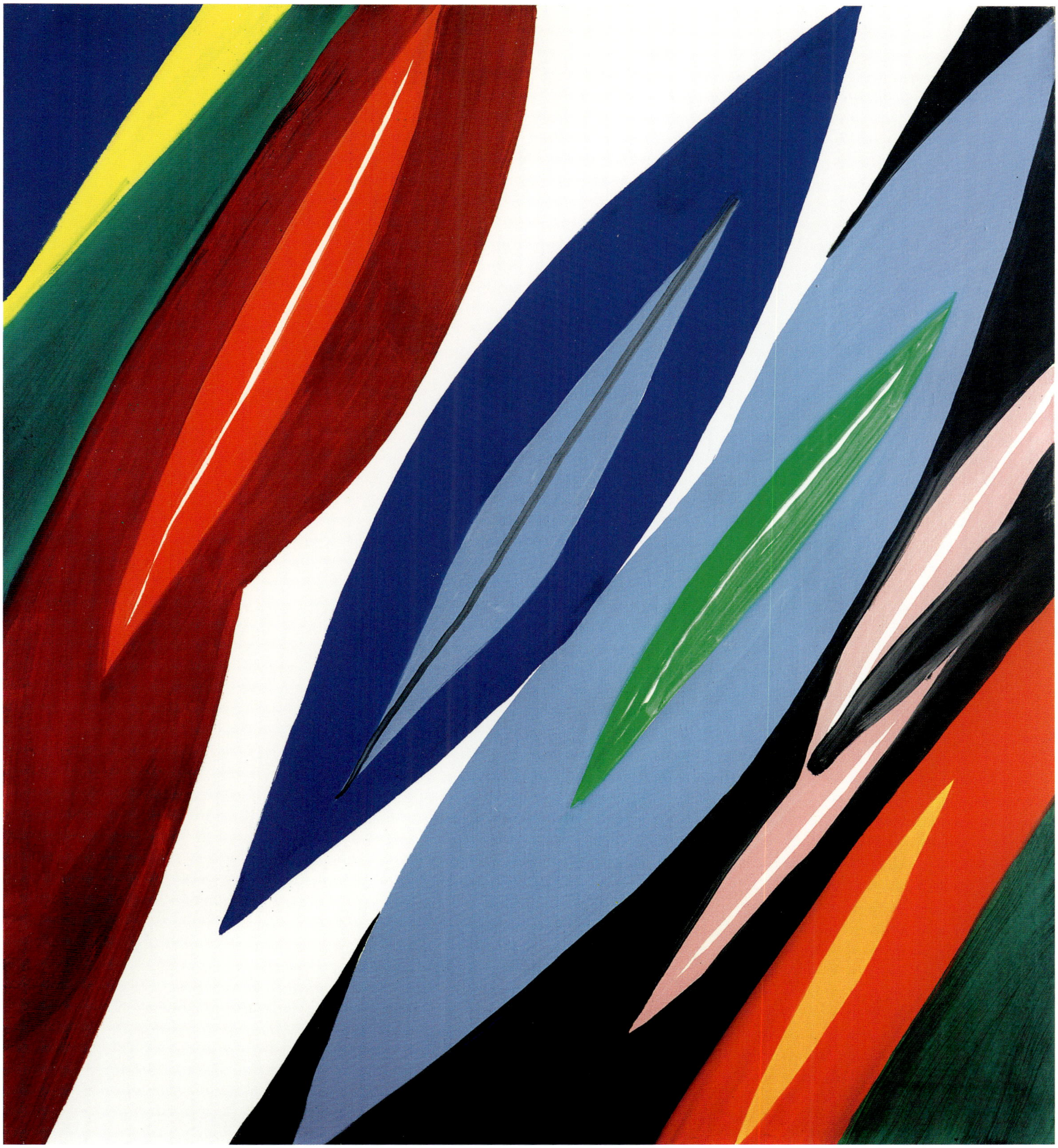

Postscript

Amongst the simple, elemental forms of Nay's last paintings one finds a motif that appears like an eye closing. Haftmann observed these 'magic eye signs' of the last works: 'an old threatening script sign in Nay's iconography looked out again and brought the dance of the round disks to a rigid halt or actually loaded it with the weight of the cultic'.[236] The 'script sign' was not always so threatening, and may be traced as a leitmotif throughout Nay's career that draws the diverse periods together.

The most schematic depictions of the human form in his early Surrealist period reduce the body to a single elongated form, defined as human only by an eye, such as with *Winkender mit einem Auge* (Waving with One Eye, 1932), or embryonic forms with a single dark eye. Eyes survive the dissolution of the body and remain floating in the dunes in the landscapes of the mid-1930s, becoming a form of punctuation, a single dark spot, in the human figures that populate the 'Lofoten' paintings. This is not a thinking but a staring eye, not seductive or searching, but blank, knowledgeless; a mere sign. In the early 1940s the eye is more often closed, only to return after 1945 as a much stronger symbol, giving for the first time a sense of inner life, of thoughtfulness. A compelling comparison for this use of the motif, particularly after 1945, is found in the sculpture of Henry Moore, where the eye motif performed a similar function, indicating self-aware life.[237]

By the time of *Kythera* (Kythira, 1947), the eye motif had become dominant, and began to take on a disembodied, spiritual quality. As a motif developed through the 'Fugal' paintings it is often nothing more than a way of punctuating the pictorial space, yet the origins of the eye motif are clear. The use of simply drawn representational eyes in some works of this period, such as *Der Clown zeigt sich* (The Clown Appears, 1951), seems a clear reference to Miró; in other works, as Siegfried Gohr has suggested, the comparison to be drawn is with Picasso's endless variations on an eye-like form.[238]

Then, at the beginning of the 1950s the eye motif disappears, or at least becomes submerged within landscape-like images, as in *Vom vulkanischen Grau* (Of Volcanic Grey, 1953). It was with this departure of the human element that Nay's work went through its most difficult period in the middle of that decade. But already in 1954, with the emergence of the disk-motif in the 'Disk' paintings, the path begins to be cleared for the final transformation of the eye motif, and the final flourishing of Nay's vision of painting as an emblem of humanity. In 1958, for example in *Blau und Violett* (Blue and Violet, 1958) it appears as a black dot floating amongst the disks, a disembodied pupil; it then dilates and eventually dominates the picture space, as in *Umbra* (Umber, 1959). This is not a seeing eye, but a being eye, ontological rather than psychological, to recall Stravinsky's theory of post-tonal music, as well as Heidegger's more obscure writings on the question of being. It is a simmering form that suggests the painting itself as a self-conscious object, looking as much as it is looked at.

236 Haftmann, 'Epilogue', in *E.W. Nay. A Retrospective*, *op. cit.*, p.18.
237 See Ludwig Baron Döry, 'Begegnung mit Nay', in *Die Hofheimer Jahre*, *op. cit.*, pp.141–57. Nay valued Moore's work highly, at a time when the latter was being promoted in Germany as an emblem of British culture and democracy. See Stonard, *op. cit.*
238 *Ernst Wilhelm Nay*, *op. cit.*

The 'Eye' paintings are the culmination of this story, and of the notion of the human body in Nay's work. Into the 1960s they suggest a frantic, thirsty type of vision, or, as with *Weiße Quelle* (White Source, 1963), a form of primitive wonder, like eyes opened for the first time. They crowd the canvas and clamour for attention, having finally escaped from polite repression, overbearing in their omniscience, as with the Documenta paintings in 1964. Then, at their height, they suddenly fizzle out, explode, or simply disappear. The frantic quality departs, and the being, seeing eye becomes incorporated with what is seen, taking its place as a higher form of symbolic punctuation. Eyes retreat into the shadows, looking out from dark swathes of pigment, often constituted by forms silhouetted against the bare canvas, as with *Nachtblau* (Night-Blue, 1965). There is no mistaking their melancholy compared with the fervour of the 'Eye' paintings that had come just before. In the final works of 1967 and 1968, they flicker on and off, appearing occasionally as narrow slits, eyes wide shut perhaps, or images of thoughtfulness and *Innerlichkeit* – inwardness.

The persistence of the eye motif shows Nay's underlying obsession with the intelligence of vision. It is an obsession that connects him with the riven decades through which he lived, suggesting an escape into the present based on the immediacy of visual perception. The dissolution of the body in the mind is the oldest idea in art, but during the twentieth century this sublimation was also an escape from the body politic. Like all artists, Nay was an exile, but more than many others he stayed true to his chosen home of painting, and not once did he look back. In the words of a poem by Saint-John Perse that was close to his heart, *'L'exil n'est point d'hier! L'exil n'est point d'hier!'*[239]

239 'Exile is not of yesterday! Exile is not of yesterday!' in Saint-John Perse, *Exile and other poems*, trans Denis Devlin, Bollingen Foundation, New York, 1949, originally published as *Exil, suivi de Poème à l'étrangère; Pluies; Neiges*, Gallimard, Paris, 1945, p.14.

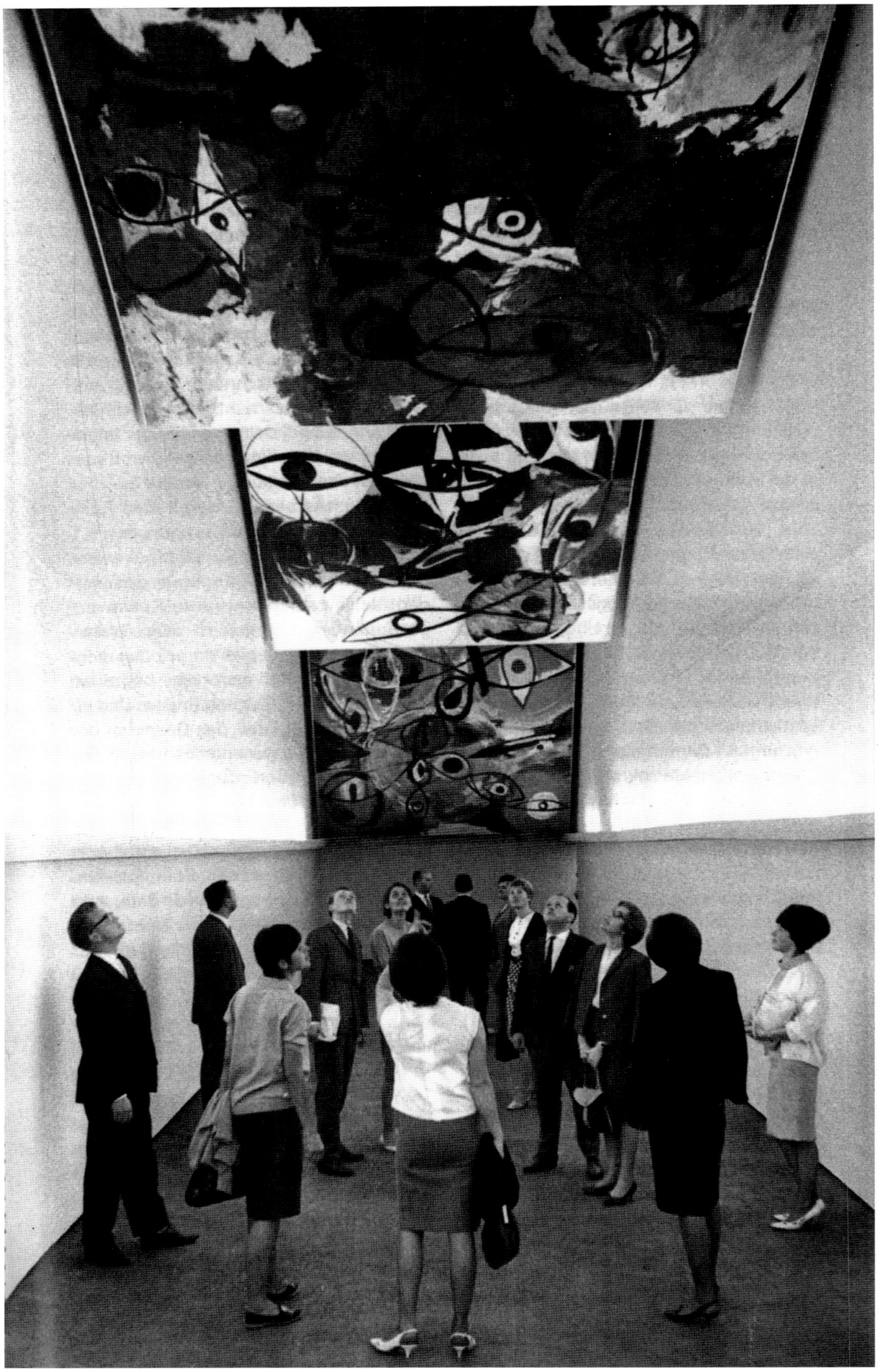

Presentation of E.W. Nay's *Drei Bilder im Raum* in the Fridericianum at Documenta III, Kassel, 1964

Pamela Kort

Ernst Wilhelm Nay and the Issue of Content in Abstract Painting

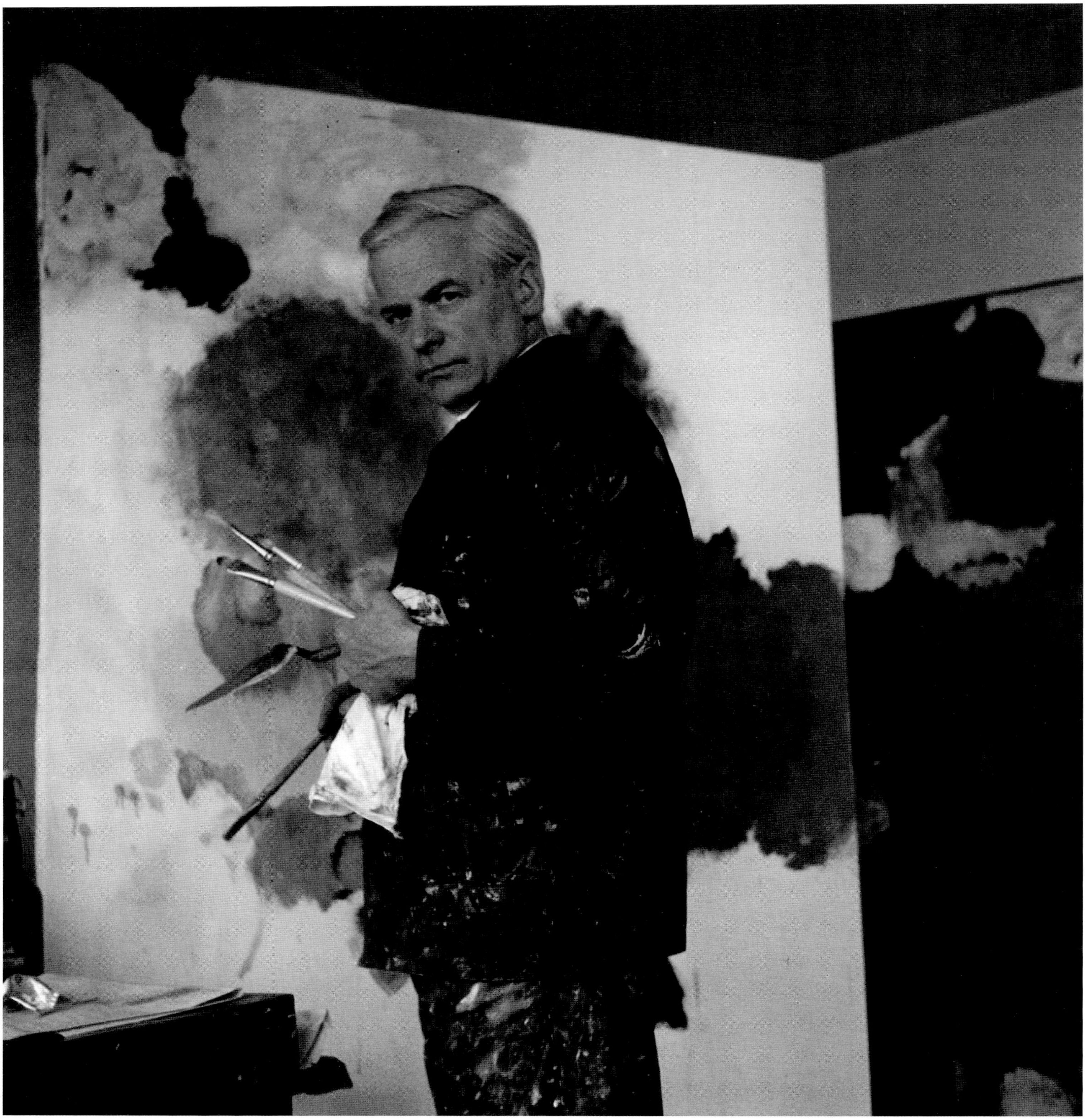

E.W. Nay in his studio, Cologne, 1958

By 1959 Ernst Wilhelm Nay had become Germany's most successful abstract painter. Such was his standing that Albert Schulze Vellinghausen opened his review in the *Frankfurter Allgemeine Zeitung* of Nay's retrospective that year at the Kunstverein in Düsseldorf with this flabbergasting statement: 'Ernst Wilhelm Nay is absolved from discovery and its process, which is always somewhat strenuous for all involved. He is spared such tactlessness. There is no need to contribute to his fame for the sake of making him more famous.' Superfluously or not, Schulze Vellinghausen went on to praise the exhibition anyway, crediting Nay's recent 'grandiose' abstract paintings for endowing it with a 'truly extraordinary' quality.[1] As perhaps the most erudite critic writing for one of Germany's most prestigious daily newspapers, Schulze Vellinghausen's opinions counted.[2]

Two years later, the continued hoopla around Nay and other so-called *Wirtschaftswunder* ('Economic Miracle') artists compelled in part the painters Georg Baselitz and Eugen Schönebeck to formulate what came to be considered two of the most remarkable artistic manifestos written since the close of the Second World War.[3] The language and semi-abstract images of their *Pandemonium* manifestos, clearly evoke just how fed up they were with the cultural mechanisms that pumped up and sustained artists' reputations, Nay being for them the prime example. Baselitz's critique of the *externals* who 'have practiced art historical additions ... spoken persistently of final strokes' and 'fallen into ecstasy too rapidly' suggests the follies and shortcomings of critics.[4] Schönebeck took on instead the 'double moral standards' of the professors at the Hochschule für Bildende Künste in Berlin-Wilmersdorf, from which he had just graduated. These are the 'colleagues' who 'approach each other with outstretched arms',[5] who encouraged their students to experiment with Nay's version of abstraction, while resenting his success. Seeking to gain a foothold, Schönebeck and Baselitz mailed the initial manifesto announcing their first self-staged show to everyone they could think of. Will Grohmann, Berlin's most important critic, was at the top of their list. They could have kicked themselves when he actually showed up, during one of the few moments they absented themselves from the ice-cold provisional exhibition space.[6] Having missed their chance, they went back to their easels and continued to read about Nay in the daily newspapers.

It wasn't until mid-1964 that the tide of accolades finally began to ebb. That June, three monumental new paintings by Nay were featured in a spectacular installation designed by Arnold Bode at Documenta III (p.154). By suspending the brightly coloured canvases diagonally from the ceiling of a corridor-like passage, Bode hoped that those who moved through the space would 'bring into being a total picture that was both more and other than the sum of its three parts'.[7] Unfortunately, the effect that ensued was more of a controversial rather than visual nature. In September 1964 a lengthy article appeared in the weekly newspaper *Die Zeit* that questioned not just the importance of Nay's abstract painting, but the integrity of those critics who upheld it. Schulze Vellinghausen's name was the first to appear, together with an excerpt from one of his texts in which he rapturously praised Nay's method of painting. Isolated from its original context, the quote was made to look ridiculous. Apparently the author had been biding his time for some years: the statement came from Schulze Vellinghausen's 1959 review of Nay's retrospective at the Kunstverein in Düsseldorf. Quotations extolling the artist taken from older texts by Grohmann and Werner Haftmann, who had curated Documenta since its inception, followed in quick succession.[8] Never mind that a gloss preceding the *Die Zeit* article disclosed that it had been written by a younger abstract painter,[9] or that a subsequent attack in Berlin's daily newspaper *Der Tagespiegel* also came from another less successful artist.[10] Both knew how to play upon long-simmering doubts in Germany – reservations that dated back to the first years of the twentieth century – about the quality of its modern art.

While the authority of the cultural authorities remained intact, Nay soon came to feel that his artistic reputation had been seriously damaged. In May of 1966 he responded to a letter from the editor of *Die Zeit*: 'You expressed ... the hope that through the passage of time, the article from back then by a "fanatical author" might have lost its effect. Unfortunately ... you set an assassination of character into motion in your newspaper that will soon turn into a murder.'[11] Although Bode had included Nay's work in all three previous Documentas and initially planned to invite him back in 1968, he ultimately chose not to do so.[12] By the time the exhibition

This essay has benefited from discussions with Werner Hofmann and Peter-Klaus Schuster. I also want to thank Hans-Jörg Rheinburger for inviting me to the Max-Planck-Institute für Wissenschaftsgeschichte during August and September 2011, where I was able to research the section on physics. Marlène de Saussure, Magdalene Claesges and Brigitte Schlüter also provided much-appreciated research assistance. All translations are the author's own, unless otherwise indicated.

1 Albert Schulze Vellinghausen, 'E.W. Nay in Düsseldorf: Weg und Verwandlung eines Oeuvres', in *Frankfurter Allgemeine Zeitung*, 21 January 1959. Reprinted in *Anspielungen-Ausgewählte Reden, Aufsätze, Kritiken zur Bildenden Kunst, Literatur, Architektur*, Friedrich, Velber bei Hanover, 1962, pp.181–83.
2 On Schulze Vellinghausen's standing in Germany see Friederike Kitschen, 'Kommentar' in Martin Schieder and Friederike Kitschen (eds), *Art Vivant: Quellen und Kommentare zu den Deutsch-Französischen Kunstbeziehungen 1945–1960*, Akademie Verlag, Berlin, 2011, p.132. See also Karl Otto Götz's comment in '"Das Informel ist ein Prinzip": Claudia Posca im Gespräch mit Karl Otto Götz und Rissa', 12 November 1998, in *Informel: Der Anfang nach dem Ende*, Museum am Ostwall Dortmund and Harenberg Edition, Dortmund, 1999, p.239.
3 Eugen Schönebeck, unpublished interview with the author, 4 July 2011, Berlin.
4 Georg Baselitz, 'Pandemonic Manifesto I, Second Version, 1961', in Detlev Gretenkort (ed), *Georg Baselitz: Collected Writings and Interviews*, Ridinghouse, London, 2010, p.26. Eugen Schönebeck, 'Fragments For a Pandemonium', Spring 1962, in Pamela Kort and Max Hollein (eds), *Eugen Schönebeck 1957–1967*, Schirn Kunsthalle, Frankfurt, 23 February – 15 May 2011, exhibition catalogue, Hirmer, Munich, 2011, p.159.
5 Eugen Schönebeck, unpublished interview with the author, 8 August 2011.
6 Georg Baselitz, unpublished interview with the author, 21 July 2010.
7 Werner Haftmann, 'Einführung', in *Documenta III*, Alte Galerie, Museum Fridericianum, Orangerie Kassel, 27 June – 5 October, 1964, exhibition catalogue, M. DuMont Schauberg, Cologne, 1964, p.XVI.
8 Will Grohmann, 'Deutschland, Österreich, und Schweiz', in Will Grohmann (ed), *Kunst nach 1945*, M. DuMont Schauberg, Cologne, 1958, p.171; Werner Haftmann, 'Willi Baumeister und Ernst Wilhelm Nay: Eröffnungsvortrag der Austellung "Baumeister und Nay" in der Kunsthalle Basel', 27 February 1960, in Haftmann, *Skizzenbuch zur Kultur der Gegenwart: Reden und Aufsätze*, Prestel-Verlag, Munich, 1960, p.202.
9 Hans Platschek, 'Nays Scheiben – Ein repräsentativer Deutscher Maler genauer betrachtet', in *Die Zeit*, 4 September 1964, in *E.W. Nay: Bilder und Dokumente: 1902–1968*, Germanisches Nationalmuseum, Nuremberg, 29 March – 1 June 1980, exhibition catalogue, Prestel-Verlag, Munich, 1980, pp.251–54.
10 Klaus Jürgen-Fischer, 'Der Fall des Malers E.W. Nay – Ein heftig geführter Beitrag zu einer heftigen Diskussion', in *Der Tagespiegel*, 5 November 1964, *ibid.*, pp.255–57.
11 E.W. Nay, letter to Josef Müller-Marein, chief editor of *Die Zeit*, 18 May 1966, *ibid.*, p.260.

opened that summer, Nay was dead, the victim of a heart attack. Thereafter his significance to the development of postwar German art began to be downplayed, to the point that today, scarcely anyone in Germany under 50, who is not a specialist, even knows his name. In America, despite good reviews and acquisitions of his paintings by museums and private collectors since the mid-1950s, his work disappeared even more rapidly from the public sphere following his death. Ironically, although the artists who had ganged up against Nay had hoped to fell him alone, it turned out that they helped to take all of German abstract art, their own included, down with him.

Up until now, Nay's slow but steady slippage from view in Germany and America has been racked up to a series of unlucky coincidences. Firstly, the attack against him was well timed. It came just as he was on the brink of attaining the international acclaim that would have ratified his standing in Germany. Secondly, the blow was strengthened by a change in aesthetic tastes that came about just at that time. In 1964 Pop art began to flood into Europe. It wasn't long before it overran the status of non-objective painting of all kinds everywhere. Four years later, when Nay died, the student revolts began in Germany. Colourful abstract paintings were anathema to this generation, who called for more obviously socially engaged works of art. Thereafter art that was pleasing to the eye continued to be regarded in Germany with misgivings.

Apparently, too, Nay had no real followers in either country. Or at least, in this climate, if younger artists had taken note of his abstract paintings they chose to remain quiet about it.[13] And then there was the fact that no powerful international art dealer emerged after the Knoedler Gallery dropped Nay from its programme following a change of hands in the late 1960s. The initial enthusiasm for Nay's abstract art across the Atlantic was bound to peter out unless it was carefully shored up. After all, American Abstract Expressionist painting had begun to unfold a decade before Nay started to work out his own version of abstractionism; it wasn't even until 1954 that the work of New York painters associated with this school began to obtain currency in Germany.

Even the boom for German art in America and Britain during the last two decades of the twentieth century did not bring Nay's art back into the limelight there. The trajectory of his painting just couldn't be made to fit the story of the emergence of modern German art as it had thus far been constructed across the Atlantic. On the one hand, the more or less figurative paintings that he made between 1927 and 1949 were too late to be equated with first- or second-generation Expressionist art.[14] On the other, the abstract idiom that Nay cultivated later did not jive well with the increasing taste for so-called neo-Expressionist figurative painting.

Meanwhile in Germany, a backlash against abstraction began to heat up again, this time fanned by Marxist historians. The upshot was the publication in 1986 of a hefty tome examining the factors that led to allegedly 'anti-realist' painting, literature and music rapidly becoming the dominant aesthetic in Germany between 1945 and 1965. Nay, of course, had stood near or at the helm of the movement in the visual arts precisely during these years.[15] A decade later, German Informel and Tachist painters and scultpors began to be rediscovered there.[16] Nay's paintings were almost always excluded from shows and books featuring these artists, not least because his version of abstraction had put theirs in the shade during the heyday of the style in Germany.

Nay's abstract art didn't just happen to fall through the cracks in time of art-historical and curatorial practice: *it was allowed to*. Few scholars have stepped forth since 1964 to try to sort out the polemics in Germany that culminated in the denunciation of these once so appreciated paintings.[17] And almost no one has attempted to reveal why the attack was so successful, and the degree to which it resulted in obscuring what Nay had really been trying to accomplish with his art.

It was not until 1980 that an effort was made in Germany to reverse this tide of ignorance. That year saw the publication of an article by Peter-Klaus Schuster, penned on the occasion of a retrospective exhibition commemorating the gift of Nay's written papers by his estate to the Archiv für Bildende Kunst im Germanisches Nationalmuseum in Nuremberg. In his text titled *Kunst im Kontext: E.W. Nays ständige Wandlung*, Schuster not only argued for the significance of Nay's abstraction, but demonstrated that the attempt to denounce its importance had already begun in 1953.[18] Regrettably, next to no one took up the many challenging questions that his article raised.

In 2009 a large exhibition – *E.W. Nay: Bilder der 1960er Jahre* – was mounted that focused exclusively on Nay's late work. It also reconstructed, for the first time, the installation of his paintings at Documenta III that had caused so much controversy in 1964. The accompanying German/English catalogue would have been the ideal place for an essay exploring in depth the causes behind this highly charged discussion. Well aware of the job at hand, the exhibition's curator began her essay with the comment: 'One of the reasons for the lack of knowledge about his late work, even among experts, lies in its peculiar and problematic reception history.'

12 Arnold Bode, letter to E.W. Nay, 12 January 1965, in Heiner Georgsdorf (ed), *Arnold Bode: Schriften und Gespräche*, Siebehaar Verlag, Berlin, 2007, p.150.

13 In 1971 Marcia Tucker mounted the exhibition *The Structure of Color* at the Whitney Museum of Art in New York. Although it neither featured Nay's works nor mentioned his name, the title echoes one of the central theoretical premises of his art, described in his book *Vom Gestaltwert der Farbe* (roughly translated as the Structural Value of Color), published in 1955. See *The Structure of Color*, Whitney Museum of Modern Art, 25 February – 18 April 1971, exhibition catalogue, Whitney Museum of Modern Art, New York, 1970. Peter-Klaus Schuster suggests that Nay influenced not only Frank Stella but also the 'American pattern painters'. See Peter-Klaus Schuster, 'Kunst im Kontext: E.W. Nays ständige Wandlung', in *E.W. Nay: Bilder und Dokumente*, *op. cit.*, pp.15–16.

14 See for example, *Expressionism: A German Intuition 1905–1920*, Solomon R. Guggenheim Museum, New York, 1980, exhibition catalogue, Solomon R. Guggenheim Museum, New York, 1980, and *German Expressionism 1915–1925: The Second Generation*, Los Angeles County Museum of Art, 9 October – 31 December 1988, exhibition catalogue, Prestel-Verlag, Munich, 1988.

15 See Jost Hermand, *Kultur im Wiederaufbau: Die Bundesrepublik Deutschland 1945–1965*, Nymphenburger, Munich, 1986.

16 For a definition of 'Informel' and 'Tachist' see particularly Nicola Carola Heuwinkel, *Entgrenzte Malerei: Art Informel in Deutschland*, Kehrer Verlag, Heidelberg and Berlin, 2010, pp.24–29.

17 On the reception of Nay, see Friedrich Weltzien, *E.W. Nay – Figur und Körperbild*, Dietrich Reimer Verlag, Berlin, 2003, pp.21–46. See also Hans Körner, 'Utopien und Enttäuschungen – Eine Einführung in das Thema', in Hans Körner, (ed), *Flächenland: Die abstrakte Malerei im frühen Nachkriegsdeutschland und in der jungen Bundesrepublik*, Francke Verlag, Tübingen and Basel, 1996, pp.9–17.

Rather than examining the tricky unfolding of this history, however, she sidestepped the task, commenting that its premises were all but 'incomprehensible' to today's readers.[19] What follows takes issue with this.

This essay will begin with a brief account of Nay's rise to fame in Germany until 1959. By then, he had shifted from the figurative mode in which he had worked until around 1949, to an increasingly abstract style, a change largely effectuated by 1952.[20] Two years later, the *Scheibenbilder* ('Disk' paintings) began to emerge, canvases that would rocket him to the highpoint of his career (p.156). The remainder of this section will trace the highlights of the presentation of Nay's paintings in America and Britain from 1955 until his death in 1968.

The second part will focus on the in-fighting between the members of the Deutscher Künstlerbund – Germany's premiere artists' organisation at the time – about its exhibition policies. This bickering began in 1952, shortly after the group's first annual show, and continued until 1955, when its first president Karl Hofer died. What initially began as a conflict between painters working in a more or less figurative idiom and those whose works tended towards an abstraction, soon developed into a squaring off between abstract painters who were prominently featured within its exhibitions, such as Nay, and the large group of Informel and Tachist artists chiefly blackballed from them during these years. Matters were only exacerbated by the critical acclaim that Grohmann bestowed upon a select coterie of older abstractionists, all of whom were key members of the Künstlerbund. While he saw to it that their work remained in the public eye, almost without exception he refused to write in depth about Informel or Tachist art until after 1955.[21]

Haftmann's *Malerei im 20. Jahrhundert* came into print in 1954, followed six years later by the publication of a lengthy monograph on Nay.[22] The third section of this text will focus on the method and rhetoric that Haftmann used in his books to argue for the importance of Nay's postwar abstract art. Three problematic strands characterise his approach: the alignment of these paintings with prewar 'Nordic modernism' in Germany; an equation of them with Gottfried Benn's 'world of expression' (*Ausdruckswelt*) and concept of 'inner necessity' (*innere Notwendigkeit*); and the claim

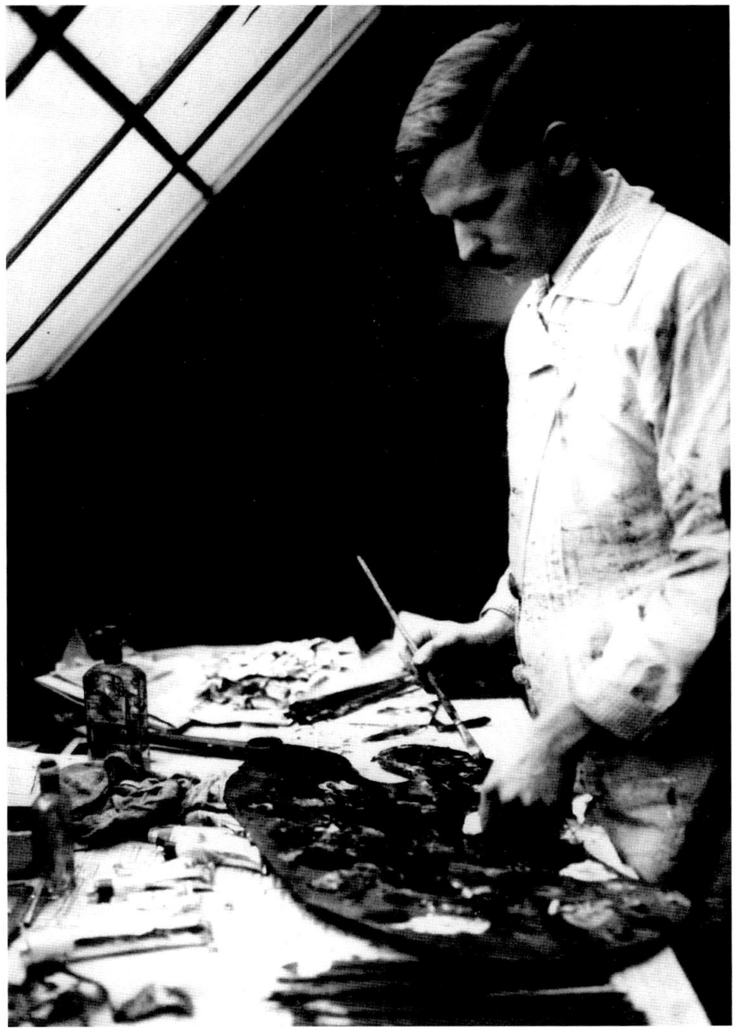

E.W. Nay in his Berlin studio, 1931

18 Schuster, 1980, *op. cit.*, pp.7–16.
19 See Ingrid Pfeiffer, 'E.W. Nay – Gegenwärtigkeit und Zeitlosigkeit' and 'E.W. Nay – Topicality and Timelessness', in *E.W. Nay: Bilder der 1960er Jahre*, Schirn Kunsthalle, Frankfurt, 22 January – 26 April 2009, exhibition catalogue, Hirmer Verlag, Munich, 2009, p.7. In a separate booklet issued in connection with this show, Dirk Schwarze briefly outlined the so-called *Documenta-Streit*, without, however, attempting to explain its origins. See Dirk Schwarze, *Die Kunst der Inszenierung oder Als Arnold Bode Ernst Wilhelm Nay in den Himmel hob*, Siebenhaar Verlag, Berlin, 2009, pp.49–59.
20 These dates follow the chronology established by Aurel Scheibler in *Ernst Wilhelm Nay: Werkverzeichnis der Ölgemälde*, 2 vols, M. DuMont and Museum Ludwig, Cologne, 1990. See particularly, vol.1, p.294; vol.2, pp.6, 62.
21 Martin Schieder, *Im Blick des Anderen: Die Deutsch-Französischen Kunstbeziehungen 1945–1959*, Akademie Verlag, Berlin, 2005, p.139. See also Götz, 1998, *op. cit.*, p.235 and Bernard Schultze, 'Das Informel ist eine Keimzelle gewesen: Claudia Posca im Gespräch mit Bernard Schultze', 23 December 1998, in *Informel: Der Anfang nach dem Ende*, 1999, *op. cit.*, p.267. See also Dina Sonntag, 'Bibliographie Will Grohmann', in *In Memoriam Will Grohmann: 1887–1968 Wegbereiter der Moderne*, exhibition catalogue, Staatsgalerie Stuttgart, Stuttgart, 1987, pp.58–64.
22 Werner Haftmann, *Malerei im 20. Jahrhundert*, Prestel-Verlag, Munich, 1954, and Werner Haftmann, *E.W. Nay*, M. DuMont, Cologne, 1960.

that such work need have no content other than its own elements. All of these approaches would be misconstrued to varying degrees by German artists and critics during the 1960s to argue that Nay's abstract painting was essentially retrograde. Although Haftmann's monograph on Nay was never translated into English, his *Painting in the Twentieth Century* came into print, however, in 1960.[23] This book, together with the texts that he wrote for almost all of Nay's one-man gallery exhibitions in America and the catalogue of his first solo show in England, shaped an English-speaking take on the artist. Although Haftmann was one of Nay's few confidants, the artist did not necessarily sanction his views, although he allowed them to stand.

The final section will examine what Nay wanted to achieve with his abstract art and why this went largely unnoticed. He was deeply concerned with achieving paintings that paralleled developments in the natural sciences, physics and mathematics. With them he aimed to educe a painted realm that appealed to a consciousness outside of the constructs of measurable time and space. Such paintings, nevertheless, were stimulated by pressing questions particular to the time and place in which they emerged.[24] Far from turning away from the precarious human condition in post-World-War II Germany, he tried to deal with it through the painterly medium of form and colour.

Nay in Germany, America and Great Britain (1925–68)

Ernst Wilhelm Nay first appeared on the German art scene in 1925. That year, Karl Hofer offered the 23-year-old a stipendium at the Hochschule für Bildende Künste in Berlin, where he was teaching. Soon afterwards word had begun to circulate that Nay was Hofer's most promising student.[25] He left the Hochschule three years later, convinced that he had progressed sufficiently to be able to work independently. The Preussische Akademie der Künste awarded him a prize in 1931 that also included a nine-month stay at the Deutsche Akademie (Villa Massimo) in Rome. His next 'honour' was of rather a different nature. In 1937, he became the youngest artist to be included in the defamatory Munich show, *Entartete Kunst* (Degenerate Art). Two paintings of the ten works that the National Socialists had confiscated from public museum collections were included in the section of that exhibition in which abstraction was equated with insanity.[26] And with that, his promising career came temporarily to a screeching halt in Germany. Not so in America: that year his works appeared for the first time in a group show at Curt Valentin's Buchholz Gallery in New York. In 1939, Buchholz lent one of these paintings to the exhibition *Modern German Art* at the Springfield Museum of Fine Arts in Illinois.

In Germany, Nay began military service in 1940, first as an infantryman and after 1941 as a cartographer. Fortunate enough to survive the war, Nay was even able to paint intermittently between 1942 and 1944. During those years, he worked in an atelier in Le Mans, France, that the amateur French sculptor Pierre Térouanne had put at his disposal. Almost immediately upon being released as a private first-class soldier from an assembly camp in Eger (today Cheb) in 1945, he returned to painting. In October of 1946, just a half a year after Joseph Beuys entered the Kunstakademie in Düsseldorf, his teacher Ewald Mataré wrote to Nay inquiring whether he would be interested in a teaching position there. Nay was not to be tempted: he felt he must concentrate on his painting instead.[27]

In 1948, Nay's art was presented for the first time in a high-ranking international show. That year, and again in 1950, he participated in the 24th and 25th Venice Biennales and took part as well in the 1950 *Pittsburgh International Exhibition of Paintings* at the Carnegie Institute. 1950 also saw the mounting of a retrospective of Nay's work at the Kestner-Gesellschaft in Hanover. Two years later, the Haus am Waldsee in Berlin also presented a retrospective exhibition.

Meanwhile, Nay's abstract paintings were included in the first important shows of German art mounted abroad. Among the highlights were the showing of three of his new abstract paintings in *A Hundred Years of German Painting* at the Tate Gallery in London in 1956, the presentation of two such works in *German Art of the Twentieth Century* (1957) at The Museum of Modern Art in New York and subsequently at the City Art Museum of St Louis, and the exhibition of four recent paintings in the Smithsonian Institute's travelling exhibition *German Artists of Today*, which toured America between 1959 and 1961.

1955 had turned out to be a watershed year for Nay. It saw a retrospective of his work in Germany at the Hamburger Kunsthalle, followed by the inclusion of eight paintings in the first Documenta in Kassel, and the award of Hamburg's prestigious Lichtwark prize. The year also marked his first solo show in the United States, at the Kleemann Galleries in New York. During the next four years, exhibition after exhibition was mounted in Germany. In 1959 this history reached its apogee: a retrospective of Nay's work was held at the Kunstverein in Düsseldorf and seven of his recent abstract paintings were prominently featured at Documenta II.

Meanwhile, in New York the Kleemann Galleries gave him a second solo show in 1958 and a third in 1959. Nay crossed the Atlantic with his wife to celebrate the opening of the latter exhibition in November 1959. He returned to America three more times: for the

23 Werner Haftmann, *Painting in the Twentieth Century*, trans Ralph Manheim, Lund Humphries, London, 1960.
24 Gert Schiff was one of the first authors to note this. See Gert Schiff, 'Gefährdung und Meisterschaft: Zu E.W. Nay Ausstellungen in Hamburg und Hanover', in *Frankfurter Allgemeine Zeitung*, 18 April 1955, p.8. See also Schuster, 1980, *op. cit.*, pp.12–13.
25 See Karl Hofer, letter to Grassmann, 2 July 1947 in Andreas Hüneke (ed), *Karl Hofer: Malerei hat eine Zukunft, Briefe, Aufsätze, Reden*, Gustav Kiepenheuer, Leipzig & Weimar, 1991, p.283: 'Nay was not just my student but the most talented one.'
26 Peter-Klaus Schuster, 'The "Inner Emigration" Art for No One', in Christos M. Joachimides, Norman Rosenthal and Wieland Schmied (eds), *German Art in the 20th Century: Painting and Sculpture 1905–1985*, Royal Academy of Arts, London, 11 October – 22 December 1985, exhibition catalogue, Royal Academy of Arts, London, 1985, pp.461–62. See also Dagmar Grimm, 'Ernst Wilhelm Nay', in *Degenerate Art: The Fate of the Avant-Garde in Nazi Germany*, Los Angeles County Museum of Art, 17 February – 12 May 1991, exhibition catalogue, Los Angeles County Museum of Modern Art, Los Angeles, 1991, p.313.
27 Ewald Mataré, letter to E.W. Nay, 16 October 1946, and E.W. Nay, letter to Erich Meyer, 24 December 1946, both in *E.W. Nay: Bilder und Dokumente*, *op. cit.*, p.97.

opening of his show at Knoedler & Company in 1962, and again in 1963 and 1966, travelling on several occasions to Chicago, Los Angeles and San Francisco. Artists too across the Atlantic were eager to meet him: he was received by the likes of Mark Rothko, Robert Motherwell and his talented painter-wife Helen Frankenthaler. Interested in their versions of abstraction, Nay greeted the opportunity to exchange ideas with them, despite his limited English.[28]

Nay had two more one-man exhibitions at Knoedler: the first took place in 1964 followed by another in 1968. All three of them and the Kleemann exhibitions featured only the artists' newest work. And there were sales. His success was singular. As the Cologne art dealer, Rudolf Zwirner later recalled: 'The attempt to sell German art in New York or at least interest American colleagues in it completely failed. The traumatic experiences of Germany's past continued to be felt too strongly. Only Ernst Wilhelm Nay was able to exhibit in the 1950s and also the 1960s in New York galleries.'[29] Although this wasn't quite true – other postwar German artists, for example Willi Baumeister, had exhibited in America since the 1950s – lingering deep-seated anti-German sentiments indeed dampened a widespread embrace of their art. Nay's last one-man exhibition in the United States took place posthumously at the Goethe Center in San Francisco in November of 1968. It featured work from the final eight years of the artists' life made in a variety of media. Although he had a first solo show at the New Gallery London in 1960, it was not until 1991 that Fischer Fine Arts in London presented a second solo exhibition, followed by a third in 2007 at Karsten Schubert, London. To date, a museum retrospective of his paintings is yet to take place in either country.

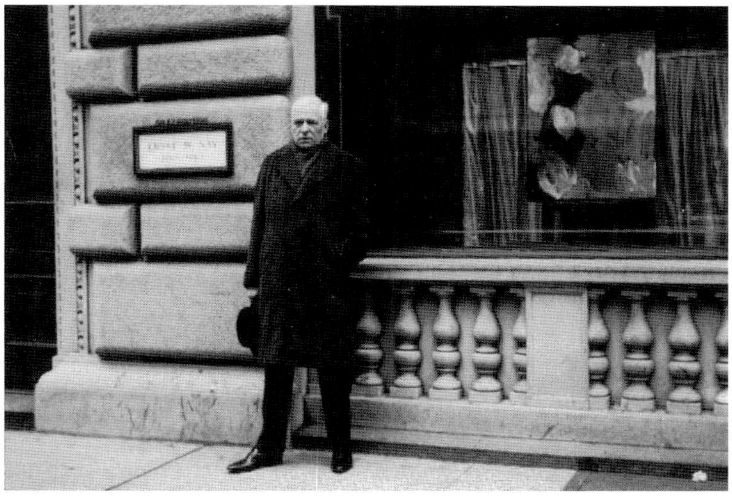

E.W. Nay outside the Knoedler Gallery, New York City, on the occasion of his exhibition, 1962

Exhibition Politics: The Deutsche Künstlerbund and Will Grohmann (1951–55)

One of the earliest articles written in English in which Nay's name crops up was 'Art in Berlin: Summer, 1951', written by the German émigré art historian Hugo Munsterberg and published in the *College Art Journal* late that year. It is worth dwelling for a moment on the event that seems to have most inspired its writing: the first annual exhibition of the Deutscher Künstlerbund since 1936, when it was outlawed by the National Socialists. The exhibition, which took place at Hochschule für Bildende Künste in Berlin's Western sector from 1 August until 1 October 1951, convinced Munsterberg that the Künstlerbund had once again become 'Germany's leading artists' society'. He went on to characterise the show in these terms:

28 See Christiane Lange, 'Nay in Amerika', in Siegfried Gohr (ed), *Nay – Variationen: Retrospektive zum 100. Geburtstag*, Kunsthalle der Hypo-Kulturstiftung, Munich, 27 September – 24 Novermber 2002, exhibtion catalogue, M. DuMont, Cologne, 2002, p.31.
29 Rudolf Zwirner, 'Deutsche Nachkriegskunst im Kontext des internationalen Kunstgeschehens: Erinnerungen eines Kunsthändlers', in Eckhart Gillen (ed), *Deutschlandbilder: Kunst aus einem geteilten Land*, Martin-Gropius-Bau, Berlin, 7 September 1997 – 11 January 1998, exhibition catalogue, M. DuMont, Cologne, 1997, p.581.

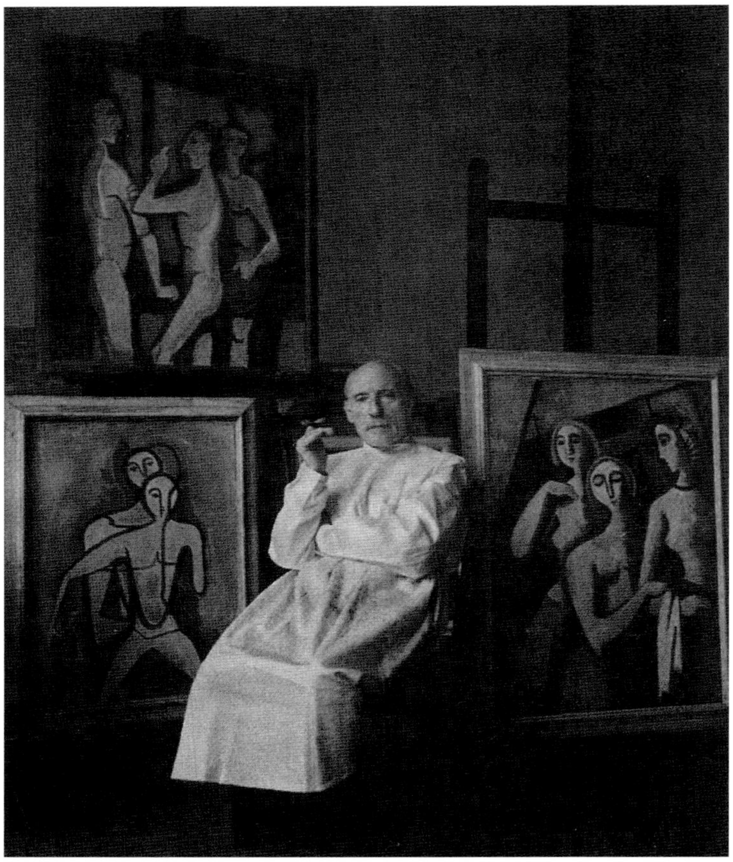

Karl Hofer, 1954

'The general impression was one of an active and vital creative spirit with the emphasis on abstraction ranging all the way from abstract expressionism to pure abstraction of the non-objective variety.' Nevertheless, he noted somewhat ruefully that the first prize had gone to the 73-year-old Karl Hofer, whose figurative work 'lacks the power and beauty of the landscapes and figure pieces of his earlier period'. In contrast, he applauded the awarding of the second prize to the abstract painter Fritz Winter, whom he described as 'the most original and creative artist working in Germany today'. Shortly afterwards he came to Nay, writing that the artist 'has turned to a purely abstract expressionism with bold, flat colors and sharply delineated shapes' that packed an 'almost brutal vigor'.[30] The comment is an early example of a tendency to discuss Nay's style using the misnomer Abstract Expressionism, a designation that not only stuck but would be misused by those who attacked him in the German press in 1964.[31]

Less than 12 months later, Grohmann reported in *Die Neue Zeitung* that 'Nay belongs to the dozen artists that count.'[32] This was quite a statement, coming from a critic who was widely considered to be the 'pope' of the art world.[33] Grohmann went on to note that though the paintings that Nay had shown at the 1951 Künstlerbund exhibition were 'a little cold and dry in their geometricising abstraction', his more recent non-objective work on view in the Haus am Waldsee evidenced 'the enormous distance between him and the so-called "abstractionists", whose work is just as empty as the so-called "Realists" from former times and today'.[34] Although he refrained from naming just who these 'empty' abstractionists were, there is little doubt that Hofer was the painter he most equated with the 'realists from former times'.

Born in 1887, Grohmann had built his art-historical reputation steadily during the 1920s by focusing particularly on the work of Paul Klee, Wassily Kandinsky and Ernst Ludwig Kirchner. Since 1936 and continuing until the end of the Second World War, he had written book reviews and cultural articles for weekly National Socialist magazines *Die Neue Linie*, *Das Reich* and *Die Pause* among others. Of a more or less highbrow nature, they communicated nationalistic and geographical sentiments in keeping with party lines.[35] After 1945, he returned to his hometown Dresden, where he became director of the Staatliche Werkakademie. In the winter of 1947 Hofer invited Grohmann to teach art history at Berlin's Hochschule für Bildende Künste, which the artist directed.[36] Soon afterwards Grohmann was granted a professorship there. It was not

30 Hugo Munsterberg, 'Art in Berlin: Summer, 1951', in *College Art Journal*, vol.11, no.2, winter 1951–52, pp.110–12.
31 See Jürgen-Fischer, 1964, *op. cit.*, p.256. See also Lange, 2002, *op. cit.*, p.32.
32 Will Grohmann, 'E.W. Nay im "Haus am Waldsee"', in *Die Neue Zeitung*, Berlin-Dahlem, n.117, 20 May 1952, p.7, in *E.W. Nay: Bilder und Dokumente*, *op. cit.*, p.118.
33 Diether Schmidt, 'Erinnerung aus der fünften Zone', in Eckhart Gillen und Diether Schmidt (eds), *Zone 5. Kunst in der Viersektorenstadt 1945–1951*, Berlinische Galerie, Berlin, 1989, p.31.
34 Grohmann, *E.W. Nay: Bilder und Dokumente*, 1952, *op. cit.*, p.118.
35 Monika Wucher, 'Dr. Grohmann's Empfehlungen. Leitmotiv moderner Kunstpublizistik im Nationalsozialismus', in Eugen Blume and Dieter Scholz (eds), *Überbrückt: Ästhetische Moderne und Nationalsozialismus Kunsthistoriker und Künstler 1925–1937*, Verlag der Buchhandlung Walther König, Cologne, 1999, pp.109–23.
36 Karin Maur, 'Will Grohmann Wegbereiter der Moderne', in *In Memoriam Will Grohman*, *op. cit.*, p.9.

long before he also became the chief cultural critic for the Berlin edition of *Die Neue Zeitung*, an American-subsidised newspaper, based in Munich. Far from supporting 'figurative' trends in painting, however, he sang the praises of several abstract artists whom he had known before the outbreak of the war, Willi Baumeister, Winter and Nay chief amongst them.

Critical of the uneven quality of artworks presented in the Künstlerbund's first annual exhibition, early in 1952 Baumeister began to lobby for revisions to its selection process. By 23 March of that year Hans Uhlmann, Theodor Werner and Winter joined him in sending a letter of complaint to the Künstlerbund. In it they denounced the all-inclusive exhibiting policy of the Künstlerbund's president, claiming that this contradicted the elitist line of the association's original charter. They demanded that all work submitted should be subject to jury decisions, rather than merely the work by non-members who had been invited to send it for consideration. They also argued for the addition of a critic or art historian on the jury, who could bring a distanced expertise. The man they had in mind was, of course, Grohmann. Finally, they insisted on a more frequent inclusion of younger painters' works, as well as experienced external directors for their annual shows.[37] Although he was not amongst the signatories of the letter, Nay, as well as Georg Meistermann and Ewald Mataré, belonged to the group of self-named 'oppositionalists'.[38] All let it be known that if they did not get their way, they would not participate in the annual shows. Concerned, the managing directors and Hofer agreed within a month to their demands as regards jury procedure, but would not hear of including a critic in an artists' organisation.[39]

Problems within the Künstlerbund reached a new high point early in 1953, when Max Pechstein and the lesser-known artist Wolf Hoffmann sued the association for 'damage to sales possibilities' caused by the jury voting against the inclusion of their work in that year's exhibition in Hamburg.[40] Both men, who painted in a more figurative idiom, accused the Künstlerbund of falling under the 'dictatorship of the abstractionists' – a clash chronicled in July of that year in the weekly magazine *Der Spiegel*.[41] While it is true that since 1953 the Künstlerbund's jury had been composed of more abstract artists than figurative ones, within the exhibitions themselves there was no notable abundance of abstract work.[42] Nevertheless, such malicious name-calling had apparently been

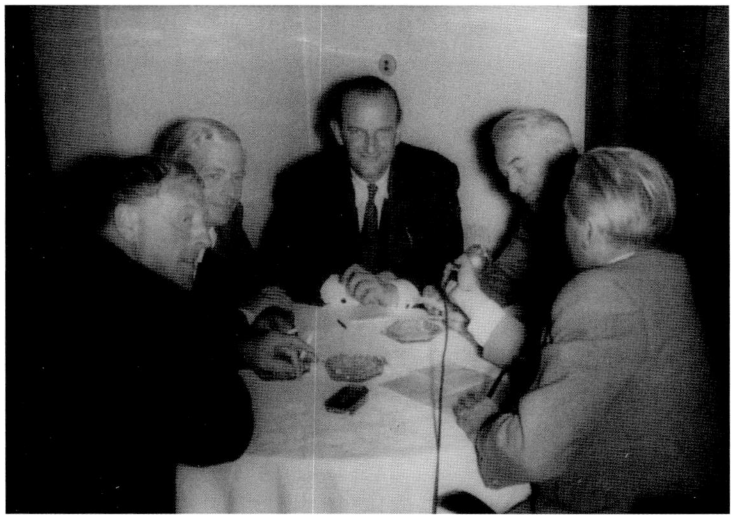

(left to right:) Ewald Mataré, E.W. Nay, Georg Meistermann and Will Grohmann in conversation at the first annual exhibition of the Deutscher Künstlerbund, Berlin, 1951

Jury session for the Deutscher Künstlerbund's second annual exhibition, (left to right: Joseph Fassbender, Karl Scmidt-Pottluff, Ewald Mataré, Adolf Hartmann, Georg Meistermann, Karl Hartung, Ernst Schuhmacher, Erich Heckel), 1952

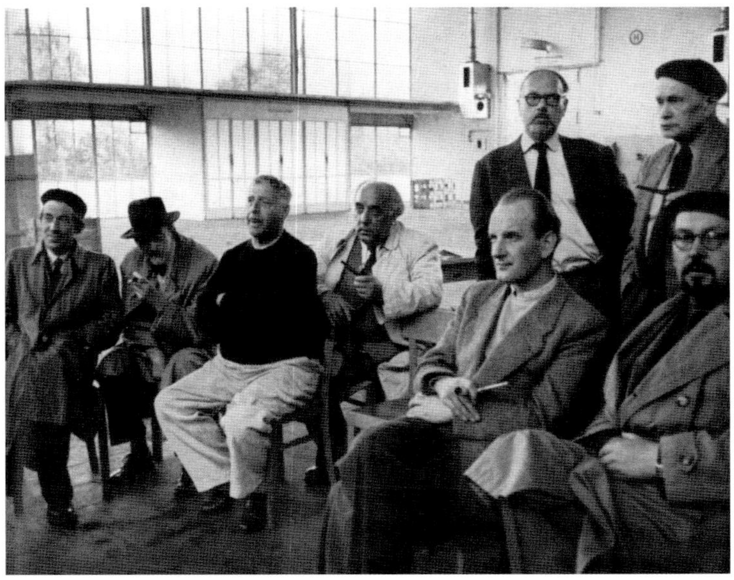

37 See Myriam Maiser, 'Der Streit um die Moderne im Deutschen Künstlerbund unter dem ersten Vorsitzenden Karl Hofer', PhD dissertation, Kunsthistorisches Institut der Freien Universität, Berlin, 2007, pp.32, 103, 108. See also Christine Fischer-Defoy, '"Klee und das in seinem Gefolge Entstandene ist alles andere wie abstract"—Die Auseinandersetzung zwischen Karl Hofer und Willi Baumeister in Deutschen Künstlerbund', in Hans-Werner Schmidt (ed), *Willi Baumeister Karl Hofer: Begegung der Bilder*, Museum der bildenden Künste, Leipzig, 19 December 2004 – 27 February 2005, exhibition catalogue, Kerber Verlag, Bielefeld, 2004, pp.185–86.

38 See Maiser, 2007, *op. cit.*, pp.104–05.

39 *Ibid.* On Grohmann's reaction, see *ibid.*, p.107.

40 The 1953 jury consisted of Baumeister, Arnold Fiedler, Ernst Geitlinger, Karl Hartung, Max Kaus, Karl Kluth, Hans Kuhn, Georg Meistermann, Ernst Schuhmacher, Herbert Spangenberg, Fritz Winter, Erich Heckel, Gerhard Marcks, Edwin Scharff and Toni Staedler, of which only the work of the last four was figurative in essence. See *ibid.*, pp.138–43.

41 Anonymous, 'Streit: Rabiat wie ein Religionskrieg', in *Der Spiegel*, no.29, 15 July 1953, pp.27–30.

42 Maiser, 2007, *op. cit.*, p.245.

making the rounds for some time, as evidenced in an article Grohmann had published in the *Die Neue Zeitung* in June of that year. There he drew attention to the growing tendency to brand abstract painters, and those like himself who advocated their style, as an 'Abstrakte SS'.[43] The so-called *Streit um die Moderne* between Hofer and Grohmann, which reached an apogee in the first months of 1955, would revive and intensify the language of this skirmish.

More than a little annoyed, in his review of the Künstlerbund's 1953 exhibition, which ran from 9 May to 12 July 1953 at the Kunsthalle in Hamburg, Grohmann wrote in *Das Kunstwerk*: 'The art school professors and their friends dominate the board and jury; the younger generation is not represented. The two youngest are Fritz Winter (b.1905) and Georg Meistermann (b.1911).'[44] Haftmann added his voice, too, writing in the *Frankfurter Allgemeine Zeitung*: 'The Künstlerbund is beginning to get too old ... [it] should increase the number of invitations to younger artists as far as possible.'[45] Soon, other critics joined in the fracas, pointing out that younger painters affiliated with Informel and Tachist trends had gone missing.[46] This was far from inconsequential for these artists. By 1953 the Künstlerbund had become the most prestigious artistic platform to present and sell new work in Germany. In comparison, Munich's annual *Grosse Kunstausstellung* was primarily regarded as a commercial exhibition.[47]

Meanwhile, Nay had become a much more important artist in Grohmann's eyes. In a review of the 1953 annual show, published in *Die Neue Zeitung* and titled 'Drei Maler hohen Ranges: Willi Baumeister, E.W. Nay, und Fritz Winter sind die Akzente' he praised these three painters' very different abstract works as the best in the exhibition.[48] The same month, Haftmann closed his review of the show in the *Frankfurter Allgemeine Zeitung* with this line: 'In all of this one wonderful voice sings completely alone – E.W. Nay.'[49]

In her dissertation about the Künstlerbund's exhibitions between 1951 and 1955, based on archival research, Myriam Maiser sums up the exhibition policies of the Künstlerbund as follows:

> In the realm of abstraction the Künstlerbund espoused already prominent German artists such as Baumeister, Meistermann, Nay, Winter ... without including other known and new talents to a considerable degree. Isolated works of Informel painters appeared in only one exhibition. Fred Thieler (b.1916), Hans Platschek (b.1923) and K.R.H. Sonderborg (b.1923) amongst them. Work by those pressing to the front of the line, mostly young Informel German artists, were not included in the annual exhibitions of the Deutsche Künstlerbund through 1955.[50]

The irregular invitation of younger painters to submit works was partly due to the desire of some of their colleagues to keep them out of the organisation. Only those who had been invited three times by the jury and had at least one painting included in the annual exhibition could become members.[51] Even though Nay was never amongst the jurors, the prominent place he was accorded in such shows and the positive reviews that followed were grounds enough for spiteful envy.

It was not long before a call for a new charter for the Künstlerbund's jury policies resulted in a face-off between Baumeister and Hofer. Matters reached a new climax in October of 1954. That month, one after another, Nay, Baumeister and Winter left the Künstlerbund, using as their excuse a derogatory comment that Hofer had purportedly made to the press about 'how easy' it was to make abstract art. Regardless of the fact that his words had been distorted, by then his objections to abstract art were sufficiently well-known to his colleagues to make their secession from the Künstlerbund seem appropriate.[52] Their exit, however, was actually a last, if unsuccessful, ruse to try to force Hofer to resign as president, thereby enabling a reorganisation of the Künstlerbund with Baumeister as its president. Once again, Grohmann brought the quarrel to a broad-based public through an article published in *Die Neue Zeitung* on 4 November 1954.[53] Needless to say, as would be noted in the press, the lack of paintings by Baumeister, Nay and Winter in the annual 1955 show compromised its quality as never before.[54]

Here, note should be taken that the tendency amongst scholars to reduce the growing debate between Baumeister and Hofer to aesthetic polarisations brought about by the Cold War – an argument that equates abstraction with democratic values in West Germany, and realist tendencies with the socialist ideology of the former East – not only over-simplifies matters but ignores schisms between several generations of abstract painters working in the West.[55] For example, although Nay had been willing to align himself with Baumeister's drive for a reorganisation of the Künstlerbund since 1952, by then two years had passed since he had privately denounced the latter's abstract paintings as 'epigonic'.[56] In 1953 he also condemned the 'art of the soul' (*Seelenkunst*) made by ZEN 49 – Willi Baumeister, Rolf Cavel, Gerhard Fietz, Rupprecht Geiger, Willy Hempel, Brigitte Meier-Denninghoff and Fritz Winter to name merely its founding members – as not just 'based upon Kandinsky' but 'nearing an end'.[57] Additionally Nay wanted nothing to do with various younger Informel and Tachist artists, whether they be those affiliated with Quadriga in Frankfurt – Karl Otto Götz,

43 Will Grohmann, 'Die drei Tricks in der Diskussion um die heutige Kunste', *Die Neue Zeitung*, Frankfurt am Main, no.150, 27/28 June 1953, p.9.
44 Will Grohmann, 'Der Deutsche Künstlerbund Hamburg 1953: Einge Bemerkungen zur Ausstellungspolitik', in *Das Kunstwerk*, Frankfurt am Main, vol.2, no.7, 1953, p.51.
45 Werner Haftmann, 'Vom Standort der deutschen Kunst: Die Ausstellung des Deutschen Künstlerbundes in Hamburg', in *Frankfurter Allgemeine Zeitung*, no.117, 23 May 1953, p.BuZ4.
46 Maiser, 2007, *op. cit.*, p.172.
47 Anonymous, 'Streit: Rabiat wie ein Religionskrieg', in *Der Spiegel*, no.29, 15 July 1953, pp.28–29.
48 Will Grohmann, 'Drei Maler hohen Ranges, Willi Baumeister, E.W. Nay und Fritz Winter sind die Akzente', in Maiser, 2007, *op. cit.*, p.134.
49 Haftmann, in *Frankfurter Allgemeine Zeitung*, *op. cit.*
50 Maiser, 2007, *op. cit.*, p.173
51 Anonymous, 'Rabiat wie ein Religionskrieg', in *Der Spiegel*, 15 July 1953, p.27.
52 Fischer-Defoy, 2004, *op. cit.*, pp.187–89. See also Maiser, 2007, *op. cit.*, pp.217–20.
53 Will Grohmann, 'Krise des "Deutschen Künstlerbundes"', in *Die Neue Zeitung*, Berlin-Dahlem, no.257 4 November 1954, p.7. Also in *E.W. Nay: Bilder und Dokumente*, *op. cit.*, p.124.
54 Maiser, 2007, *op. cit.*, pp.194–95.
55 See Yule Heibel's critical remarks on this tendency in her *Reconstructing the Subject: Modernist Painting in West Germany 1945–1950*, Princeton University Press, Princeton, NJ, 1995, p.91.
56 E.W. Nay, memorandum dated 14 January 1950, in *Lesebuch: Selbstzeugnisse und Schriften 1931–1968*, M. DuMont, Cologne, 2002, p.55.
57 E.W. Nay, memorandum dated 13 September 1953, *ibid.*, p.76.

Otto Greis, Heinz Kreuz, and Bernhard Schultze – the Düsseldorf-based Gruppe 53 – Peter Brüning, Karl Fred Dahmen, Albert Fürst, Winfred Gaul, and Gerhard Hoehme among them – or the so-called Junger Westen, an artists' organisation based in Recklinghausen that included Gustav Deppe, Thomas Grochowiak, and Emil Schumacher as well as others. As far as he was concerned, his abstract painting had next to nothing in common with their aesthetic.

In 1954, Haftmann's *Malerei im 20. Jahrhundert* (Painting in the Twentieth Century) appeared on the market, soon becoming a best-seller.[58] Following the appearance in 1955 of a second hefty volume of illustrations accompanied by abbreviated text passages, *Malerei im 20. Jahrhundert* began to be embraced in Germany as the 'bible' of art history.[59] In its pages Haftmann barely mentioned the work of German Tachist or Informel artists. Instead, he argued that the increasingly abstract style that Nay had cultivated since 1950 singled him out as Germany's most important painter.[60] Klaus Jürgen-Fischer, a little known Informel artist, took Haftmann to task for this in a lengthy article, '*Was ist Tachismus?*' published late in 1955 in *Das Kunstwerk*. He alleged that though couched in 'spontaneous' and 'Tachist' language, the point of departure for Nay's abstract paintings was actually 'geometrical ornamental figurations'. Far from automatic, their 'structure required a strict compositional procedure'. Why then, he wondered, would Haftmann grant the 'first place in modern art' to a painter in his *Malerei im 20. Jahrhundert* whose work combined 'two contrary pictorial principles'?[61]

Meanwhile in the mid-1950s in Paris, the prominent gallerist René Drouin had become interested in mounting an exhibition about postwar trends in German non-figurative art. Above all, he wanted to show work by young artists, rendered in the 'most expressive' gestural style, which evidenced the 'greatest degree of liveliness'.[62] In order to ferret out such painters, as well as those better known in Germany, he solicited the advice of three experts: Will Grohmann, John A. Thwaites and Carl Linfert. The latter primarily networked in the Rhineland, where since 1949 he had taken over the evening programming of the Nordwestdeutscher Rundfunk. Thwaites knew the art scene in Bavaria like the back of his hand. He had helped to found ZEN 49 in Munich after quitting the British diplomatic service in 1949. He remained in Munich until 1955, when he moved to Düsseldorf, where those artists affiliated with Gruppe 53 found his endorsement. Critical of Nay's standing in Germany, he didn't hesitate to take a swipe at the artist in writing whenever he could.[63]

Drouin's exhibition, *Peintures et sculptures non-figuratives en Allemagne d'aujourd'hui*, which ran from 7 April to 8 May 1955 in the former clubhouse of the Cercle Volney, was the first large exhibition of abstract German art in France after the close of the Second World War. The exhibition featured 98 artworks by 34 painters and three sculptors. Among them were not just Baumeister, Meistermann, Nay, Werner and Winter, but also many Tachist and Informel artists. By then, Carl Buchheister, Götz and Thieler had all been given one-man gallery shows in Paris.[64] As it turned out, it was particularly the work of the latter two, along with paintings by Schultze and Sonderborg, that stole the show at the Cercle Volney. Grohmann chose, however, not to report this in his review of the exhibition in *Der Tagespiegel*. Instead he wrote:

> It's hard to say which painters the French like best; they seem to be hooked on personalities who are controversial in Germany, Bernard Schultze for example, or W. Wesel, Fred Thieler or the younger Hamburg artist Sonderborg. That doesn't mean, however, that they overlook the quality of those painters whom we value, but that they value the rest more than here in Germany.[65]

The Parisian critics' reviews, however, left no doubt which painters they favoured, judging work by Nay, Meistermann and Winter as pale in comparison.[66] Grohmann's article infuriated many of these artists, still largely unrecognised in Germany. Götz, for example, whose name Grohmann hadn't even bothered to mention, commented in a letter to the French art critic and painter Édouard Jaguer: 'Grohmann doesn't have the courage to say that we are the stars of the German show ... That is mean.'[67]

More or less parallel to the Cercle Volney exhibition, the Galerie Creuze presented *Phases de l'art contemporain. Première confrontation internationale de l'art expérimental à Paris*, in which the works of such international artists as Pierre Alechinsky, Lucio Fontana and Sam Francis were juxtaposed with paintings by Buchheister, Götz and Schultze.[68] More than a thousand visitors were said to have attended the opening, drumming up even further interest in the Cercle Volney exhibition.[69] Far from being galvanised into action, however, German museum officials reacted with hesitation. While initially the Staatsgalerie Stuttgart had indicated that it would also present the Cercle Volney exhibition, in the end its director decided against doing so. Even when the exhibition opened at the Düsseldorf Kunstmuseum on 25 June 1955, it was not celebrated in the German press. Throughout its eight-week run, it

58 *Malerei im 20. Jahrhundert* saw a second printing in 1957, and a third expanded version in 1962, before being released in a fourth newly enlarged edition in 1965. Thereafter it continued to be reissued, going into a ninth edition in 2000.
59 Werner Haftmann, *Malerei im 20. Jahrhundert: Tafelband*, Prestel-Verlag, Munich, 1954. See also Harald Kimpel, 'Werner Haftmann und der "Geist der französischen Kunst"', in Martin Schieder and Isabelle Ewig (eds), *In die Freiheit Geworfen: Positionen zur Deutsch-Französischen Kunstgeschichte nach 1945*, Akademie Verlag, Berlin, 2006, p.133.
60 Haftman, *op. cit.*, p.465.
61 Klaus J. Fischer, 'Was ist Tachismus?', in *Das Kunstwerk*, vol.5, no.9, V1955/56, pp.19–20.
62 Martin Schieder, 'René Drouin und seine Ausstellung "Peintures et sculptures non figuratives en Allemagne d'aujourd'hui" 1955 in Paris', in Uwe Fleckner, Martin Schieder and Michael F. Zimmermann (eds), *Jenseits der Grenzen: Französische und deutsche Kunst vom Ancien Régime bis zur Gegenwart*, vol.3, *Dialog der Avantgarden*, M. DuMont, Cologne, 2000, p.184.
63 Beate Eickhoff, *John Anthony Thwaites und die Kunstkritik der 50er Jahre*, Verlag und Datenbank für Geisteswissenschaften, Weimar, 2004, pp.206–07.
64 Schieder, *Jenseits der Grenzen*, 2000, *op. cit.*, pp.184–85.
65 Will Grohmann, 'Osterreise über die Grenzen: Deutsche Kunst in Paris – Kandinsky in Bern', in *Der Tagespiegel*, no.2922, p.4. Also in Schieder, *Im Blick des Anderen*, 2005, *op. cit.*, pp.139–40.
66 Schieder, *Jenseits der Grenzen*, 2000, *op. cit.*, p.192.
67 Karl Otto Götz, letter to Édouard Jaguer, 29 April 1955, *ibid.*, p.140.
68 See Schieder, *Jenseits der Grenzen*, 2000, *op. cit.*, p.191. Schultze, Bucheister, Götz and Greis had already been invited to show their newest paintings alongside those by Alchensky, Camille Bryen, Asger Jorn and Roberto Matta at *Première Exposition Phases* at the Studio Paul Facchetti, which opened on 22 January 1954 in Paris. See Schieder, *Im Blick des Anderen*, 2005, *op. cit.*, pp.157–58.
69 Schieder, *Jenseits der Grenzen*, 2000, *op. cit.*, p.191.

was seen by barely 6,000 visitors.[70] In the interim almost 130,000 visitors flocked to the first Documenta, which had opened in Kassel.[71] Although Haftmann included a large group of paintings by the more established abstractionists in Germany – Nay, of course, amongst them – he did not include a single canvas by a German Tachist or Informel painter.[72]

The upshot was predictable. Marginalised by their fellow artists from the annual Künstlerbund shows, left out of Germany's most important book about the significance of postwar aesthetic trends there, and all but ignored by official exhibition makers, many of these younger artists began to quip about their more successful colleagues. Already by 1954 Nay was near the top of their list. Never mind that two years before he had added his voice to those 'oppositionalists' in the Künstlerbund arguing for the inclusion of newer talent. While a seemingly unstoppable avalanche of kudos showered over Nay in Germany, scarcely a drop of recognition was ladled out to Tachist or Informel painters.[73] In Paris, however, then still the art capital of Europe, their work had begun to make headlines. In the wake, for example, of the showing of several of his new paintings in *Première Exposition Phases* at the Studio Paul Facchetti in 1954, Götz wrote to Jaguer: 'Here [in Paris] the big painters, the Nays, Meistermanns, and Winters, these types, rightfully shy away from exhibiting, because the criticism they would receive could break one of the spikes off their crowns.'[74] In Nay's case at least, the accusation was not particularly true. He had been interested in a showing in Paris since 1948, but apart from participating in the *Salon de Mai* in 1950, nothing came of his efforts until his work was included in the Cercle Volney exhibition in 1955.[75] It was this fact, together with the resolute internationalism of the soon to be founded Zero group, that lent credence to the later allegation that Nay was nothing more than a provincial German painter.

Meanwhile, in January of 1955, the growing confrontation between Hofer and Grohmann began to sizzle and fry, culminating in a red-hot exchange between them in the Berlin press.[76] In his article 'Der Mut, unmodern zu sein' which appeared on 11 February 1955 in *Der Tagespiegel*, Hofer commented:

> Every new phase of art requires its defence in written and spoken words. Nevertheless, it shouldn't get to the point of the kind of intolerance prevalent today ... Indeed, alarmingly, such behavior approaches that of the Nazi state with its Gauleiters and SS. A Goebbels is already at hand; a Führer probably too. Oh, saintly Klee, if you only knew what is taking place under the banner of your name.[77]

Although Hofer did not elaborate, given the illusion to Klee there is little doubt that he was referring to Grohmann and Haftmann. Both had not only recently published monographs on Klee, but had also used his famous phrase 'art makes visible' (1920) to defend the aims of the postwar abstract artists they supported.[78]

The struggle between Hofer and Grohmann and the artists aligned with him, however, was only superficially intertwined with their differences regarding painting styles. It was the dispute about the establishing of exhibiting policies, membership rules and a viable charter within the Künstlerbund that really fuelled their confrontation.[79] Hofer died in April 1955, possibly helped into his grave by the exchange. Baumeister, who was a decade younger, unexpectedly followed him a few months later. After that, there was no further discussion of Grohmann's possible integration into the Künstlerbund. The same aggressiveness that characterised his critique of Hofer's views – which disregarded the honour long associated with his name – would also typify the even more disrespectful tone with which Nay would be assailed in the German press less than ten years later.

In October 1955, Eugen Schönebeck arrived at the Hochschule für Bildende Künste in Berlin, entering Hans Kuhn's class in his second semester. Describing the atmosphere there, he commented later: 'the name Nay was on everyone's lips'. Several drawings evidencing his experimentation with the possibilities of Nay's 'Disk' paintings are amongst his earliest works to survive.[80] Georg Baselitz joined Hann Trier's class a year later. About this time he recalled: 'I soaked up everything that my professor, Trier, presented to me: Bauhaus, abstraction, Nay's writings – whose theories I worked out in coloured pencils – then I read Kandinsky, Malevitch and so on.'[81] By 'Nay's writings' Baselitz meant *Vom Gestaltwert der Farbe*, a small booklet published by Prestel-Verlag in 1955.[82] Thereafter, both Schönebeck and Baselitz chose, however, to cultivate a style of painting until at least 1960 more in line with Tachism than Nay's brand of abstraction.

Meanwhile, Informel painters continued to struggle to get their work shown in Germany – Jürgen-Fischer and Platschek amongst them. Up until 1959, things had looked relatively promising for them. Both had participated in the Cercle Volney exhibition in Paris, and in 1956 Jürgen-Fischer was given a one-man show at the Kaiser-Wilhelm-Museum in Krefeld. Platschek was also one of the few Informel painters whose work had been included in an early Künstlerbund exhibition. Although the jury had chosen to exhibit several of his paintings in the annual 1954 exhibition, the follow-

70 *Ibid.*, p.195.
71 Manfred Schneckenburger (ed), *Documenta: Idee und Institution*, Bruckmann, Munich, 1983, p.29.
72 See Franz Roh, *Streit um die Moderne: Auseinandersetzung mit Gegnern der neuen Malerei*, Paul List, Munich, 1962, p.40.
73 Karl Otto Götz, '"Das Informel ist ein Prinzip": Claudia Posca im Gespräch mit Karl Otto Götz und Rissa', 12 November 1998, in *Informel: Der Anfang nach dem Ende*, *op. cit.*, p.234.
74 Karl Otto Götz, letter to Édouard Jaguer 18 March 1954, in Schieder, *Im Blick des Anderen*, *op. cit.*, p.158.
75 For E.W. Nay's interest in showing in Paris, see, for example, the letter from Nay to Erich Meyer, 2 December 1948 in *E.W. Nay: Bilder und Dokumente*, *op. cit.*, p.104.
76 Karl Hofer, 'Der Mut, unmodern zu sein', in *Der Tagespiegel*, 11 February 1955, p.5. This article is a condensed version of Karl Hofer, 'Zur Situation der bildenden Kunst', in *Der Monat*, vol.77, no.7, February 1955, pp.425–32. Both in *Karl Hofer: Malerei hat eine Zukunft, Briefe, Aufsätze, Reden*, *op. cit.*, pp.348–58. Will Grohmann, 'Respekt vor den Tatsachen: Ein Wort für die moderne Kunst', in *Der Tagespiegel*, 18 February 1955, p.4 and 'Die Kritiker ist für die Kunst', in *Der Monat*, vol.78, no.7, March 1955, pp.545–48.
77 Hofer, 'Der Mut', 1955, *op. cit.*, p.356.
78 Werner Haftmann, *Paul Klee: Wege bildernischen Denkens*, Prestel-Verlag, Munich, 1950, and Will Grohmann, *Paul Klee: Leben und Werk*, Kohlhammer, Stuttgart,1954.
79 Heibel, 1995, *op. cit.*, p.174, fn.32.
80 Eugen Schönebeck, unpublished interview with the author, 16 July 2007.
81 George Baselitz, in conversation with Heinz Peter Schwerfel, 1989, trans Fiona Elliot, in *Georg Baselitz: Collected Writings*, 2010, *op. cit.*, p.179.
82 Although that book had been translated into English by 1962, it never found a publisher. See Bob R. Martin, letter to Elisabeth Nay, 25 July 1962, in *E.W. Nay: Bilder und Dokumente*, *op. cit.*, p.140.

ing year the works he sent at their behest were rejected.[83] Miffed, he refused their request that he should once again submit work for consideration for the 1956 show. Instead, that January, he testily dashed off a letter to them in which he not only criticised their adjudicators, but stated that he saw no reason to send work that might possibly be rejected again.[84] Two years later, he had cause for more disappointment with the publishing of the lavishly illustrated *Neue Kunst nach 1945*. Grohmann, who had edited the volume, also wrote a long chapter in it about developments in German, Austrian and Swiss art. In it he devoted several dozen pages to discussing work by Informel and Tachist artists. Platschek's name, however, only cropped up in passim.[85]

In the interim, Haftmann had been gearing up for the second Documenta in Kassel. Although Grohmann and his artist cohorts had failed to make his voice known inside the Künstlerbund, Haftmann asked him to join the Documenta advisory board for the 1959 exhibition, subsequently renewing the offer for the 1964 show. Informel and Tachist art finally gained official acceptance at the 1959 German Documenta. In no sense, however, did this kind of art 'triumph' there. Instead, it was marginalised once again by its exhibition in an unlit space just under the roof. While Jürgen-Fischer was not invited, Platschek, showed three recent paintings there. Seven canvases by Nay were presented in the well lit galleries below, including the monumental painting *Das Freiburger Bild*. On 7 July 1959 he jotted down his impressions of the show. His first comment was 'Tachism is dead.'[86] Nevertheless, Haftmann included many of the younger Informel and Tachist artists featured in the 1959 Documenta, once again in the 1964 Documenta; Platschek, however, was not among them.

The chance to get even with the official art establishment in Germany presented itself in the wake of the mixed reception of the third Documenta. Perhaps the most vehement article was Jürgen-Fischer's 'Im Zeichen des Informalismus. Auf der documenta III kommt die neue Malerei zu kurz', published that summer in *Die Zeit*. Here, he accused Bode, the exhibition's director, of having attempted to bestow upon Nay 'world-wide recognition'. Although Jürgen-Fischer found Bode's installation of three of Nay's gigantic new paintings from the ceiling of the Museum Fridericianum ingenious, he blamed the 'bias of the Documenta advisory board' for having caused him to focus on the wrong painter. Instead of confirming Nay's talent, he claimed that the installation 'cemented his artistic collapse'. In so doing it also exposed the existence of a 'national misunderstanding' about the artist's significance.[87] Silently, both Jürgen-Fischer and Platschek blamed this phalanx for ignoring their works, to the point that both had been forced to find additional means of supporting themselves. While since 1955 Jürgen-Fischer had devoted himself increasingly to editing *Das*

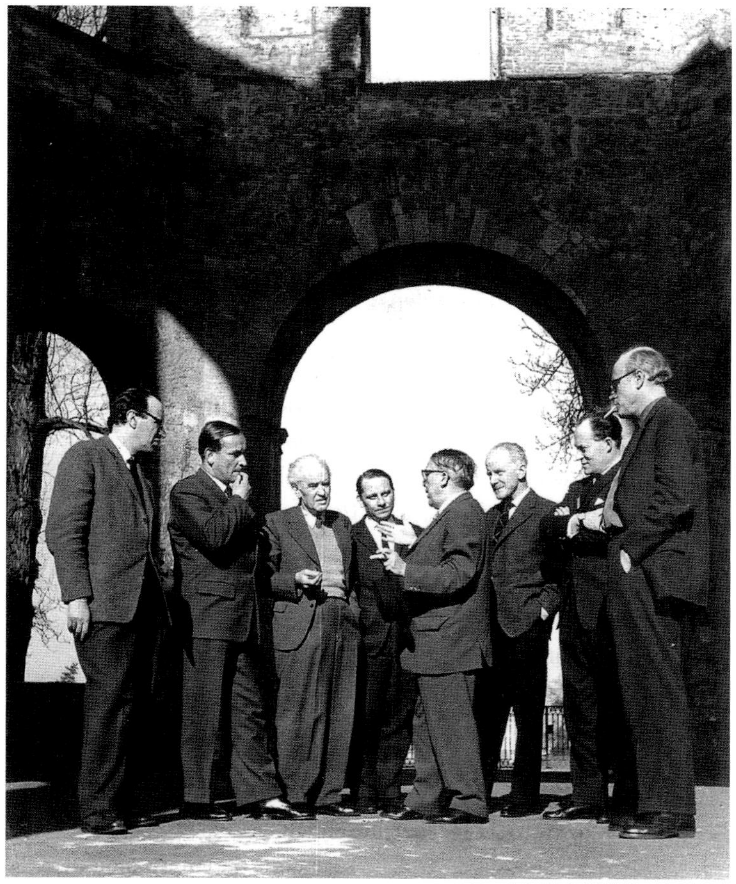

The advisory board of Documenta II in the ruins of the Orangerie (left to right: Ernst Goldschmidt, Werner Haftmann, Will Grohmann, Herbert von Buttlar, Arnold Bode, Ernst Holzinger, Eduard Trier and Werner Schmalenbach), 1959

83 Maiser, 2007, *op. cit.*, pp.173–74, 177, 195.
84 Hans Platschek, letter to E. Seel, 25 February 1956, Archiv Deutscher Künstlerbund, no.31P, in Maiser, 2007, *op. cit.*, p.208.
85 Will Grohmann, 'Deutschland, Österreich, und Schweiz', in *Neue Kunst nach 1945*, Will Grohmann (ed), M. DuMont Schauberg, Cologne, 1958, pp.151–218.
86 Nay, memorandum of 7 July 1959, in *Lesebuch*, *op. cit.*, 2002, p.189.
87 Klaus Jürgen-Fischer, 'Im Zeichen des Informalismus: Auf der documenta III kommt die neue Malerei zu kurz,' in *Die Zeit*, 10 July 1964, no.28, in Schneckenburger, *op. cit.*, pp.81–82.

Kunstwerk, Platschek began in 1959 to write books about art as a sideline.

Undoubtedly encouraged by the swipe his colleague had taken at Nay, Platschek wrote an even more vicious article, which was published on 4 September 1964 in *Die Zeit*. In this cleverly argued text, Platschek even went so far as to accuse Haftmann of using language to laud Nay's paintings that was reminiscent of the lingo of National Socialist ideologues. Next he came after the artist himself, proposing that his postwar shift from mythical subjects to abstract disks was nothing more than a clever tactical move; despite their new look, the paintings remained anchored in sentiments that had helped enable Fascism.[88] The implication was that Haftmann and Nay were not just old Nazis, but dangerous ones, not least because they were currently leading the art world around by its nose. Such slander went far beyond the linguistic slingshots first taken at Grohmann in 1953 and later in 1955, which had equated his vigorous support of abstraction with the aggressive tactics of the SS.

Even though it must have been obvious to most readers that Platschek had overshot the mark, his words hit a sensitive nerve. For one thing, a broad-based public had long been suspicious of the merit of abstract art, not least because it wasn't easy to understand. Added to this was the fact that the articles appeared just when national attention was increasingly focused on the Auschwitz Process unfolding in Frankfurt. And finally, those in the know realized that Platschek had hit upon aspects of the history of modern art in Germany that at the time they would perhaps have preferred left unsaid.

Werner Haftmann, 'Nordic Modernism' and E.W. Nay (1934–60)

At this juncture it is helpful to recall the status of the discipline of art history in Germany after 1945. Not only had modern painting and sculpture come to a grinding halt there since 1933, but after that date art historians either had to accommodate their work to themes sanctioned by National Socialist cultural authorities or quit the discipline. Born in 1912, Werner Haftmann began to study art history in Berlin just as Adolf Hitler came into power. The following year, at just 22 years of age, Haftmann started to write for the magazine *Kunst der Nation*. The six-page journal, which appeared twice monthly from 1 November 1933 until 15 February 1935, provided a platform for the articulation of pro-Expressionist sentiments at a moment when these were still allowed in Germany.[89] Enabled by Joseph Goebbels, *Kunst der Nation* was in a sense born out of a political struggle for power with Alfred Rosenberg, an encounter that unfolded around the definition of modern art in National Socialist Germany. As long as the question remained open, a new kind of Expressionist art still had a future there. Sympathetic to Expressionist art, Goebbels particularly admired Emil Nolde and Ernst Barlach. In December of 1933, on the occasion of Edvard Munch's seventieth birthday, he even went so far as to recognise the Norwegian artist as a representative 'northern-folkish art-maker'.[90] Two years later, when it turned out that Hitler would not tolerate any straying from the line of officially accepted art, Goebbels withdrew his support from the magazine and it folded.[91] By then, Haftmann had published three articles in its pages.[92] All of them were aimed at trying to prevent the banning of Expressionist art espoused by Rosenberg's Kampfbund für deutsche Kultur.

One example is an October 1934 article titled 'Geographie und unsere bewusste Kunstsituation. Abhandlung zur Frage des West-Östlichen'. In it Haftmann described the work of Franc Marc in these terms:

> Of course, Marc used the structural forms of a Western painter, but the inner form (the internal painting intention) disassociated itself from Western thinking, in so far as it replaced a rational outlook with a metaphysical-pantheistic mindset ... Now the greatness and strangeness of the East stood before the German artist and called him to come to terms with it.[93]

Haftmann then alleged that future art in Germany would 'synthesise' Western and Eastern impulses, driven by an 'inner necessity' to bring forth a 'distinctly developed German art form'. It was this aim, he asserted, that informed the work of artists currently developing a new kind of Nordic Expressionism, Barlach and Nolde among them.[94]

Like others who wrote for *Kunst der Nation* – Alfred Hentzen, Paul Ferdinand Schmidt and Herbert von Einem among them – Haftmann aimed to connect new Expressionist trends in art, loosely known as 'Nordic modernism', with characteristically 'German' art, thereby isolating and elevating it from 'foreign' international trends in the sense expounded by the National Socialists.[95] In this, he seems to have followed to some extent the generational theory of Wilhelm Pinder, who had argued just a few months before in *Kunst der Nation* for a 'Nordic' or 'Viking' bent as a fundamental feature of German art. Pinder's agenda, however, was to establish national stylistic continuities so as to define what constituted German art.[96]

88 Hans Platschek, 'Nays Scheiben – Ein repräsentativer Deutscher Maler genauer betrachtet', in *Die Zeit*, 4 September 1964, no.36, in *E.W. Nay: Bilder und Dokumente*, *op. cit.*, pp.251–53.
89 Dieter Scholz, 'Otto Andreas Schreiber, die "Kunst der Nation" und die Fabrikausstellungen', in Blume, *op. cit.*, p.92.
90 Christian Saehrendt, *Ernst Ludwig Kirchner: Bohème-Identität und nationale Sendung*, Peter Lang, Frankfurt am Main, 2003, p.197. See also Peter Paret, *An Artist Against the Reich: Ernst Barlach 1933–1938*, Cambridge University Press, Cambridge, 2003, p.61.
91 Paret, 2003, *op. cit.*, p.72.
92 Werner Haftmann, 'Form und Wirklichkeit: Exkurs über deren Einheit in der modernen Kunst', in *Kunst der Nation*, 1 August 1934, vol.2, no.15, p.1; Werner Haftmann, 'Geographie und unsere bewusste Kunstsituation. Abhandlung zur Frage des West-Östlichen' in *Kunst der Nation*, 2 October 1934, vol.2, no.20, pp.3–4; Werner Haftmann, 'Zu Vielfältigkeit Deutscher Kunst', in *Kunst der Nation*, 2 December 1934, vol.2, no.24, pp.1–2.
93 Werner Haftmann, 'Geographie und unsere bewusste Kunstsituation', *op. cit.*, p.3. Also in Eckhart Gillen, 'Die Zwischenkriegsgeneration auf der Suche nach einer Synthese aus expressionistischen "Ballungen" und klassizistischer Ordnung', in Blume, *op. cit.*, pp.21–24.
94 Haftmann, 'Geographie und unsere bewusste Kunstsituation', *op. cit.*, p.4.
95 See Werner Haftmann, *Verfemte Kunst*, M. DuMont, Cologne, 1986, p.22 Although he discussed several of his colleagues' association with the magazine in this book, Haftmann refrained from mentioning that he had also been a contributor.

Haftmann's lines also indicate a careful reading of Gottfried Benn's 'Bekenntnis zum Expressionismus' (Confession of an Expressionist). This text first appeared in November 1933 in *Deutsche Zukunft*, just as the initial issue of *Kunst der Nation* was printed. Like the art historians who defended Expressionism in that magazine, Benn directed his article against the denunciation of painterly Expressionism as 'degenerate'. In 1934, in a slightly expanded version of the article, he alleged that 'out of the chaos of their life and times' all Expressionists of his generation 'had experienced an evolution subject to the most urgent inner necessity not given to other generations, an evolution toward a new order and new historical meaning'.[97]

In 1933, however, Benn had already fallen under the sway of National Socialism; he would continue to align himself with its objectives until July 1934. Pinder became a committed National Socialist no later than 1935, when he accepted a professorship in Berlin, persisting in his allegiance to the party until the end of the war.[98] After *Kunst der Nation* went under in 1935, Haftmann chose to give up writing about modern art. Instead, in 1936 he completed his dissertation on *Das italienische Säulenmonument* at Göttingen Universität. He then accepted an assistantship at the Kunsthistorisches Institut in Florence, where he remained until 1939. Although the opportunity arose in the final days of 1939 for him to become Hans Sedlmayr's assistant at the University in Vienna, he declined the job, citing 'intellectual freedom' as his reason. Haftmann was just able to publish his dissertation, before being conscripted into war service in 1940.[99] Shortly after the close of the war, he was released from an American military camp. He served for a while as a freelance journalist, publishing articles in various newspapers, before assuming a post as an art history lecturer at Hamburg's Staatliche Hochschule der Künste in 1950, a position that he retained for the next five years.

It is therefore not so surprising that the tenor of what Haftmann would write about Nay's work after the war would be indebted to his concerns as a young doctoral student before it broke out.[100] As it turned out, Pinder's *Das Problem der Generationen in der Kunstgeschichte Europas* (1926), not only continued to hold Haftmann's attention in 1935, but informed the methodology of his *Malerei im 20. Jahrhundert*, published almost 20 years later.[101] Pinder's concepts of generational difference and the undulating character of a historical continuum helped Haftmann make a case in that book for the imminent emergence of 'a style of great range', rooted in aesthetic developments that had unfolded in the 'two decades' between the world wars. It had been the 'imperturbable faith' of such artists as Nay and Winter in the 'higher necessity of their work' that kept it alive in the bleak years of war. Thereafter a 'new generation' took up 'the long sequence of artistic ideas and works that began with Cézanne' and 'in an unbroken' manner pressed ahead with them.[102]

Above all, however, after 1945 Haftmann continued to believe deeply in the synthesis of Northern and Eastern art that he had prophesied in 1934. It was this that he credited Nay with having achieved in his painting. In *Malerei im 20. Jahrhundert* he described, for example, Nay's post-1952 work in the following terms, words repeated verbatim in the 1960 English translation of the book:

> And now, as we might logically expect, the Western horizons of the constructors Poussin and Gris are gradually eclipsed and there emerges a Northern and Eastern realm where such painters as Munch, Nolde and Kandinsky have their place. If these paintings make the viewer think of the early works of Kandinsky or Nolde or Expressionism, the grain of truth contained in such a comparison lies in the fact that the Nordic world of expression has here achieved a new birth.[103]

Nay, too, had for a while embraced the idea of a new type of painting that would 'develop in the Nordic-Germanic world'.[104] Aware of this, in 1937 Carl Georg Heise convinced Munch to subsidise a short stay by Nay in Norway. The 'Lofoten' pictures that emerged soon afterwards were amongst the most expressive images that Nay was ever to make. By the close of the war, however, he had lost interest in the potential of so-called 'Nordic modernism'. For example, in 1948 he commented to a young artist that although Nolde's art was embedded in a 'vitalist' energy he too wanted to exploit, it was lacking in 'form', a quality just as important to the art of the future.[105] By 1950 Nay had come to feel that postwar art had two departure points: the evocation of the 'hallucinative' and 'unconscious', a tendency he equated with the paintings of Kandinsky and Klee and the 'tectonic, imaginative awareness of pictorial form' that for him originated in the work of Paul Cézanne and the Cubists. His own paintings, he claimed, proceeded from the latter.[106] Nevertheless, even in the 1965 edition of *Malerei im 20. Jahrhundert* Haftmann continued to emphasise the importance of the 'Nordic world of Expressionism' for Nay's post-1952 paintings.[107]

And yet, Haftmann's discussion of the National Socialists' misuse of the term 'Nordic' in the 1954 edition of the book reveals that he was far from unaware of just how fraught his own use of the same term could be.[108] In his monograph on Nay he only slightly

96 Stefan Germer, 'Kunst der Nation: Zu einem Versuch die Avantgarde zu nationalisieren', in Bazon Brock and Achim Preiss (eds), *Kunst auf Befehl? Dreiunddreissig bis Fünfundvierzig*, Klinkhardt & Biermann, Munich, 1990, p.36.
97 Gottfried Benn, 'Expressionism and the Third Reich', in Victor H. Miesel (ed), *Voices of German Expressionism*, Prentice-Hall, Englewood Cliffs, NJ, 1970, p.199.
98 Daniela Stöppel, 'Wilhelm Pinder: 1878–1947', in Ulrich Pfisterer (ed), *Klassiker der Kunstgeschichte*, vol.2, *Von Panofsky bis Greenberg*, C.H. Beck, Munich, 2008, pp.8–9.
99 Sabine Fastert, '"Ich habe als europäischer Historiker geschrieben über europäische Malerei": Werner Haftmanns Prinzipien der Kunstbetrachtung', in Stephan Albrecht, Michaela Braesel, Sabine Fastert, Andrea Gottdang and Garbriele Wimböck (eds), *Kunst – Geschichte – Wahrnehmung: Strukturen und Mechanismen von Wahrnehmungsstrategien*, Deutscher Kunstverlag, Munich and Berlin, 2008, p.321, fn.1.
100 Gillen, 1999, *op. cit.*, p.24.
101 On the indebtedness of Haftmann's method to Pindar, see Werner Hofmann, 'Der Stilentwurf des 20. Jahrhunderts', in *Merkur*, vol.9, no.7, 1955, p.681. On Haftmann's concern with Pinder in 1935, see Fastert, 2008, *op. cit.*, p.316.
102 Haftmann, *Malerei im 20. Jahrhundert*, 1954, *op. cit.*, pp.426–29, 434–35; *idem*, *Painting in the Twentieth Century*, 1960, *op. cit.*, pp.306–07, 312–13.
103 *Ibid.*, p.468; Haftmann, *Painting in the Twentieth Century*, 1960, *op. cit.*, p.365.
104 E.W. Nay, letter to Carl Georg Heise, 1 February 1935, in *Lesebuch*, *op. cit.*, p.14.
105 E.W. Nay, letter to Dietrich Voigt, 19 September 1948, *ibid.*, p.46.
106 E.W. Nay, manuscript of an interview with the Nordwestdeutsche Rundfunk, 5 April 1950, in *Lesebuch*, *op. cit.*, p.56.
107 Werner Haftmann, *Malerei im 20. Jahrhundert*, *op. cit*, p.505.
108 Haftmann, *Malerei im 20. Jahrhundert*, 1954, *op. cit.*, pp.423–24.

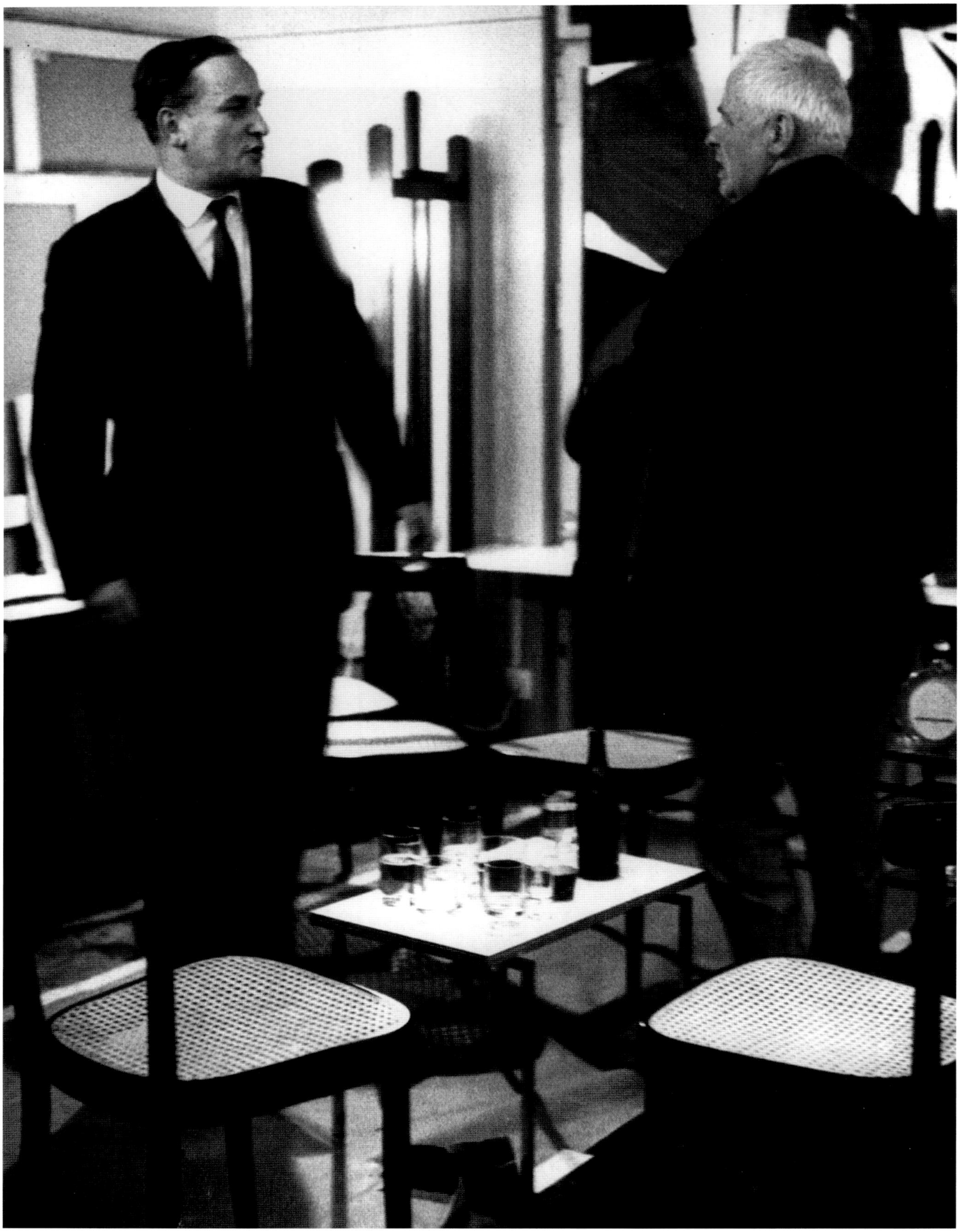

E.W. Nay and Werner Haftmann in the studio, 1964

changed his tune, suggesting that the artists' concern with the 'north-eastern world of expression' – that of Kandinsky and Nolde – culminated in 1952.[109] This did not stop him, however, from rapturously describing the paintings that Nay made in the midst of the war and continuing until 1947 in these terms: 'In the magical light that shines out of the coloured planes and in the unreality of the rhythmically moving pictorial space, a mythical quality always rings through.' Thirty pages later, Haftmann summed up this period of work:

> It is this, the western component in Nay, that also completely retains an intellectual connection to the ideas of the French colourists – to Matisse and Delaunay. The north-eastern world of expression may also be valued as the fundamental component in Nays pictorial fantasy and with that the often noticed proximity to Nordic Expressionism.'[110] Nay apparently saw nothing wrong with such passages, although he had frequently corrected others during the book's writing. Instead, after reading the final draft of the manuscript, he returned it to the author stating: 'Fully enthusiastic and in agreement'.[111]

Obviously, then, Haftmann's propensity to explain Nay's post-1945 painting from a perspective more in tune with views on modern art emergent around 1910 was at least partly in keeping with the artist's own views. On the occasion of Haftmann's receipt of Hamburg's 1962 Lessing-Prize, and the concurrent reissuing of a book of his selected essays – *Skizzenbuch zur Kultur der Gegenwart* (1960) – Werner Hofmann published a review of the book in the monthly journal *Merkur*, in which he pointed out the contradictory nature of Haftmann's ideas on contemporary art. In it he argued that Haftmann 'follows an approach to the history of ideas, not accidentally embedded in the years in which Expressionism blossomed'. By this, he meant that Haftmann's view of art as resultant from 'inner necessity', and the 'compulsion to express' harked back to Benn's texts. Not one to truck with Benn, Hofmann found such a methodology not only hopelessly outdated, but irresponsibly metaphysical at a moment that called for hard and fast terms.[112]

'The Documenta-Streit' (1964)

Two years later, Hans Platschek arrived on the scene, publishing, 'Nays Scheiben – Ein repräsentativer deutscher Maler genauer betrachtet' in *Die Zeit.* What was really just a series of wise-cracks was so cleverly formulated that it sparked off a heated debate in the press. The young artist began his article by chastising Albert Schulze Vellinghausen, Will Grohmann and Werner Haftmann, albeit without specifically naming them, for producing 'clichés' about Nay as though they were working with printer's stereotypes rather than judiciously writing. Next he tried to prove just how empty their comments were by making a mockery of *Das Freiburger Bild*, Nay's most famous painting.[113] There seems little doubt that he remembered how prominently this monumental canvas had been displayed at the 1959 Documenta (p.154), where his own work had been relegated to the small space just below the roof of the Fridericianum.[114]

Platschek then turned to Haftmann, quoting at length the passages from his monograph cited above. Next he twisted the meaning of Haftmann's claim in his *Malerei im 20. Jahrhunderts* that 'the Nordic world of expression... achieved a new birth' in Nay's post-1952 abstract paintings so as to imply that these paintings continued to convey the 'same ideology' as his earlier work, i.e. the *Ausdruckswelt* of Gottfried Benn's brief flirtation with Fascism.[115] Although thoroughly off-base, there was just enough truth in such statements to ferment debate.

Haftmann had indeed maintained a deep conviction in the significance of the 'irrational' potential of the 'north-eastern world of expression' for Nay's post-1945 paintings.[116] Nay too, had long been interested in Benn's inventive language, particularly his concept of the *Ausdruckswelt*. The concept, in fact, is inseparable from the central theoretical principle of his art: the structural value (*Gestaltwert*) of colour. Note for example, the following sentences, which he jotted down in a notebook in 1952:

> The first half of the Twentieth century strengthened modes of operation [in painting]; the second half, which stands under the rubric of the world of expression [*Ausdruckswelt*], is beginning to reinterpret functionalism in religious terms ... The surface [*Fläche*] is the only form-giving world of painting. In this form-giving world the world of expression makes itself known ... The art of the second half of the Twentieth century is the form-giving world as the world of expression, the form-giving world of surface out of colour and the world of expression.[117]

And yet, as Platschek was certainly well aware, the title *Ausdruckswelt* that Benn had given to his 1949 book, was nothing if not programmatic. With it, Benn had been meant to underscore that the 'teachings of the world of expression', which for a while had led him to commit himself to Fascism, had by 1945 become his means of 'overcoming Nationalism, racism and history, as well as human and individual sorrow, which is our born patrimony'.[118] It was precisely such dialectics that informed Benn's ideal of artistic

109 Haftmann, *E.W. Nay*, 1960, *op. cit.*, p.151.
110 *Ibid.*, pp.95, 121.
111 E.W. Nay, letter to Werner Haftmann, 31 July 1960, cited in *E.W. Nay: Bilder und Dokumente*, *op. cit.*, p.173.
112 Werner Hofmann, 'Werner Haftmanns Widersprüche', in *Merkur*, vol.172, no.16, 1962, p.592. Werner Hofmann, conversation with the author, 16 October 2011.
113 Hans Platschek, 'Nays Scheiben', in *E.W. Nay: Bilder und Dokumente, op. cit.*, pp.251–52.
114 See Winfred Gaul, '"Jeder Stil wird zur Sackgasse": Claudia Posca im Gespräch mit Winfred Gaul', 21 October 1998, in *Informel: Der Anfang nach dem Ende*, *op. cit.*, p.254.
115 Haftmann, *Malerei im 20. Jahrhundert*, *op. cit.*, p.468; Haftmann, *Painting in the Twentieth Century*, *op. cit.*, p.365. See also Platschek, 'Nays Scheiben', in *E.W. Nay: Bilder und Dokumente*, *op. cit.*, pp.252–53.
116 See also Haftmann, *E.W. Nay*, 1960, *op. cit.*, p.12.
117 E.W. Nay, memorandum dated 23 April 1952, in *Lesebuch*, *op. cit.*, p.62.
118 See Walter Jens (ed), 'Gottfried Benn', in *Kindlers Neues Literatur Lexikon*, Kindlers, Munich, 1998, p.511. Gottfried Benn, *Ausdruckswelt: Essays und Aphorismen*, Limes-Verlag, Wiesbaden, 1949, pp.7–8.

commitment. Haftmann not only upheld this stance, but in part aligned his own method with it. Note, for example, the title – *Wege zur Ausdruckswelt* – that he accorded to the second section of his *Malerei im 20. Jahrhundert*.

Ignoring these nuances, Platschek continued his attack, now misconstruing the implications of Haftmann's next statement about Nay's abstract art: 'These new paintings no longer express anything but themselves. The thematic, humanistic, mythical elements have fallen away. The painting is a purely artistic affair.'[119] Left unqualified, the phrases opened up the painter's work to the charge that it was devoid of content and therefore must be purely decorative. Two months later, Jürgen-Fischer contended precisely this in 'Der Fall des Malers E.W. Nay – Ein heftig geführter Beitrag zu einer heftigen Diskussion', published in *Der Tagespiegel*. There he claimed that although work by contemporary artists was bringing about a 'global reassessment' of 'authentic ornament', Nay is 'working in the field of painting on the degeneration of ornament into the lax arabesque, which has already repeatedly brought about flimsy collapses in art history'.[120] Such a vilification of Nay's abstract art, which depended in part upon the equation of 'ornament and crime', was anything but new.[121] Ultimately, however, it was not really the artist's paintings, but the featuring of them time after time in special shows and the raining down of prizes upon them with which Jürgen-Fischer really took issue. At the end of the article he lamented that it had been left to such painters as he to 'topple' the 'hollow monuments' that an 'oligarchy' had 'set before their noses', so 'monstrous' as to 'block communication'.[122] Read between the lines, the insinuation was that 'Der Fall des Malers E.W. Nay' was comparable to the Wilhelminian 'Fall Böcklin'.[123] In both cases, 'incompetent' critics had 'duped' a broad-based public into admiring allegedly 'bad' painters.

Platschek's next charge – that Nay's abstraction was brought about by a need to suppress reality and therefore was regressive in essence – was so outlandish that it gave people something to fluff up their feathers and cluck about. Near the end of his article he struck a particularly spiteful blow, condemning Nay's recent work as 'standing for an immutability that does not correspond with a reality: his disks encourage acceptance as a surrogate for it. As such they proffer a backward-looking utopia.'[124] Such an allegation was not only false, but short-circuited. Nay no more looked away from reality in 1955 than he had done a decade earlier when he began to move slowly towards abstraction. If anything, it had been the fracturing of reality in postwar Germany that caused him increasingly to cultivate an abstract idiom of painting. Already late in 1946, the painter Heinz Trökes had penned the following incisive statement about Nay's most recent paintings, published in *Das Kunstwerk*:

> E.W. Nay, who comes out of Expressionism, has created out of this a new pictorial world, using strong colour rhythms, and clear, prismatic forms that are not simple decoration but rather multilayered like our modern life, but which show the rupture without veiling it.[125]

Nay not only came 'out of Expressionism', but initially out of Surrealism as well. Several of his 1932 paintings were clearly indebted to the collotypes of Max Ernst's *Histoire Naturelle* (1925) (p.174).[126] Despite its title, Ernst's *Histoire Naturelle* had nothing to do with the natural evolution of forms in nature.[127] Their make-believe 'scientific' quality was one of the reasons that Nay liked them. Writing about the importance of Ernst's work to the development of his own painting, he explained in 1931 to Paul Westheim: 'What I want: Interpretation of the preternatural world, which as an organic law is present within us.'[128] In point of fact, Ernst's cycle of prints presented a fictional take on a world in which nature as we know it has come to an end.[129] After the close of the Second World War and the bombing of Hiroshima such an idea took on increased relevance.

E.W. Nay: 'The Aperspectival World View' (1949–68)[130]

In 1949 Nay came across a book that would help him build an aesthetic system intended to communicate a consciousness about time and space that was nothing if not forward-looking. That study was the first volume of Jean Gebser's *Ursprung und Gegenwart: Die Fundamente der aperspektivischen Welt* (The Ever-Present Origin: Foundations of the Aperspectival World).[131] In its very first lines, the Swiss cultural philosopher explained that in counter-distinction to 'those who have heralded the decline of the West' he

119 Haftmann, *Malerei im 20. Jahrhundert*, 1954, *op. cit.*, p.468; Haftmann, *Painting in the Twentieth Century*, 1960, *op. cit.*, p.365.
120 Jürgen-Fischer, 1964, *op. cit.*, p.256.
121 See Schuster, *E.W. Nay: Bilder und Dokumente*, 1980, *op. cit.*, pp.11–12. See also Adolf Loos, 'Ornament und Verbrechen', a lecture held on 21 January 1908 in the Akademische Verband für Literatur und Musik in Vienna. In Franz Glück (ed), *Sämtliche Schriften in Zwei Bänden*, vol.1, Herold, Vienna, 1962), pp.276–88. See also Markus Brüderlin, 'Die Einheit in der Differenz: Die Bedeutung des Ornaments für die abstrakte Kunst des 20. Jahrhunderts von Philipp Otto Runge bis Frank Stella', PhD dissertation, Bergische Universität, G.H. Wuppertal, 1994.
122 Jürgen-Fischer, 1964, *op. cit.*, p.257.
123 See particularly, Julius Meier-Graefe, *Entwicklungsgeschichte der modernen Kunst*, vol.2, Verlag Jul. Hoffmann, Stuttgart, 1904, p.452.
124 Platschek, in *E.W. Nay: Bilder und Dokumente*, 1964, *op. cit.*, p.253.
125 H. Trökes, 'Moderne Kunst in Deutschland', in *Das Kunstwerk*, vol.1, no.8/9, 1946/47, p.75, quoted in Heibel, 1995, *op. cit.*, p.109.
126 Haftmann, *E.W. Nay*, 1960, *op. cit.*, pp.53–54.
127 Pamela Kort, 'Arnold Böcklin, Max Ernst and the Debate around Origins and Survivals in Germany and France', in Pamela Kort and Max Hollein (eds), *Darwin: Art and the Search for Origins*, Schirn Kunsthalle Frankfurt, 5 February – 3 May 2009, exhibition catalogue, Wienand, Cologne, 2009, pp.42–44.
128 See E.W. Nay, 'Aus einem Brief an Paul Westheim', in *Das Kunstblatt*, vol.15, no.4, Berlin, 1931, pp.97–98, in *Lesebuch*, *op. cit.*, pp.11–12.
129 Ralf Konersmann, 'Max Ernst und die Idee der Naturgeschichte', in Karin Orchard and Jörg Zimmermann (eds), *Die Erfindung der Natur. Max Ernst, Paul Klee, Wols und das surreale Universum*, Sprengel-Museum Hanover, 27 February – 8 May 1994, exhibition catalogue, Rombach, Freiburg im Breisgau, 1994, p.163.
130 E.W. Nay, letter to Will Grohmann, 29 February 1956, cited in *Lesebuch, op. cit.*, p.132
131 Jean Gebser, *Ursprung Und Gegenwart: Bd. 1: Die Fundamente der aperspektivischen Welt; Beitrag zu einer Geschichte der Bewusstwerdung*, Deutsche-Verlags Anstalt, Stuttgart, 1949. Jean Gebser, *The Ever-Present Origin: Part One: Foundations of the Aperspectival World: A Contribution to the History of the Awakening of Consciousness* and *Part Two: Manifestations of the Aperspectival World: An Attempt at the Concretion of the Spiritual*, trans Noel Barstand, Ohio University Press, Athens, OH, 1985.

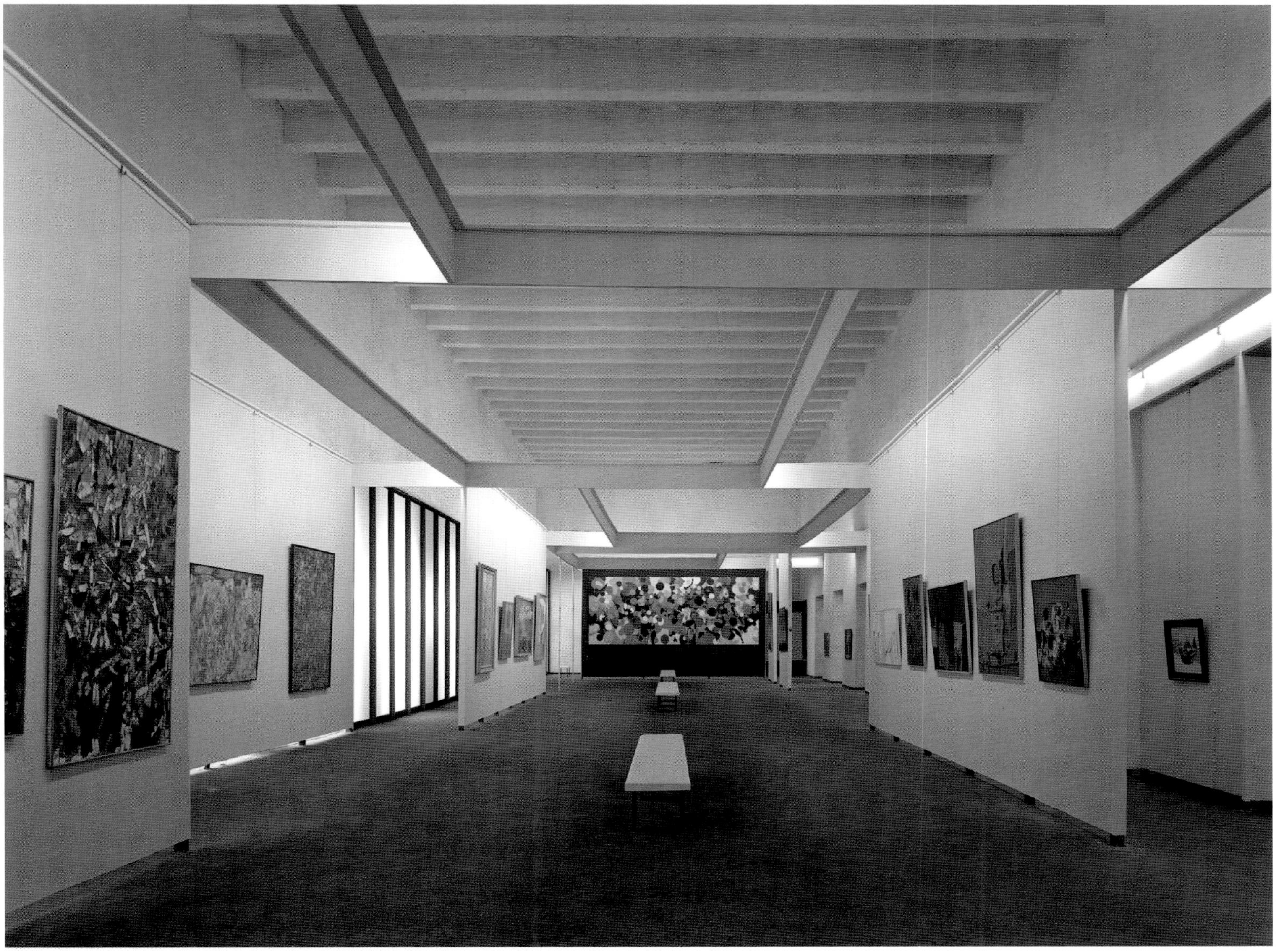

View into the main room at
Fridericianum at Documenta II,
Kassel, with E.W. Nay's *Das Freiburger Bild* centre stage, 1959

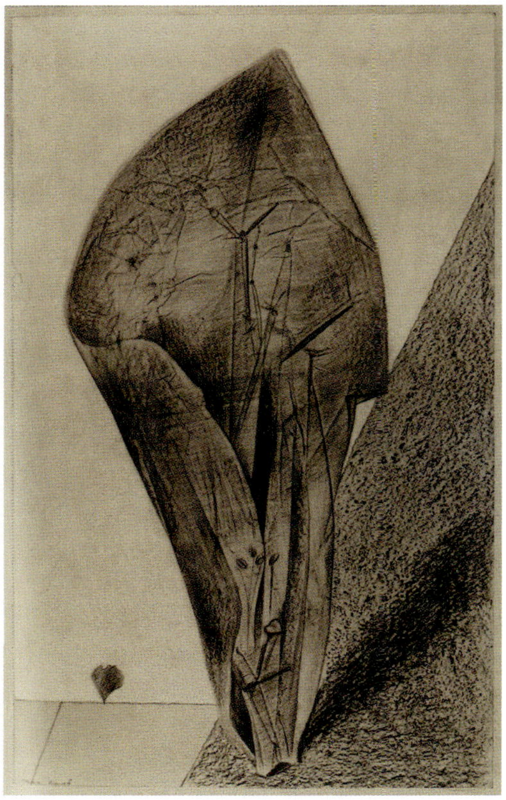

Max Ernst
elle garde son secret (Historie Naturelle print 10), 1925
Frottage, pencil, gouache on paper
42.7 × 26 cm · 16¾ × 10¼ in

E.W. Nay
Fisch und Muschel, 1932
Oil on canvas
60 × 48 cm · 23⅝ × 18⅞ in

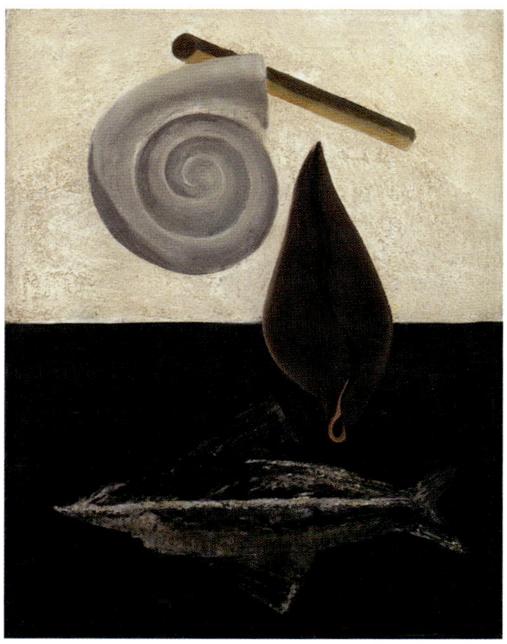

was convinced of the certainty of the 'emergence of a new era of mankind'. In his view, recent works of art confirmed that the necessary transition to a new 'integral' structure of consciousness had already begun to take place.[132] In this process perspective played a decisive role. No wonder, not just Nay, but soon other artists too, eagerly took up his books.

Nay made no secret of his interest in the meaning of Gebser's concepts for his art, although few seem to have taken notice of this.[133] The following comments from a talk he gave on the occasion of the opening of his exhibition on 8 June 1949 at the Frankfurter Kunstkabinett Hanna Bekker vom Rath, indicate that he began to read Gebser's book soon after its publication:

> Artistry is not concerned with the magical, the mystical, the mythical, nor philosophy and not at all with psychology. It's not through absolute intuition that artistry is effectuated, but through the clear and original European consciousness ... It is the aperspectival, autonomous, four-dimensional picture.'[134]

Far from losing interest in the complicated book, two years later Nay was still digesting it. Let us consider, for example, the following lines written by Nay about his work for the 1951 catalogue of the first exhibition of the Deutscher Künstlerbund:

> It seems to me that our time, however, is beginning to discover the dynamic-rhythmic form of the picture expressed in the aperspectival three-dimensionality of the corporeal form-picture ... Pictures that withdraw from the disruption of psychology's speculative elements, of reflexion, of intellectualism, require the cabala of the language of form. To create the latter is the artist's business; to recognise it, that of the viewer who wants to experience the pictures.[135]

His use of the word 'aperspectival' at once directs attention to Gebser's ideas. Even as late as 1990, *Duden's Fremdwörterbuch*, connected the term with this author: 'Aperspectival means: without limitation to the observer's contemporary perspectival point of view (from the world-vision [*Weltsicht*] of the Swiss philosopher Jean Gebser, whose world outlook incorporates the notion of time as a "fourth dimension").'[136] Then there is the matter of what the artist meant by: 'Pictures that withdraw from the disruption of psychology's speculative elements'. There seems little doubt that with this phrase Nay intended to suggest that art cannot be interpreted using such 'speculative' postulates as the unconscious. This, too, was in keeping with Gebser, who maintained in his book:

132 Jean Gebser, 1949, *ibid.*, pp.3–4; Gebser, 1985, pp.1–2.
133 On the importance of Gebser to Nay, see Magdalene Claesges-Bette, 'Die Geburt des Elementaren Bildes aus dem Geist der Abstraktion: Versuch einer Deutung der theoretischen Schriften von Ernst Wilhelm Nay', PhD dissertation, Philosophische Fakultät der Universität zu Köln, 2001, pp.97–105.
134 See E.W. Nay, 'Rede zur Eröffnung der Ausstellung 'Nay', cited in *Lesebuch*, *op. cit.*, pp.49, 50.
135 E.W. Nay, in *Deutscher Künstlerbund 1950: Erste Ausstellung Berlin 1951*, Hochschule für Bildende Künste Berlin, 1951,
in Heibel, 1995, *op. cit.*, p.71.
136 Claesges-Bette, 2001, *op. cit.*, p.97, fn.356.

'There is no so-called unconscious; there are only various modalities (or intensities) of consciousness.'[137] And finally, one might ask how 'recognition' can be achieved by 'the viewer who wants to experience the pictures'. That answer is also to be found in the pages of Gebser's book, in the section in which he describes 'numinous experience'.[138] There, Gebser asserted that 'as the possibility diminishes for numinous experiences from nature there is a proportionate increase for such experiences from art as created by man'. The state of 'recognition' that Nay's paintings demand from the viewer commence with what Gebser characterises as a resolving and balancing of 'the power immanent in us – the soul – and the power that resides in things – the *numinosum*', which enables an insight into 'the fundamental structure of the World'.[139] It is this insight – one beyond the constrictions of measurable notions of time and space – that Nay hoped his abstract paintings might reveal.

In 1953, the second volume of Gebser's *Ursprung und Gegenwart: Die Manifestationen der aperspektivischen Welt* (The Ever-Present Origin: Manifestations of the Aperspectival World) was published.[140] That year, on the occasion of a lecture at the Landeskunstschule in Hamburg, Nay stated:

> With the opening of our century, a transformation to a view of the world that regains a genuine concept of space and time begins. Jean Gebser, the Swiss philosophic writer, states: 'True space is not measurable – it is spirit.' In the place of a measurable concept of space and time [the concept of] intensity steps forward.[141]

The entire lecture was published in 1959, in *Abstrakte Maler lehren*, a book edited by Gustav Hassenpflug.[142] Nay's concern with Gebser's ideas persisted; on 29 February 1956 he wrote these lines to Grohmann: 'Jean Gebser speaks about the aperspectival world-view [*Weltbild*], which at once calls for a new level of consciousness.'[143]

Actually, Gebser had maintained already in the first volume of *Ursprung und Gegenwart* that it was 'neither a matter of a new world-view [*Weltbild*], nor of a new conception of the world [*Weltvorstellung*]', but of a 'new reality', [*neue Wirklichkeit*] which is 'integral' in essence.[144] Gebser invented the term 'aperspectival' to indicate the capacity of human beings to effectuate a 'mutation' from the dominant mode of consciousness – 'mental' – with its dualistic reasoning processes to a higher structure of consciousness, which is 'integral' in essence. While 'mental consciousness' is governed by perspectival seeing, 'integral consciousness' is space and time free; it unfolds in the fourth dimension. Such a notion certainly appealed to Nay, because it held out the promise of an aesthetic as yet widely untapped in Germany. Whereas in America, France and Italy, the debate around the fourth dimension – had reached an apogee by 1929, in Germany relatively few artists were interested in its prospects.[145] Instead, they had engaged themselves with of the concept of the fourth dimension advanced primarily by the turn-of-the-century occultist, Rudolf Steiner. Nay, who like Gebser had lived to see the misuse of 'mysticism' by the National Socialists and its disastrous consequences, would have nothing of this. He strongly believed that 'art does not come out of religions or their substitutes'.[146]

In 1957 Gebser agreed to write a short foreword to a catalogue of an exhibition of Nay's work presented in Cologne at the Galerie Der Spiegel (p.180). In his text he judged the artist's recent paintings as both 'luminous, vibrating and concentrated, as well as a simultaneously harmonic dormant manifestation of a shining vital life-feeling; the sustaining elements of this art, which correspond today to the formation of conscious structures, become visible in these pictures'. He closed the article with the comment that the pictures represented a 'breakthrough' that 'might have a broader meaning for our time'.[147] Few, however, were willing to investigate the implications of such words.

Nay's interest in Gebser's theories was far from singular. Such critics as Franz Roh and John A. Thwaites also read his books in the 1950s, as well as artists as diverse as Willi Baumeister, Theodor Werner, Rupprecht Geiger and Joseph Beuys.[148] Haftmann, too, thanked the Swiss cultural philosopher in the foreword of *Malerei im 20. Jahrhundert*. Although he never referred to him again by name in the book, his characterisation of the outcome of Nay's assimilation of Juan Gris's aesthetic – the yielding of an 'aperspectival four-dimensional image' – was, of course, a coded reference to Gebser.[149] Grohmann was familiar as well with Gebser's *Abendländische Wandlung: Abriss der Ergebnisse moderner Forschung in Physik, Biologie und Psychologie. Ihre Bedeutung für Gegenwart und Zukunft* (1943), which he mentioned in the chapter he wrote in *Neue Kunst nach 1945* as important to the painter Theodor Werner.[150] While Werner Hofmann too had read Gebser's books, initially he

137 Jean Gebser, 1949, p.327; Gebser, 1985, p.204.

138 Nay began to use the word 'numinose' in his memorandums and lectures in 1949. See E.W. Nay, 'Rede zur Eröffnung der Ausstellung "Nay" Frankfurter Kunstkabinett Hanna Bekker vom Rath, Frankfurt a. M.', 8 June – mid-July 1949, in *Lesebuch*, *op. cit.*, p.49 and Nay, memorandum dated c.1949, *ibid.*, p.54.

139 Jean Gebser, 1949, *op. cit.*, pp.324, 327; Gebser, *The Ever-Present Origin: Part One*, *op. cit.*, pp.202–03.

140 Jean Gebser, *Ursprung und Gegenward: Bd. 2: Die Manifestationen der aperspektivischen Welt; Versuch einer Konkretion des Geistigen*, Deutsche-Verlags Anstalt, Stuttgart, 1953.

141 E.W. Nay, 'Hamburg 27.11.1953: Vortrag an der Hamburger Landeskunstschule', in *Lesebuch*, *op. cit.*, p.86.

142 E.W. Nay, 'Gestaltwert der Farbe, Vortrag an der Hamburger Landeskunstschule', in Gustav Hassenpflug (ed), *Abstrakte Maler lehren*, Ellermann, Munich and Berlin, 1959, pp.53–59.

143 E.W. Nay, letter to Will Grohmann, 29 February 1956, cited in *Lesebuch*, *op. cit.*, p.132.

144 Jean Gebser, *Ursprung und Gegenwart*, 1949, *op. cit.*, pp.14–15. Gebser, 1985, *op. cit.* pp.1–2.

145 Linda Dalrymple Henderson, *The Fourth Dimension and Non-Euclidean Geometry in Modern Art*, Princeton University Press, Princeton, NJ, 1983, p.XXII.

146 E.W. Nay, letter to Günther Franke, 11 February 1950, in *Lesebuch*, *op. cit.*, p.56. See also G.L. Mosse, 'The Mystical Origins of National Socialism', in *Journal of the History of Ideas*, vol.22, no.1, January–March 1961, pp.81–96.

147 Jean Gebser, [No title], in *E.W. Nay*, series Geh durch den Spiegel Galerie der Spiegel, Cologne, October 1957, np.

148 On the interest in Gebser of Geiger, Roh and Werner, see Dirk Teuber, '"ZEN 49, dieser Name passt mir nicht": Zum Selbstverständnis einer deutschen Künstlergruppe', in Jochen Poetter (ed), *Die ersten zehn Jahre – Orientierung*, Staatliche Kunsthalle, Baden-Baden, 6 December – 15 February 1987, exhibition catalogue, Staatliche Kunsthalle Baden-Baden, Baden-Baden, 1987, p.53, fn.90. On Baumeister's interest in Gebser, see Will Grohmann, *Willi Baumeister: Leben und Werk*, M. DuMont Schauberg, Cologne, 1963, p.11, in Teuber, 1989, *op. cit.*, pp.46, 53, fn.96. On Thwaite's interest in Gebser, see Eickhoff, *op. cit.*, p.169. On Beuys's concern with Gebser see Johannes Stüttgen, 'Zeitbegriffe bei Jean Gebser und Joseph Beuys', in *Beiträge zur Integralen Weltsicht: Jahrbuch der Internationalen Jean Gebser Gesellschaft*, vol.XI, 1996, pp.41–67; Eva and Wenzel Beuys, *Atlantis: Joseph Beuys 3 Aktionen 1964–1965*, Steidl-Verlag, Göttingen, 2008, pp.81, 83, 85, 95, 96; Magdalena Holzhey, *Im Labor des Zeichners: Joseph Beuys und die Naturwissenschaft*, Reimer, Berlin, 2009, pp.32, 149, 159.

149 Haftmann, 1954, *op. cit.*, pp.13, 466; Haftmann, *Painting in the Twentieth Century*, *op. cit.*, pp.12, 364; aperspectival is here mistranslated as non-perspective.

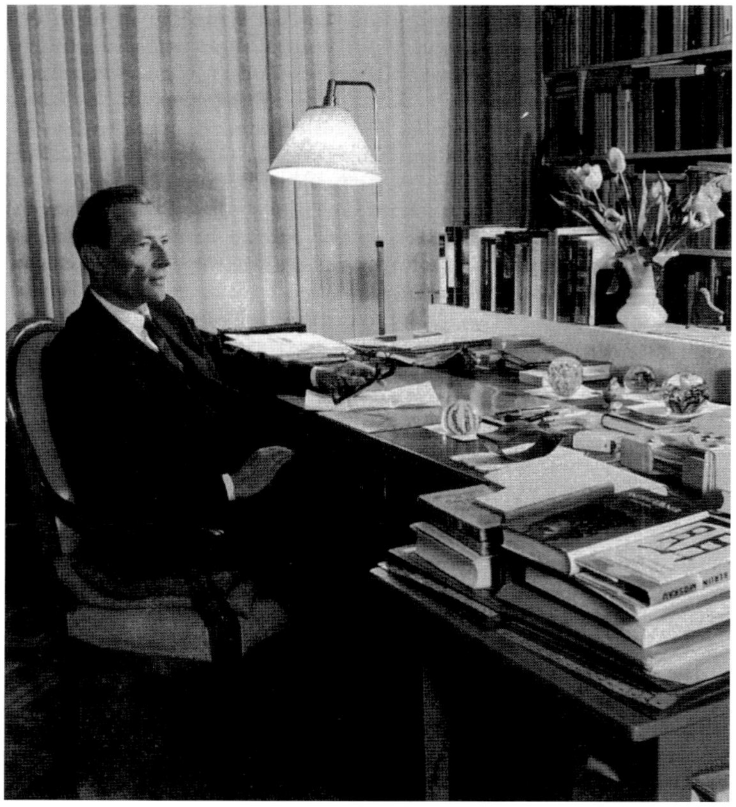

Jean Gebser at his writing desk, Bern, c.1957

was not particulary impressed by them.[151] Eventually, however, he realized how much the books had actually affected him, acknowledging in 1998 that: 'I owe more to his two-volume work *Ursprung und Gegenwart* than to the art-historical apologists of modernity.'[152]

A memorandum amongst Nay's writings dated to 1949 reveals that concurrent with his reading of *Ursprung und Gegenwart* he had begun to explore the ideas two physicists – Pascual Jordan and Louis de Broglie – fundamental to Gebser's books. It was particularly de Broglie's concern with the interaction of 'light and matter' and Jordan's exploration of the 'borderline area between matter and spirit' that caught and held the artist's attention. Although hard to decipher, the note suggests Nay's attempt to establish parallels between the presence of a three-dimensional object, its optical and sensory perception, and the degree to which scientific findings prove that a more all-embracing vision of it – as Gebser claimed – was indeed possible.[153] In his 1960 monograph about the artist, Werner Haftmann refrained from mentioning the importance of Gebser to Nay's aesthetic. Instead he claimed that it had been Nay's reading of Jordan and de Broglie that helped him to attain a kind of 'spatial figure' (*Raumfigur*) in his post-1955 paintings. He then went on to describe its attributes as follows:

> This spatial figure is aperspectival and lies outside the definitional realm of Euclidian space – [making known] an aperspectival, non-Euclidian continuum of space. It corresponds in a remarkable parallel manner with the notion of space in physics ... Lighting up here and there equivalences to the ideas and models of a modern scientific spirit, of a new manner of figuring reality, were no small thing to Nay.[154]

Haftmann's characterisation of Nay's 'spatial figures' as 'aperspectival', reveals that he was well aware that not just de Broglie and Jordan, but Gebser as well – and to a much greater degree – had helped Nay to transform his interest in physics and philosophy into an aesthetic theory. His reticence to name Gebser as one of the artist's more important sources, both in his *Malerei im 20. Jahrhunderts* and his monograph on the artist, was undoubtedly due to his unwillingness to risk any possible marring of his or Nay's reputation, by referencing an author, who had never even finished high school. One of the upshots was a slow fuelling of the suspicion that critics such as he, who drew parallels between abstract art and science, were actually only seeking to legitimise otherwise weak paintings.[155] Hofmann voiced precisely such misgivings in his 1962 review of Haftmann's *Skizzenbuch zur Kultur der Gegenwart*:

150 Grohmann, 1958, *op. cit.*, p.166. Jean Gebser's *Abendländische Wandlung* was reissued in 1956 by the Ullstein-Verlag.
151 Werner Hofmann, 'Geschichtsdeutung als Leidenschaft', in *Merkur*, vol.10, no.6, June 1956, p.615.
152 Werner Hofmann, *Die Moderne im Rückspiegel: Hauptwege der Kunstgeschichte*, Verlag C.H. Beck, Munich, 1998, p.8.
153 E.W. Nay, memorandum dated 1949, in *Lesebuch*, Verlag C.H. Beck, Munich, p.53.
154 Haftmann, *E.W. Nay*, *op. cit.*, p.179. On Nay's reading of Jordan and de Broglie see Haftmann, *E.W. Nay*, *op. cit.*, pp.132, 179.
155 See Jost Hermand, 'Modernism Restored: West German Painting in the 1950s', in *New German Critique*, no.32, spring–summer 1984, p.31.

> The picture that Haftmann sketches of the first actual 'world culture' is intended to prove the accordance of art and intellectual history and to give to our age a harmonic integral structure. According to this, art exists in tune with science. Both increase our knowledge of creation ... But is it not much more the case that it is only after having completed a work that artists then seek to secure the legitimization of science?[156]

Far from true, Nay was deeply preoccupied with twentieth-century developments in physics, not the least because they so thoroughly informed Gebser's point of view. All three of his books – *Abendlandische Wandlung* and the two volumes of *Ursprung und Gegenwart* – not only reacted to this history, but took it a step further, by proposing in positive terms its implications for the future of man. The volumes were fully in tune at the time with the reading proclivities of a broad-based public. Almost as soon as the Second World War ended, scores of books and articles began to appear that were aimed at making the effect of recent discoveries in physics understandable to the masses. Within the veritable flood of information, the number of articles written by Jordan in particular stands out.[157] *Abendlandische Wandlung* was not only sufficiently popular as to be reprinted in 1945 and 1950, but was soon picked by the mass-market Ullstein Verlag. They reissued the book again in 1956 as part of a series about modern physics.

It wasn't long before artists and defenders of abstract art began to draw upon these sources. Baumeister was one of the earliest to do so. In an article entitled 'Bild und Weltbild', published in *Prisma* in June 1947, he wrote: 'Faced with a new image of the world the following questions are justified ... If anything, isn't non-objective art largely a parallel to today's science? ... He [the painter] does not make a picture after nature, but one like natural processes.'[158] That same year, the art critic Kurt Leonhard published *Die heilige Fläche: Gespräche über moderne Kunst*. In the second dialogue, titled 'Der neue Mensch und das neue Bild', a painter – very probably Baumeister – his student, an art historian and a poet exchange views about physics. The painter states: 'I too have in recent days looked into the subject of the new sciences. And I must say that at every turn I have found confirmation of the deep necessity for a new art.'[159]

Artists such as Max Bill and Wolfgang Paalen, as well as Camille Bryen and Georges Mathieu, soon began to write about their own interest in physics.[160] And yet even though Nay had long underscored that his painting evolved 'parallel to the modern natural sciences, mathematics, and physics' – a phrase from the last handwritten note he would jot down – little attempt has been made to coordinate this assertion with the work of a panoply of artists and writers who also upheld such a view.[161] At least one of the reasons for this was the propensity of his postwar critics to emphasise Nay's special status in Germany as the sole painter there capable of generating a completely new aesthetic.[162]

Ultimately Haftmann's refusal to specify how exactly Nay's paintings were related to ideas from the writings of de Broglie, Jordan and Gebser obscured one of the most significant impulses of the painter's abstraction: the relationship of his art to the growing debate during the 1950s in Germany about the so-called space-time continuum. In September 1955, for example, the art historian Arnold Hauser argued in a lengthy article with the telling title 'Der Begriff der Zeit in der neueren Kunst und Wissenschaft' as follows: 'All of modern art is fixated with the idea of the reciprocal action and combination of space and time.'[163] Although Hauser then went on to focus upon film as the primary evidence of this, his statement applied equally to concerns amongst painters. It was this fact that had already led Will Grohmann to state in his 1954 Darmstadt lecture that a good critic must understand the present, 'for example, what space-time is'.[164] By this Grohmann meant that he must at least be familiar with ideas that Gebser had put forward in both volumes of *Ursprung und Gegenwart*, embedded in the issue of a 'space-time' continuum. Like Haftmann, however, he did not elucidate upon the actual importance of Gebser's ideas for Nay's art.

If there is one artist in postwar Germany whose work was as bound up with the natural sciences as Nay claimed his to be, it was Joseph Beuys (p.178). Beuys' 'expanded concept of art' took the 'object' as its starting point, it was not things in themselves, but the invisible connections they call forth that was its subject. Nay proceeded instead from the painterly realm of form and colour, using these qualities to evoke a new kind of perceptual awareness. As he put it in 1956: 'Today artwork that is painting comes into being when a cognisance of aperspectival space joins with the agent of genuine surface so that, technically speaking, the locking into place of both operations without external interference causes more to happen than was reckoned with, namely art.[165] Beuys, too, had become interested during the 1950s in connections between his work and physics, although his point of departure had initially been Steiner's ideas, not Gebser's.[166] Just as Beuys was beginning to draw theoretical connections between the processes of chemical and social transformation, Nay had given form to images that to some suggested the chemical conversion of material into energy. In a memorandum from 1956, Nay summarised the reaction of several scientists at the Chemisches Institut der Universität to his *Freiburger Bild* (p.117) with which they came into contact daily: 'The red emptiness in the middle of the picture, so they said, is built up similarly to the manner in which one conceives the coming into existence of stars: the middle empty, but hot, out of which an energy mass is created that is energetic.' Nay found the discussion

156 Hofmann, 'Werner Haftmanns Widersprüche', 1962, *op. cit.*, p.593.
157 Elisabeth Emter, *Literatur und Quantentheorie: Die Rezeption der modernen Physik in Schriften zur Literatur und Philosophie deutschsprachiger Autoren (1925–1970)*, Walter de Gruyter, Berlin and New York, 1995, pp.180–83.
158 Will Baumeister, 'Bild und Weltbild', in *Prisma*, no.8, 1 June 1947, p.15.
159 Kurt Leonhard, *Die heilige Fläche: Gespräche über moderne Kunst*, Deutsche Verlags-Anstalt, Stuttgart, 1947, p.74, in Emter, 1995, *op. cit.*, p.195.
160 Emter, 1995, *op. cit.*, pp.189–90.
161 E.W. Nay, memorandum dated 30 March 1968, in *Lesebuch*, *op. cit.*, p.322.
162 Weltzien, 2003, *op. cit.*, p.31.
163 Arnold Hauser, 'Der Begriff der Zeit in der Neueren Kunst und Wissenschaft', in *Merkur*, vol.9, no.9, September, 1955, p.811.
164 Will Grohmann, in Eickhoff, 2004, *op. cit.*, p.168.
165 E.W. Nay, letter to Will Grohmann, 29 February 1956, p.132.
166 See Götz Adriani, Winfried Konnertz and Karin Thomas, *Joseph Beuys*, M. DuMont Schauberg, Cologne, 1973, pp.41–46 and p.19.
167 E.W. Nay, memorandum dated 17 November 1956, in *Lesebuch*, *op. cit.*, p.161.

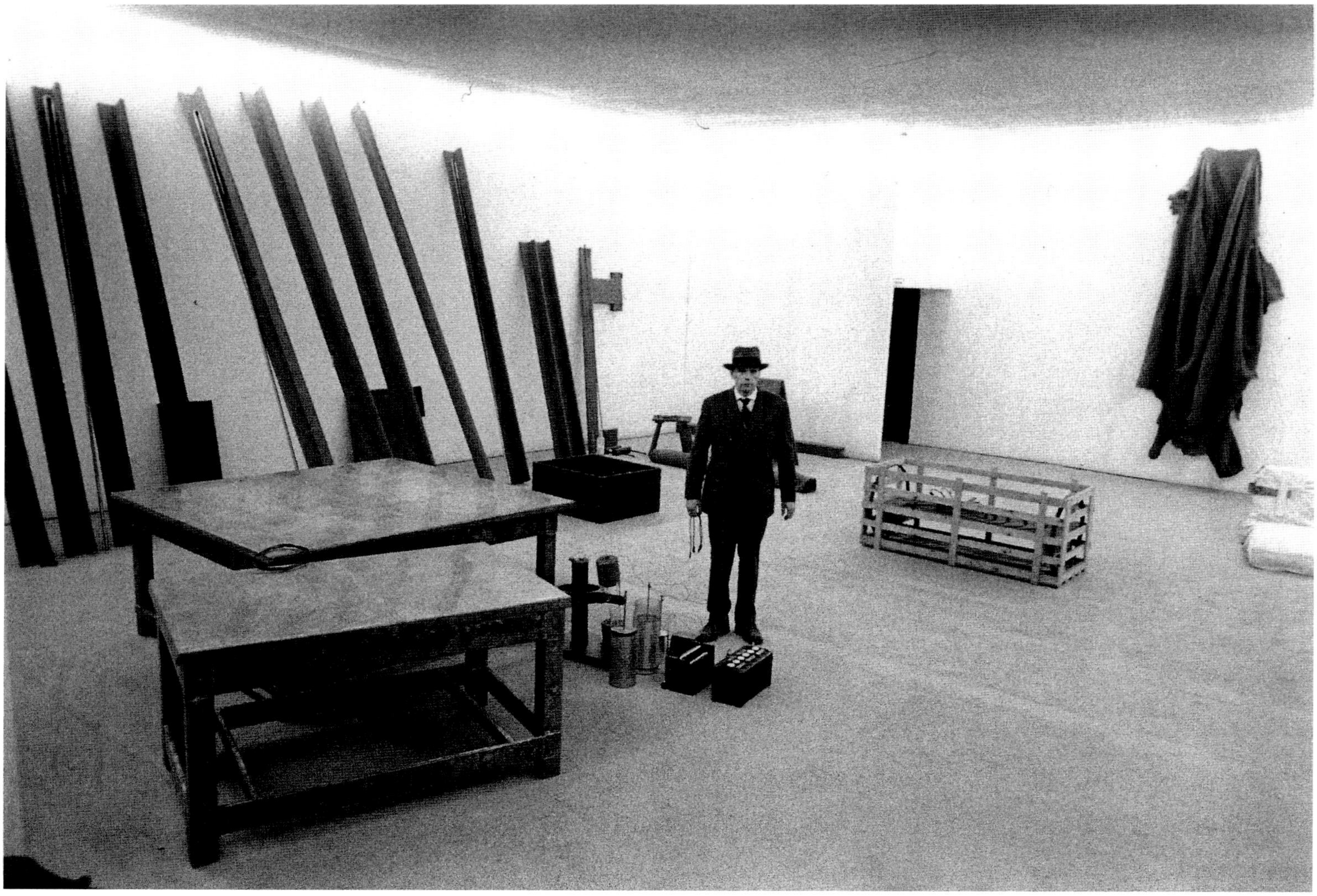

Joseph Beuys at the opening of
Raumplastik, Documenta IV, Kassel,
1968

highly stimulating, writing that it had 'possibly enabled a new definition of the question of "art and nature" to be revealed'.[167]

By then, Nay's approach to painting had long since been seen as approximating the activity of a scientist experimenting in a laboratory. After a visit to Nay's atelier in Le Mans, France, in the midst of the war, Ernst Jünger noted in his diary: 'Before his pictures I had the strong impression of laboratory work, of promethean creation, out of which new forms flow.'[168] Jünger, who had trained as an entomologist, was in a position to know. Nay came across this 1943 account no later than 1949, when Jünger began to publish his diaries under the collective title *Strahlungen*. He certainly did not fail to notice that Jünger's notations had been deeply informed by connections that he drew between the behaviour of light as made by modern physicists and his own style of writing. What counted for him was the dual nature of the real, meaning both its perceptible and indiscernible aspects.[169] Haftmann, too, saw Nay as something of a scientist, writing in 1948: 'my deepest human "yes" to Nay is my sense of him as being a worker in the laboratory of mankind'.[170] It was precisely such a badge of artistry that Beuys would increasingly build upon, beginning in 1964 in Germany.

That fateful year, as will be recalled, saw the presentation of Nay's *Drei Bilder im Raum* in a special section of Documenta III titled *Bild und Skulptur im Raum* (p.158). Initially, Nay had wanted nothing to do with the radical installation stratagems employed in this part of the exhibition. Never one to shun experimentation, however, he eventually came around, and delivered three 400 × 400 centimetre canvases made to order for the space in which they would be exhibited. A diary entry written during the time he was working on the paintings indicates that his long-standing interest in Gebser's ideas played no small role in his having finally agreed to Bode's daring idea of hanging them from the ceiling. It reads in part: 'Annulment of perspectival space ... annulment of dimension ... space and time as an indefinable unity'.[171]

Beuys had also been invited to submit three drawings to the 1964 Documenta. He lobbied until he was granted permission to add three *Bienenkönigin* (1952) wax sculptures and the bronze work, *SåFG-SåUG* (1953–58).[172] Beuys was not only invited back to the next Documenta, but given a gallery of his own. The objects assembled in that room – *Stelle (Fettfilzplastik) vollständig mit Hochspannungswechselstrom aufgeladener Kupferplatte* (1967) among them – their collective title *Raumplastik*, and his characterisation of them – 'it is actually the organs of men in this room that are represented in a completely translated form' – irritated more than a few of his followers, who felt Beuys had betrayed the central aim of his aesthetic – the making of politically commited art – in favour of science.[173] True or not, from this point on, Beuys made Documenta, which until 1965 had perhaps served as Nay's most important exhibiting arena, his chief aesthetic forum.[174]

Beuys picked up, as it were, where Nay had been forced to leave off. Although Beuys's art also had Expressionist roots, he was able to successfully play this fact down, after becoming professor at the Kunstakademie Düsseldorf in 1961.[175] Beuys saw to it that he became the primary spokesman about his art. A born strategist of sorts, after 1963 he aligned his art with primarily younger, international Fluxus artists, before becoming a kind of one-man movement. His timing was also just right. By 1968 socially engaged works of art had taken centre stage. The connection of art with technology also began to garner the attention of museum directors. With his actions, drawings, and sculptures, Beuys effectively evoked the dangers that could be unleashed by developments in technology, without becoming specific. He also came up with a manner of addressing Germany's burdened past, by cultivating what might be termed an aesthetic of pain.[176] Through his art Beuys subtly advocated that only through exposing the 'wound' that is Germany could a sharpening of consciousness be attained, thereby opening up the possibility of a more utopian future.

Nay took the opposite tack. He used the traditional vehicle of painting to educe from the viewer what he felt could be a more productive way of looking at the world. For Nay, the way to an 'integral' consciousness – also sought to some degree by Beuys[177] – was through the production of beautiful rather than shocking forms. As he explained to Grohmann in a 1956 letter:

> [Take the example of] a sick man who goes to a doctor, who should heal his pains ... He will have to treat its origins. Abolish the pains! And you say, 'and on top of it the pictures are beautiful'. Thus – the beauty of the paintings abolishes the existent pain. And the question of the origins remains to be put ... The anxiety, the pain, will be gently deflected through the beauty of the pictures, guiding the viewer to the origins of the anxiety and pain. This origin will not be sought in a subjective, psychological region, not in a vital sphere; it will not be sought after through the question of the rapport of men in itself and to oneself, but instead in the issue of the relationship of man to space and to a consciousness of space ... A work of art brings this process about through colour, the most unfathomable, most uncontrollable value.[178]

If we take Nay at his word, he was convinced that colour and form were more useful in alleviating pain than cultivating an ability to mourn. For him, content and form in painting were identical, a point of view that may have been prompted by his reading of Benn, and which had informed his work since at least 1939. Nearing the end of his life, he judged that it was partly for this reason that his

168 Ernst Jünger, '1 May 1943', in *Strahlungen*, Heliopolis-Verlag, Tübingen, 1949, p.318. In Weltzien, 2003, *op. cit.*, p.202.
169 Emter, 1995, *op. cit.*, pp.140–41.
170 Haftmann, 1948, *op. cit.*, np.
171 E.W. Nay, memorandum dated 24 January 1964, in *Lesebuch*, *op. cit.*, pp.252–53.
172 Veit Loers, 'Die plastischen Arbeiten der documenta 3', in Veit Loers and Pia Witzmann (eds), *Joseph Beuys: Documenta Arbeit*, Museum Fridericianum, Kassel, 5 September–14 November 1993, exhibition catalogue, Edition Cantz, Stuttgart, 1993, pp.49–63.
173 Johannes Stüttgen, 'Die documenta-Beiträge von Joseph Beuys als plastisch-logische Einheit (von innen betrachtet)', *ibid.*, pp.13–19.
174 On Nay's installations at the first three Documentas, see Schwarze, 2009, *op. cit.*, p.52.
175 Pamela Kort, 'Beuys: The Profile of a Successor', in Gene Ray (ed), *Joseph Beuys: Mapping the Legacy*, DAP, New York, 2001, pp.25–31.
176 Holzhey, 2009, *op. cit.*, pp.21–23.
177 Joseph Beuys, *Das Geheimnis der Knospe zarter Hülle: Texte 1941–1986*, Schirmer and Mosel, Munich, 2000, p.157.
178 E.W. Nay, letter to Will Grohmann, 29 February 1956, in *Lesebuch*, *op. cit.*, pp.131–33.

art was so difficult to understand.[179] And so it was that Beuys, who had long been opposed to painting, had the last word.

In England, however, the critic Lawrence Alloway had argued as early as 1960 for the holistic dimensions of Nay's art. In a review of Nay's exhibition at the New London Gallery that year, published in *Art International*, he had this to say:

> An alternative approach to the 'meaning' of painters like Nay and [Sam] Francis lies in the meaning of decoration ... The experience of Nay's painting must be holistic, for one can neither separate a subject from the painted forms nor give reasons for the particular configuration of each work. They are neither illustrative nor self-expressive. At present, this kind of painting, in which formality and content are inseparable – decorative in the most demanding sense of the word – tends to get discussed in a critical vocabulary inherited from times when subject matter and technique were more usefully divisible than they are now.[180]

Nevertheless, by the mid-1980s the view had come to prevail that the lack of recognisable content in Nay's paintings not only made them politically irresponsible, but that such work encouraged the widespread tendency in Germany to suppress its fraught past.[181] To top it off, the vibrant and resplendent colours of his abstract paintings led to their assessment as too beautiful to be anything but decorative.[182]

The opposite, however, was true. Nay was drawn to Gebser's work for at least two reasons, both of which responded to the social-historical milieu of post World War Two Germany. Firstly, Gebser's book gave back to art a redemptive task, which Hans Sedlmayr's widely read 1948 book, *Verlust der Mitte* (Art in Crisis, The Lost Centre), had all but cancelled out.[183] Aware of this, Gebser argued instead: 'those who in their mental limitation and spatial captivity reiterate the cliché of "loss of the middle" will be unable to recognize the new consciousness structure ... Since the whole is space-time-free, it knows no middle ... The loss of the middle is not a loss, but a gain of the whole.'[184] It was this condition, according to Gebser, that constituted the integral consciousness towards which contemporary man was striving. With *Ursprung und Gegenwart* he hoped to beat back any tendency towards a regression to the magical and mythical structures of consciousness that had opened the way to National Socialism and the destruction of the Second World War. Although Nay insisted throughout his life that 'art cannot be political or socially critical', his concern with making paintings that might help activate a new level of consciousness in man was far from devoid of social intention.[185]

179 E.W. Nay, memorandum dated 24 January 1964, in *Lesebuch*, *op. cit.*, p.253. See particularly Claesges-Bette, 2001, *op. cit.*, pp.113–15.

180 Lawrence Alloway, 'London Letter'; see 'Guttoso, Nay, and others', in *Art International*, vol.4, no.10, 31 December 1960, p.73.

181 See for example, Günter Grass, *Geschenkte Freiheit: Rede zum 8. Mai 1945*, Akademie der Künste, Berlin, 1985, pp.13–14. See also Christine Fischer-Defoy, '"Falsche fünfziger": Gespräch über Karl Hofer und die Kunstdebatte der fünfziger Jahre mit Günter Grass', in Christine Fischer-Defoy and Karl-Hofer Gesellschaft (eds), *Ich habe das Meine gesagt!: Reden und Stellungnahmen von Karl Hofer zu Kunst, Kultur und Politik in Deutschland 1945–1955*, Nicolai, Berlin, 1995, pp.41–42.

182 See for example, Martin Damus, *Kunst in der BRD: 1945–1990*, Rowohlt, Reinbek bei Hamburg, 1995, p.142.

183 Hans Sedlmayr, *Verlust der Mitte*, Ullstein, Frankfurt am Main and Berlin, 1948.

184 Gebser, 1953, *op. cit.*, p.330; Gebser, 1985, *op. cit.*, p.479.

185 E.W. Nay, memorandum dated June 1965, 'Auf der Insel Kreta entstandene Niederschrift', in *Lesebuch*, *op. cit.*, p.261.

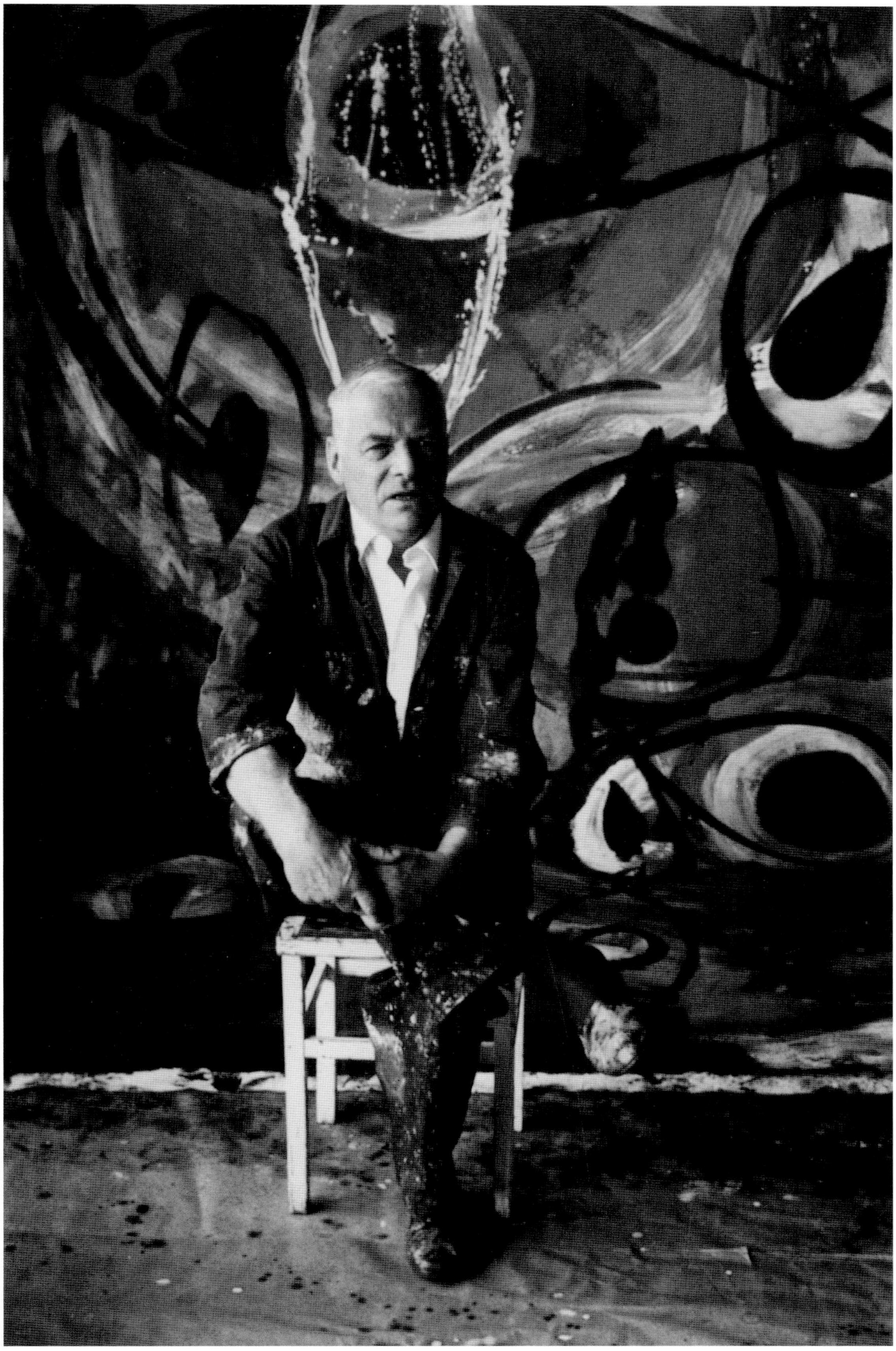

E.W. Nay in front of *Documenta Bild A (Rot-Grün)* in his studio, Cologne, 1964

Index

Abendländische Wandlung 181
Abstract Expressionism 118, 162
Adenauer, Konrad 91, 94
Adorno, Theodor W. 8, 10, 75
Aënors Hochzeit (Aeneas's Wedding) 57, 69, 70, 73
Alloway, Lawrence 184
Alpha (Alpha) 117
Ankunft der Fischer (Arrival of the Fishermen) 39, 43
anti-realist painting 162
Appen, Karl von 21
Arndt, Adolf 76
Arndt, Ruth 76, 94, 97
art of the soul (*Seelenkunst*) 168
Auffindung Moses (The Discovery of Moses) 54, 55
Ausdruckswelt (world of expression) 163, 175
Axle 145

Baluschek, Hans 21
Barlach, Ernst 28
Baselitz, Georg 7, 11, 140, 161, 170
Baudissin, Count Klaus von 39
Baumeister, Willi 71, 74, 94, 118, 167
Baumgart, Fritz 55
Beckmann, Max 18, 52
Begräbnis (Burial) 21, 25
'Bekenntnis zum Expressionismus' (Confession of an Expressionist) 172–73
Benn, Gottfried 40, 163, 172–73, 175, 183–84
Berlin Akademie der Künste 117
Berlin Nationalgalerie 21, 39
Berlin Secession exhibition 22, 34
Betts, Paul 94
Beuys, Joseph 7, 11, 117–18, 140, 164, 181, 183
Bild und Skulptur im Raum (Paintings and Sculptures in Space) 140, 183
Bildnis Franz Reuter 18, 19, 22
Bildnis meiner Mutter 20
Bill, Max 181
Blau und Violett (Blue and Violet) 156
Blaue Reiter exhibition 18
Blumenkohlstilleben (Gemüsestillben) (Still Life with Cauliflower) 22–23, 27
Blumenthal, Hermann 28
Blüten (Flora) 95, 101
Bode, Arnold 140, 161
Bornholm, E.W.N. 23
Boulez, Pierre 90
Braque, Georges 21
Brecht, Berthold 10
Breker, Arno 28
Broglie, Louis de 116, 180, 181
Brooks, Harry A. 118
Bryen, Camille 181
Buchholz gallery 39, 164
Buchholz, Karl 39
Budczies, Arnold 53
Building Dwelling Thinking 118

Carnegie Institute 164
Cavel, Rolf 168
Cercle Volney gallery 169, 170
Cézanne, Paul 21, 173
concrete painting 145
Constructivist art 17
cosmic unconsciousness 76, 91
The Craft of Musical Composition 90
cubism 173

Damenbildnis (Portrait of a Woman) 21, 22
Darmstadt Secession exhibition 73
Das Kunstblatt 8, 21, 22, 28
Das Licht (The Light) 144
Das Problem der Generationen in der Kunstgeschichte Europas 173
David und Bathsheba (David and Bathsheba) 91, 92
Degenerate Art exhibition see *Entartete Kunst*
Delauney, Robert 146
Der Angler (The Fisherman) 40, 46
Der blaue Boll 28
Der Clown zeigt sich (The Clown Appears) 156
Der Fall des Malers E.W. Nay 176
Der Garten des Herrn Térouanne (Mr Térouanne's Garden) 56, 67
Der Hirte I (The Shepherd I) 76, 87
Der Morgen (The Morning) 145, 148–49
Der Sturm 21
Der Sturm gallery 8, 17
Der Ursprung des Kunstwerkes (Origin of the Work of Art) 75
Deutsche Akademie (Villa Massimo) 28, 71, 164
Deutsche Kunstgemeinschaft gallery 21
Deutscher Künstlerbund see Künstlerbund exhibition
Deux enfants sont menacés par un rossignol (Two Children Frightened by a Nightingale) 29
Diamant 116, 117
Diamant Rot (Diamond Red) 117, 125
Die alten Meister der modernen Kunst in Deutschland (The old masters of modern art in Germany) exhibition 95
Die Nacht (The Night) 144
Die Sängerin (The Singers) 40
Disk painting (*Scheibenbild*) 97, 115, 116, 117, 118, 144, 156, 163
Dittmayer, Hans 56
Dix, Otto 29, 71, 73
Döbel, Karl 21
Documenta I 10, 15, 75, 97, 117, 144, 161, 164, 170
Doumenta II 75, 97, 115, 118, 144, 164, 171
Documenta III 15, 74, 75, 140, 144, 145, 157, 158, 161, 162, 171, 175–83
Documenta Bild A (Rot-Grün) (Documenta Painting A (Red-Green)) 140, 141
Documenta Bild B (Blau-Rot-Gelb) (Documenta Painting B (Blue-Red-Yellow)) 140, 143
Documenta Bild C (WeiB-Schwarz-Grau) (Documenta Painting C (White-Black-Grey)) 140, 142
Domnick, Ottomar 74
Doppelspindel-Blau (Double-Spindle-Blue) 146, 155
Drei Bilder im Raum (Three Paintings in Space) 140, 183
Dressler, August Wilhelm 18
Drouin, René 169
Dünenlandschaft (Dunescape) 35, 37
Dunkler Widerhall (Dark Echo) 97
Eichhorn-Bild (Eichhorn Picture) 55
Eigenbrödler (eccentrics) 21
Einem, Herbert von 172
Elchkopf (Elk Head) 8, 29, 33, 34, 35
Entartete Kunst (Degenerate Art) exhibition 7, 8, 21, 24, 39, 52, 72, 164
Ernst, Max 8, 28, 29, 176, 178
Erster Deutscher Herbstsalon exhibition 18
E.W. Nay: Bilder der 1960er Jahre exhibition 162
Expo 58–50 ans d'art moderne 117
Expressionism 7, 15, 21, 28, 74, 118, 144, 162, 172, 176
Eye paintings 119, 140, 144, 157

Fee (Fairy) 94, 99
Femme Rose (Pink Woman) 76, 85
Fietz, Bernard 168
Fietz, Gerhard 95
Figurale – Nauikaa (Figural Nausicaa) 94, 98
The Firebird 90
Fisch und Muschel (Fish and Mussel) 29, 30, 178
Fischer in der Brandung (Fishermen in the Waves) 39, 45
Fischer Fine Arts exhibition 165
Fischerboote an der Hafenmole (Fishing Boats at the Harbour) 21, 23
Fischerdorf Teju auf Bornholm (Fishing Village of Teju on Bornholm Island) 23, 26
Flag in Orange Field 145
Flechtheim, Alfred 34
Flechtheim gallery 34
Francis, Sam 144
Franke, Günther 8, 34, 53, 54, 76, 94, 117
Frankfurter Allgemeine Zeitung 161, 168
Frankfurter Kunstkabinett Hanna Bekker vom Rath 178
Frankfurter Kunstverein 15, 144
Frauen im Sund (Women in the Sand) 53, 61
Freiburger Bild (The Freiburg Painting) 114, 115, 116–17, 118, 121, 144, 175, 177, 181
Freundlich, Otto 146
Fridericianum exhibition 144, 158, 175
Friedrich, Casper David 146
Fritsch, Ernst 18
Fugal paintings 90, 95, 156
Führerbild (Fuhrer portrait) 53

Galerie Creuze 169
Galerie Der Spiegel 94, 179
Galerie Dr Werner Rusche 76
Galerie Ferninand Möller 94–95
Galerie Franz 76
Galerie Gerd Rosen 73
Galerie Günther Franke 73
Galerie Les Contemporains 117
Gallwitz, Klaus 71
Gebser, Jean 176, 178, 179, 180, 184
Gehlen, Arnold 114
Geiger, Rupprecht 168
Georg, Heinrich 40
George, Waldemar 8
German Art of the Twentieth Century exhibition 8, 117, 164
German Artists of Today exhibition 164
German Impressionism 21
Gespräch (Conversation) 76, 81
Gilles, Werner 40

Girl with a Mirror 144
Goebbels, Joseph 34, 172
Gohr, Siegfried 72, 144
Golding, John 15
Gosebruch, Ernst 23, 34, 35, 72
Grassin 54
Grohmann, Will 76, 94, 95, 161, 165–72, 175, 181
Grosse Kuntstausstellung exhibition 168
Grosz, George 17–18
Grufß an Scharoun (Greetings to Sharoun) 97
Gruppe 47 11
Gruppe 53 168–69
Gsellius bookshop 17
Gutbrod, Karl 14

Haftmann, Werner 10, 34, 70, 73, 75, 91, 114, 116, 117, 144, 146, 156, 161, 163, 164, 168, 171, 172–75, 180, 181, 183
Hagemann, Carl 21, 34, 35, 40, 52, 54
Hamburger Kunsthalle 34
Hamburger Kunstverein 97
Hard Edge painters 145
Hasenpflug, Gustav 179
Haubrich, Joseph 94
Haus am Waldsee exhibition 95, 164
Hauser, Arnold 181
Heckel, Erich 7
Heibel, Yule 74, 75, 91
Heidegger, Martin 11, 75, 91, 118
Heise, Carl Georg 22–23, 173
Hekate-Bilder (Hekate paintings) 8, 9, 10, 72–73, 74, 76, 79, 95
Heldt, Werner 10, 40
Hempel, Willi 168
Hentzen, Alfred 34, 172
Hentzen, Anne 73
Hero paintings 140
Hero und Leander 91
Herrmann, Herbert 55
Highway 145
Himmelsrichtung (Heavenward) 144
Hindemith, Paul 90
Hinterzimmer gallery 76
Histoire Naturelle 176
Hochschule für bildende 18, 161, 164, 165, 170
Hofer, Karl 18, 21, 22, 23, 28, 94, 163, 164, 166, 170
Hoffmann, Wolf 167
Hofheim studio 70–72, 73, 76
Hofmann, Werner 175, 180
Holzinger, Ernst 71
A Hundred Years of German Painting 117, 164

Improvisation 39
Informel painters 162, 163, 168, 169, 170, 171
Insel und Mond (Island and Moon) 28, 29

Jargon of Authenticity 75
Jawlensky, Alexej von 54
Jetztzeit (Now-time) painting 14
Johns, Jasper 145
Jordan, Pascual 180
Junge Maler exhibition 21
Jünger, Ernst 8, 40, 52, 55, 56, 57, 183
Junger Westen 169
Jürgen-Fischer, Klaus 144, 168, 170, 171, 176
Justi, Ludwig 39

Kandinsky, Wassily 39, 54–55, 94, 95, 173
Kartenspieler (Card Players) 21, 22
Kelly, Ellsworth 145
Kerkovius, Ida 94
Kestner-Gesellschaft exhibition 97, 164
Kiefer, Anselm 7
Kirchner, Ernst Ludwig 7, 8, 10, 17, 18, 21, 35, 40, 95
Klee, Paul 8, 17, 28, 29, 94, 95, 97, 173
Kleeman Galleries 97, 117, 164, 165
Kleeman, Henry 97
Klein, Bernhard 18
Klüser, Bernd 117
Knoedler & Company exhibition 118, 165
Kokoschka, Oskar 18
Komposition mit vier Frauen (Composition with Four Women) 55, 63
Komposition vor Blau und Gelb (Composition on Blue and Yellow) 144
Königin auf Thron (Enthroned Queen) 8, 57
Körperdiskurses (discourses surrounding the body) 75
Kuhn, Hans 54, 170
Kunst im Kontext: E.W.Nays ständige Wandlung 162
Kunstgeschichtliche Grundbegriffe (Principles of Art History) 75
Kunstgewerbeschule (School of Arts and Crafts) 18
Künstlerbund exhibition 94, 163, 165–72, 178
Kunstmuseum, Düsseldorf 169
Kupka, Frantisek 146
Kythera (Kythira) 76, 82, 156

Lammert, Willi 28
Lampe, Fräulein 55
Land der fünf Sonnen (Land of the Five Suns) 55
Land und Meer (Land and Sea) 55, 145
Landeskunstschule lectureship 95
Landschaft mit Telegrafenmasten (Landscape with Telegraph Poles) 21
Landschaft Promenade (Landscape Promenade) 22
L'art abstrait, ses origins, ses premières maîtres 15
Lawdor, Standish D. 117
Leeb, Susanne 91
Legende (Eduards Tod IV) (Legend (Eduard's Death IV)) 73
Lehrter Bahnhof exhibition 18
Leonhard, Kurt 181
Lessing-Prize 175
Licht in Dunkel (Light in Darkness) 119
Lichtwark prize 97, 164
Liebespaar (Lovers) 23, 24
Liegende Frau (Recumbent Woman) 76
Lineamentenbilder (lineament paintings) 97
Linfert, Carl 169
Lob des Grau (In Praise of Grey) 95, 103
Lob des Grün (In Praise of Green) 119, 133
Lofoten paintings 156, 173
Los Angeles County Museum of Art 15
Lucie-Smith, Edward 118
Lühdorf, Hans 54, 56
Lurçat, Jean 28

Maiser, Myriam 168
Malerei im 20. Jahrhundert 163, 169, 173, 175, 176, 179, 180
Malerei und Plastik in Deutschland (Painting and Sculpture in Germany) 39

Malverbot 8
Mann, Thomas 10, 35
Mann vor Bergsee (Man Beside Mountain Lake) 38, 39, 96
Männer und Rad (Men and Wheel) 28–29
Marc, Franz 7, 52
Marks-Hansen, Beate 35
Mataré, Ewald 164, 167
Matisse, Henri 146
Matter and Light 116
Matthieu, Georges 181
Meier-Denninghoff, Brigitte 168
Meistermann, Georg 95, 167, 168
Melzer, Moritz 17
Memling, Hans 28
Menschen am Strand (Figures on a Beach) 41, 51
Menschen in den Lofoten (Frauen am Meer) (Figures in Lofoten) (Women by the Sea) 8, 40, 49
Merleau-Ponty, Maurice 75
Metagrau (Meta-Grey) 118, 131
Meteor (Meteor) 144
Mettel, Hans 71
Meyer, Erich 23, 34, 70, 76, 94
military service, Nay's 8, 14, 52–57
Minima Moralia 11
Mit federndem Grün (With Resilient Green) 96–97, 111
Mit rotem Arm (Orestie) (With Red Arm (Orestes)) 56, 65
Mit Silberpunkten (Silver Points) 95, 105
Modern German Art exhibition 164
Moholy-Nagy, László 17
Möller, Ferdinand 94–95
Moore, Henry 156
Morin 54
Munch, Edvard 14, 39, 41
Munsterberg, Hugo 165
Museum Behnhaus (Lübeck) 22, 23
Museum der Gegenwart 40
Museum of Modern Art, The, New York 164
Musikalische Poetik 90
Myers, Bernard 91
Mythische Tierbilder (mythical animal paintings) 34
mythischer wirklichkeit (mythical reality) 55

Nachtblau (Night Blue) 145, 147, 157
Nay, Elly 22, 23, 35, 53, 73, 94
Nay, Johannes (father of E.W.N.) 16
Nay, Otto (brother of E.W.N.) 17
Nay-Scheibler, Elisabeth 16, 96, 115
Nay's disks – a closer look at a German painter 144
Nazi era 10–11, 21, 34, 35, 39, 40, 116–17, 144, 165, 172, 173, 175
Neue Figuration 144
Neue Münchener Sezession exhibition 22
Neue Nationalgalerie 10
Neue Realisten & Pop Art (New Realism & Pop Art) exhibition 140
neue Wirklichkeit 179
The New American Painting exhibition 117
New London Gallery 118
Nierentisch design culture 94
Nimptsch, Uli 28
Nolde, Ada 40
Nolde, Emil 40, 52, 117

Nono, Luigi 90
Nordic modernism 163, 172–75
Novembergruppe (November Group) 8, 17
Nussbaum, Félix 28

Op art 145
Orphist paintings 146

Paalen, Wolfgang 181
Painting in the Twentieth Century 164
Pandemonium manifestos 161
Parabel (Parable) 117, 129
Paths to the Absolute 15
Pechstein, Max 17, 167
Peill collection 76
Peintures et sculptures non-figuratives en Allemagne d'aujourd'hui exhibition 169
Periscope (Hart Crane) 145
Pfahler, Karl Georg 145
Pfeiffer-Watenphul, Max 28
Phiole (Phial) 146
Picasso, Pablo 8, 28, 144
Pinder, Wilhelm 172, 173
Pittsburg International Exhibition of Paintings 164
Platschek, Hans 144, 170, 171, 172, 175, 176
Poetics of Music in the Form of Six lessons 90
Polke, Sigmar 7
Pollock, Jackson 115, 117
Polychromatisch II (Polychromatic II) 146
Pop art 145, 162
postwar Germany 10–11, 70–76
Poussin 23
Premiere Exposition Phases exhibition 170
Preussische Akademie der Künste 164
Provinzial-Museum (Hanover) 22
Prussian Academy of Arts Spring exhibition 18, 21, 22, 34
Purrmann, Hans 8

Quell (Source) 144

Rath, Hannah Bekker vom 40–41, 57, 70, 91, 94, 178
Rauhreif (Hoar Frost) 29, 31
Raumgedanken 56
Rauschenberg, Robert 145
Reck-Malleczewen, Friedrich 40
Reichskammer der bildenen Künste 41
Reichskulturkammer 34
Reimann, Albert 8
Reimann-Schule 17
Rhythmen und Kürzel (Rhythm and Code) 119, 139
Rhythmic paintings 90, 95
Richter, Gerhard 7, 8, 11, 140
Roederstein, Ottilie 70
Roh, Franz 18, 179
Rohan, Prince 40
Rondo (Rondo) 117, 127
Rösler, Louise 71
Rössing, Karl 28
Rotklang (Red Sound) 119, 135
Rousseau, Henri (Douanier) 8, 18
Royal Academy of Arts 8
Rüdlinger, Arnold 118
Ruth Meffert portrait 18

Salon de Mai 170
Sandweg (Pathway) 21, 23
Sao Paulo Biennale exhibition 117
Scharl, Josef 28
Scharoun, Hans 114, 117
Scheffler, Karl 18
Scheibe, Richard 40
Scheibenbild (disk painting) style 97, 115, 116, 117, 118
Schlemmer, Oskar 35, 117
Schmidt, Paul Ferdinand 72
Schmidt-Rottluff, Karl 8, 28, 40–41
Schmitt, Carl 29, 40, 41, 52, 55, 56, 145
Schnitzler, Georg von 40
Schnitzler, Lilly von 40
Schönebeck, Eugen 161, 170
Schulkollegium, Munster 145
Schulpforta 16, 17
Schultze-Naumburg, Paul 144
Schuster, Peter-Klaus 72, 76, 162
Schwarz, Heinrich 21
Schwarze, Dick 140
Schwarzer Daimant (Black Diamond) 29, 32
Schwitters, Kurt 17
Sedlmayr, Hans 173, 184
Segelboote nachts auf dem Meer (Sailing Boats at Night on the Sea) 35, 42
Selbstbildnis (Self-Portrait) 17, 53, 59
Seuphor, Michael 15
Sibylle (Sibyl) 70, 74, 77
Sinus (Sinus) 145, 151
Skizzenbuch zur Kultur der Gegenwart 175, 180
Sombart, Werner 40
Sommer (zwei Frauen) (Summer (Two Women)) 53–54
Soutine, Chaim 8
The Spiritual in Art: Abstract Painting 1890–1985 15
Springfield Museum of Fine Arts 164
Spuren und Perlen (Traces and Pearls) 96, 109
Städel Museum 71
Sternbalance (Star Balance) 115, 123
Stockhausen, Karlheinz 90
Stravinsky, Igor 90, 91, 156
Streit um die Moderne 168
Studio Paul Facchetti 170
Surrealism 8, 28–29, 70, 76, 91, 145, 176
Symphonie in Weiß (Symphony in White) 97, 113, 116, 118

Tachist painters 162, 163, 168, 169, 171
Térouanne, Pierre 8, 54, 164
Teuber, Hermann 23
Theo Champion, Werner Gilles, E.W. Nay and Lilly Steiner exhibition 34
Thiemann, Hans 95
Thwaites, John Anthony 144–45, 146, 169, 179
Tochter der Hekate I (The Daughter of Hekate I) 8, 9, 72, 74
Tochter der Hekate II (The Daughter of Hekate II) 76, 79
Traum (Dream) 144
Trier, Hann 170
Trökes, Heinz 176
Two Heads 97

Uhde, Wilhelm 8, 18
Uhlmann, Hans 94, 167
Ursprung und Gegenwart: Die Fundamente der aperspektivischen Welt (The Ever-Present Origin: Foundations of the Aperspectival World) 176, 179, 180, 181, 184
Usinger, Fritz 96

Valentin, Kurt *see* Buchholz, Karl Vellinghausen, Albert Schulze 161, 175
Venice Biennale exhibitions 115, 164
Verlust der Mitte (The Lost Centre) 184
Villa Massimo, Rome (Deutsche Akademie) 28, 71, 164
Vinnen, Karl 144
Voight, Dietrich 71
Völkischer Beobachter article 34
Vom Gestaltwert der Farbe (On the Design Value of Colour) 96, 170
Vom Vulkanischen Grau (Of Volcanic grey) 96, 107, 156
Von Nolde bis Nay exhibition 53
Vorstadtstrasse 22

Walden, Herwarth 8, 17, 21, 22
Weiße Kuh (White Cow) 34, 36
Weiße Quelle (White Source) 119, 137, 157
Weiße Sphinx (White Sphinx) 91, 93
Weltzien, Friedrich 72, 75, 91, 96
Wendl, Max 28
Werner, Theodor 95, 167
Westheim, Paul 8, 21, 22, 28
Wiederaufbaukultur (Reconstruction culture) 72
Winkender mit einem Auge (Waving with One Eye) 156
Winter, Fritz 74, 95, 144, 167, 168
Winterliche Mondlandschaft (Winter Moon Landscape) 21
Wölfflin, Heinrich 75
Wols 144
world of expression (*Ausdruckswelt*) 163, 175
Wunderwald, Gustav 21

ZEN 49 group 74, 75, 168
Zero Group 140
Zwei Figuren (Two Figures) 76, 89
Zwirner, Rudolf 165
Zwischen Widerstand und Anpassung (Between resistance and acquiescence) exhibition 35

Selected Bibliography

* For an extended bibliography see E.W. Nay's catalogue raisonné, 1990

2012
Ernst Wilhelm Nay: Das Polyphone Bild. Gouachen, Aquarelle, Zeichnungen, exhibition catalogue, Kunstmuseum, Bonn; Museum Liner, Appenzell and Mönchehaus Museum, Goslar (2012–13)

Dr. Magdalene Claesges (ed), *Ernst Wilhelm Nay: Werkverzeichnis. Aquarelle – Gouachen – Zeichnungen. Volume 1 (1919–1948)*, Hatje Cantz Verlag, Ostfildern

2009
E.W. Nay: Bilder der 1960er Jahre, exhibition catalogue, Schirn Kunsthalle, Frankfurt a.M. and Haus am Waldsee, Berlin

Dirk Schwarze, *Die Kunst der Inszenierung, oder, Als Arnold Bode Ernst Wilhelm Nay in den Himmel hob*, Siebenhaar Verlag, Berlin

2004
E.W. Nay – Aquarelle und Gouachen 1937–68, exhibition catalogue, Pinakothek der Moderne, Graphische Sammlung, Munich; Folkwang Museum, Essen and Musée d'Art Moderne et Contemporain, Strasbourg

2003
Friedrich Weltzien, *Ernst Wilhelm Nay – Das Körperbild der vierziger Jahre*, Reimer Verlag, Berlin

2002
Nay – Variationen. Retrospektive zum 100. Geburtstag, exhibition catalogue, Kunsthalle der Hypo-Kulturstiftung, Munich and Kunstsmuseum, Bonn (2002–03)

Dr. Magdalene Claesges (ed), *E.W. Nay – Lesebuch. Selbstzeugnisse und Schriften 1931–1968*, DuMont, Cologne

2001
Dr. Magdalene Claesges, *Die Geburt des Elementaren Bildes aus dem Geist der Abstraktion. Versuch einer Deutung der theoretischen Schriften von Ernst Wilhelm Nay*, dissertation, Cologne

2000
E.W. Nay: Aquarelle, Gouachen, Zeichnungen, exhibition catalogue, Kunsthalle, Emden and Saarland Museum, Saarbrücken

1998
Ernst Wilhelm Nay, exhibition catalogue, Stedelijk Museum, Amsterdam; Gemäldegalerie Neue Meister, Dresden and Wilhelm-Lehmbruck-Museum, Duisburg

1995
Yule Heibel, *Reconstructing the subject: modernist painting in Western Germany, 1945–1950*, Princeton University Press, Chichester

1994
Ernst Wilhelm Nay – Die Hofheimer Jahre 1945–1951, exhibition catalogue, Städtische Galerie im Städel, Frankfurt a.M. and Museum der bildenden Künste, Leipzig, Hatje Cantz Verlag, Ostfildern

1990
E.W. Nay: Retrospektive, exhibition catalogue, Josef-Haubrich-Kunsthalle, Cologne; Kunsthalle, Basel and Scottish National Gallery of Art, Edinburgh (1990–91)

* Aurel Scheibler (ed), *Ernst Wilhelm Nay: Werkverzeichnis der Ölgemälde*, 2 Vols., DuMont, Cologne

1985
Bilder kommen aus Bildern: E.W. Nay, 1902–68, Gemälde und unveröffentlichte Schriften aus vier Jahrzehnten, exhibition catalogue, Museum Haus Lange, Krefeld; Westfälischer Kunstverein, Munster and Kunstverein, Hamburg

1984
Elly (Helene) Nay, *Ein strahlendes Weiß: Meine Zeit mit E.W. Nay*, Selbstverl. d. Verf., Berlin

1980
E.W. Nay 1902–1968, Bilder und Dokumente, Archiv für Bildende Kunst am Germanischen Nationalmuseum Nürnberg (ed), exhibiton catalogue, Germanisches Nationalmuseum, Nuremberg; Haus der Kunst, Munich; Bayer AG, Leverkusen; Wilhelm-Hack-Museum, Ludwigshafen and Neue Galerie, Kassel, Prestel-Verlag, Munich (1980–81)

1976
Nay – Zeichnungen, exhibition catalogue, Jahrhunderthalle Hoechst, Höchst; Neue Galerie, Kassel; Kunsthalle, Tubingen; Galerie Der Spiegel, Cologne and Schloß Detmold, Lippische Gesellschaft für Kunst, Detmold (1976–77)

1975
Karlheinz Gabler, *Ernst Wilhelm Nay – Die Druckgraphik 1923–1968*, Belser, Stuttgart and Zurich

1962
E.W. Nay – 60 Jahre, exhibition catalogue, Museum Folkwang, Essen

1960
Werner Haftmann, *E.W. Nay*, DuMont, Cologne (expanded edition: DuMont, Cologne, 1991)

1955
Ernst Wilhelm Nay, *Vom Gestaltwert der Farbe – Fläche, Zahl und Rhythmus*, Prestel-Verlag, Munich

Acknowledgements

This book would not have appeared without the original encouragement and support of Elisabeth Nay-Scheibler, and the E.W. Nay Foundation in Cologne. For my part, I am deeply indebted to Christian Klein, Brigitte Schlüter and Magdalene Claesges from the Foundation for their vital advice and kindness. Many thanks also to Aurel Scheibler, whose excellent catalogue raisonnée is an essential work of reference. Karsten Schubert, who first suggested this book, was instrumental in realising the project through the auspices of Ridinghouse, and I wholeheartedly thank both him and Doro Globus for their assistance at all stages of research, writing and production. Mark Thomson has designed and produced a handsome book, a joy to pick up and read. Many thanks to Pamela Kort for her excellent and extremely well-informed essay on the reception of Nay outside of Germany, which greatly furthers our understanding of the artist. It is apt that Norman Rosenthal introduces this volume, as it was the image of Nay's painting *Gespräch* on the front cover of the legendary exhibition *German Art in the Twentieth Century*, organised by Rosenthal at the Royal Academy in 1989, that first drew Nay to the attention of many outside Germany.

For assistance with research I would like to thank in particular Birgit Joos at the Deutsches Kunstarchiv in Nuremberg; a phenomenal resource for any serious scholar of German art. I would also like to thank for their essential assistance in research: Jürgen Becker, Silvia Diekmann, Kristin Hartisch, Lasse Jacobsen, Antje Kalcher, Birte Kleemann, Antje Mansbrügge, Jens Niederhut, Peter Nisbett, Dietmar Schenk and Maria Stein-Steinfeld. An illuminating conversation with Ingrid Pfeiffer at the Schirn Kunsthalle, Frankfurt, at the time of her exhibition of the late paintings gave a great boost to research in its early stages. For extremely insightful conversation and encouragement I am also very grateful to Michael Werner.

John-Paul Stonard

We wish to acknowledge the exceptional support of the E.W. Nay Foundation. The foundation's chair, Mrs Elisabeth Nay-Scheibler, responded to our initial proposal with great enthusiasm and has been a continuous source of encouragement and invaluable advice.

Ridinghouse

Photo credits

Stefan Moses, Munich: pp.4, 174, 185, 191, back cover
Heinpeter Schreiber, Cologne: pp.9, 20, 25, 26, 33, 46, 49, 51, 63, 65, 69, 77, 79, 82, 87, 98, 99, 103, 109, 113, 133, 137, 139–43, 151, 155
Archive E.W. Nay Foundation, Cologne: pp.10, 16, 17 (top), 23 (bottom), 56, 72, 163
Hans Lülsdorff, Atelier Weite, Cologne: p.12
Simon Vogel, Cologne: pp.38, 105
Baron Döry: p.71 (top)
Eva-Maria Czakó: p.71 (bottom)
Johanna Schmitz-Fabri, Cologne: p.74
Else Ahrweiler, Dusseldorf: p.115
Werner Lengemann, Kassel: p.158
Florence Henri: p.160
E.W. Nay Archiv and Archiv des DuMont Literatur und Kunstverlag: p.165
Life: p.166
Günther Becker: pp.171, 177
Avisag Tüllmann: p.182

Nay collection credits

Private collection: pp.9, 20, 25–27, 32, 33, 38, 43, 46, 49, 53, 54, 59, 63–69, 77, 82, 85, 89–99, 103, 113, 131, 133, 155
Nationalgalerie, Berlin: pp.17 (bottom), 45
Hamburger Kunsthalle, Hamburg: pp.19, 36, 147
Brusberg Fine Art Berlin: p.29 (bottom)
Private Collection Hannover, courtesy Brusberg Fine Art Berlin: pp.30, 178 (bottom)
Private collection, Essen: pp.31, 127
Staatsgalerie Stuttgart: pp.37, 116
Private collection, Cloppenburg: p.41
Collection Goller: p.51
Kunstmuseum Düsseldorf: p.61
Private collection, Hannover: p.79
Westfälisches Landesmuseum für Kunst und Kulturgeschichte, Munster: p.81
Private collection, Munich: p.87
Museum Ludwig, Cologne: pp.101, 129
Private collection, Rheinland: pp.105, 139
Private collection, Düsseldorf: p.107
Sprengel Museum, Hanover: p.109
Private collection, Switzerland: p.111
Land Baden-Württemberg, Chemisches Institut der Universität Freiburg: pp.120–21
Wilhelm-Lehmbruck-Museum, Duisburg: p.123
Milwaukee Art Museum: p.125
Städel Museum, Frankfurt: pp.135, 151
Tate, London: pp.137, front cover
Private collection, on loan to Bundeskanzleramt, Berlin: pp.141–43
Der Regierungspräsident, Munster: pp.148–49
Rheinisches Landesmuseum, Bonn: p.153

Other credits

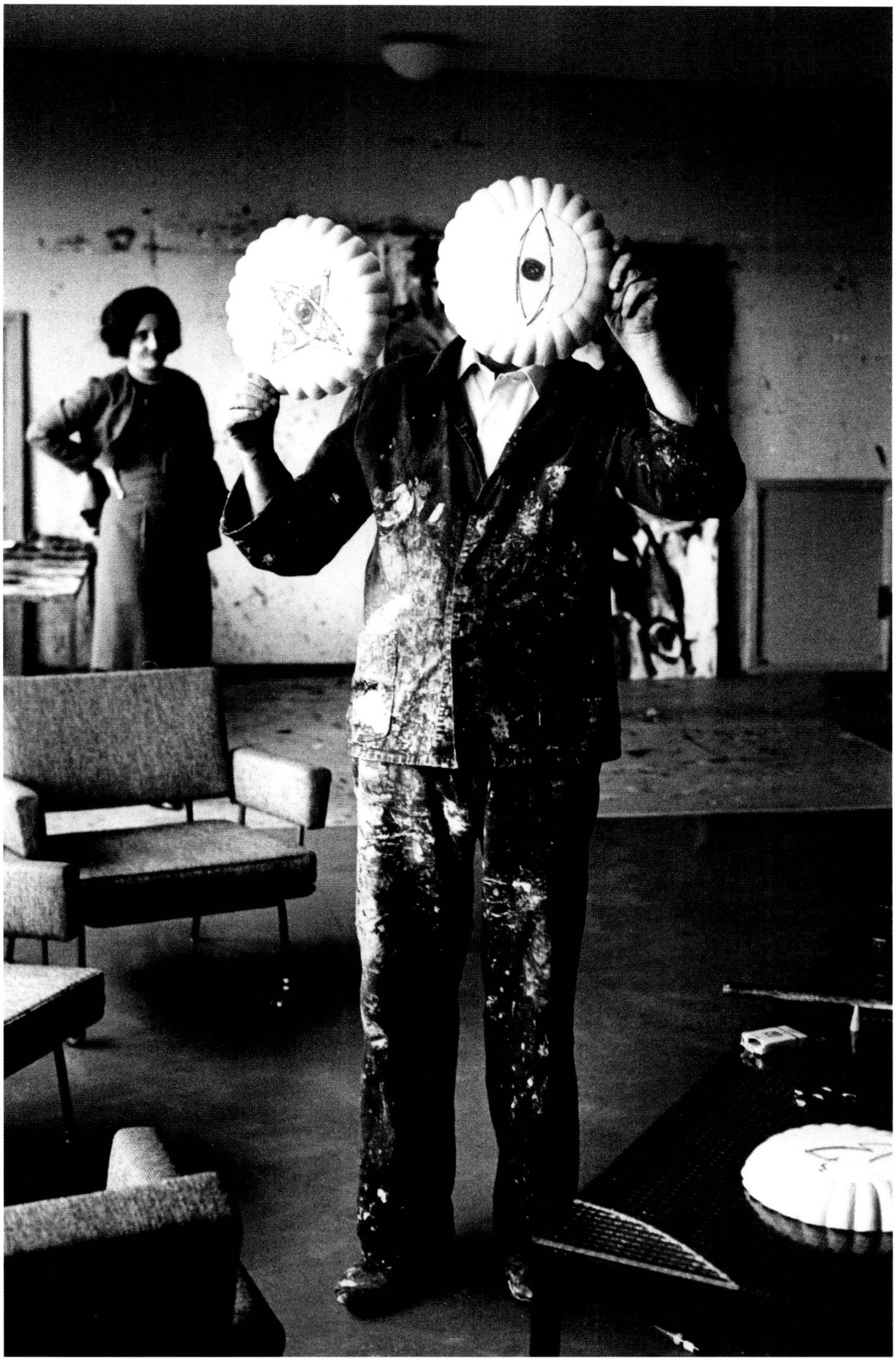

E.W. Nay in his studio in Cologne with
"eye-motif" on party plates, c.1964, his
wife Elisabeth in the background

Published in 2012 by Ridinghouse

5–8 Lower John Street
Golden Square
London W1F 9DR
United Kingdom
www.ridinghouse.co.uk

Distributed in the UK and Europe by
Cornerhouse
70 Oxford Street
Manchester M1 5NH
United Kingdom
www.cornerhouse.org

Distributed in the US by
RAM Publications
2525 Michigan Avenue Building A2
Santa Monica, CA, 90404
United States
www.rampub.com

British Library Cataloguing-in-Publication Data
A full catalogue record of this book is available from the British Library

ISBN 978-1-905464-54-8

Ridinghouse Publisher: Doro Globus
Editorial Assistant: Louisa Green
Copy-editor: Melissa Larner
Proof-reader: Dorothy Feaver

Designed and produced by Mark Thomson
Assisted by Rob Payne
Set in Arnhem Pro
Printed by Grafos sa, Spain